INSIDE

LightWave 3D

Dan Ablan

Contributing Authors:
Patrik Beck
Mike DeSantis
Bill Fleming
Bob Hood
Prem Subrahmanyam

New
Riders

New Riders Publishing, Indianapolis, Indiana

Inside LightWave 3D

By Dan Ablan, Patrik Beck, Mike DeSantis, Bill Fleming, Bob Hood, and Prem Subrahmanyam

Published by:

New Riders Publishing

201 West 103rd Street

Indianapolis, IN 46290 USA

Copyright ® 1998 by New Riders Publishing

Printed in the United States of America 1 2 3 4 5 6 7 8 9 0

Library of Congress Cataloging-in-Publication Data

97-80765

ISBN: 1-56205-799-5

Warning and Disclaimer

PUBLISHER	Jordan Gold
EXECUTIVE EDITOR	Alicia Buckley
DIRECTOR OF EDITORIAL SERVICES	Lisa Wilson
MANAGING EDITOR	Brice Gosnell

DEVELOPMENT EDITORS
Laura Frey
Ed Metzler

PROJECT EDITOR
Katie Purdum

COPY EDITOR
San Dee Phillips

TECHNICAL EDITORS
Arnie Cachelin
Doug Nakakihara

SOFTWARE PRODUCT DEVELOPER
Steve Flatt

SOFTWARE ACQUISITIONS AND DEVELOPMENT
Dustin Sullivan

TEAM COORDINATORS
Stacey Beheler
Michelle Newcomb

MANUFACTURING COORDINATOR
Paul Gilchrist

BOOK DESIGNER
Glenn Larsen

COVER DESIGNER
Dan Armstrong

COVER PRODUCTION
Casey Price

DIRECTOR OF PRODUCTION
Larry Klein

PRODUCTION TEAM SUPERVISOR
Laurie Casey

GRAPHICS IMAGE SPECIALISTS
Steve Adams
Debi Bolhuis
Kevin Cliburn
Sadie Crawford
Wil Cruz
Tammy Graham
Oliver Jackson

PRODUCTION ANALYSTS
Dan Harris
Erich J. Richter

PRODUCTION
Jeanne Clark
Cyndi Davis-Hubler

INDEXER
Cheryl Jackson

About the Authors

Dan Ablan, author of the best-selling *LightWave Power Guide*, brings you yet another down-to-earth instructional book for the serious LightWave artist. He has been animating with LightWave 3D for over seven years. He has created animations for broadcast television, numerous videos, and print. Dan is a graduate of Valparaiso University with a degree in Broadcast Journalism, and a minor in Photojournalism. Dan's animation company AGA Digital Studios, Inc., is located in the Chicago area and produces 3D animation for corporate clients and advertising agencies. LightWave 3D is an integral part of AGA Digital Studios, Inc. Dan has been writing about LightWave for years in magazines such as *LightWave Pro*, *Video Toaster User*, and currently his articles can be found monthly in *3D Design* magazine. He has a videotape training series through ProWave, and you can also find Dan traveling around the U.S. teaching LightWave 3D at various seminars.

Patrik Beck is currently creating animated shorts and is the special effects director for several independently produced films. He has been self-employed as an independent contractor creating and writing about animation for the last 10 years. He has degrees in electronics and theatre arts. Patrik was a ballroom dance instructor and a salesman at Radio Shack, and has been performing as a professional musician for the last 20 years. He lives in Milwaukee, Wisconsin, with his wife, Cathy, dog Woofer, cat Leslie, and two perfectly rendered children, Mariah and Christian.

Mike DeSantis is a freelance animator/web designer whose main client is GE Capital. He is a graduate of the Art Institute of Philadelphia's Graphic Design program, but he taught himself 3D animation later. After winning three international awards with Ray Dream Studio, he started using LightWave when version 5.0 was released. A strong background in traditional drawing and painting has helped Mike in developing 3D modeling and animation skills. Adrenaline Imaging can be reached at AdrenCG@aol.com, and the web address is http://www.adrenaline-cg.com.

Bill Fleming is a 3D Chaotician who has worked as a photorealistic 3D consultant for multimedia, broadcast, and film. He currently manages Komodo Studio, a leading 3D studio that specializes in photorealistic 3D effects for the broadcast and film industries. He has written many advanced LightWave tutorials and is a contributing editor to *LightWavin'* magazine.

Bob Hood is a Senior Software Engineer currently working for NewTek, Inc., on the LightWave 3D development team. He has been working with computers and developing software since the early 1980s, and has been doing so professionally for more than

12 years. Bob has amassed experience in a wide variety of computer-related disciplines, and has worked on many large, international software development projects as both a team member and a team leader. Computer language design, telecommunications, and 3D computer graphics and animation are particular interests of his. His first computer was a Commodore VIC-20, and his first software development work was done in 6502 Assembly language.

Prem Subrahmanyam is a native of the city of Tallahassee, Florida, where he lives with his wife and six children. As a graduate of Florida State University with a degree in computer science, Prem fell in love with computer generated imagery during his stint at FSU, where he insatiably devoured computer graphic magazines at the FSU library. Upon graduation, he was employed as a graphic artist and animator at a local production company for several years before branching off into freelance graphic design, animation, and contract programming. While most of his clients have been local or regional, Prem has done graphic design work for such national clients as Dun & Bradstreet and ACCO North America. However, Prem is perhaps best known for the LightWave plug-ins that he has designed—Surface Effectors/DSFX (a plug-in enabling dynamic surfacing effects in LightWave) and Relativity (a plug-in that brings the power of mathematical expression relationships between items in LightWave).

Trademark Acknowledgments

Dedication

For Maria. —Dan

Acknowledgements

Dan Ablan wishes to thank the talented and dedicated team of editors at New Riders Publishing. Laura Frey has worked tirelessly to whip this book into shape under tight deadlines and many headaches. Needless to say, she did it. A warm thanks is extended to Alicia Buckley for keeping an eye on the project and maintaining the standards of a New Riders Inside book. Without them, this book would not be the outstanding resource that it is. In addition, Dustin Sullivan has worked diligently to produce a robust accompanying CD for the book. Thanks, Dustin! Thank you to Katie Purdum for worrying about conventions and keeping everything consistent. Thank you to Stacey Beheler and Michelle Newcomb for handling the acquisitions and also to New Riders' production team for making the book look great. This book would not be complete without the hard work of Ed Metzler's editing, as well as the work of Technical Editors Doug Nakakihara and Arnie Cachelin. Thanks, guys, you are the best kind of safety nets! Not to go unmentioned, Dan thanks his family (brother Jerry, too) and Brian "the Boy" Paluch for the wonderful support over the years. Lastly, Dan wishes to thank his wife, Maria, for her patience and especially her support during the sleepless nights, long weekends, and summer days missed while completing this book. Sagapo Matia Mu.

Contents at a Glance

Table of Contents

Part I

GETTING STARTED

Chapter 1

CONFIGURING AND PREPARATION

When you sit down in front of your computer, think about what's most important while you are working. Are you comfortable? Are you too close or too far from the monitor? Too often, no one discusses the effects of a good working environment for 3D animators. Typically, most technical manuals and books never go beyond telling you what sort of system you should have and how many megabytes of RAM you need to install. Of course, these are important issues, but your surroundings and work atmosphere are just as important (if not more so). This first chapter discusses the following information:

- Your workstation environment
- Necessary information for running LightWave 5.5 on your computer
- Information on installing the software
- The latest features of and changes to LightWave 5.5

Before you start, you should read the Installation guide that ships with LightWave 3D 5.5. If you have a new video display device, get familiar with its operation so that you can easily change screen resolutions and colors.

Your Workstation Environment

3D animation is fraught with elements. You should always consider each element with every project you take on. A very important issue that could not only help your animations, but also your well-being, is ergonomics. Configuring a decent LightWave workstation also means configuring the system externally—the position of your computer monitor, a comfortable chair, the right temperature, and the appropriate lighting are all elements you need to consider when setting up your workstation.

Simply put, your working environment (whether at home or the office) transcends into your animations. More importantly, it can affect your creativity.

Installing and Configuring LightWave 3D

Two situations come into play with your LightWave software. Either you will perform a complete install of LightWave or just upgrade from a previous version. If you are installing LightWave for the first time, you must first take care of the hardware lock, or dongle. After the dongle is in place, you can begin installing LightWave. If you are an existing user of LightWave, you already have your dongle attached to the back of the computer (making the upgrade of your LightWave software painless).

This section examines the requirements your system needs to successfully run LightWave 3D 5.5 (including the dongle), along with some helpful recommendations on RAM and processors that can help you put together a faster workstation.

The Dongle

The dongle is a topic of discussion among many animators these days. Basically, your LightWave software will not run without the dongle. This small piece of plastic attaches to the parallel port on the back of your computer. It protects the software manufacturer from a copy of its software "accidentally" being installed on more than one machine.

Dongles, for the most part, aren't too much trouble. Once in a while, however, along comes a dud that the manufacturer needs to replace. One problem that can arise when working with a dongle is that many programs use them. If your main workstation has a few programs on it, you may have a dongle chain 4 or 5 lengths long. They all still function, but you might need a support at one end to hold them up.

Because the dongle is a pass-through device, animators who have parallel ZIP drives from Iomega or printers can attach these devices to the back of the dongle. Many users attach the dongle to a printer switch box, which is connected to the computer by a cable. This makes switching incompatible dongles or peripherals easier, and enables you to place valuable dongles or sets of dongles in more convenient or more secure locations.

NOTE

Don't be afraid to use a printer with the dongle. Although there are inconsistent reports that some users have had bad experiences with dongles not working when hooked with a printer, many LightWave users keep a permanent dongle/printer configuration without trouble.

WARNING

Whatever you do, be certain that your computer is turned off before attaching the hardware lock (dongle) to the back of your computer. The same rule applies when attaching printers or peripheral devices to the back of the dongle.

Although unconfirmed at this writing, you should be aware of a potential problem. Some LightWave animators have claimed that by performing a "new hardware search" through Windows 95, their dongles were internally destroyed. Consequently, LightWave would not run. Don't perform this system check with your dongle on. The time it takes to return a dongle to have it repaired is not worth the risk.

NOTE

The dongle is static sensitive, so be careful when handling it.

After the dongle is attached to the back of the computer and your peripherals (if any) are attached once again, power up your system. Follow the installation instructions that came with your LightWave software. If LightWave fails to run after installation, check the following:

- **The hardware lock is not fully attached.** Check the connection on the parallel port. Be careful of static electrical discharge. Look before you touch. If the dongle is loose, power down the system and reattach.

- **The parallel port is not configured properly.** Check to see whether you have more than one parallel port. Identify the port your dongle is attached to and make that port the default parallel.

- **Sentinel driver not found.** The Sentinel software is not installed. Follow the instructions within the LightWave reference manuals for installing the correct version of the dongle software driver.

- **If all else fails, try something simple.** Reboot the computer. Every once in a while, resetting the system mysteriously corrects odd problems.

- **None of the above.** If nothing mentioned above works, you may have a bad dongle. For this, give your local LightWave dealer a call, or direct your questions to NewTek, Inc. They can guide you in the right direction to get your dongle and software up and running.

System Requirements

Believe it or not, system requirements for LightWave are not as demanding as other software applications. Granted, LightWave runs like any other graphics software package—the more processing power, the more memory, and the more disk space you have, the better off you are. You can, however, easily begin animating with the basics. Because computer technology and systems have dropped in price so much in the past few years, it is truly unbelievable what you can do for a few thousand dollars these days. With just this small amount of capital, you can slide right into your own animation station. But where do you begin?

Ask yourself this question: What is more important, memory or processor? If you said memory, you are correct. Too often, animators and even everyday computer users think they are getting the best computer possible by purchasing the most expensive system. They neglect, however, to upgrade the memory. Of course, a faster processor gives you faster rendering. If you don't have enough memory to complete a scene the way you would like, however, you are getting nowhere. A Pentium 133, for example, with 80 MB of RAM and a 256 KB cache proves to be a better workstation and runs more efficiently than a Pentium 200 with 16 or 32 MB of RAM. The following table lists some minimum requirements for LightWave workstations:

You need	PC	Macintosh
Processor	A 486/Pentium or DEC Alpha or a MIPS R4400 or later	A PowerPC
Operating system	Windows NT 3.5 or higher or Windows 95	Mac OS 7.5
Minimum RAM (recommended)	32 MB	32 MB
Hard drive space (recommended)	500 MB	500 MB
CD-ROM drive	Required	Required

NOTE

Please note that the recommended requirements are suggested for basic performance and rendering. You can find actual minimum requirements for system configurations in the NewTek reference manuals.

Operating systems take up memory. Software takes up memory. The amount of complexity in your work also takes up memory. With your new-found knowledge from this book, however, you can often save money by purchasing a lesser processor with more RAM than the opposite. At the time of this writing, a Pentium 150 with a standard 16 MB of RAM was selling for around $900–$1,000. Add more RAM, say 64 MB for $300, and a 4 MB video card for $200, and you've got a very nice computer system for $1,500. With LightWave and an animation recorder, you can make up that cost in one or two logo animation jobs.

Memory Concerns

Many computer users don't realize how important memory is to a good working computer system. As anyone can tell you, however, the more memory the better. As technology dramatically changes the face of computing, software applications are being written to do more and more, faster and better. The trade-off is memory. This is evident by the price drops in memory over the past few years. In the spring of 1995, a 16 MB SIMM (single memory chip) cost close to $600. By the spring of 1997, you could buy the same 16 MB SIMM for $89.

You can get away with only 16 MB of RAM for a basic LightWave workstation, but this is a bare minimum. To get satisfactory performance from LightWave, 32 MB to 64 MB are recommended. More RAM is necessary if you want to run another program while running LightWave (a paint program such Adobe's Photoshop, for example). Images you use within LightWave are held in memory while rendering, and the more complex your object and scenes are, the more memory you need. If you can increase your system memory to at least 64 MB of RAM, you can work comfortably on most everyday projects. If you can upgrade to 128 MB of RAM, you will do even better. If you can upgrade to 256 MB of RAM, you will be the envy of your friends and colleagues.

Hard Disk Concerns

This book recommends at least a 500 MB hard drive—not because the LightWave software takes up that much space, but because the work you generate will. If you have as little as 10 MB, you can install the LightWave program files. A larger hard drive, however, means that you won't be limited in storage space for images and rendered sequences. Typically, most basic computer systems you purchase today ship with at least an 800 MB to 1 gigabyte hard drive. Higher-end workstations ship with as much as 6.5 GB of storage and more.

Even though you may have tons of storage space, you still need to back up your work when working with your hard drive. Too often, animators with larger hard drives forget to back up because they always have room to store more. Animators with smaller hard drives need to clean out their drives more often to make room for new work; this forces them to back up. Many, however, just forget to back up. Remember to back up your work. The few minutes you take now can save you hours upon hours in the future.

Don't worry about backing up your LightWave program, just your work. Be certain to back up your objects, images, and renders, though. You can always reinstall LightWave from the NewTek CD-ROM.

A removable disk such as an Iomega ZIP or JAZ drive is a good unit to have for hard drive backups. The ZIP holds 100 MB of data, and the JAZ holds 1 gigabyte. Another great way to back up your work is with a CD-ROM recorder. CD recorders sell for under $600 (about the same as a JAZ drive), and you can purchase blank CDs for as little as $5. A CD-ROM can hold approximately 650 MB of data. The benefit of a CD recorder is that your work is permanent. Moreover, a CD-ROM drive can be found in most computer systems these days. Thus you can copy your work to your home computer or install it on a new computer very easily.

Video Driver Concerns

After LightWave 5.0 shipped, the phrase OpenGL became very common. OpenGL (Graphics Library) enables computer systems to display full shaded 3D models on-screen. Due to the complexity of instructions calculated in the video display, a simple 2 MB video card became the bare minimum. LightWave 5.0 integrated OpenGL support, enabling the animator to see his 3D objects in full color without rendering.

Now LightWave 5.5 takes a bigger step and offers OpenGL texture support. Before 5.5, users with a 4 MB video card had a decent setup. Now that the software allows the use of textures within OpenGL, a stronger video display is recommended. Figure 1.1 shows how OpenGL looked in LightWave 5.0. Figure 1.2 shows how the OpenGL texture support looks in LightWave 5.5. Figure 1.3 shows a rendered version of the same object.

As these images show, there is not a huge difference between OpenGL with textures and the rendered image, other than the shadows and backdrop. Keep in mind that shadows, reflections, bump maps, and other calculated information won't be displayed until time image is rendered. For basic objects with applied image maps, however, the OpenGL texture support is a significant improvement in 5.5. Figure 1.4 shows the new OpenGL Texture button located under the Options Panel.

FIGURE 1.1
LightWave with OpenGL display, similar to the capability of version 5.0.

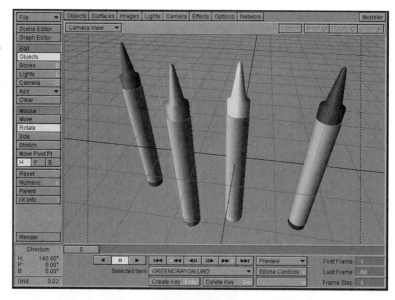

FIGURE 1.2
LightWave with OpenGL texture display, new to 5.5.

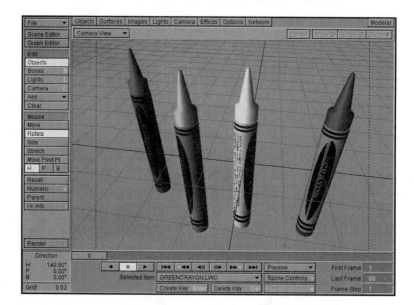

FIGURE 1.3
A rendered image from the same scene.

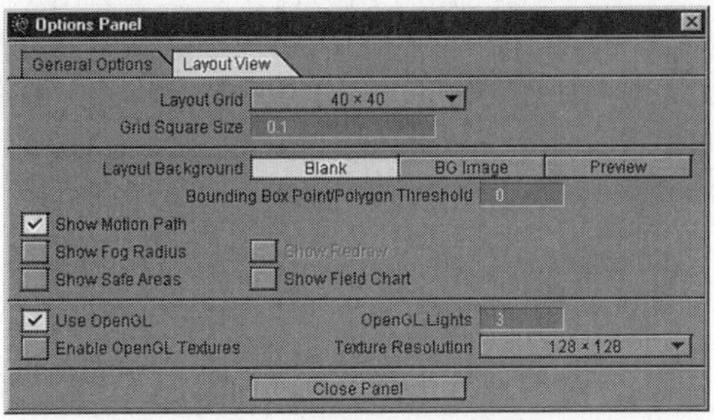

FIGURE 1.4
In addition to turning on OpenGL, LightWave enables you to turn on OpenGL Texture, found under the Options Panel.

To get decent results with this powerful new feature, it is recommended that you use at least a 4 MB video card. These cards range anywhere in price from $200–$400. Cards are available designed specifically for 3D animators and OpenGL. Cards such as the Oxygen have 8 or 12 MB of video memory and make the OpenGL redraws significantly faster. Check with your local LightWave dealer for high-end OpenGL cards. Be prepared to spend about $1,000 or more.

This new OpenGL texture feature has some user control, more than on and off. You can choose between different texture resolutions for the OpenGL display. The higher the resolution, the slower the display will be. The resolutions are as follows:

- 64×64

- 128×128

- 256×256

- 512×512

Figure 1.2 used an OpenGL texture resolution of 512×512. In addition to being able to display image maps instantly, LightWave 5.5 also enables you to move, rotate, size, and position the images directly in Layout. Look for further information on texture reference objects in the section titled "The New Tools" that appears later in this chapter.

The Configuration Files for LightWave and Modeler

The LightWave and Modeler configuration files (Lw.cfg and Lwm.cfg) are two simple files found within the NewTek/Programs directory. These files contain the necessary information for the programs' operations such as default frame count, installed plug-ins, and so on. The following is an example of a partial Lw.cfg file:

```
LWCO
0
ContentDirectory C:\NEWTEK
ScenesDirectory Scenes
ObjectsDirectory Objects
HierarchiesDirectory Scenes
SurfacesDirectory Surfaces
ImagesDirectory Images
OutputDirectory Images
AnimationsDirectory Animations
MotionsDirectory Motions
EnvelopesDirectory Envelopes
PreviewsDirectory Previews
CommandDirectory C:\SN\Command\
TempDirectory C:\NEWTEK\PROGRAMS\Temp\
StatusFilename (none)
MaxObjects 1000
MaxSurfaces 1000
MaxImages 200
MaxLights 1000
```

```
DefaultSceneLength 60
DefaultFPS 30.000000
DefaultTension 0.000000
DefaultPixelAspect 2
DefaultSegmentMemory 8670000
DefaultZoomFactor 2.200000
DefaultOverlay 0
RenderThreads 1
RenderProgress 1
RenderDisplayDevice 0
AutoFrameAdvance 0
FrameEndBeep 0
OutputFilenameFormat 3
SerialPortName COM1:
RecordSetup1 (none)
RecordSetup2 (none)
RecordCommand (none)
RecordDelay 0.000000
FirstFrameDelay 0.000000
UnitSystem 1 4
AutoKeyAdjust 0
AutoKeyCreate 1
AbsolutePointer 0
LeftButtonSelect 1
DefaultGridNumber 40
DynamicUpdate 1
BoundingBoxThreshold 13726
QuickMotionPathFrames 30
ShowSafeAreas 0
ShowFieldChart 0
LayoutViewLibrary 1
LayoutViewLights 1
LayoutViewTextures 1
LayoutViewTextureSize 7
ScreamerNetCPUs 1
ActivationDelay 0
DataOverlayWarning 1
RenderTimeWarnings 1
OverwriteWarnings 2
FileType Objects *.*
FileType Images *.*
FileType Animations *.*
Plugin ImageSaver Alias(.als) C:\NEWTEK\PLUGINS\LAYOUT\Hiipsave.p
➥Alias(.als)
Plugin ImageSaver BMP(.bmp) C:\NEWTEK\PLUGINS\LAYOUT\Hiipsave.p
➥BMP(.bmp)
Plugin ImageSaver BMP_256(.bmp) C:\NEWTEK\PLUGINS\LAYOUT\Hiipcmap.p
```

Certain functions within LightWave are saved to the Lw.cfg and Lwm.cfg files when quitting the program. Some of these functions are OpenGL, Left Button Select, Render Display Device, and others.

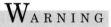

WARNING

Do not edit the configuration files while LightWave is running.

Preventative Measures

With any work on which you are about to embark, it's good to have a plan. This book emphasizes project planning. In this section, planning plays a roll in configuration and preparation.

Preventative measures within your configuration are simple. More than just setting up a decent workstation with a virus checker, preventative measures also include how your hard drive is organized. It is important to take the time to organize your hard drive so that files, images, objects, and scenes all have a folder to call their own.

The following sections discuss system backups and their usefulness to your work, as well as the importance of saving and deleting files.

System Backups

Beyond an organized system, a good working backup system is a must. You should back up your system often, preferably once every week if you turn over a lot of work. Backing up your work will save you hours in the long run. Part of backing up your system should also include reformatting your hard drive.

It's a good idea to back up your work every six months or so, and then to reformat the entire hard drive on your system. Then reinstall the operating system, utilities, and of course LightWave. From there, copy your work files back over from the backup. Voilá, you've got a nice clean system. In addition to having a cleaned out drive, you have also wiped out fragments left by constant hard-drive use, making your system more efficient.

Saving and Deleting

When installing the newest version of LightWave, or a new plug-in for that matter, it's a good idea to create a separate folder. This folder should be created for the previous versions of the software or plug-in. You don't want to ever write over an existing file—you never know when you might need it.

Saving cannot be stressed enough. Save! Save! Save! Did you also know that it is important to save? Okay, you get the point. The reason this is stressed so strongly is because the time it takes to click one button, or make one keystroke, is so small, but rebuilding or reanimating an object or scene can take hours, days, or worse. Save your work in steps. If at any point you then decide that where you're at is not working, you can revert back to the preceding saved version. If you don't do that, you must start all over.

Before you begin deleting anything, be absolutely certain that you are done with it. Ask yourself why you're deleting the file. Is it really taking up much space? Don't be too anxious to delete any file when using LightWave. Much of the work you do in LightWave can be pulled apart and used within other animations. You can take pieces from one animation and put them into others. Also, most LightWave files (images excluded) take up little hard-drive space.

A great thing to do is invest in a removable media device such as ZIP or JAZ from Iomega, or purchase a CD-ROM burner. Here's a quick price range for units such as these:

Unit	Price Range	Media Size	Media Cost
ZIP Drive	$150–200	100 MB	$15–20
JAZ Drive	$450–500	1000 MB	$95–115
CD Recorder	$399–600	650 MB	$4–8

These are just a few ideas for backing up your work. You can also use other types of devices for backup, such as tape drives or optical drives.

NOTE

Of course, if you signed non-disclosure and proprietary agreements for an animation, you probably won't be able to reuse any parts of that animation in others.

Introducing LightWave 5.5

Now that the formalities are out of the way, you can finally see what the newest version of LightWave has to offer. You will notice a vast improvement throughout LightWave's Layout and Modeler. Improvements have been made to many areas, including the interface, existing features such as Inverse Kinematics and Bones, and much more. Plug-ins have been updated, and many new plug-ins have been added. Read on to take a guided tour of NewTek's LightWave 3D 5.5.

This section covers the new features of LightWave in detail, including hands-on exercises to help you become comfortable with Version 5.5.

The New Interface

The most noticeable differences in the LightWave 5.5 interface are the new colors and buttons. You can also now modify the interface palette in the Lwcom.cfg file.

Many of the functions within the Layout and Modeler interfaces now include keyboard equivalents right on the buttons. Out of the many 3D packages available, LightWave's interfaces are about the easiest to navigate. This is because standard Windows "icons" are not used. Too often, programs have icons to represent buttons, some of which are cryptic and not very clear. LightWave's interfaces have maintained clearly labeled buttons throughout the program. Kudos to NewTek for keeping this format. As you read on, you will learn that the new 5.5 interface in both Layout and Modeler make the animator's job easier, and that certain areas have been moved to better locations.

Layout

LightWave is available for the Intel Windows platform as well as others, and computer users are accustomed to a full-color interface. Still, LightWave through Version 5.0 maintained a gray and somewhat dull interface, in which the colors could not be modified. Although extremely functional, the Layout interface became archaic. Figure 1.5 shows the LightWave 5.0 interface, still resembling Versions 4.0 and 3.0.

FIGURE 1.5

As good as the software was, the LightWave interface up through Version 5.0 remained a vision of the past.

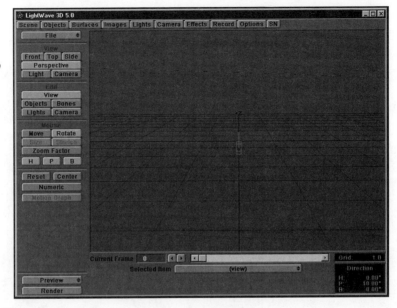

Now, NewTek has polished the LightWave interface without damaging its functionality. Figure 1.6 shows the new 5.5 Layout.

FIGURE 1.6

LightWave 5.5 sports a new interface with more colors and smarter positioning of some functions.

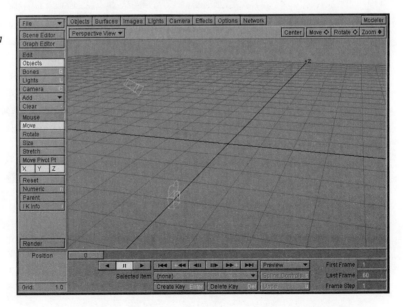

Modeler

Accordingly, LightWave's Modeler has adopted the same new interface. Figure 1.7 shows the new Modeler interface.

FIGURE 1.7
LightWave Modeler 5.5 shows itself off with a new look as well.

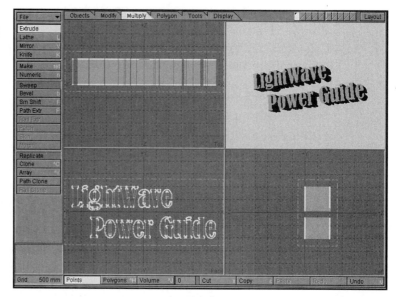

In addition to Modeler's new look, buttons for layers have been modified as well. These new buttons are larger, making layer selection easier to do. Another huge improvement in the 5.5 Modeler interface is the OpenGL display colors. Version 5.0 introduced OpenGL in Modeler's preview window, enabling users to see fully shaded versions of what they were modeling. The background had two options, black or a sky blue. Now, 5.5 enables the user to select any color from the spectrum. This chosen color is written to the Modeler configuration file upon quitting the program. When the program is started again, the colored OpenGL interface automatically applies.

You can read about many other Modeler changes as well as new plug-ins in Chapter 4, "Modeler Techniques." Part of the rearrangement in the new LightWave 5.5 interface, which makes your navigation around the screen easier, is within the panel buttons.

The Panel Buttons

The panels within LightWave have found some new improvements as well. Some panels have been added to; others have been moved to different locations. The panel buttons have matured with LightWave over the years. The first two versions of LightWave didn't even have panel buttons in Layout. Now, however, the panel buttons are slightly varied with Version 5.5—more refined and more functional.

The Layout Panels

The panels within Layout function the same way they did in previous versions of LightWave. Two things have changed, however: the Record Panel is no longer included, and the SN Panel (ScreamerNet) is now labeled Network. Figure 1.8 shows the new panel buttons in Layout.

FIGURE 1.8
Layout's panels have been updated, and some panels have moved.

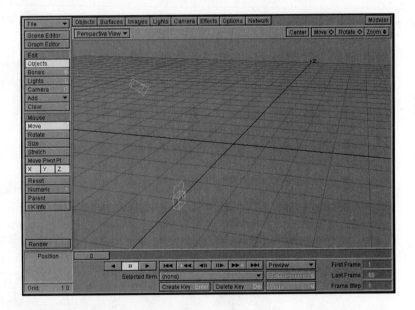

You can now find the Record Panel functions under the Render Panel. Figure 1.9 shows the new Render Panel.

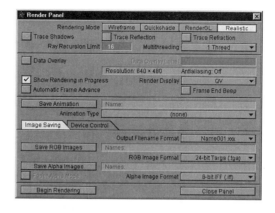

The Layout Panel buttons have experienced certain other changes as well.
Certain areas used to request the user to click on another button to access
yet another panel, such as the Surfaces Panel plug-ins. Now, LightWave's
familiar tabs are incorporated into the panels. Figure 1.10 shows the
Surfaces Panel with the new Basic Parameters tab. Users access plug-ins
from this area.

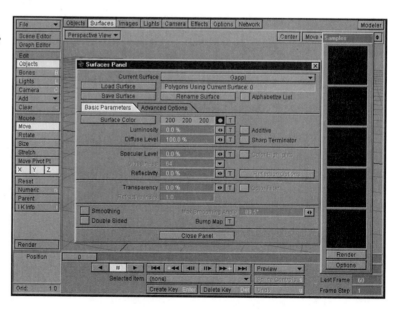

This new feature makes it much easier to add plug-ins, especially those that
need to be applied to many surfaces within a scene. Other panels, such as the
Objects Panel, incorporate this change as well.

Lastly, the new panels in 5.5 are moveable around the screen. This is a handy improvement over the past versions of LightWave where an open panel blocked the entire work screen. This is useful because many adjustments made in those panels cause interactive updates in Layout, which remains active as well.

Figure 1.11 shows the Options Panel slid over and down to the lower-right corner of the screen.

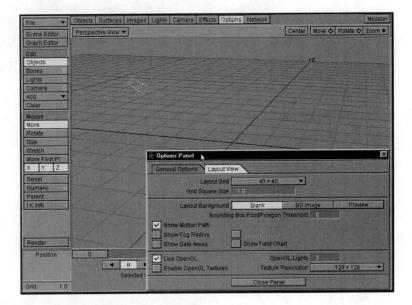

FIGURE 1.11
LightWave 5.5's new panels are now moveable.

The Modeler Panel Buttons

The Modeler Panel buttons have improvements as well. One of the most noticeable improvements is the appearance; the Modeler Panel buttons now look similar to LightWave's tabs. Figure 1.12 shows the Modeler Panel buttons.

Other panel changes in Modeler include a few new buttons such as the Multiply Panel's new Knife feature button.

Modeler's buttons within the panels also include the keyboard equivalent label on each button.

FIGURE 1.12
Modeler's panel buttons now use the tab look.

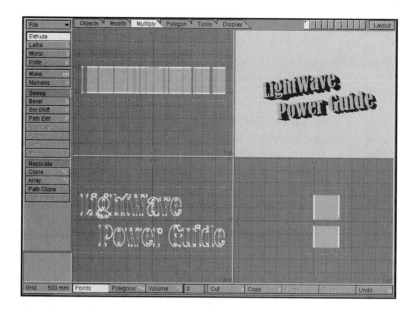

Panels Within Panels

As mentioned earlier, LightWave 5.5 has added panels within panels, otherwise known as tabs. Figure 1.13 shows the Objects Panel in which the Deformations tab is a panel within a panel and separate from the Appearance Options tab.

FIGURE 1.13
Previously accessed by clicking on another button, the Deformations area is now a tab within the Objects Panel.

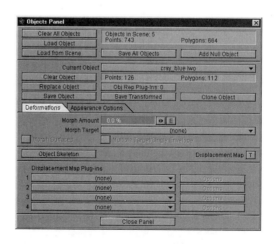

You can find embedded panels in the Surfaces Panel as well, where the panel within a panel separates the Basic Parameters and Advanced Options.

The New Tools

As with any software upgrade, users want to know what the new tools are. LightWave 5.5 offers quite a few new tools, making the price well worth the money. It ships with many cool new features including a "lite" version of Dynamic Realities Particle Storm software, the long-awaited Morph Gizmo plug-in, a Volumetric lighting plug-in, as well as many other tools.

The following sections discuss the new Deformation tools, the Morph Gizmo plug-in, and the new volumetric lighting plug-in called Steamer. Also, you can see an overview of the Particle Storm Lite included with 5.5.

Modeler Tools in Layout

One of the coolest new sets of tools added to LightWave 5.5 is the Deformation tools. Animators have been requesting more of LightWave's modeling functions to be incorporated into Layout. The addition of the Deformation plug-in successfully answers some of the user requests.

Adding the Deformer.p file adds six new plug-ins to the Objects Panel's Deformation tools. These tools are Bend, Pole, Shear, Taper, Twist, and Vortex. If you are familiar with any one of these tools in Modeler, you will enjoy using them in Layout.

The premise of these tools is to help the user eliminate steps needed to animate. An animator wants to sway a palm tree, for example, to simulate a severe storm for a local television station. He needs to animate this because he accidentally broke the station's only video camera. So, off to his computer he goes. Before LightWave 5.5, he would have had to either add a series bone structure to the tree, possibly with an Inverse Kinematics chain, or bend the tree in Modeler, saving out each bent tree as a separate object, and then morph between them. Whichever way he went, it would have taken some time. Also, a morph sequence would not properly bend a tree, because morphs work in a linear fashion. The tree needs to curve.

The Deformation Plug-Ins

Enter the Deformation plug-in tools. Figure 1.14 shows the palm tree in Layout at frame 0. Notice that two Null objects are added to the top and bottom of the tree.

FIGURE 1.14

Frame 0 of an animation setup with three objects: a tree and two Null objects.

Figure 1.15 shows frame 30 in the same animation. The palm tree bends to the right.

FIGURE 1.15

Frame 30 shows the same tree bent over via control of a Null object.

Bending the tree this way took two keyframes. To set up this basic scene, follow these steps:

THE MAI TAI TREE

1. Load the Tree object from the Landscape directory found in the NewTek folder on your hard drive. When you installed LightWave, this directory was created.

2. Add two Null objects by selecting Edit, Objects from the left side of the Layout screen. Next, click on and hold the Add button to add one null, and repeat. Feel free to rename them if you like to **base** and **control** in the Objects Panel. This isn't necessary, however, for the tool to work.

3. In Layout, move the first null, or base null, to the base of the tree by choosing the Null object from the Selected Item menu at the bottom of the screen. Select Mouse, Move from the buttons along the left side of the screen. Click in the Layout window and drag into place.

4. Move the second null, or control null, to the top of the tree.

5. Remember to create keyframes for each of these objects.

6. Open the Objects Panel and select the tree as the current object.

7. Click on the Deformations tab, and select the Deform: Bend displacement map plug-in.

8. Click on the Options button, and select the first (or base null) as the Effect Base. Select the second (or control null) as the Effect handle. Click on OK, and close the panel.

9. Select the second null and move it about. Anything happen? Did the tree bend? Probably not. One more step is needed.

10. Click on the Options Panel to open it. Select Auto Key Adjust and Auto Key Create under the General Options tab. Close the panel and go back to Layout. Now move the null. Is the tree bending?

TIP

If you'd like to see the tree bend as you move it and not have it jump to Bounding Box mode, change the Bounding Box Point/Polygon Threshold. To do this, go to the Options Panel and select the Layout view. The tree is 2091 points. Set the Threshold value to 2100. This tells LightWave to not jump to Bounding Box mode unless the point/polygon count rises above this value. When you move the Null object in Layout, you will see the tree bend in real time.

The Auto Key Adjust and Auto Key Create features should be used with caution. These tools are written to the LightWave configuration file upon closing the program. Forgetting to turn these off can seriously mess up your scene. Accidentally moving or adjusting an object with these settings on instantly creates the change. You should not use the Auto Key features in regular scene setups.

Another feature of the Deformation tools is that the Base Null object acts as the origin of control. If you move the Base Null object halfway up the tree, for example, and then move the Top Null object, the tree will bend only from the middle (see fig. 1.16).

FIGURE 1.16

The Base Null object determines a starting point for the Deformation plug-in effect.

These basic settings work the same way for the other five Deformation plugins: Pole, Shear, Taper, Twist, and Vortex.

You can read more about these Modeler functions in your LightWave reference manuals. A better way to see how they really work, however, is to set up your own scene. Follow the steps in the preceding exercise, but use the other Deformation plug-ins to see what you come up with!

Morph Gizmo

Morph Gizmo is the character animator's answer to easy character animation, especially with faces. Morph Gizmo is included with 5.5, and is Generic Plug-in type found under the Options Panel. Figure 1.17 shows the Morph Gizmo interface.

FIGURE 1.17

Morph Gizmo ships with 5.5 and is a fantastic new tool for animators looking to escape traditional morphing techniques.

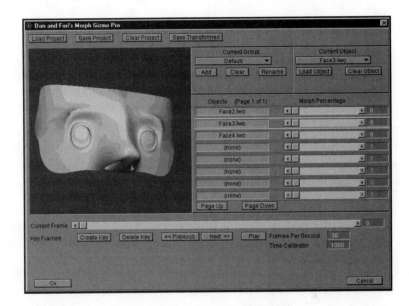

Gizmo enables you to take multiple morph targets and set a timeline between any one or more objects at varied percentages. Consider, for example, that you have made a character that has small eyes, large eyes, offset eyes, a squashed nose, a smile, and so on. Each one of these variances are different objects. Setting traditional morphing techniques would be time-consuming, difficult, and overall, not very fluid. By using Morph Gizmo, you can morph the character with small eyes to the character with large eyes while the mouth is morphing from a smile to a frown.

It's really not as complicated as it sounds. Perform the following steps to get an idea of how this cool plug-in works.

USING THE MORPH GIZMO PLUG-IN

1. Load the Morph Gizmo plug-in.

2. Select Load Object, and load the Face1.lwo object from the accompanying CD. This will become the Original or Base object.

3. Select Load Object again, and this time load the Face2.lwo object. This object is exactly the same as the first face, except that the eyes are closed.

NOTE

It's important to remember that even with Morph Gizmo, the point order and polygon count must remain the same from object to object.

4. Face2.lwo now appears under the Objects list. You don't see the Face1.lwo object listed because it is the Original and Base object.

5. Click on and hold the Morph Percentage slider, and move to the right. Watch the face blink its eyes.

This is a very basic use of Morph Gizmo, but the principle is the same for one object, 100, or more. To animate the eyes blinking over time, you create a keyframe for the different positions from the Key Frame controls at the bottom of the Morph Gizmo interface.

6. After your keyframes are set, use the Save Project button at the top of the screen, and save the project with the .giz extension.

7. Click on OK to close the Gizmo Panel. Go to the Objects Panel and load the same Face1.lwo object.

8. Click on the Deformations tab, and then select Displacement Map Plug-In Morph_Gizmo_Render. Click on the Options button next to it, and load the .giz file you just saved in Morph Gizmo.

This project loads the displacement information into Layout. After you get the okay that the scene has been loaded, close the panel and make a preview. Notice that the face's eyes are blinking, just as you had set up in Morph Gizmo. Also notice that only one object is loaded. This is a nice feature of Morph Gizmo, helping you to avoid cluttering your scene with a series of Morph objects.

Again, this is just a basic overview of Morph Gizmo, enough to get your interest piqued. You will use Morph Gizmo more in Chapter 14, "Facial Animation and Morph Gizmo."

Other Changes in Layout

Some other notable changes to the Layout interface in 5.5 are worth mentioning. Figure 1.18 shows the updated left side of the Layout screen.

FIGURE 1.18

A few changes have been made to the buttons along the left side of the Layout screen.

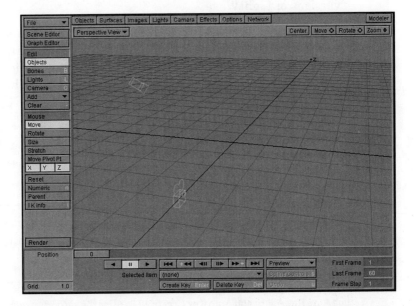

First, notice that the View button has been moved. It is now above the Layout screen and is a drop-down menu. Secondly, two new buttons are added at the top left of the screen. Scene Editor and Graph Editor are what used to be the Motion Graph Panel. The Scene Editor was formerly known as the Scene Panel.

Also notice the drop-down Add button. Here, you can easily add additional objects or Null objects when the Edit/Object button is selected. If you select the Edit/Bones button, the Add drop-down menu gives you the option to Add Bone, Add Child Bone, and two new features: Draw Bones and Draw Child Bones. When Edit/Light is selected, the Add drop-down menu offers the addition of lights.

The Draw Bones feature is explained in Chapter 13, "Bones and Character Animation."

Down toward the bottom of the buttons, notice that the Parent and Target buttons have been relocated. Many of the changes in 5.5 are simple common-sense rearrangements, such as the Parent and Target buttons. Also, the single row of buttons is less confusing than the double row found in earlier versions of LightWave.

At the very bottom-left corner, you will see the Information Panel that was previously located on the opposite side of the screen. Taking the Information Panel's original place are the frame information indicators: First Frame, Last Frame, and Frame Step. These areas have been brought out from the Scene Editor.

Directly below the Layout screen, a new timeline slider has been added. This bar now has a number on it, which can be toggled from Frame Number to SMTPE Time Code to Time in Seconds. You can find this selection within the Scene Editor.

On the new Layout screen, you will see a Forward Play, Pause, and Reverse Play set of buttons next to the timeline slider. This area enables you to step through an animation forward, or reverse automatically.

TIP

Setting Auto Key Adjust and Auto Key Create while using the automatic timeline player button records your actions. Try moving something around in Layout after clicking on the Forward Play button.

Take a few minutes and click around the new interface to familiarize yourself with the new additions and changes.

LightWave Object Files

LightWave's object files are proprietary to LightWave. The .lwo extension tells you that you are working with a LightWave object as opposed to a DXF or 3DS file. LightWave objects have not really changed, so if you have objects from your Amiga LightWave 3.0 setup that you'd like to now use in LightWave 5.5, you will have no trouble. Of course, keep in mind that an Amiga floppy disk cannot be read in a PC or Macintosh. From time to time, however, you may find that you come across an object of a different format altogether.

Compatible Object Types

Even though LightWave uses LWO type files, you are not limited to just that. LightWave can import 3DS and DXF files into Modeler. This is very useful because some of your clients may generate architectural objects, logos, or similar objects that you need to use in LightWave.

Modeler automatically converts any non-LightWave object files.

NOTE

If an object does not have an .lwo extension, the load requester in Modeler won't see it. Be certain to change the file type to All Files when loading objects of a different type.

LightWave also ships with an Object Exporter plug-in for Modeler. This plug-in enables you to save out an LWO object as a 3DS file, DXF, or Wavefront object. You can find this plug-in, called Translator, under the Tools, Custom menu.

LightWave 3D and Multiprocessor Systems

LightWave 5.5 now ships with multithreading capabilities for multiprocessing systems. Figure 1.19 shows the new addition to the record panel.

FIGURE 1.19

Multiprocessor systems are taken advantage of by LightWave 5.5's new multithreading feature.

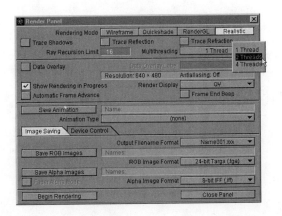

Basically, if you are working with a dual Pentium Pro, for example, you set the multithreading function to two threads to maximize your system's processing power for rendering.

Summary

This chapter gave a brief introduction to LightWave 5.5, presenting information on the dongle, system requirements, and new interface. It did not, however, stop there.

This chapter discussed the importance of a good working environment for your LightWave workstation. It's important to your physical well-being as well as your creativity to have a decently set-up workspace. You read that installing the software, either for the first time or as an upgrade, is relatively painless, and the dreaded "dongle" issues were demystified. Some of the major new features in LightWave 5.5 were spelled out, and you learned about some preventative measures to make your work go smoother.

Now read on. Chapter 2, "Concepts and Theories," discusses a few concepts and theories of which you should be aware.

Chapter 2

CONCEPTS AND THEORIES

Using any 3D animation program requires more than just computer knowledge. You can find many 3D artists whose varied backgrounds play an important role in their work. Concepts and theories are often the less exciting areas of study for animators. In actuality, however, a well-rounded background in video and film can give the 3D animator a strong advantage over those without such a background. By reviewing concepts and theories of video, film, lighting, color, and motions, you develop a stronger foundation for your animation work. Concepts deal with ideas and perspectives. Theories are standard practices that you can employ throughout the creative process.

This chapter covers the following concepts and theories:

- The importance of video and film to animators
- Lighting theory
- Color theory
- Motions

The Importance of Video and Film to Animators

No written rule states that you must know video and film to be an animator. Inevitably, however, you must know basic video and film techniques to excel in 3D animation. Most animation instruction manuals ignore the camera; therefore, so does the animator. In completing a top-notch animation, the camera should play a main role in the process.

NOTE

Chapter 11, "Cameras," discusses camera angles and techniques in more detail.

As a guideline to your future as a 3D animator, whether professional or hobbyist, understanding the importance of video and film to animation is one of the most important keys to reaching the best results. The same goes for still photographers. Understanding framing and angles can turn a mediocre photo into an outstanding photo. Figure 2.1 shows a typical photograph poorly framed.

Now take a look at figure 2.2. Here, the photograph takes into account the people, as well as their surroundings.

Taking this one step further, an integral part of a Hollywood film production is the cinematographer. Even with million-dollar actors, explosions, plane crashes, and beautiful sets, the movie won't be nearly as entertaining or comfortable to watch if the cinematographer doesn't perform the job. This is what you need to remember when animating in LightWave, or any 3D program.

Key to the cinematographer is the gaffer. The gaffer is the person on the set in charge of lighting. Neither a creative angle, a breathtaking view, nor an Academy Award-winning performance can be fully appreciated if the lighting is wrong. As photographers know, light is the breath in their photographs. Video and film producers use light creatively to convey the right message or desired look. Animators have the same tools in their LightWave software, enabling them to re-create what the gaffer does.

FIGURE 2.1
A typical photograph poorly framed.

FIGURE 2.2
A photograph that is framed well. Notice the use of the surroundings in the background.

Lighting Theory

Lighting for video and film is also an integral part of every production. Light can create different moods, from pleasant and peaceful to dank and scary. If you've ever taken a film class, you may have read about the workings of D.W. Griffith or Alfred Hitchcock. They used camera angles and unconventional lighting to achieve their desired effects and moods. Again, this can all be translated into your 3D animations.

LightWave has an exciting layout design in that you now have five lights to choose from. You can set up these lights just the way you would in the real world, yet without ladders or electrical outlets. You can effortlessly hoist a spotlight up 2 meters as a blue fill light. Or you can place a point light 200 meters away, replicating the sun's intense rays.

These light sources are exactly the tools you need to generate computer images that can be as interesting and effective as old D.W. Griffith's movies. With a basic understanding of warm and cool lights, angles of light, and ambient intensities, you will be on your way to outstanding visuals. The following is a brief breakdown you can use throughout your animations:

- Warm lights are colored more brown, beige, orange, and so on.
- Cold lights are colored more blue and gray.
- Single lights from above often cast a heavenly feel.
- Single lights from below cast an ominous and dark feeling.
- A distant blue light cast onto a scene can generate a feeling of daylight.

Take a look at the following four figures. These figures demonstrate different lighting conditions on the same subject. Figure 2.3 shows an object lit with basic 3-point lighting. You can use this look for simple logo creations or industrial animations.

Figure 2.4 shows the same object with one bright point light set at a distance with some intensity falloff. Here, more of a sunlit face appears.

This last example shows the same object lit with one spotlight underneath the chin. This gives somewhat of an eerie or creepy feeling.

FIGURE 2.3
A 3D object lit with basic 3-point lighting, similar to what is used in a television studio.

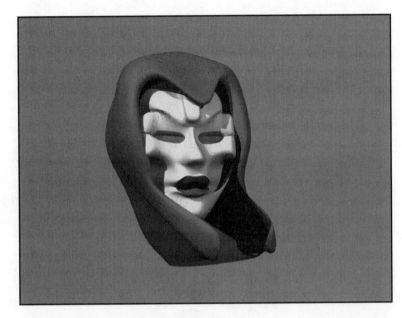

FIGURE 2.4
The same object lit with just one point light, set to a yellowish color, and moved far away to simulate sunlight.

FIGURE 2.5
*The object is lit with
one spotlight from
below to convey a
creepy feeling.*

These are just some of the ways lighting can change the look of your animation. More elaborate scenes with more lighting effects produce even greater results. As you read through and practice the tutorials throughout this book, be certain to take note of the light positions, colors, types, and intensities.

The World of Light

There's much more to understand about lighting than just simple placement. Light is everywhere and changes the look and mood in all that it touches. Think of a cold, hard office and the type of lighting it holds— off-white fluorescent lighting. If you've ever seen the movie *Joe vs. The Volcano* with Tom Hanks, you would have seen that the director brought this type of lighting in to convey the exact mood for the office environment in which Joe worked. Now think of a home environment. The lighting is incandescent canister lights, or sometimes track lighting, or basic everyday lamps are used. This establishes a warm, comfortable mood. The color and temperature of the incandescent light bulbs is more inviting than a cold office lighting environment. Consider this when lighting your LightWave animations.

NOTE

Always remember that you can re-create reality inside your computer. Study your surroundings and mimic them with LightWave.

When considering light, comprehending the color spectrum is a bonus. The
color of light is only perceived based on the pigment of the material reflecting
it. When white light passes through a prism, its spectrum of component
colors becomes visible in the form of a rainbow. Although the colors are
spread smoothly, it is convenient to pick a few sample points along this
spectrum to characterize a given color. This is how the human eye sees it. The
eye has three types of light receptors attuned roughly to pick up red, green,
and blue. The colors of the rainbow are often remembered as ROYGBIV, or
red, orange, yellow, green, blue, indigo, and violet. The primary colors are
red, green, and blue. You will notice the RGB color values throughout
graphics and animation programs, including LightWave.

Because light in the real world is so varied, you can spend a lifetime studying
it. The man-made light in a studio often does not show the full range of color
a model's dress may have. By taking that same dress outdoors into the bright
sunlight, you would reveal practically every imperfection in the fabric.
Sunlight varies throughout the day, changing from soft and warm in the
morning, to bright and hot at midday, and then back to soft again in the
evening. Within your LightWave animations, sunlight is the hardest light to
reproduce. What helps "sell" the look is not only the light, but the materials
and ambient light. Ambient light and LightWave are discussed in the "Real
Light" section a little later in this chapter.

Another element of light in the real world is the atmosphere. Not always
noted, the atmosphere is what causes the spectacular visual skylines,
sunsets, and sunrises you often see. In computer animation, the "spectacular" or breathtaking views aren't easily translated. Nature is the most
difficult thing to reproduce when it comes to computer animation. Advancements in technology and programming, however, have enabled animators to
take their first steps toward re-creating Mother Nature. Volumetric lighting
is now included with LightWave 5.5 and offers the animator a new set of tools
for atmospheric effects such as clouds, fog, mist, and more. Figure 2.6 shows
a scene where volumetric lights help create a low-lying ground fog, an effect
not so easy to create before volumetrics.

NOTE

Be certain to check out Chapter 10, "Lighting and Atmospheres," for tutorials on Steamer, LightWave's new volumetric plug-in.

FIGURE 2.6
LightWave's new volumetric lighting helps re-create realistic atmospheres.

Don't ever stop looking at the world around you. The small inconsistencies in textures such as stone and dirt and the graceful curves of the clouds can be your outline for beautiful 3D creations.

When time allows, be certain to pick up a book on color and light theory to study the topic more in depth.

The Computer World of Light

It may seem that everything you just read is not important to you and your LightWave scenes. In actuality, it's very important. Light, color, video, and film techniques are a primary foundation for 3D animation.

In the computer world, LightWave works to imitate nature. The tools are available to you to generate real-world situations in a digital environment. Although these tools are simply algorithms written by smart programmers, the end result is a visual re-creation of the real world.

The computer world of light gives you reigning power in some respects. That is to say, you can control the elements such as a sunny day or a cloudy day. You can decide how the office should be lit, and where to put that cool new lamp in your living room. All this is possible without an electric bill either! To reconstruct a light with a computer simulation, it helps to acknowledge how light works in the real world.

Real Light

Most people don't pay attention to how light is cast in the real world. The color and shadows of everyday light are often taken for granted. Setting up lights within a 3D computer environment requires you to think much more about light and its properties. One notable property that should be considered is ambient light. Simply put, ambient light is the area within your scene not directly hit by the light source—the dark areas of the scene. No set value determines the "right" ambient light setting in LightWave. This book can, however, recommend to you some good values to start with. The default value for ambient light is 25 percent. You can find the Ambient Light setting within the Lights Panel (see fig. 2.7).

FIGURE 2.7

The Ambient Light control within LightWave's Lights Panel.

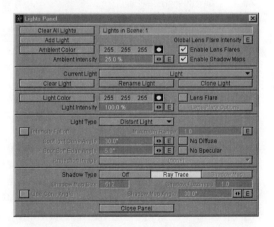

Another property that needs to be considered is how light is absorbed in the real world. Red objects absorb green and blue light, in turn reflecting what our eyes see as the color red. In the real world, the color reflected is often cast onto surrounding objects. This "bounced" light is called radiosity. A few 3D programs have begun to include radiosity rendering within their software. LightWave does not yet have this power, but it may in the future.

Don't worry about radiosity in LightWave. Chapter 10 teaches you how to "fake" radiosity effects.

If you've worked with ray tracing at all, such as shadows, reflections, or refraction in LightWave, you know how much more realism can be achieved by using these three properties. One more added property to those would be radiosity. Figure 2.8 convinces your eye that this is true to life; just like the real world, radiosity comes into play and bounced light is recorded.

FIGURE 2.8
A room with radiosity. This room looks realistic.

Real light is the perfect resource for your animations. Lighting can change the entire look of your animation. Studying the way light falls onto land, water, and the atmosphere gives you an army of insight for your future animation projects. After you have studied real light, you can take that information and translate it into artificial light.

Artificial Light

This type of light doesn't necessarily mean computer-generated light. The light you have on your desktop or from the headlamps on your car or the ceiling fixtures in your office are all artificial light sources. Computer-generated light is modeled after these lights, and you will find that indoor lighting may be some of the easiest lighting to reproduce in LightWave.

Earlier in this chapter, incandescent light and fluorescent light was mentioned. These two sources are most common. Many times, however, you will find colored lights in the real world. Perhaps you have seen blue and yellow lights in a park fountain, or maybe those multicolored lights used for holiday decorations? Colored lights can add dramatic effects to a well-lit 3D animation. Colored lights are most commonly used for moods, such as sunsets, campfires, daylight, or stage lighting. Fluorescent lights are common in large stores, offices, gymnasiums, schools, and warehouses to name a few. Incandescent light is used in homes, dens, television studio control rooms, and art galleries, for example.

LightWave offers the capability to color any light source to any color of the RGB spectrum. Figure 2.9 shows the color selector in the Lights Panel.

FIGURE 2.9
Colored lights can be added easily in LightWave from any RGB value.

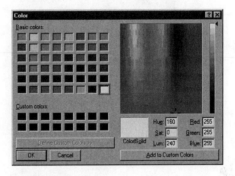

Your ability to change light color can be beneficial in that soft-colored fill lights can be added for increased effects. Spreading a lot of white light onto a subject washes it out. Think of a rock concert stage, or a school auditorium. Not only are there bright white lights, but colored lights as well, usually yellows, reds, and blues. You can put the same setup directly into your 3D animations. Figure 2.10 is a simple scene that has four lights. Two main lights are used to basically light the scene. One red light is set behind the car to add color to the area behind the car to simulate reflections of the brake lights. A warm off-white light spreads across the backdrop.

Without the colored lights, the scene would look a little off. Adding a few lights, some of which are colored, gives the scene a more realistic feel.

Light temperature is also an important factor when it comes to lighting. In the real world, *Kelvin temperature* is the term used to describe the intensity of a light source. The sun on a sunny day, for example, is measured at 10,000 degrees Kelvin, whereas a cloudy day measures at 7,000 degrees Kelvin. In the artificial world, Kelvin temperatures can be associated with LightWave's intensity values. Figure 2.11 shows the Light Intensity area within the Lights Panel.

FIGURE 2.10
Out of four lights in this scene, two colored lights are placed for added warmth.

FIGURE 2.11
Kelvin temperatures are similar to intensity values in LightWave.

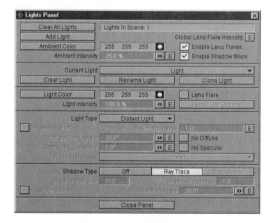

NOTE

Intensity values can range well above 100 percent, as well as below 0 percent.

You don't need to become a lighting expert or join a gaffer's union to understand lighting in LightWave. But a basic foundation of some of the principles behind light and color can help you create your own moods and environments within the 3D world. What you create and how you create it is totally up to you. *Inside LightWave 3D* intends to guide you through some alternative ideas and insights, and hopefully stir your imagination to the possibilities you have at your fingertips.

Color Theory

You can find color theory in many books at your local library or bookstore. This is because color and the applications of color are so wide-ranging. For this book, it's better to concentrate on how color is created and translated within the LightWave environment.

RGB

You should understand color through the basics of RGB—red, green, and blue. Mixing these colors can create any color within the spectrum.

Figure 2.12 shows the Color Selection Panel typical of many windows applications and LightWave.

FIGURE 2.12
The color palette in which you can select RGB values.

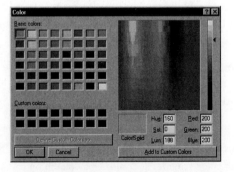

TIP

The Windows color palette selector is new to LightWave 5.5. For those die-hard LightWave veterans who prefer LightWave's own RGB sliders, hold down the Shift key when pressing a color selector, such as Surface Color.

It's hard to believe that the mixing of three colors can create so many different effects. But color theory such as this is basic introductory material to anyone who has studied art or photography. Figure 2.13 shows three spotlights pointed at a wall. (It's not very intriguing.)

FIGURE 2.13

Three spotlights, red, blue, and green, are pointed at a wall. Nothing special here.

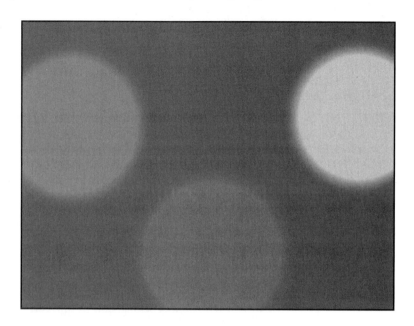

Take a look at figure 2.14. The three spotlights have crossed paths. Notice that the red and blue make purple, and the blue and green make yellow. If all three colors are mixed, you go back to a whitish color, as you can see in the center of the spots.

Changing the hue, saturation, and value of each red, blue, and green value creates different colors. To find the right color for your situation, simple trial and error is a good place to start.

NOTE

Although color schemes and values may match on paper, the best way to fully judge a color is to see it in its final form. If a client hands you a set of RGB values, what comes out may not look like what the client originally wanted. Trust your judgement and use your eyes—they are your best tools for determining the proper color.

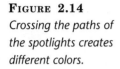

FIGURE 2.14
Crossing the paths of the spotlights creates different colors.

You should be aware that when RGB color is converted to CMYK, colors sometimes shift dramatically. If your computer monitor isn't calibrated to the printing house specifications, you could end up with something different than planned. Be certain to check out Chapter 16, "Output Options and Techniques," for more specific information on CMYK and printing of LightWave images.

One last thing to note about color theory. Experiment. Don't worry so much about numbers and values, and go with what looks good to you. In the end, it's the visual presentation, not the values within the computer, that sell your animation.

The Print World

As a LightWave 3D animator, you will often deal with people from the print world. You may be one yourself, branching on into 3D, the next logical step. Whichever the case, you will often work from preprinted materials that already have color values assigned to them. Having colors already picked out for your animation may not always be a good thing.

Typically what you see in print is not what will come out from the computer. The way a computer and video/animation recorder handle images and color information is different than that of a print press. Take Jim the Artist, for example, who has worked feverishly to get his boss's new logo ready for the big sales and service meeting. The last thing to do is complete the corporate video with a 3D animation. They come to you and show you the logo. Being the pro that you are, and because you bought *Inside LightWave 3D*, you know that you can whip out this animation in a couple of days. Jim the Artist is thrilled; you will be saving his hide, too. He hands you a set of Pantone colors, a standard coloring system in the print graphics industry. You take the RGB values from the Pantone sheets, and enter them into the color selector for the client's logo.

The render looks nothing like the print! What do you do? You eyeball it. Hollywood films are visually color corrected by a color timer. A color timer is someone who has mastered the art of adjusting film exposure times. This accounts for disparities in film stock, film processing, and so on. Tweaking is always necessary at nearly every step. Even the color sections in this book were visually adjusted before printing so that the intended color comes through. This may sound unprofessional, but on the contrary, it's not. One's own vision is the best color converter.

Another situation you may run into is when your animation needs to go to print. Your client has asked you to design a 3D version of his company's logo to be added to his business cards. You show the client the 3D still via floppy disk and an imaging program such as Adobe's Photoshop. Your client loves the logo and approves it. From here, your print resolution render is sent to the print department, which in turn prepares a plate for the printer to make the business cards. When the cards come back, the color that was once thought of as bright and cheerful is now dull and dingy. This is because computers and video handle color differently than printing presses do. To correct the situation, you make necessary adjustments to the intensities and hues.

Now your client wants one more favor—he wants this logo incorporated into a business presentation.

Color for Presentations

Using LightWave for presentations is a fast growing use for the popular program. Presentations these days are often presented from a laptop computer. When this is the case, color is not as much of an issue as is file size. Be certain to read about resolutions later in this chapter.

Using a LightWave animation in a presentation is a great way to spice up a meeting. When it comes to color and presentations, it's important to know how the presentation will be shown: either through a computer monitor or a projection screen. If the presentation is being shown through a computer monitor, you can rest easy in that the color you create on your computer screen will look the same on another screen. Granted, brands of monitors and makes of computers differ. Often, however, a simple adjustment of the monitor's own calibration is all that needs to be done. If the presentation is being projected, however, keep the following few things in mind:

- Be prepared for a shift in color from your LightWave test renders to the final presentation projection. Often, hues tend to shift but can be corrected through the controls on the projection unit.

- Be prepared for an image that won't be as bright when projected. Presentations run through a projection unit can often loose color and become muddy. To correct this, be certain that the projection unit's contrast and brightness controls are brought up.

- When creating graphics and animations for presentation, use contrast. Use a dark background such as navy blue, for example, for yellows and white 3D elements. Contrast in your animations will prove effective when used within a presentation.

Color from Computer to Video

Converting color from computer to video is a heated topic of discussion between producers and animators. Each party believes its color is the most pure in form. The computer artist believes that the computer color cannot be wrong because it's from a computer and totally accurate. The video producer believes that his color is true to life and matches the real world.

In actuality, what you need to know is that there is a difference between the two, and there always will be. Colors shift, and as mentioned before, different machines handle color differently. Your best weapon is your eyes. If you think the color within your animation looks perfect, but suddenly becomes too yellow when put to video, just adjust the values. Don't worry that the computer image doesn't look right. If the final image on video looks accurate and the client is happy, go with it.

You can, however, take the following preventative measures to aid in your quest for complete color:

- When working with a video producer, discuss the color issue and be aware that there is sometimes a noticeable difference. If your video producer is not familiar with computers and color schemes, spend some time together at your workstation.

- Have the video producer generate color bars that you can use to balance the color within your computer.

- Be prepared for a little trial and error. Often, animations translate beautifully to video. Other times, they don't. A little experimentation to see how your computer-generated images translate to video can provide color information to both you and your client.

When you get your feet wet in the world of computer animation, you will eventually deal with artists from corporations or producers from video companies. Each has his or her own methods and reasons for why or how something should be done. When animating for them, get all the information you can about their project. This includes color samples of their artwork, and where they intend to use your animation. Be certain to have them view a test of your renders to make sure that the color is what they want. From there, you can start considering the motions in your animations.

Motions

Video and film techniques, light, and now motion. These are the three most important elements you will always be working with in 3D animation. A study of video and film techniques added to knowledge of light and color and put together with proper motions equal a great animation.

The Importance of Motion

With the release of LightWave 3D with the Video Toaster in the early 90s, a flood of 3D animation began to emerge from every aspect of video production. Cable television, wedding videos, corporate video productions, and more all began to incorporate 3D animation.

3D animation was so new and cool to look at that most people didn't pay too much attention to movements, timing, light, or color. But as the years passed, viewers have become smarter, technology is faster and stronger, and animators demand more for their creative efforts. Previously, you could see either a fast moving logo or model with hard starts and stops. Characters were almost robot-like, no matter what shape or form they were. If the camera moved, it was often jerky and too fast.

With the advancements in software, technology, and education, computer animations are now better lit, more fluid, and very realistic in terms of motion.

The importance of motion to your animations means more to the final piece than you would think. Motion is so natural for human beings, but replicating even the slightest hand gesture or the simplest glance can easily take an animator days to complete. The models you build are important, as is the 3D environment and the lighting. The motions, however, are the icing on the cake, contributing to the overall mood and feeling of the animation piece.

Your client, for example, needs a spooky graveyard animated for a video project. The objects look good and the lighting is fine, but with the wrong camera moves, the animation is not nearly as effective. Smooth, sliding camera moves are not as convincing as quick pan to the right with LightWave's added motion blur. A standard height throughout the animation is not as scary as moving the camera along the ground.

NOTE

Camera moves are often overlooked as part of a top-notch animation. Be certain to check out Chapter 11 for tutorials on camera techniques.

The Study of Motion

Motion, like color theory, can be studied for years. A quick way to learn how to find out how something moves is to watch it. That's all you need to do. If you understand your software and how to set a figure or object into a desired position, you can animate motion. The animators at Pixar for Disney's *Toy Story* can be seen on company home videos performing some of the toy's moves themselves. Ask yourself, how would a toy soldier get around if his boots were nailed to a board? The animators at Industrial Light and Magic who created the fantastic visuals for the *Jurassic Park* movies used real footage of animals to study their motions. Do you know how a dinosaur moves? Neither did they, so they found some video of the closest living relatives, such as elephants, lizards, giraffes, and so on.

In a way, you may find this sort of "study" cheating. There is no cheating in animation, however, except when the actual work is not your own. Mimicking the motions of people and animals is what animation is all about. With 3D animation, you are re-creating reality, or better, creating your own reality. Study the way you get out of bed in the morning. Watch people open doors, and how they turn their bodies. Watch animals run and walk, and watch how they sleep. These are the things to study to master motion in LightWave, or in any 3D program.

N OTE

For tutorials on motion, don't skip Chapter 5, "Layout and Animation Techniques," and Chapter 13, "Bones and Character Animation."

Motion Capture

Another way to create realistic motion in your animations is to use motion capture. Motion capture is a tremendous asset to animators when it comes to animation. In essence, motion capture systems take physical data from human or animal movement, and then translate that information into usable motion data within a 3D program. Up until the mid-90s, motion capture was reserved for the very high-end clients, such as multimillion-dollar moviemakers, and the top ad agencies. Like everything else, however, technology improves and computer systems become better, cheaper, and faster. Now, motion capture is relatively accessible to the everyday 3D animator.

Motion capture systems vary. Some have wires and electrodes placed on key joints and limbs of the live object. Others use laser light to record data. Figure 2.15 shows a human actor hooked up to a motion capture system.

FIGURE 2.15

A motion capture system in action, hooked to a human subject. The motions of the human actor are recorded in the computer and applied to the computer model.

Many animators, however, are against the use of motion capture. Some feel that it is not the true art of animation. And, they're right. It's not. It is, however, a unique way of animating and bringing the real world into the imaginary world. At times, using motion capture is the only way to go to get the job done and make the client happy.

NOTE

Be certain to check out Chapter 13 for more information on motion capture in LightWave.

Motions and LightWave

LightWave 5.5 has many new features, one of which is the capability to work with motion capture systems. LightWave 5.5 has motion capture support for Wavefront and Acclaim motion data. These two formats are industry standards, and are available from most of the motion capture studios. Increasingly, they provide LightWave format motion files as well.

Animators often don't like working with motion capture data because it is very difficult to edit and adjust. If you don't like the motion, it is best to get the actor to do it again! As the tools evolve, this will, presumably, become less of an issue.

Figure 2.16 shows a jog sequence, copied from a motion capture system. Certain frames have been modified slightly, and the original run cycle was then replicated four times. From there, four frames offset each jog cycle.

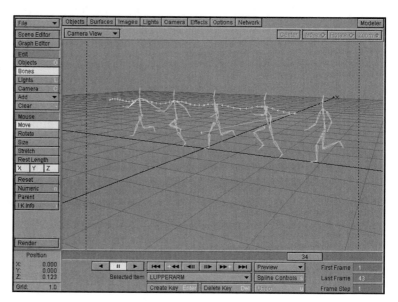

Keyframing

The motion capture files taken into LightWave are generated into keyframes. Keyframes can be thought of as placeholders for motions of objects, lights, or the camera. Setting a key at a certain frame tells the item to "stay there." A frame in LightWave is one complete picture, as it is in film. A series of frames makes animation.

With computer animation, keyframing is somewhat automated. Assume, for example, that you have made a classic animation of the space shuttle for a NASA video. If you keyframed the ship every step of the way from ground to space, you wasted your time. Setting a starting and ending position for the space shuttle is all that you need to do. LightWave generates the "in-between" frames. For an animation such as this, you may decide to add a few frames somewhere near the middle—to tilt the ship slightly. The ship then continues through its final keyframe.

Try keyframing something of your own by performing the following steps.

THE BASIC MOVES

1. From the *Inside LightWave 3D* CD, load the Inside.lwo object from the Chapter 2 directory.

2. Place the object to the back and bottom of the screen.

3. Press the Enter or Return key to bring up the Create Motion Key Panel. Click on OK to create the key for the selected item.

4. Now go to frame 60 by pressing the f key on your keyboard, and entering **60** in the Requester.

5. From the Camera view (press 6 on the number keypad), use the right mouse button (Macintosh users use Control and the mouse) to move the object to the top of the screen. Again, press Enter or Return to create a keyframe at 60 for the selected item.

6. Now make a preview from the Preview drop-down menu at the bottom of the screen (see fig. 2.17).

FIGURE 2.17

The Preview drop-down menu is located at the bottom of the screen.

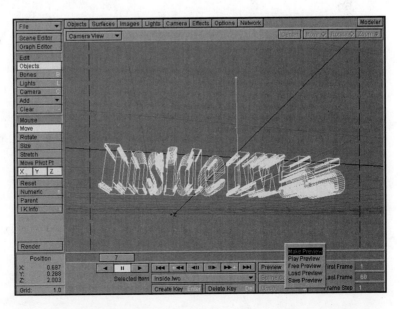

7. Play back the preview. LightWave has created the motion between the first and last keyframe.

8. Now take it one step further. Go to frame 30 by pressing the f key again and entering **30**. Move the object back on the Z axis by using the left mouse button. Now create a keyframe at 30, and again make a preview.

Now you will see the object rise up, swing back, and then come forward again to the original resting position. Congratulations, you've just made an animation with keyframes.

Although this is basic animation information, the point here is that motion requires time and understanding. Even messing around with a simple logo just to explore different motion paths is a good thing to do now and again. Look for more intricate keyframe techniques in Chapter 5.

Summary

Concepts and theories are two significant ways to enhance your learning and growth as a 3D animator. Without a concept, you cannot go as far with your creativity. Learning about color concepts, camera concepts, and lighting concepts enables you to come up with your own powerful concepts for that next great animation job.

Theories are a foundation for you. Theories of how light refracts, of how light is reflected, or of how the RGB color spectrum relates to you as a 3D animator form a foundation you must have. *Inside LightWave 3D* was written to teach you more about the software, and more importantly, to open your mind to more ideas, more learning, and more creativity. This chapter was kept to a minimum so that you can spend more time in the chapters to follow, creating animations for yourself and not just reading about it. If you are ready, sit up, get a cool drink, and turn the page to see Chapter 3, "LightWave in Action."

On the CD-ROM:
ColoredLights.lws
InsideLWLogo.lws
Jog.lws
Lights_OldLady.lws
RGB.lws

Chapter 3

LightWave in Action

It's always exciting to get a new program or software update so you can spend hours clicking around to see exactly what the software can do. With so many elements to LightWave 5.5 for you to explore, perhaps the best way is to dive right in to a few practical tutorials. Before that, however, read this chapter to become familiar with project planning, animation creation, and the types of animations you can create. The tutorials in this chapter familiarize you with the new interface and tools. In this chapter, you'll learn about the following:

- Planning your projects

- Creating LightWave animations

- Types of animations you can create with LightWave

- LightWave for print and advertising purposes

- LightWave for technical and industrial animations

- Developing game animations

Planning Your Projects

Although it is tempting to open LightWave and begin you projects right away, a few simple steps exist that you should take to help your project run smoothly. This section describes some of the planning methods you can use when working with clients or creating animations for yourself.

First, be sure to get all the facts from your client before you begin working on an animation. If you are simply creating an animation for yourself, be sure to think out the entire animation and jot down notes before you begin. This painless step can save you quite a bit of time once the project begins.

Working with Clients

From time to time, even the producers can't iron out what they want. This is where your keen sense of management comes into play. Here are a few tips to keep in mind when working with clients to save time, money, and your sanity.

- Be sure to plan out the entire animation no matter what the client tells you. Know what is expected, due dates, lengths, and rates for additional last minute changes. More importantly, make sure you and the client have a clear understanding of what the animation will consist of.

- Work out an animation agreement before any work begins. If your client won't sign, take a walk.

- Be fair, but stand your ground. Create a set of guidelines for yourself and stick to them.

- Get 50% of your fee up front before any work begins.

- Have a storyboard of the complete animation signed off on by the client before any work begins.

Don't be afraid to stick with these guidelines; they are practical and necessary. You are the one who is paying for the computer system and software. You are the one with the overhead, and you are the one spending hours in front of a computer screen. Raise your standards, but don't take yourself too seriously.

Organizing Your Directories

After a project and price are agreed upon, create working directories for your objects, images, and scene files. Proper organization of your work for each and every job you do will save time and mistakes. Here's a brief idea of a directory structure:

```
C:\Clients
      \DansCandyCo
          \Scenes
          \Objects
          \Images
          \Previews
```

NOTE

You can also use the sample directory structure as the content directory within LightWave. Setting the Content Directory under the Options panel to C:\Clients\DansCandyCo will enable LightWave to easily find all the objects and images within the scene.

From here, you can back up this directory to a removable media device, such as a tape drive, ZIP or JAZ drive, or burn it to a CD-ROM. Back up every step of the way, not just at the end.

WARNING

If you work with LightWave on different platforms, such as a Macintosh and a PC, spaces in file names should not be used. Also, even though Windows NT uses long file names, some LightWave workstations do not. Try to keep file names under eight characters, for cross-platform reasons.

Last in your project planning are the storyboards. Planning your animation project involves many elements, but visually seeing what you are about to create truly helps expedite the process.

Creating Storyboards

Storyboards are not the most exciting part of creating a 3D animation. Storyboards are like the outlines your high school English teacher made you do before you wrote a paper. Storyboards take on the same characteristics, but they are definitely a major plus in the planning of a masterful LightWave animation.

Your client, for example, requires that you create an animation with a one square mile area outside a major city. You take the job and know exactly what to do. You haven't made storyboards, but you have notes from the meetings. Suddenly, after days of rendering, you forget one very important building in the animation, and you must go back and redo that particular shot. With a storyboard, each shot in your animation is worked out on paper first. The room for error is diminished, and you can confidently tackle your project. Not using a storyboard is like driving across the country without a map. Local trips may not need a map, but longer ones do, just like your 3D animations.

A storyboard is simply a sketch of the scenes throughout your animation. Film producers have walls and walls of storyboard sheets to guide them through the film production process. You don't need to be this elaborate for most animations. Figure 3.1 shows an empty storyboard frame.

You don't need to be a sketch artist to generate a storyboard. A stick figure pencil drawing with a good description is about all you need. Figure 3.2 shows what a basic storyboard can look like. Feel free to look at this image closer by pulling it off this book's CD-ROM.

When to Use Storyboards

Use storyboards often, but they are not mandatory with each project you embark upon. The following is a quick tip list for when to use storyboards:

- Projects for clients
- Long-term projects

- Lengthy animations with complex scenes

- Legal animations

FIGURE 3.1

A typical storyboard frame used for either video or animation.

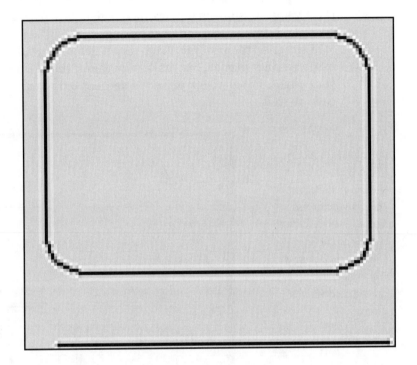

If you are working on a simple project for yourself, don't worry about creating a storyboard. Often, just messing around with LightWave for an afternoon can generate some of your best work. Like anything, you tend to excel in what you do often. If you get into the habit of making storyboards, you will inevitably make them faster, better, and more often. It will become a routine part of every animation. The results are that you will please the client without making careless mistakes, and use the time for creativity, not backtracking.

Altering Storyboards

So you've decided to do it right from the start. You've worked out an arrangement with your client; he's paid 50% up front and has been a big help working with you planning the storyboards. It's been a great collaborative effort, and the animation is going to be spectacular.

What if, however, there is a change? What do you do? Because you have a storyboard, or a script for that matter, does not mean it's written in stone. You must remember that a storyboard is merely a visual outline of the project ahead. Altering or varying the visuals is nothing out of the ordinary because certain situations arise during an animation that make the original idea either better or worse. From there, a change would definitely need to be made. Change is good, but make sure that if there is a change, you run it by your client. Otherwise, you've wasted not only your time, but the client's time as well.

FIGURE 3.2

An animator's rough storyboard—crude-looking, but effective. This storyboard was created using Microsoft Word. You can use primitive shapes in Word or LightWave to generate storyboard sheets.

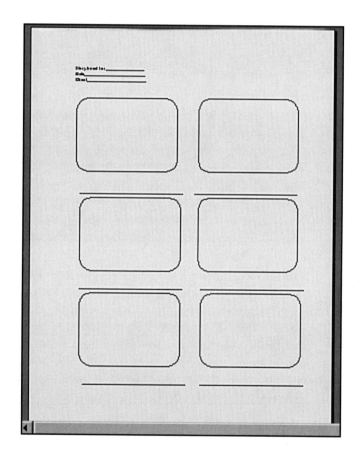

Varying from the Storyboard

The storyboard you create might turn out to be a great piece of work. You might even want to frame it because it's so good. That doesn't mean, however, that you can't vary from it.

One of the benefits of creating a storyboard is that you generate a foundation for the animation and can visually see the beginning, middle, and end. By doing this, you alleviate the need to wonder what you are going to create, and you can focus on the job. From here, you can create with more ideas and enhancements.

Creating Animations for Video

Those who see 3D and eventually get into the business are anxious to create their first 3D animation. Animations have the same foundation no matter where they will be used. If you are animating strictly as a hobbiest, are creating a corporate flying logo, or are working in a Hollywood studio for next month's made-for-TV movie, a LightWave animation is virtually the same anyway you look at it.

Each LightWave animation has the same basic components. A LightWave scene holds the complete information of the project. A LightWave scene file tells your computer what objects are included, what motions they posses, what camera settings are being used, resolutions, recording parameters, and which plug-ins need to be applied. Any element associated with the animation is recorded as a scene file. It is important to note, however, that a LightWave object file retains the information associated with it. That is an object's surface and accompanying image maps are saved with the object file. To better explain it, Table 3.1 shows a breakdown of what is saved with a scene file and what is saved with an object file.

TABLE 3.1

What Is Saved in Scene Versus Object Files

Scene Files Contain	Object Files Contain
Scene information	Object surfacing
Motions	Object plug-ins
Keyframes	Image maps associated with objects
Lighting	
Plug-ins used	
Camera positions and lenses	

continues

TABLE 3.1, CONTINUED

What Is Saved in Scene Versus Object Files

Scene Files Contain	Object Files Contain
Recording information	
Displacement Maps	
Image sequences	
Bones and IK	
Envelope settings	
Clip Maps	

NOTE

Saving a LightWave scene does not save the surfaces of an object. Be sure to use the Save Object selection from within the Objects Panel to save an object's surface settings and image maps. Using the Save All Objects command from the Objects Panel records all surface settings for objects.

If you are simply creating fun animations for yourself, you should realize that the people working in the Hollywood studios using LightWave are doing the same thing you are. The difference is that they work with better objects, surfaces, and usually systems. They also have years of experience creating animations. What you should realize, however, is that they are working with the same software you are, loading objects, saving scenes, and creating images. Learn to know what power you have at your fingertips, and to open your mind to the possibilities of the endless creative visions you can create.

Animating for Video Production

A common application for LightWave animations is for video production. This can be any sort of production from home videos to weddings, to corporate training videos, to television programs. The following brief tutorial takes you through a simple creepy graveyard scene, something that can be used for video distribution or as an introduction to a cable television special. You'll learn about the following:

- Setting up a scene and surfaces

- Loading and placing objects in a scene

- Modifying simple ground and sky objects you can reuse

- Lighting for nighttime skies

- Creating lightning

- Creating rain

- Animating the camera

Animations such as this are good to learn from for many reasons. The sky you'll set up can be manipulated slightly to achieve an entirely different look. The rain can be used as snow, depending on where in the world you live. The ground can become a dusty desert or a mountain range with a few clicks of the mouse.

SETTING UP THE GRAVEYARD SCENE

1. Go to the Options Panel, and set the Content Directory to the area where this book's CD-ROM files are. For example, C:\INLW\Projects\Chap3 would instruct Lightwave to look for objects and images there, rather than to the C:\Newtek directory. You can set this content directory to look for your CD as well.

2. Begin by starting LightWave's Layout. Go to the Objects Panel and press Load Object.

3. Go to the Chapter 3 directory on this book's CD-ROM. Load the GroundBump.lwo file. This object is a premade Ground object for you to surface on your own.

NOTE

New to LightWave 5.5 is the Add button in Layout. By being in the Edit Object mode, you can simply click the Add drop-down button to add an object or a Null object to the scene. You also can add Lights and Bones the same way. This saves the step of entering the panels.

With the Ground object loaded, you now have automatically set the grid size for the animation as well. This is because when you first create a scene, the grid will always end up in a size relative to the largest object, which, in this case, is the ground. This is an automatic feature of LightWave. A workaround to this is to load the main object and then save the scene. Reload the scene, and when larger objects are added, the grid size won't change.

TIP

Going to the Options Panel and then changing the Grid Square Size within the Layout View tab can change the Grid Size in Layout. If your camera or object moves too fast with a mouse adjustment, your Grid Square Size is too large. If an object or the camera doesn't seem to move at all with a mouse adjustment, your Grid Square Size is too small. Figure 3.3 shows the Layout View tab. The Grid Square Size adjusts the size of the grid seen in the Layout window. Its size also affects the increments of movement and rotation of items in a scene.

FIGURE 3.3

The Layout View tab within the Options Panel where you can adjust the Grid Square Size.

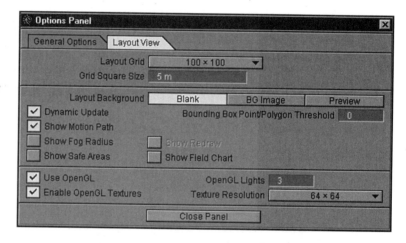

4. In addition to the Ground object, load the Tombstone object (Tombstone.lwo) three times and load the Cloud object (Cloud.lwo) into Layout, also from the book's CD-ROM, Chapter 3 directory. You should change the grid size to 100 m. This will help the accuracy and placement of objects.

5. Begin setting up the scene by first placing the tombstones. This will be a little tricky because the ground object is not level. A good way to see better is to turn on OpenGL preview for the ground object (if you're working with LightWave 5.0 or higher). This will make the ground solid and help you place the stones. Access the OpenGL Display through the Options Panel, under the Layout View tab.

6. Move the tombstones into place, one toward the front of the ground, one toward the back, and one off to the side. Create keyframes for each object to hold them in place. Figure 3.4 shows an example of how the tombstones can be placed. Notice the slight banked camera angle on them. Duplicate this camera angle with a bank of about –10.

FIGURE 3.4
Tombstones are loaded three times and scattered about the graveyard.

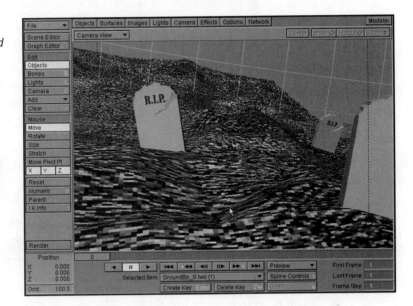

NOTE

You must also tell LightWave's Scene Editor to show the individual or all objects as OpenGL objects, wireframe, or Textured OpenGL objects. Do this by entering the Scene Editor, and choosing the Show All Objects As selection. You can do this individually also in the Scene Editor by clicking in the second column next to the object's listing in the scene overview.

7. Now you need to size up the clouds. Select the Cloud object, and size it up to about 9 or 10 times for all axes. Do this by selecting the cloud as the current object, and then pressing size from the mouse menu buttons on the left-hand side of the screen. Press n to call up the Numeric Requester, and enter the new size values. The Cloud object should encompass the Ground object.

8. Move the Cloud object into place by viewing it from the side. You may have to zoom out the view a bit to see the clouds by pressing the command

(,) key. Create a keyframe to lock it in place. Press the 3 on the keypad to jump to the Side (ZY) view. Move the cloud object so that it encompasses the Ground objects, as in figure 3.5.

FIGURE 3.5

The Cloud object in place covering the ground elements. Here, it can be seen as the circle around the entire scene.

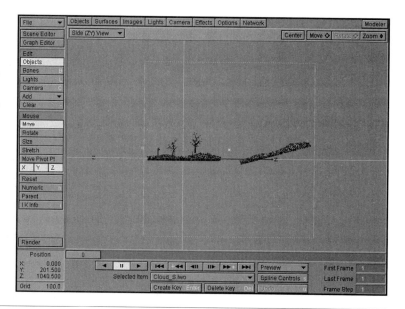

Now you need to surface the objects. The ground basically needs some dirt, fractal noise, and a brownish-green color. These values are totally random; you can have fun creating a grimy, dirty ground. The following steps work through the surfacing of the objects in the scene.

SURFACING THE OBJECTS

1. Continue from the previous exercise. Load the Ground.tga, SandDirt.tga, and DirtBump.tga files from this book's CD-ROM. You can place each of these on the Ground object for a different type of look. Surface the ground with these images.

2. Select the Ground as the current surface in the Surfaces Panel. Click the T button next to Surface Color to enter the Texture Panel. Select Planar Image Map as the current surface. Use Ground.tga as the Texture Image. Keep Pixel Blending, Width and Height Repeat on. The texture Axis is Y, and the Texture size is X = 1500.0, Y = 90.0, and Z = 800.0. Turn Smoothing on.

NOTE

LightWave 5.5 now supports different units of measurement in Layout. Make sure your units are set to meters for this tutorial from the Options, General Options area.

3. Go a step further and use the same Texture Size and Texture Image settings as in step 9 for the Diffuse Texture. Again select the T button, but this time next to the Diffuse value setting in the Surfaces Panel. Use the brightness levels in the image to set varying diffuse levels across the surface. This creates a more natural-looking image map.

You can also use the same settings to apply a bump map. Set the bump map values within the Texture Panel next to Bump Map at the bottom of the screen.

When rendered, this simple Ground object will work fine for your graveyard animation. To learn more about surfacing properties and how you can alter this object, read Chapter 8, "Textures and Materials," for in-depth information. Figure 3.6 shows the rendered Ground object.

FIGURE 3.6
The Ground object after a Color texture, Diffuse texture, and bump map were applied.

4. For the clouds, surfaces need to be a little more specific. Use the following data:

Surface Color	140,160,255
Surface Color Texture	
Texture Type	Fractal Noise
Texture Opacity	100%
Texture Size	X 50
	Y 6
	Z 50
Texture Velocity	X 0.05
	Y 0.02
	Z -0.2
Texture Color	158,172,186
Frcquencies	10
Contrast	2.0
Small Power	0.5

5. Click Use Texture for the Surface Color Texture, and create some soft, dark blue and gray streaked clouds. The image on the CD was created with the following values. Feel free to adjust the values for different looks.

Luminosity	30%
Diffuse Level	0%
Specular Level	0%
Transparency	40%
Transparency Texture	
Texture Type	Fractal Noise
Texture Opacity	100%
Texture Size	X 45
	Y 5
	Z 45
Texture Velocity	X 0.2
	Y 0.07
	Z -0.8
Texture Value	100%
Frequencies	10
Contrast	2.0
Small Power	0.5

These values will produce some soft dark blue streaked clouds. However, if you use the default LightWave background, your dark blue clouds will render over the dark black sky. Although surfacing is covered more in depth in Chapter 8, it's appropriate to mention here because much of the success of this cloud surface depends on the scene's backdrop colors. Since the cloud object is transparent, you will see right through it. What's behind will be the backdrop colors. This is why it's appropriate to set the colors to a blue sky, or similar.

6. From the Effects Panel, select the Backdrop and Fog tab. Here, you can change the sky color to match the clouds better. Remember that you just made the clouds transparent, so the sky will show through. Experiment with different colors and settings. The image for the book used the following settings for a Gradient Sky. You can enter these values under the Effects, Backdrop, and Fog tab. Click on Gradient Backdrop.

Zenith Color	37,36,62
Sky Color	32,38,85
Ground Color	32,38,85
Nadir Color	107,63,1
Sky Squeeze	5.0
Ground Squeeze	5.0
And for the fog settings:	
Fog Type	Nonlinear 1
Minimum Fog Distance	500
Maximum Fog Distance	2500
Minimum Fog Amount	0%
Maximum Fog Amount	75%
Backdrop Fog	On

Do a quick test render, and you'll see that you now have an evening sky with visible clouds. Change the color of the gradient backdrop and you'll have a different look.

In order for your scene and animation to be of professional caliber, you need to add the little details. In the next exercise, you add mountains in the background, scary dead trees, and rain. Mountains are very easy to create because instead of creating an entirely new object, you can use the ground object as a mountain range. The dead trees are simply tree models with the leaves removed. You can easily vary the tree shape by adding and removing branches. You create the rain by simply loading the rain object that ships with LightWave.

ADDING DETAILS TO THE SCENE

1. Continue from the previous exercise. Load the Ground.lwo object again from the Chapter 3 directory on this book's CD-ROM. Because of the added fog in the scene, the first Ground object blends seamlessly into the second Ground object, or now the mountains. Move the second Ground object back behind the first Ground object, and rotate it slightly on the pitch, as shown in figure 3.7.

TIP

You can take this one step further and load the second Ground object into Modeler and rename the surface from ground to mountain. Resave the object as Mountains.lwo, and then apply a surface and texture to it. Briefly, the mountain surface, if you decide to change it, should be similar to the ground's surface, but more blue and brighter. Try diffusing the Ground.tga image with a whitish-blue surface color. Figure 3.7 shows the Ground object in position used as a mountain range.

FIGURE 3.7

The same Ground object is used twice to make a mountain range.

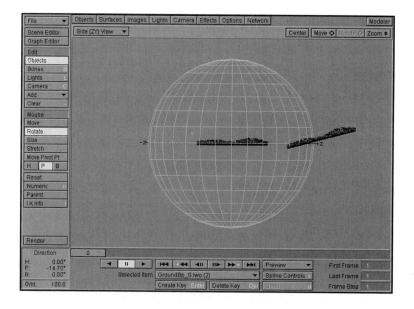

2. Part of every good scary graveyard are a few dead trees. Load the Tree object (Tree1.lwo) into Layout from the Chapter 3 directory on this book's CD (see fig. 3.8).

FIGURE 3.8

A basic Tree object suddenly becomes a scary dead tree once the leaves are removed. Find this object in the Chapter 3 directory of this book's CD-ROM.

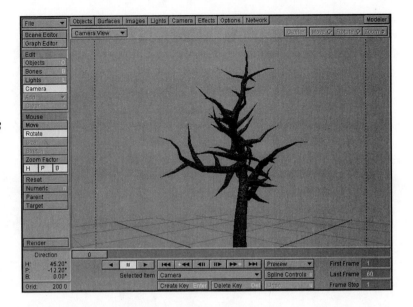

You may want more than one tree. You can use the same tree two or three times, or you can load Tree2.lwo from this book's CD-ROM. Just be sure to rotate each one so that they don't appear the same at any angle. You can also size up the tree, and warp it a bit with the stretch function in Layout.

Another way to create different versions of this tree is to cut off some of the branches in Modeler and move the points of remaining branches. Also, you can use the Vertilectric plug-in from Blevins Enterprises to create some cool-looking, random dead trees.

3. Place the tree(s) around the ground as you see fit. You only need a few trees, so be sure not to clump them together. These trees are already surfaced, so don't worry about adjusting them.

When placing the trees, be sure to keep an eye on where they are in relation to the ground. Because the ground object is not completely flat, it's easy to make a mistake in placement and your tree could be too low, or even float above the ground. Once in place, remember to create a keyframe at zero for each object. Figure 3.9 shows how the scene looks so far with the trees placed and fog rendered.

4. Now you need some rain. You can do this by loading the rain scene that ships with LightWave from NewTek. You can find this scene in the Misc Directory in your NewTek folder. From the Objects Panel, use Load From Scene to import an existing scene into a current scene. Click NO to loading the existing Lights when prompted.

5. The Null object in this scene has the rain columns parented to it, allowing you to size the rain to fit the current scene. Select the Null object, and size it numerically with a value of 300.0 on the X, Y, and Z axes.

TIP

This rain is simple to reproduce. In Modeler, you can create a large block of single point polygons by using the LW_RandPoints plug-in. From there, you can turn the points into single point polygons through the LW_Points2Polys plug-in.

The rain scene is already set to go when you take the original LightWave rain scene using Load From Scene in the Objects Panel. However, here's a quick explanation of how it works. Two columns are loaded into layout and placed one on top of the other. Each is moving steadily downward. When the first column passes the ground plane, it quickly dissolves out, travels to above the other rain column, and dissolves back in. The same thing happens to the second rain column. This creates a constant cascading rainfall.

6. When you render the rain, be sure to turn on Particle Blur at about 50% in the Camera Panel. This finishes the illusion of rain. Figure 3.10 shows the rain rendered with Particle Blur, the tombstones in place, and the mountains in the background.

FIGURE 3.10
Single point polygons with Particle Blur create a nice rain effect.

The lighting in this scene now needs to be adjusted. If you remember back when you created the clouds, you set a fractal noise transparency map. If you render out this scene, you really don't see the clouds too well. This is because no light is set to illuminate the clouds. The following steps walk you through lighting the scene.

LIGHTING THE GRAVEYARD SCENE

1. Go to the Lights Panel and click Add Light. Change the default Intensity to 80%. Change the Light Type to Point, and change the Light Color to

192,205,204 RGB. Click Lens Flare, select the Lens Flare Option, and enter the Lens Flare Panel. Select Rename Light and name it Moon.

2. Use the following settings to create a glowing moon. Figure 3.11 shows LightWave's Lens Flare settings.

Flare Intensity = 140%
Turn On   Fade Off Screen
                                             Fade Behind Objects
                                             Central Glow
                                             Random Streaks

Streak Intensity = 3%
Streak Density = 5.0

FIGURE 3.11
The Lens Flare Panel within LightWave.

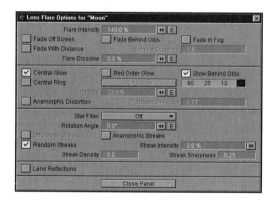

3. Return to Layout and select the Moon Light as the current light. Move it beyond the Cloud object, back on the Z-axis. Move the Moon Light back on the Z-axis behind the graveyard. Keep it low so it stays in the frame. This is an arbitrary location, so place it to your liking.

Now render a small test. The sky is more illuminated and the clouds are now visible. You can adjust the background colors and the clouds to create any amount of sky effects. For example, a brighter blue to orange gradient will create a sunset mood.

TIP

Experiment with these basic settings. You can manipulate them to create many different looks.

Finally, your last step in animating a scary graveyard scene is to create some nice camera moves using Motion Blur. The scenario of a traveling camera through a scary graveyard truly puts the final touches on an animation like this. Start with the camera at frame 0. At frame 0, the camera is up in the sky, above the trees. As the animation starts, it slowly travels down to reveal the first tombstone. The following steps go through animating the scene.

ANIMATING THE GRAVEYARD

1. Position the camera at about 836.324 on the Y-axis. This setting is up to you, but use this value as a reference. Rotate the camera so that the graveyard is in view. The camera should rest just above the graveyard, as in figure 3.12.

FIGURE 3.12
The first keyframe for the camera. This is what the shot will be when the animation begins.

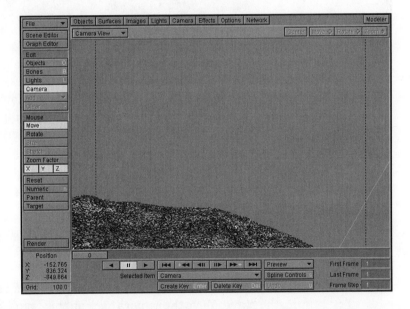

2. You want the camera to take about 5 seconds to travel down to the ground, so using the right mouse button (hold Ctrl plus the mouse for the Mac), bring the camera down on the Y-axis so that it is sitting just above the ground. Bank it about 10 degrees to offset the look. Create a key here at frame 150. Figure 3.13 shows the second keyframe.

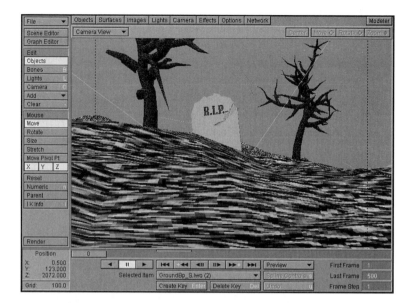

3. Now you want the camera to move in toward the first tombstone. The entire animation is short, about 500 frames, or 16.6 seconds. You need to travel by two tombstones in that time, without rushing through. Move the camera in on the Z-axis so that it's sitting just in front of the tombstone, as in figure 3.14. Create a keyframe here at 220. Feel free to rotate the bank of the camera slightly again.

TIP

When the camera gets to the third keyframe, notice the angle. Instead of just moving the camera in to show the tombstone, bank the camera to the left or right to give an uncomfortable feeling. Also, remember to check out Chapter 11, "Cameras," for more camera techniques.

4. At this point, you want the viewer to be scared and suddenly pull back from the grave. Move the camera back on the Z-axis. Don't go as far back as the previous keyframe though. Create a keyframe there at 230. This is only 10 frames up from the second keyframe because you want the camera to suddenly jerk back.

5. From there, the camera swings away, so create another keyframe 10 frames later at 240, with the camera rotated 40 degrees to the right. Again, these camera positions don't need to be exact. The idea here is to get a feel for setting up camera moves that go beyond a start and stop.

FIGURE 3.14

The camera has moved in toward the tombstone at the third keyframe.

6.   With the camera turned to the right at frame 240, move it in close to the next tombstone. Create a keyframe there about 3 seconds later at frame 340, remembering to bank the camera slightly.

7.   Again, the camera jerks back over ten frames. Back up the camera and create a keyframe at 350. Next, rotate the camera to the left, pointing at a tree. Create a keyframe here at 360.

8.   Similar to the tombstones, move the camera in toward the tree, banking it slightly as you go. Create a keyframe for the camera at the base of the tree at frame 460. If the camera movements from 360 to 460 appear too smooth for a graveyard, create a keyframe in between, say at 428, and bank the camera in another direction. This will offset the motion path a bit and make for a more appropriate graveyard camera move.

9.   Rotate the camera up, and move it into the sky for a last keyframe at 520. Figure 3.15 shows the camera at frame 360, before the camera moves in closer to the tree.

FIGURE 3.15

The camera has moved in toward a tree before turning up into the sky.

You can see a rendered version of this animation on the book's CD-ROM. View the AVI file called Gravyard from the Chapter 3 directory. You also can load this scene from the book's CD and check out the keyframes.

Although basic, the previous exercise has eye-catching results. This is because you have a complete picture, more than just an object over a black background, or a flat ground with a standard blue sky. Even a basic animation like this has a little personality because of the clouds, the fog, the angles, and the camera moves. Remember these methods in all your animations, and you'll begin to step ahead of your competition. The following sections cover some other great applications for LightWave animations.

Developing Game Animations

Before the success of LightWave on the PC and Macintosh, LightWave was not a common tool with video game developers. Now the speed, power, and affordability of LightWave on common workstations make it an ideal candidate for 3D video game creation.

LightWave animations in game development are found in two areas. The first is the animated opening sequence. Usually, the final animation is compressed to a playable computer file with sound, such as an AVI. The second is in the creation of models and image maps used for sets and characters within the games themselves. Using LightWave to create AVI files has few limitations, other than length.

When preparing to create an animation for a video game, the rules are different from the ones for video production. First and foremost, storyboards play a big role in these types of animation. The animation for a video game is created to introduce the story in a timely, but effective, manner, not just for show. Having the animation planned out before work begins is a good first step.

From there, if LightWave will be used to create objects and characters in the game, animators need to seriously consider the polygon count in each and every object. The problem is how to make an object look good without many polygons. The answer is in the design of the character and its surfacing.

Animating for Video Games

Animating for a video game is as much fun as playing one because you can tell the characters what to do.

Animators for video games often follow these guidelines:

- Polygon counts must remain low on each object. This is because in order for the elements within a video game to react in real-time, a low polygon count requires less computation time within the gaming system. Additionally, low polygon counts enable programmers and artists to add more elements throughout the game.

- Image maps should remain very low in size as well. Image maps throughout a video game work best with images under 100KB in size.

- Movements can be as complex as you want; you can even use motion capture.

The challenge in animating for video games comes from creating the best-looking and most realistic characters and scenes, while maintaining memory constraints and speed. The less information there is within a scene, the faster the video game can run. A true video game artist and animator knows exactly how to keep polygon counts low and image maps small, but still turns out a fantastic-looking game.

Other Applications of LightWave

LightWave experts will tell you that LightWave 3D is used in more diverse industries than any other 3D program, including television, movies, forensic animations, and architectural animations. The following pages will take you on a tour of the areas in which LightWave 3D can be used.

Animating for Television

In the previous section, you saw how LightWave can be used for video production. Often, video productions are presented on television, either local cable, regional cable, or broadcast. This section, however, talks about LightWave for television on a larger scale. Take a look at your local television commercials, national television programs, and national television commercials. You will see 3D animations for the M&M commercials from Wil Vinton Studios, Babylon 5 from Foundation Imaging, the Titanic mini-series from Digital Muse and more, all of which were created directly for television using LightWave.

Video is typically rendered at roughly 752×480 pixels. LightWave's resolutions support pixels up to 8000×8000, which means renders are more than suitable for television and film.

Animating for Movies

Because of the high rendering resolutions LightWave can produce, the software is widely used for television and movie trailers. In addition, it is used because of its low price, its Windows NT operating system (particularly on the DEC Alpha system), affordable Alpha/MIPS workstations, and ScreamerNet for Network rendering. You may have seen the previews to the second James Bond 007 thriller with Pierce Brosnan, which used LightWave to generate the effects. Long time LightWave animator John Gross's Digital Muse produced the animations. LightWave's film market is definitely growing, with companies such as Digital Muse and Digital Domain involved as some of the major players. You can plan on seeing more and more LightWave each time you head to the movie theatres.

Forensic Animation

Although a small market for LightWave animations, Forensic usage of 3D is growing rapidly. Figure 3.16 shows an image of a heart animated for forensic use in a medical lab.

FIGURE 3.16
LightWave used for forensic animation, to show the human heart and lungs.

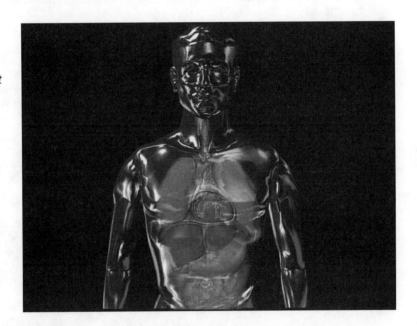

Forensic animation benefits greatly from 3D animation because artists can literally rebuild scientific data, internal organs, and recreate the scene of an accident. If you think about it, one small LightWave animation can take a criminal off of the streets or let a wrongly accused man go free. LightWave can be a powerful tool when put to use.

Architectural Animation

Users of AutoCAD are certainly familiar with the top results from 3D renders of soon-to-be-built buildings. LightWave animators also enjoy the same pleasure, but on a much larger scale.

LightWave enables an animator to take an architect's AutoCAD file, the original computer generated blue print, and add ray-traced shadows, lighting effects, and more. Animated walkthroughs of buildings, or even corporate districts, can save enormous amounts of money because people can visualize what will be built. Investors can see where their money will go, and engineers can see how their work will play a role to the surrounding elements. Figure 3.17 shows an actual city block in Chicago. Franklin Stevenson built this object for the Illinois Medical District. Here, the complete one-square-mile district is rebuilt from an architect's AutoCAD file.

FIGURE 3.17

A true replica in LightWave of a one square mile district in Chicago. Models by Franklin Stevenson. Rendering by Dan Ablan.

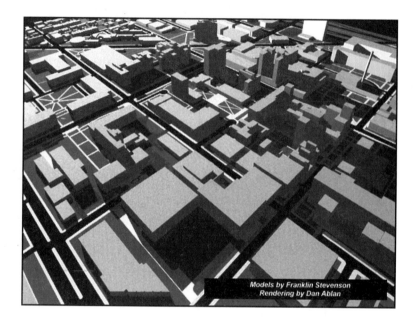

LightWave can be used for just about anything you can imagine. The methods may be different than other programs, but often, the results exceed expectations. LightWave is so wide ranging that even video game creators are using it to build 3D graphics for video games. Beyond that, artists are using it to create 3D art for print and advertising campaigns.

LightWave for Print and Advertising

When you think of LightWave, the first thought would be animation. But 3D imagery is so popular, many advertisers are turning to artists for 3D stills for magazine ads, billboards, 3D art, and even covers of books.

The cover of this book is a perfect example of LightWave 3D used in print. The image was generated specifically for the cover. In doing so, author Dan Ablan worked with these elements in mind:

- The image should be fast-looking and colorful.

- The final image must be able to be cut and pasted into another piece of work. The object has to be rendered on a single-color background, so the final car image is easy to remove individually.

- The resolution must be high enough for print, at least 3000 pixels.

Figure 3.18 shows the formula car before rendering over a basic blue (0,0,255 RGB) background. Simple planning of where the image will be used is essential to the project before it begins. This is crucial because the resolutions needed for print and advertising are much higher than resolutions for video, almost four times as large. That means, your single frame render will take four times as long as a video render. However, the LightWave Layout design can remain virtually the same, as seen in figure 3.18.

FIGURE 3.18
One frame of a formula race car is rendered for use on the cover of this book.

Rendering over a basic background, such as a 255 RGB Green, allows the final artist to cut and paste easily. If the car had been rendered as part of a scene, cutting it out in a 2D paint program, such as Photoshop, would be very difficult. Also, using a color value like this (bright green) is unlikely to appear elsewhere in the image. Using plain black or white as a background can make cropping and image more difficult since shadows are close to black in color, and highlights are close to white. Cleanly selecting the rendered portion of the image would be more difficult on a black or white background.

The same principle applies when rendering a 3D image for advertising. As shown in figure 3.19, a simple product bottle is rendered over a plain background. The advertising agency wants it floating over clouds, perhaps even moving clouds. They only need the 3D rendered bottle from you, the rest is put together by their in-house artists.

FIGURE 3.19
A household cleaning bottle is rendered over a plain background so that artists can later cut it out for a print ad.

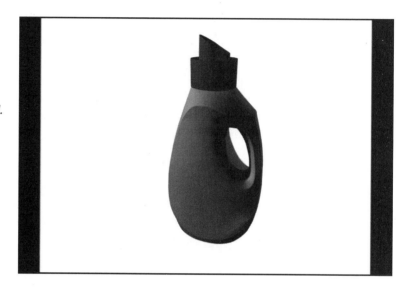

This type of work is easy to do, and it pays well. Yet, a more challenging approach would be to place the product within a 3D set. Figure 3.20 shows the bottle on a 3D backdrop, lit with standard three-point lighting.

FIGURE 3.20
The 3D bottle is rendered in a virtual set. This is more of a complete look and more fun to create.

Creating advertisements such as this can be used for either still imagery or moving animations. Also, a project like this looks great on your demo reel!

Creating images for print and advertising have two key factors you need to consider: realism and resolution. The two Rs are what you need to remember when putting together still or moving 3D images for print and advertising. All other LightWave knowledge you have can be applied. Realism relies on lighting, shadows, textures, and surroundings, all elements talked about throughout this book. Resolution and image size is the next step to understand.

Resolution and Image Size

Image resolutions can be challenging. Although the output often looks the same in the end, resolutions are different for print than they are for video, film, computer AVI, or QuickTime movies. It's up to you to figure out what resolution is too much or not enough for the project at hand. *Inside LightWave 3D* includes a small chart of resolutions and uses.

Type of Media	Resolution
AVI or QuickTime movies	300×200 pixels
Video, SVHS, BetaSP, D2	752×480 (note, 720×486 works too for PVR users)
Film	From 2560×1920 up to 8000×8000

Film resolutions can vary depending on the printer. Where 2560×1920 may be enough for some uses such as magazine images, often resolutions of 3000 or more are needed for cover images of magazines or books. This is an area that will become specific when you need to create something. Generally, the editor of the magazine or art director at an ad agency will tell you what resolution they want you to use. This also means that aspect ratios may change. The standard 4×3 ratio used commonly for video is not always used in print.

Pixel Aspects

When rendering your images, you need to be aware of the Pixel Aspect in LightWave. Different systems use different pixel aspects, specifically square pixels versus rectangular or elongated pixels. If your rendered image or animation is headed for video tape or television, you will want to use a different pixel aspect than square, such as D2. If your image or animation is staying within the computer or going to a Macintosh, you should use square pixels.

The pixels that make up the image are scaled because a computer monitor's ration is more square than a television's is. You need to adjust accordingly to your output.

Technical and Industrial Animations

There's one more area LightWave is commonly used for: technical and industrial animations. Before computer prices dropped, and before 3D imagery was so accessible and affordable, technical illustrators either spent huge amounts of money to have 3D animations created out-of-house, or used drawings to present their message. Smaller industrial firms simply could not afford the luxury of 3D.

Today, things are much different. 3D industrial animations are not a luxury but a necessity. 3D animation in the technical and industrial arena is beneficial to companies for safety, instruction, and communication. You can create an animation in which a water filtration system has been entirely rebuilt in 3D, for example. During the course of the animation, pieces of the system dissolve out, revealing the inner workings of the machine. This helps salespeople in the field understand exactly how their products work. It also helps engineers with future improvements and concepts.

Technical and industrial animations are not limited to complex machinery, however. Technical animations can be the simple workings of two gears, or the creation of light sources in a new office building. There's even some technical animations on your LightWave CD from NewTek. Check out the circuit board scenes within the Computer scenes directory.

Summary

Learning how to plan your projects is one of the most important skills you can master as an animator. You should also become familiar with LightWave's strengths and options in the different animation fields, such as video, games, forensics, and so on. The following list recaps the important points to keep in mind as you plan your projects:

- Get all the facts from your client before you begin working on an animation.

- Don't be afraid to stick with the guidelines you and your client establish; they are practical and necessary.

- Create working directories for your objects, images, and scene files.

- A storyboard is merely a visual outline of the project ahead.

- The speed, power, and affordability of LightWave on common workstations make it an ideal candidate for 3D video game creation.

- Creating images for print and advertising have two key factors you need to consider: realism and resolution.

- Learn what power you have at your fingertips and open your mind to the possibilities of the endless creative visions you can create.

Perhaps you are doing technical animations for advertising or industrial animations for television. Whichever the case, turn the page and read Chapter 4, "Modeler Techniques," for in-depth object creation coverage.

Chapter 4

MODELER TECHNIQUES

Once mastered, LightWave's Modeler opens up worlds of possibilities for you and your animations. Often, when you see a complex model, it's overwhelming to comprehend how basic geometric shapes such as boxes, balls, discs, cones, and curves can create a believable 3D model. But, once you break things down into separate elements, you'll better understand the steps needed to model an object. Working in LightWave's Modeler will help you understand how to build physical objects.

LightWave's Modeler is a polygonal and spline-based modeling system. Polygonal modeling relies on the creation of polygons made from points, whereas splines are curves. Whichever method you use to create a model, LightWave's Layout needs a polygonal model for rendering. Therefore, a spline-based model needs to have its curves "frozen" into polygons before rendering in Layout. With most modeling projects, you will use many of the LightWave's included tools—primarily, MetaNURBS and Boolean operations—for many of your objects. In this chapter you'll learn about:

- Modeler orientation and specifications
- Understanding your goal in Modeler
- Points, polygons, and layers
- LightWave and splines
- MetaNURBS approach
- Modeler plug-ins

Understanding Modeler's Orientation and Specifications

Before you begin a complex model, you should understand some of Modeler's preliminary settings, such as the views, grid size, and display. These settings not only will help you with your modeling but will help you follow along throughout this book's exercises.

Modeler's Points of View

In Modeler, you'll see four points of view. These default views are most common and rarely need to be changed. At the upper left corner, you see the Top view. When you load an object, this view shows the top of the object. The upper right corner is the Preview view, which has different settings controlled from the Display Options Panel. The bottom left view is the Face view. When you load an object, the view looks down the Z-axis, usually at the face of the object. Lastly, the fourth view at the bottom right side of the interface is the Side view. This view looks down the X-axis as if looking at the left side of an object. You can reconfigure the views through the Display Options Panel, which you can access by pressing d on the keyboard. The Orientation drop-down menu offers variations to the view such as an XY view, XZ view, and so on. Here, you can also change the four views in Modeler to one single view. This single view can be a Face view, Side view, Top view, or Single Preview view.

Be sure to refer to your *LightWave User Guide* and *LightWave Reference Guide* to see the other settings you can program to the numeric keypad. You have different save options for different orientations as well.

The Grid Size

At the bottom left-hand side of the Modeler screen, you'll see a small information window. At the bottom of that is information that says Grid and shows a number. This is the Grid Size. The Grid Size number in the Information Panel is the actual amount between each square grid. For example, if you have a 1 meter grid and the windows in Modeler are 5 grids tall, the Modeler window is 5 meters. So, if you were building a computer mouse to scale, this grid size would be too big.

You can change the Grid Size by pressing the comma key (,) to zoom out or the period key (.) to zoom in. Try always to model your objects to scale. Although it's not necessary, if you begin creating a good size library of objects, you should have no trouble fitting different objects from different projects into your scenes. If you create a lamp that is 10 meters tall, for example, and a month later build a desk that is actual size, the lamp would be much too large for the desk. You would then have to size and scale the lamp. Building it to scale from the start is a better way to go.

Units

LightWave Modeler 5.5 enables you to create objects in the following measurements:

- Nanometers
- Microns
- Millimeters
- Meters
- Kilometers
- Megameters
- Gigameters
- Centimeters
- Inches
- Feet
- Miles

You can set Modeler's unit system to Metric, English, or SI. SI stands for System International. Modeler will automatically convert to Metric or English depending on the unit system selected. You should get in the habit of using SI along with meters as the unit system for this book's projects and most of your work. This system will work well for you whether you are in America, France, Italy, Spain, or elsewhere. Metric is also fine to use because it has the same System International. You can find these options also under the Display Options Panel by pressing the d key on the keyboard.

Changing the Preview Type

While you're in the Display Options Panel, you'll see a drop-down menu for Preview Type. This controls the type of preview you will see in Modeler's preview window. The options are

- None
- Wire
- Frontface (polygons)

- Solid

- OpenGL Sketch

- OpenGL Flat Shaded

- OpentGL Smooth Shaded

- Quickdraw 3D (Mac Users)

Load an object into Modeler and test the different views. If your video display supports 65,000 colors or more, you may choose to keep the OpenGL Smooth Shaded preview open. Using OpenGL display requires more than an 8-bit display.

New to LightWave 5.5 is a configurable colored backdrop for OpenGL display. Under the Display tab, you'll see a button labeled Backdrop. At the bottom of this window is a new Requester that enables you to choose any color from the spectrum as your Modeler's preview backdrop display color. This is quite beneficial when surfacing objects and differentiating between objects and the backdrop. Remember that you can assign any of these Preview Type displays to a preset control on the numeric keypad by pressing Ctrl and a number.

NOTE

The color you choose for the Preview display and the type of display you select will be saved with the LightWave configuration file. So, the next time you start Modeler, your previous display options will automatically come up.

There are a few elements in Modeler that you won't change often, such as polygon creation mode (quadrangles, triangles, or automatic), curve division, grid units, or grid snap. But you should be aware that you have the ability to make these changes should a situation arise. What's also important is your goal in Modeler and how you go about creating high-quality objects.

Understanding Your Goal in Modeler

The most helpful piece of advice this book can stress is to plan your model. Know what you want to create before you begin creating it. This applies to setting up an animation as well as modeling.

You must always keep the final project in mind when you model; not the final model, but the final project. Where will the object you modeled be used? How close up will it be rendered? Is it for broadcast, film, or for home video? Knowing where the model will end up will help your modeling practices, your time, and your sanity. Often, it's not necessary to model a complete object. For example, Scooter Productions has hired you to animate a dusty desert town. You need to animate a shoot-out, so part of the project will require you to build a general store, saloon, and a few other typical old-west buildings. Throughout the animation, the scene will take place in the street. Not once do you need to animate above the buildings, or in them, or behind them. Model what you need, not what you think you'll need.

In a Hollywood set, the old-west buildings are only fronts held up by two-by-fours. The same can be said for LightWave, minus the two by fours. If all the animation calls for is the front of the buildings, there's no need to build a complete building. There's no need to build an interior or a backside, or a roof. Of course, if you ever need to use the full building in a future animation, all you need to do is add on the rest of the building to your existing model.

Purists will tell you that building only a portion of the model is "cheating." This book is telling you to work smarter, not harder. If you modeled only a portion of the building, you have still done the work necessary to get the job done.

Understanding your goal in Modeler is key. Know what you want, and know where you're going, and learn the tools within Modeler to get you there.

Physical Models

With any modeling task, it's always a bonus to have a physical model in front of you. The tools you need to complete a project are not only within your LightWave software, but on your desktop as well. Granted, it's not always possible to have the Golden Gate Bridge in front of you when modeling your own replica. In cases such as these, you can sometimes find miniature models in gift shops, catalogs, or museums. Depending on what you're modeling, you can find many useful physical models in toy stores.

Certain situations, though, require more than a physical model. For instance, perhaps you want to animate your favorite honeymoon spot. In that case, a photograph can work very well.

When working from a photograph, you have some creative freedom because not all of the elements are right in front of you. However, you might find that working from a photo works as well as a model. Photographs are also good for situations when you need to re-create an indoor environment, such as a hotel lobby or an office. A photograph helps with details such as moldings, carpet color, lighting fixtures, door trims, and more. All of these elements help make your animation more convincing.

Computer Models

When physical models or photographs aren't available or suitable, you may find computer models for your project. Computer models are widely available from a variety of sources. Many companies offer 3D objects for sale in LightWave format, such as ViewPoint Datalabs, 3namd3D, or 3Dcafe to name a few. You can also use the free datasets on the CD accompanying this book.

You can find other pre-existing computer models on the web at locations such as:

http://www.lehigh.edu/~tep3/b5-objects.html

http://www.infografica.com/3dbank/s2.html

http://www.viewpoint.com/indexb.html

http://avalon1.viewpoint.com/

http://www.infografica.com/3dbank/links.html

http://www.zygote.com/

http://www.mediom.qc.ca/creator-studio/home.html

http://www.acuris.com/

This is only a few of the many web sites growing rapidly on the Internet for 3D objects and animation. Be sure to view the legal information on each site regarding usage and copyrights.

TIP

If you don't have access to the Internet, now would be a good time to get it. The Internet allows you an enormous creative resource for 3D models, ideas, and communication with other 3D artists.

Scanned Models

Even if you have a 3D model of the object you want to include in your project, you can still waste a lot of time and money modeling it from scratch. It might make more sense to scan the object into your computer. Modeling from photographs is key. However, if you have access to a 3D scanner, you can electronically enter data to build a 3D model. Using a scanner takes out much of the guesswork when working from photographs.

Scanning, in the most common sense, means to place something thin onto a flatbed scanner to record a scanned image. Things you would typically scan on a flatbed scanner are pictures, textures, and logo designs. These are all elements that you can use in LightWave. But scanning physical models is a different beast all together. 3D scanning requires more expensive equipment—and sometime more patience. Instead of bringing an image into your system, you are physically bringing in a 3D model. This is usually done in two ways. The first way is to use a 3D laser scanner. This type of scanning requires a physical object to be placed inside a box. Lasers are cast across each axis of the model and that data is translated into the computer.

The second method, tracing the contours of a physical model, which is more affordable for the independent animator, requires a steady hand and a good bit of patience. Figure 4.1 shows a 3D scanner from MicroScribe.

FIGURE 4.1
Using a typical 3D scanner to trace the contours of a physical model.

Using a device like a 3D scanner can really keep costs down in the long run. If you have many models to generate, an investment such as this one might be a good option for you. You'll need to check with your local reseller for current pricing on 3D scanners, but you can estimate the cost to be anywhere from $2,500 and up.

This is only one example of a 3D scanner. As the industry grows and changes, more products emerge. Search the Internet for more 3D resources both for purchase and scanning units.

TIP

It's a good idea to go to at least one trade show every year, if not more. SIGGRAPH is a yearly conference on computer graphics where you can find almost anything relating to graphics, multimedia, and 3D.

Understanding Points in Modeler

When modeling any object, the foundation begins with points. Using LightWave Modeler is sometimes like playing connect-the-dots. The dots, being the points, are joined to create a solid object (polygon) that can be rendered. Every object you create will be composed of points and polygons. Figure 4.2 shows a simple illustration of two stages. First, a set of points is generated. Second, the points are connected one after the other in order to generate a polygon. A collection of polygons creates an object.

FIGURE 4.2
The left side of this image shows only the points of an object. The right side shows the points after they've been selected to make a polygon.

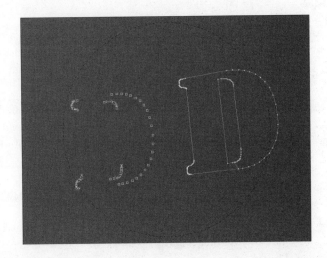

You may already be familiar with the process of selection and deselection of points and polygons in Modeler. In the next few pages, however, the information refers to the process and reasons for selection and deselection of points and polygons. To begin, take a look at the bottom of your Modeler 5.5 interface. There are three buttons labeled Points, Polygons, and Volume, as in figure 4.3.

FIGURE 4.3

The selection tools are at the bottom of the Modeler screen.

You will use these three buttons in almost every project you create in Modeler.

In this brief exercise, you will learn how to:

- Create points
- Select points to make a curve and polygon
- Move and add points
- Delete points
- Create polygons
- Adjust points and polygons

NOTE

Always remember to keep the Caps Lock off when working in Modeler. Macintosh users, remember to hold down that Command key in conjunction with the mouse button to access right mouse button features.

Points are building blocks in Modeler that are used to create objects. Points control curves and the shapes that make up a polygonal surface. Read through this exercise to work with points in Modeler.

SELECTING POINTS

1. From the Polygon tab, select Points from the Create submenu on the left side of the screen.

2. In the Face view, which is typically the bottom left view, click the right mouse button about 12 times in a complete even circle. Figure 4.4 shows what your circle of points should look like. As an alternative, you can create a disc and press the k key to kill the polygons. This leaves only the points in an even circle. Macintosh users should hold the Command key while using the mouse button for right button mouse operations.

FIGURE 4.4
A circle of points created using the right mouse button.

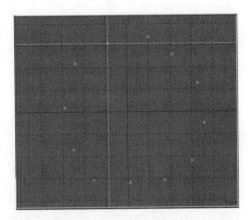

3. Now, press Ctrl+o to create a circle that has smooth lines between its points, as in figure 4.5.

FIGURE 4.5
After you create points, you will see a simple spline curve.

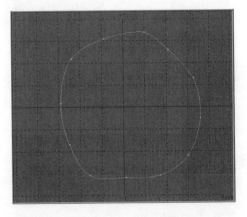

Using a spline curve, you can select, move, and drag points to easily change the shape of the circle.

4.   Select the Points button at the bottom of the interface.

NOTE

If the Points button is already selected, but nothing happens when you select a point, click on the Points button again. This will turn off any function tools on the left-hand side of the screen. The spacebar will also turn off any function tools.

5.   Click on the top right point of the circle. It should become highlighted. Now from the Modify menu tab, select the Move tool.

6.   Click and drag the point inward. Notice how the spline curves around the point, as in figure 4.6.

FIGURE 4.6
When the point moves,
the spline curves
around the point.

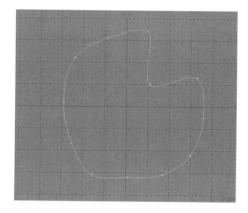

7.   Deselect the point. Press the spacebar to turn off any tools functions, such as Move. Then, click again on the point. Or you can click in a blank area on the screen, usually at the bottom of the tool bar on the left-hand side.

Remember that a click of the mouse selects a point if no points have already been selected. If the mouse button is released and then clicked again on the point, the point is now deselected. But what happens when you need to select a range of points in order? First, you would select points in order to make a curve. A curve will be generated based on the order of the points selected.

Second, if you skip a point, you do not need to start your selection all over. Simply deselect the point that was selected out of order by releasing the mouse button and clicking on it. Don't deselect the previous points but instead hold the Shift key and continue selecting.

Note

This section is here to help explain selection of points. However, the selection and deselection information applies to polygons as well. Animators typically use the Drag tool under the Modify tab to move individual points.

8. With the same circle and no points selected, choose the Drag tool from the Modify panel. This tool allows you to click and hold a point, and then drag it to the desired position. This eliminates a step in the selection process. However, Drag works with one point at a time, therefore, traditional point selection will still be used often. Drag also works in conjunction with selected points in that it limits draggable points to only those selected, if any. This is very handy when points are very close together.

This exercise guided you through the selection and deselection of points in Modeler. Understanding this is vital to your modeling skills. Practice creating, selecting, moving, dragging, and deselecting points to get more of a feel for working with points.

DragNet

DragNet is the Drag command combined with Magnet. It allows you to drag a point and have the surrounding points drag with, based on the influence set. The Drag tool eliminates the need to select and deselect points, but it only works on one point at a time. DragNet enables you to drag a predetermined section of an object without selection and deselection. As with Drag, DragNet also works in conjunction with selected points. Follow along for a quick run through DragNet.

Using the DragNet Tool

1. Back in Modeler, clean out the layers by pressing Shift+n for New and click OK.

2. From the Objects tab, select Ball from the Create submenu.

3. Press n on the keyboard to call up the Numeric Requester.

4. Press the reset button, make sure Ball Type is Globe, and click OK. You'll see a representation of the ball size in the Modeler's views. Click Make or press Enter.

TIP

If your current object is smaller or larger than your viewing area, simply press a on the keyboard to fit the object(s) to full view.

Your ball should look like the one shown in figure 4.7.

FIGURE 4.7

The basic ball, ready for DragNet.

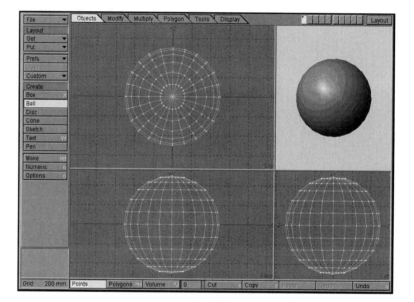

5. From the Modify tab, select the DragNet function from the Deform submenu at the bottom left of the interface. DragNet works similarly to Magnet in that the right mouse button (Mac users use the Command key) sets up a field of influence for the tool. It is important to note that the influence is greatest at the center and falls off toward the perimeter of the circle. Figure 4.8 shows the field set up for the ball.

6. Make the DragNet's range of influence about a quarter of the ball, by clicking and dragging out a range with the right mouse button.

7. Now with the left mouse button, drag any point. DragNet molds your polygons into a different shape. Figure 4.9 shows the ball object yanked to the side with DragNet.

FIGURE 4.8

You can see DragNet's range of influence in the Top view, which is set with the right mouse button. A circle represents the influence; larger circles encompassing more of the object will allow DragNet to have a greater influence.

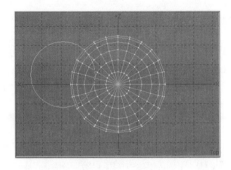

FIGURE 4.9

The basic ball, deformed with one pull of the mouse using DragNet.

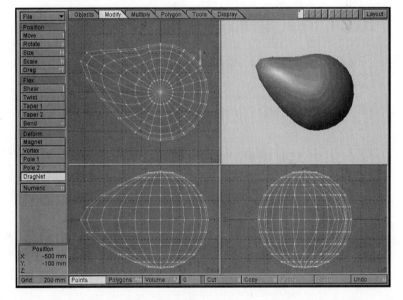

DragNet is another tool in Modeler that can help you create a desired model. DragNet, Metaform, MetaNURBS, and splines are tools that are available for you based on the project at hand. As you model and use DragNet more, you will find its usefulness is a welcomed addition to Modeler's tool set.

It's important to note that many Modeler functions, such as Move, Rotate, Size, and so on, can be applied to selected points as well as polygons. As you read about polygons, try some of the selection and deselection tips on just points to satisfy any curiosity you may have.

Working with Polygons

A polygon is any number of points connected by lines to form a solid face. Objects are made up of points and joined to make polygons, which is what LightWave sees for rendering. This section discusses the use of polygons and shows how Modeler creates them.

The creation of polygons is important to fully understand because they are the elements that complete a model. Polygons can be manipulated to create smooth rounded edges, or they can remain flat and sharp. Follow along with the next exercise to work with Polygon creation in Modeler.

CREATING POLYGONS

1. Open LightWave's Modeler, go to the Objects tab, and select the Box tool from the Create submenu. Press the n key on the keyboard to call up the Box tool's Numeric Requester. As soon as a tool is selected, such as Box, Ball, Move, Size, and so on, and the n key is pressed, that tool's Numeric Requester will pop up. Conversely, you'll find a numeric button at the bottom of the submenu as well.

2. In the Numeric Requester, press the Reset button, which will bring all values to –500mm for the Low values, and 500mm for the High values. It will also bring the segments for the X, Y, and Z axes to 1. Also note that as you use the Box tool to model, you can always reset the default size through this Numeric Requester.

3. Click OK, and then press Enter to make the box. Press a on the keyboard to fit the box to all views. Save the box as **yourbox.lwo** for use later. You should see a box like the one in figure 4.10.

FIGURE 4.10
A basic 500mm box with one segment on each side. This box has six polygons, one for each side.

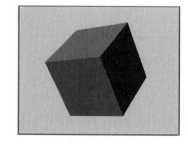

While the box created in this exercise is very basic, it is literally a building block for much of your work. You can easily start MetaNURBS models using a basic box. Later in the "MetaNURBS and Boxes" section, you'll be guided much further into this technique.

The box you created is made up of six sides, each side containing one polygon. Earlier, when points were discussed, it was noted that points make up a polygon. If you tried to save, load, and render points by themselves without any polygons in Layout, nothing would happen. LightWave renders with polygons.

You can modify this box by selecting polygons, as you did with points. Also, you can manipulate and shape this box by selecting and moving the points within it.

This next exercise will guide you through the important task of selection and deselection of polygons. Selection and deselection is key to surfacing, beveling, adjusting, and any other modeling and manipulation that you may need to do.

SELECTION AND DESELECTION OF POLYGONS

1. Load the same 500mm box created earlier (Yourbox.lwo) into all views. Select the Polygons selection button at the bottom of the Modeler interface. This tells Modeler that you want to work with polygons. Its selection means the function tools such as Rotate, Stretch, Shear, and so on affect the selected polygons.

NOTE

A very important rule to remember when selecting and deselecting is that select points and polygons will be the affected items when a function tool is used, such as Move or Rotate. If no points or polygons are selected, function tools affect all items.

2. With the Polygons button selected at the bottom of the screen, click with the left mouse button on one edge of the box. The edge will become highlighted, and a dotted line will extend from it as well. If more than one polygon becomes selected, release the mouse button, and click on the polygons to be deselected, leaving the single polygon selected. Figure 4.11 shows a box with one polygon selected.

FIGURE 4.11

Using the Polygons selection mode, one polygon is selected on the box.

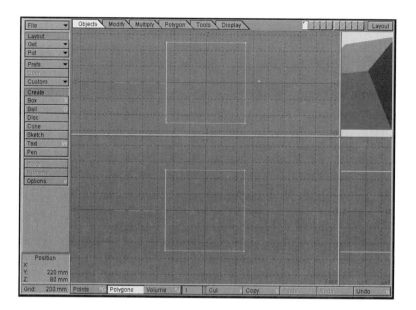

3. To estimate how many polygons are selected, you can see the value in the numeric box at the bottom center of the Modeler interface, next to the Volume button (see figure 4.12). If you want to select additional polygons, hold the Shift key while selecting the polygon.

FIGURE 4.12

The numeric indicator at the bottom of the Modeler interface will tell you how many points or polygons are selected.

Numeric box

4. With a polygon selected, press y on the keyboard to activate the Rotate tool. In the Face view, click and hold the mouse, then move it to the right. You should see the selected polygon rotate. Figure 4.13 shows the effects of rotating one selected polygon.

FIGURE 4.13
*Using the Rotate tool
on the selected
polygon results in an
odd-looking box.*

TIP ──

You can instantly deselect a polygon by pressing the / key on the keyboard. If nothing happens, press the spacebar to turn off any tools, and then press the / key.

Selecting and deselecting points and polygons may seem more complicated than it really is. As you work through projects in this book and on your own, you'll quickly pick up the idea and the process will become second nature to you. However, there is a way in which you can group selections of points and polygons. The third button at the bottom of the Modeler interface labeled Volume has two commands within it. Click on it twice and you'll see the Volume button label toggle between Exclude and Include.

Exclude and Include

The Exclude Volume command enables you to manipulate and adjust portions of objects without selecting the necessary polygons or points. Selecting Exclude Volume excludes polygons partially inside and outside of the selection area. Selecting Include Volume includes any points or polygons in and partially in the volume area. You can use both the left and right mouse buttons for selection of points, polygons, and volume. The right mouse button is used for Lasso selection. This is a quick and easy way to select a general area of points or polygons.

The Lasso Tool

The Lasso tool makes selecting a region of points or polygons easy. The left mouse button allows you to click on the desired selected point or polygon. The left mouse button in conjunction with the Volume Exclude and Include tool draws out a linear region for selection or deselection. By using the right mouse button, you can literally draw around the desired selection. Figure 4.14 shows an object with the Lasso tool's region drawn out.

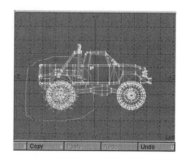

FIGURE 4.14

The Lasso tool enables you to draw around the desired selected area of points or polygons. You can see the Lasso outline, and the polygons selected can be seen in all views.

Remember to use the Lasso tool when you need to quickly select a group of points or polygons. It will save you a lot of time.

Earlier it was mentioned that function tools such as Move, Rotate, Size, and so on affect the selected points or polygons. If nothing is selected, function tools affect the entire active layer. Background layers are not affected. layers are other key elements to your Modeling foundation.

Layers

The LightWave Modeler interface provides you with 10 layers to work with. The layers in Modeler are like onion skin paper. Traditional cartoon animators constantly flip between pages to preview their previous drawing as reference. The layers in Modeler have the same functionality in that they enable you to have references when modeling. For example, your client wants you to build a car for an upcoming local television commercial. You finish the body and save your object. The next step is to create the tires. Even though the tires are part of the car, technically they are separate objects. You can select a new layer to begin working on the tires. Doing this enables you to work without a cluttered interface, but more importantly, the body of the car won't be affected by your current modeling job. However, you may need to see the body of the car as a reference for tire size, width, and placement. Modeler's layers enable you to put any number of the 10 layers in the background. This enables you to have the car on one layer for reference, while you work on the tires on another layer without affecting the Car object. Figure 4.15 shows the Layer button at the top right of the Modeler screen.

FIGURE 4.15

Modeler's Layer buttons enable you to place elements in up to 10 different layers.

If you look closely, you'll see a separation on each Layer button. This separation tells Modeler to use that particular layer as a foreground or background layer.

Foreground Layers

Foreground layers should be considered "active" layers. You can select anywhere from one to ten layers in the foreground. Selection and deselection work for all layers as they do for one.

TIP

If you work on a project with many layers, you can save the layer set through the File drop-down menu at the top left part of the screen, using the Save Layers command.

Background Layers

Background layers in Modeler should be considered your reference layers. You cannot directly save an individual object (except when using the Save Layers command) or modify anything that is in a background layer. To determine which layer is selected as a background or foreground layer, look at the position of the black dot on the layer's button. The dot indicates that the layer contains data, such as points or polygons. The black dot is always in the top-left corner. Background and foreground layers are represented by the top or bottom half of the Layer button being highlighted.

No layer is dedicated to foreground or background. You can change any layer from foreground to background as desired. Clicking on a layer button at the top selects a foreground layer. Clicking on a Layer button at the bottom selects a background layer. Holding the Shift key while selecting Layer buttons adds more than one layer. When a foreground layer is selected in conjunction with a background layer, you can use the keyboard shortcut of the apostrophe key (') to alternate between them.

Using layers has other important purposes. To perform Boolean operations such as Union, Intersect, Subtract, and Add, an object needs to be in a background layer. For example, if you want to cut a hole through an object, such as an apple, you would use two layers. In the foreground layer, you would load an apple. In the background layer, a long disc intersects the object where it will cut through. The item being affected should be in the foreground layer. The tool doing the job should be in the background layer. See the "Telephone Lines and Splines" exercise later in this chapter for a demonstration of layers.

Understanding Splines in LightWave

While LightWave's Layout renders polygons and only uses splines within motion graphs, in Modeler the spline is a very powerful tool. You can use splines in Modeler to create paths, extrusions, curved shapes, and complex objects.

Using a spline to model is simply another way to go about creating an object. Like most projects, the tools you use depend on the task at hand. When working with splines, you can benefit from using spline curves through your projects. For example, you can trace over an image of a logo in Modeler to create smooth curves. Or you can use splines to create oddly shaped polygons that require greater detail in specific areas. Spline patches are also a way to create and will be discussed further in Chapter 6, "LightWave Modeler in Action."

The following exercises will use splines and basic object shapes to build a telephone pole and cables. Your client, Sorrygent and Dumbody Engineers has hired you to re-create the scene of an accident. The situation involves a pending lawsuit over poor engineering, and you must make a convincing animation to show that their workmanship was up to standards. Therefore, a simple pole with a line attached is not nearly detailed enough. The animation calls for the camera to zoom in close to the insulator on the top of the pole where the cable attaches. In this situation, splines are the best way to model the cable.

TELEPHONE LINES AND SPLINES

1. Enter Modeler and go to a clean layer. Knowing that the telephone line is the center of attention for the animation, you need a point of reference before building it. Start by building the telephone pole. Create a disc by pressing the Disc tool under the Objects tab. Press the n key to call up the Numeric Requester, and enter these values:

Sides	48
Segments	4
Bottom	0m
Top	58m
Axis	Y
Center	
X	-8m
Y	29m
Z	8m
Radii	
X	2m
Y	29m
Z	2m

2. Click OK and then press Enter to make the telephone pole. Press the a key to fit the object in all views. You should end up with something like the example shown in figure 4.16.

3. Segments were added to the pole because the project requires the pole to sway a bit when the telephone wire is yanked off by a passing farm vehicle. However, in looking at the pole, there aren't enough segments.

Press the u key to undo the making of the telephone pole. This will leave you with the basic outline of the pole. Instead of entering the numeric requester and changing the segment value, LightWave 5.5 now offers a new interactive feature.

FIGURE 4.16
The basic telephone pole made from an elongated disc.

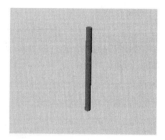

4. Press the right arrow key on your keyboard, and watch what happens to the outline of the pole. You should see segments being added to the pole. Hitting the left arrow takes away segments. This is a handy new feature in 5.5. Press the right arrow key about nine times to generate about 14 segments. Press Enter to make the pole with the added segments. This will result in a smooth bend in the pole later in the animation.

TIP

This handy interactive segment control works for Boxes as well. The right arrow adds segments on the X, while the up arrow adds segments on the Y. Left and down arrows take away segments.

Because you now have a basic telephone pole, you can go ahead to a new layer and get ready to create the telephone wire. The telephone wire is actually three wires tightly coiled together. You need to create three long thin cables, and then twist them around each other, as well as around the insulator. The Bend tool is not the right tool for this job. Splines can do it, though. You need to use the insulator as reference so the telephone cable can wrap around evenly. The engineer supplied the insulator to you, so modeling it is not that difficult. In this case, load the modeled insulator object from the Chapter 4 directory of objects on the CD accompanying this book (Insultr.lwo).

CREATING A TELEPHONE WIRE

1. Place the insulator in one layer, and select the layer with the telephone pole as a background layer. Figure 4.17 shows the insulator loaded into modeler.

FIGURE 4.17

The insulator loaded from the CD, loaded in a foreground layer. The telephone pole in the background layer appears as a black outline.

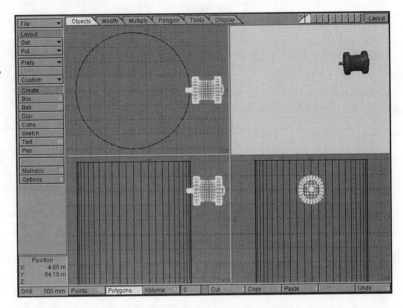

2. With the insulator in a foreground layer and the telephone pole in a background layer, press Shift+b on the keyboard. This will bring up the Boolean operations.

3. Select Union to join the insulator and pole together, as in figure 4.18. You can, however, simply cut and paste the insulator into the telephone pole's layer. This is not as clean as a union, but when rendered will appear the same.

4. Save the pole (with the insulator attached to it) to your hard drive as **Tpole.lwo**. Select a clean layer as your working foreground layer, and place the telephone pole with insulator in a background layer.

5. To make the telephone lines, you need to enlarge the grid size quite a bit to draw out the proper length of the spline. Press the letter a on the keyboard to fit the pole and insulator into view.

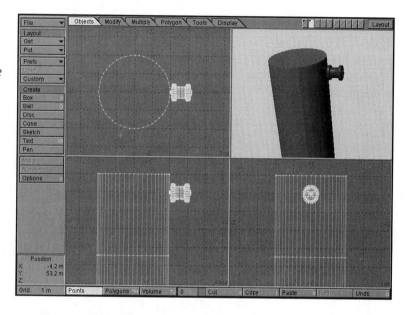

6. From the Objects tab menu, select the Sketch tool from the Create submenu items on the left-hand side of the screen. Now, in the Top view, slowly draw a line across the middle of the window. Do this by clicking the left mouse button and dragging. Press Enter to make the spline, and press the / key to deselect the Sketch tool. You should see a not-so-straight line, as shown in figure 4.19. Copy and paste this spline to another layer for later.

7. The line you just created is a spline. Now move it into place using the background elements (the pole and newly attached insulator) as references. Press t on the keyboard to select the Move tool. Click and drag upward to bring the spline into position with the insulator, as in figure 4.20.

The next step is to shape the curve. You need to wrap the curve around the insulator. But there are not enough points on the spline in the area of the insulator. You can fix this by adding points.

8. Press the Polygon selection button at the bottom of Modeler's screen, telling the program that you want to work with polygons. From the Polygon tab menu, select the Add Points function. If the button does not come up and you are unable to select it, you need to first select the item you'll be working with. Click on the spline to select it. Now you should see the Add Points function available.

FIGURE 4.19

The Sketch tool is used to draw out a spline curve.

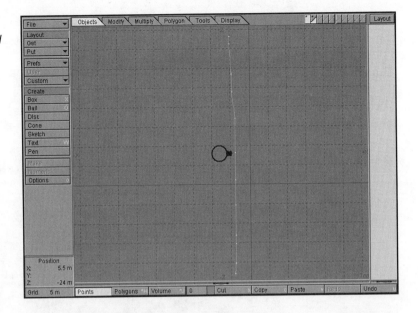

FIGURE 4.20

The spline is moved into position with the pole and insulator as reference in the background.

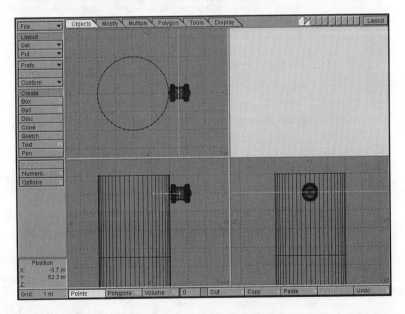

9. When you select Add Points, a small arrow pops up. With the arrow, click on the area of the spline where you want to add points. In this case, add about five points around the general area of the Insulator object. Figure 4.21 shows the five points added to the spline. Remember the

insulator and pole is in a background layer for reference. Adding points only affects the foreground layer's selected objects.

FIGURE 4.21

Five points can be added for extra control around certain areas of a spline using the Add Points function.

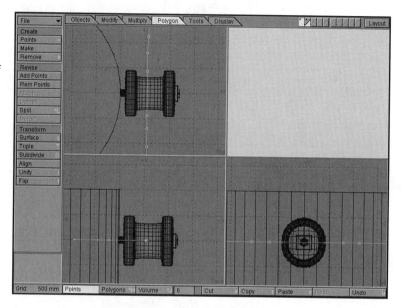

10. Now you need to wrap the spline around the insulator. The wire wrap that will hold the telephone line will be created using this spline. Deselect any points that may be selected. With Modeler's views zoomed in to see the area around the insulator, select one point near the front end of the insulator. Press t on the keyboard for Move and drag downward from the Side view. You can also move the point slightly to the right or left in the Top view. Figure 4.22 shows the point selected and dragged down.

11. Next, begin dragging points around the insulator. The telephone line will be supported by a wire, which is wrapped around the insulator.

12. Figure 4.23 shows the spline after the points were moved one at a time around the insulator from left to right. You can use Drag from the left view as well. You dragged the first point down to the bottom of the insulator. The next point was also brought to the bottom. The next point was moved to the right side of the insulator. The next point was placed back and toward the top. The point after that was moved back to the left of the insulator with one more completing the wrap.

FIGURE 4.22

One point on the spline is selected and dragged downward.

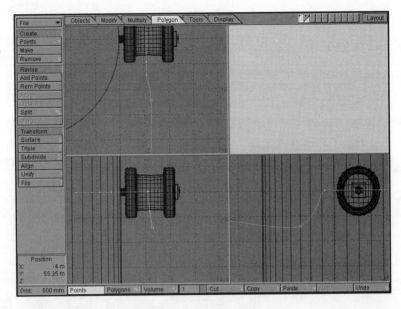

FIGURE 4.23

The added points are moved from the left view to wrap around the insulator. Remember, the insulator is only in the background so nothing done will affect it. It is simply a template to work from.

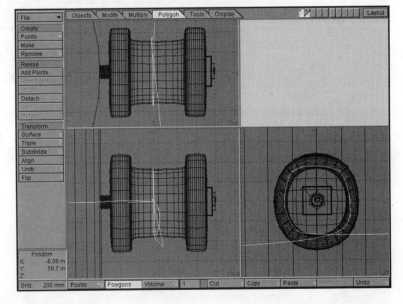

13. If you look at the spline in the other layers, it's difficult to see how the spline wraps. This is a situation when selecting the point and moving it is better than using Drag. By selecting a point, it becomes highlighted and consequently more distinguishable in all views. Select one of the top points, and move slightly to the left.

14. Select another one and move it to the left a little as well. Think of the line you are adjusting as a roller coaster doing a loop around the insulator. You need to separate the line from its own rotation so it doesn't run into itself on the way down. Figure 4.24 shows the final modifications to the spline curve.

FIGURE 4.24

A few points around the insulator area are dragged and moved to create a loop around the insulator.

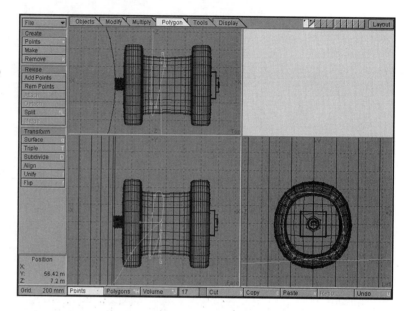

15. With that done, go to a new layer. Now you are going to make three simple discs that will become the telephone wire. You'll create the wire wrap that holds the telephone line after this. Create a disc with the following settings:

Sides	32
Segments	1
Bottom	8.0393 m
Top	8.0393 m
Axis	Z
Center	
X	-5.58 m
Y	57.08 m
Z	8.0393 m
Radii	
X	80 mm
Y	80 mm
Z	0 m

16. Click OK and press Enter to make the disc. This will become one of the three cables needed to make the telephone wire. Press the c key on the keyboard to copy the disc.

17. Move the current disc over to the right slightly, and then press v to paste the original disc back down. Figure 4.25 shows the disc created and copied.

FIGURE 4.25

One disc is created and copied to create two discs.

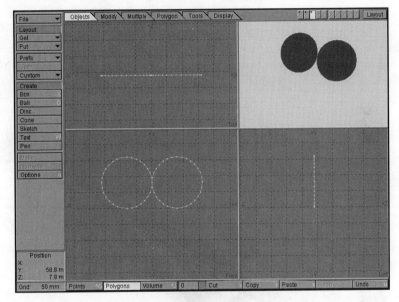

18. Lastly, select one of the discs, and press c to copy it. Press v on the keyboard to paste the selected disc. By cutting and pasting, you have the other two discs in place for a visual reference. Move the selected disc down below and directly in between the two original discs. You should have three discs like the ones in figure 4.26.

FIGURE 4.26

Three discs ready to be made into a telephone cable.

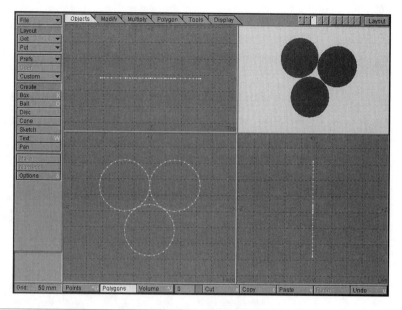

The next thing you need to do is go to the layer where you pasted the straight spline before you adjusted the points. This exercise guides you through the creation of a wrapped wire through the use of the Rail Extrude function.

USING RAIL EXTRUDE FOR WRAPPING WIRES

1. Place the pole and insulator in the background. Begin dragging each point to droop the curve into the shape of a telephone line. You can also use the Magnet tool for this.

2. When finished, make this the background layer. Move the three discs to the front part of the spline. Remember that the layer with the spline needs to be in the background layer. Move the discs to the front of the spline, at the bottom of the Top view, as in figure 4.27.

3. With the discs in place, and the spline in the background, select Rail Extrude from the Multiply menu. Select Automatic for segments, and check Oriented. Click OK and watch LightWave create your cable.

FIGURE 4.27

The three discs placed in front of the spline curve, similar to a thread and a needle's eye.

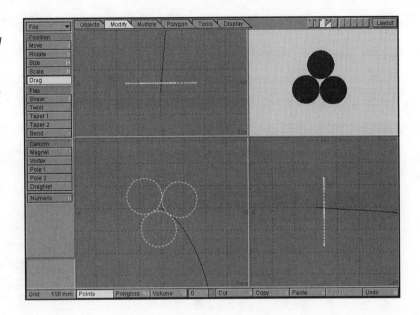

TIP

If your cable seems to do funky things and not extrude along the path of the spline, there's an easy fix. The object to be extruded, in this case, the discs, needs to be extruded in the same direction that the spline was made. Make sure that your discs are at the start of the spline, not the end, and try it again. You can flip the spline (f) to get the proper orientation.

Figure 4.28 shows the extruded disc, now a telephone cable.

4. You need to create the wire wrap that will support the telephone cable around the insulator. Make one more disc, with the following settings:

Sides	32
Segments	1
Bottom	8.6857 m
Top	8.6857 m
Axis	Z
Center	
X	-6.5 m
Y	56.1 m
Z	8.6857 m
Radii	
X	30 mm
Y	30 mm
Z	0 m

FIGURE 4.28

The three discs are extruded with Rail Extrude using the spline in a background layer as a path to follow. The result is this telephone cable.

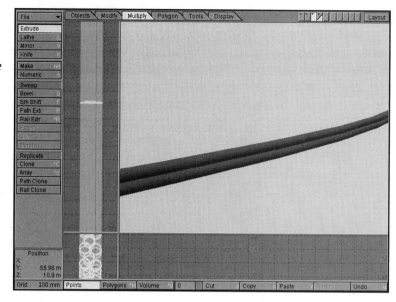

5. Click OK and press Enter to make the disc. Now for the tricky part. You need to select and move each point in the spline so that it twists around the telephone cable. Place the telephone cable in a background layer. As a helpful starting point, select the points before the loop you created earlier. With those points selected, perform a Twist from the Modify menu in the Face view. Twist the selected points and you'll see the spline twist around the telephone line. Figure 4.29 shows the twisted spline.

6. From here, slightly tweak each point so they are even around the wire (which is in the background). Remember to check all views for accuracy.

TIP

Try using OpenGL Sketch mode for a wireframe preview of both layers. Figure 4.30 shows how the Sketch view helps show where the spline wraps and intersects the telephone line. Press d on the keyboard for Display options.

7. Perform another Rail Extrude with the smaller disc and the curved spline to create the wire wrap. Figure 4.31 shows the final objects all together. The wire wrap generally should be wrapped tighter than the image shown, but this will give you a good starting point for creating with splines and selecting and deselecting points.

FIGURE 4.29
The Twist feature helps wrap the wire around the telephone cable.

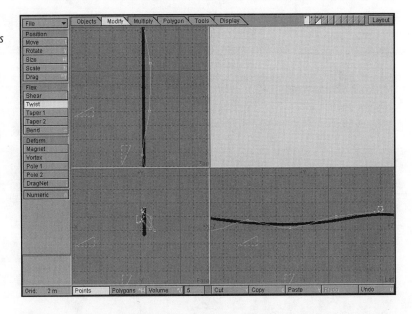

FIGURE 4.30
OpenGL Sketch mode helps decipher where the spline is wrapping or intersecting the telephone line.

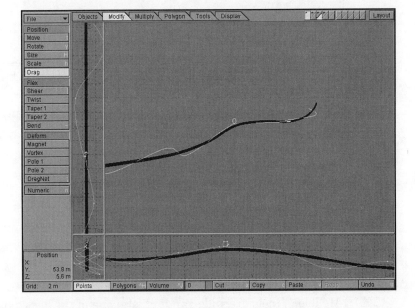

FIGURE 4.31

The telephone pole, insulator, telephone wire, and wire wrap all together with the help of some splines, layers, and selection.

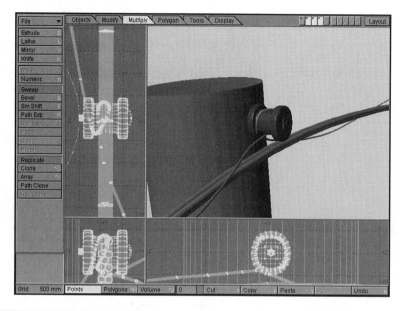

Experiment with these techniques to come up with even more cables, wires, neon signs, script signatures, mouse cables, and so on. Here are a few quick reminders for generating wire-type things with splines:

- Use the Sketch tool from the Objects menu to draw the spline.

- Use drag or point selection and move to adjust points within the spline.

- Use Rail Extrude from the Multiply menu to create wire from a single disc.

- Make sure the rail extrusion follows the same path as the spline, otherwise your extruded object will extrude in strange ways.

These techniques are examples of how you can use primitive shapes in Modeler to create more complex items. Try creating things with these tools so when the time comes for you to create intricate objects for you client, you'll know all the tools to use.

Modeler's tools are wide-ranging, and one of the best tools is MetaNURBS. MetaNURBS offers a new approach to Modeling, and you'll find that it is more versatile than splines for organic modeling.

Understanding the MetaNURBS Approach to Modeling

Introduced in LightWave 5.0, MetaNURBS practically revolutionized the way LightWave artists model. MetaNURBS is LightWave's version of Non-Uniform Rational B-Splines. In Version 5.0, MetaNURBS worked only with quad polygons, that is, polygons made up of four points. A simple box such as the one you created earlier can be generated instantly and turned into a clay-like ball with MetaNURBS. From there, you can pull, move, sketch, rotate, and deform the points and polygons to create just about any shape.

LightWave 5.5 takes MetaNURBS to a higher level, allowing the use of tripled polygons as well as quad polygons. Tripled polygons are polygons made of three points; quad polygons are made up of four points. This means you have more creative freedom and fewer oddities when creating an object. In Chapter 7, "Character Modeling with MetaNURBS," you'll be taken through a project in which you create a character with MetaNURBS. Making a face with MetaNURBS is fun and probably easier than you think.

NOTE

A non-planer polygon is basically a polygon that moves beyond the plane in which it lies, for example, a Plexiglas storm door. If you tried bending the Plexiglas, it would eventually crack and break. The same thing would occur to a flat polygon, whether it is a NURB surface or not. Adding more polygons, such as tripling, eliminates "cracking," making the polygon more malleable. Think of a polygon with more polygons as a screen door. If you bend the screen, it will bend easily and not crack or break. This is because the screen is made up of many smaller segments.

MetaNURBS and Boxes

There are different approaches to using MetaNURBS, and like other tools in Modeler, which approach to use depends on the project. Starting with the most common method, follow the next brief exercise:

METANURBS IN A BOX

This brief exercise begins with a basic box. From there, polygons are beveled, pushed, and pulled to create a simple lamp.

1. Begin by entering Modeler and saving any work you've done. Empty all layers by pressing Shift+n for New and click OK. Select the Objects tab and choose Box from the Make Create submenu. Press the n key for numeric and enter the following values:

	Low	High	Segments
X	-360 mm	340 mm	1
Y	0 m	100 mm	1
Z	-360 mm	360 mm	1

You should end up with a flat box. Press the Tab key to turn on MetaNURBS. Figure 4.32 shows what your box should look like.

FIGURE 4.32

A simple box created with one segment for the X, Y, and Z values. Pressing the Tab key turns on MetaNURBS.

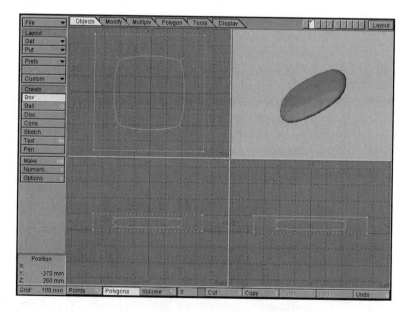

2. Now you can begin shaping your lamp. Select the bottom polygon by clicking on it, making sure that the Polygon selection button is highlighted at the bottom of the Modeler interface. When MetaNURBS is active, a patch polygon outline is visible. Even though two polygons look like they are selected, the selection indicator at the bottom of the screen reads 1, meaning only one is selected. If more than one polygon is

selected, click directly on that polygon to deselect it. The bottom polygon will become highlighted.

3. With the one polygon selected, press the b key to call up the Bevel tool. Enter an Inset value of 30mm. This will sharpen out the bottom curve. Leave all other values at zero.

4. Deselect the bottom polygon, and then select the top polygon. Be sure that just one polygon is selected. Press the b key again, and bevel the top polygon with the same inset value of 30mm.

5. Next, with the polygon still selected, bevel again, but this time enter an Inset value of 20mm.

6. The top polygon should still be selected. This is a handy feature when working with MetaNURBS and beveling. The initial polygon will remain selected as you multiply polygons. Bevel again with an Inset value of 100mm and a Shift value of 60mm. Your box should now look something like the one shown in figure 4.33.

FIGURE 4.33

A few bevels in combination with MetaNURBS, and the original box begins to look like the base of a lamp.

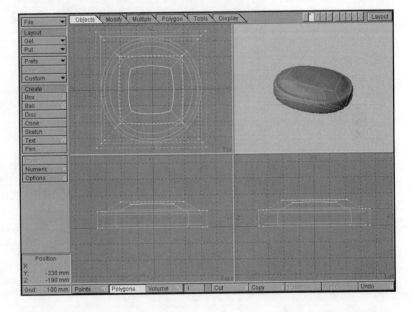

7. Again, with the top polygon selected, bevel with an Inset of 20mm, and leave all other values at zero.

8. Bevel again with an Inset value of 20mm.

9. Perform that bevel again, but this time with an Inset value of 40mm and a Shift value of 100mm. Bevel again with the same top polygon selected with an Inset value of 10mm and a Shift value of 350mm. This will create the stem for the lamp.

10. Take that same top polygon that should still be selected, and bevel with an Inset value of 10mm. Set all other parameters to 0. This will sharpen out the curve.

That's about it for the MetaNURBS lamp base. But this version won't render in Layout. As stated earlier in the polygons section of this chapter, LightWave uses polygons to render. Points and curves are not visible in rendering. At this point, you need to "freeze" the MetaNURBS curve. Do this by pressing the Freeze Curves and Patches function (Ctrl+d). Figure 4.34 shows the final object.

FIGURE 4.34

The simple box is now the base for a lamp.

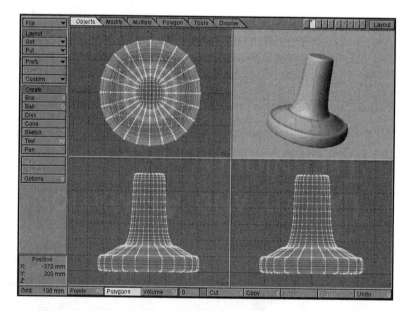

NOTE

You can change the number of polygons generated after the curves are frozen. Press o on the keyboard to enter the Data Options Panel. The Patch Division level can be adjusted. The higher the value, the more detail your final object will have. For this example, choose a patch division of about 6. Later, you'll adjust this again. Also, while you're in the Data Options Panel, change the Undo Levels to 15, the maximum allowed. These values will be written to Modeler's configuration file when you quit the program.

This is nothing elaborate, but if you take a look at the plain square box you started out with, and the final smooth shape you have now, you can see how useful MetaNURBS and boxes can be.

You can create other elements easily with MetaNURBS, some of which don't start out with a basic box. For example, follow the next project to create a lamp shade for the base you just built.

CREATING A LAMP SHADE

1. Begin in a clean layer and build a disc with the following settings:

Sides	32
Segments	1
Bottom	560 mm
Top	1.2 m
Axis	Y
Center	
X	0 m
Y	880 mm
Z	20 mm
Radii	
X	480 mm
Y	320 mm
Z	480 mm

 TIP

It's always a good idea to center your objects when possible, around the origin of the 0 axis.

2. Click OK and press Enter to make the disc. Copy and paste the disc to another layer.

3. Size the disc down slightly, about 98% of the original size, by selecting the Size function and pressing n on the keyboard. Manually enter a value of 98%.

4. The lamp shade is still solid. You sized the second object down, and if you select the layer with the original disc as a background layer, you'll see the size difference, as shown in figure 4.35.

FIGURE 4.35
*One disc is made,
copied to another layer,
and sized down from
the original.*

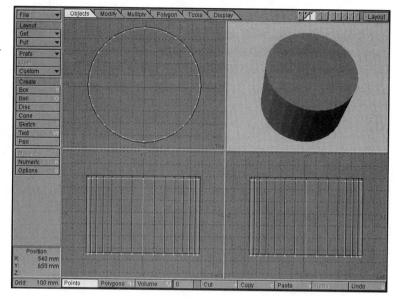

5. Select the top row of points in the smaller disc, and move them up beyond the original disc. Select the bottom set of points on the disc, and move them below the original disc's edge. Figure 4.36 shows the disc with moved points.

FIGURE 4.36
*The smaller disc points
are moved above and
below the original
discs, preparing it for a
Boolean operation.*

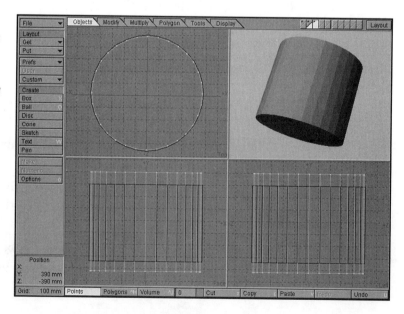

6. Now press the apostrophe key (') to flip layers. This places the smaller disc in the background and the larger disc in the foreground. Select Shift+b for Boolean Operations. Select Subtract and click OK. The small disc will cut the center out of the larger disc, as shown in figure 4.37.

FIGURE 4.37
The smaller disc is used to cut the center out of the original disc.

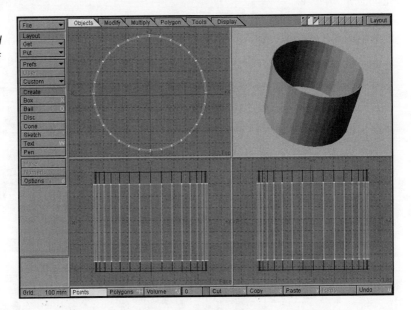

7. This object should be saved now so you won't have to redo your work should anything happen. Now, this object is not a MetaNURBS object. If you press the Tab key now, you would see an error such as the one shown in figure 4.38.

FIGURE 4.38
Attempting to use MetaNURBS on this object results in an error.

8. To eliminate this error, select the top polygon. This is the polygon along the top rim of the disc. Press Shift+t to triple the polygon. Perform this again on the bottom edge polygon. It is not necessary to triple the whole object. The sides are already quads.

TI P

Remember that to select the top polygon, you can use the right mouse button to Lasso around the polygon. Hold the Shift key and Lasso around the bottom polygon as well. You can then triple both polygons at the same time.

9. Now you can begin shaping the lamp shade. Lasso around the top set of points, and Stretch (h) them inward, similar to figure 4.39.

FIGURE 4.39

The top set of points is selected and sized down for the top of the lamp shade.

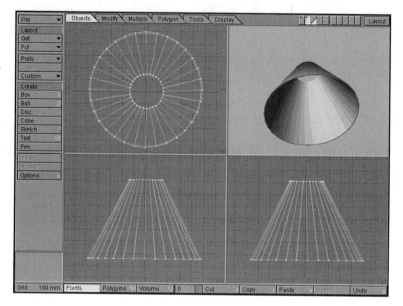

TI P

The lamp shade now is your basic household lamp shade. You can save it now to use in other animations in the future.

The next few steps will take the basic lamp shade and turn it into a fancy curved lamp shade. This will add more variety to the object.

10. Now select three or four points from the Top view. You only want to select points from the bottom of the lamp shade. Move the points from the bottom row. Move them out from the center. MetaNURBS will help create a smooth flowing lamp shade. From the three points, select the center point and move it upward. Create a shape like the one shown in figure 4.40.

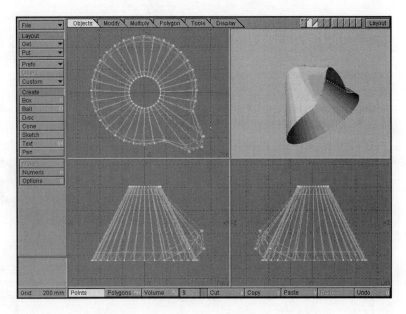

11. You can select all the points around the bottom layer and deselect every third point. Using the Stretch tool, you can curve out all side symmetrically.

12. Once you move all the points into place and are happy with the final object, remember to freeze the MetaNURBS curve by pressing Ctrl+d on the keyboard. If the final object after the freeze has too many polygons, press u on the keyboard to undo, and then press o on the keyboard to change the Patch Division level to about 2 or 3.

Join this lamp shade with the base you created earlier and then add a light in Layout. The final lamp shade object should look like the one shown in figure 4.41.

After you've frozen the curves, you can manipulate the center line of points to give the lamp shade a bit more shape. Feel free to adjust the height of the shade as well by moving the top row of points up. This object can be found under the Chapter 4 directory on the CD accompanying this book.

FIGURE 4.41

The points of the lamp shade around the base are pulled and moved to create a smooth flowing lamp shade.

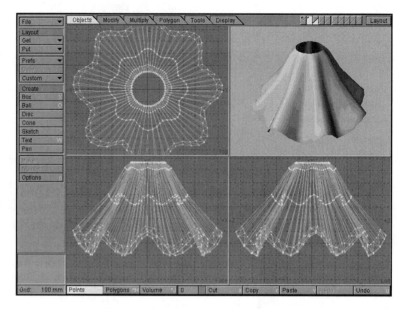

The techniques in the preceding pages are two approaches to modeling with MetaNURBS. Later in Chapter 7, you'll learn another approach, which is to work from one flat polygon and add points. Modeler also contains many plug-ins that can be helpful in your day-to-day modeling. The program ships with dozens of plug-ins, and there are also third-party plug-ins.

Expanding Your Animation Possibilities with Plug-Ins

The LightWave architecture is such that plug-ins can perform very useful and otherwise time-consuming, if not impossible, functions. You can find Modeler plug-ins under the Objects tab and Tools tab.

Because of the open architecture, there is also a constant growth market of third-party plug-ins, from software developers such as Blevins Enterprises and One and Only Media. Later in Appendix A, "Modeler and Third-Party Plug-Ins," you'll be guided through some key plug-ins and the more obscure ones.

Summary

This chapter presented resources and thoughts you should consider before embarking on that next 3D project. Modeling is a key component to your craft, and if the 3D models are good, you're halfway there. This chapter discussed:

- Working with objects
- Understanding points and polygons
- Creating complex objects with splines
- Using Modeler's layers
- Using the DragNet tool
- Working with MetaNURBS

Now, continue on to Chapter 5, "Layout and Animation Techniques," to discover the tools in Layout for creating animations with LightWave 3D 5.5.

Chapter 5

LAYOUT AND ANIMATION TECHNIQUES

Chapter 4, "Modeler Techniques," guided you through the basics of Modeler. After the last chapter, you might be thinking that LightWave's Modeler is complex enough without the headache of mastering Layout as well. You will find as you read through this chapter, however, that you can have a lot of fun working in Layout.

LightWave's Layout is your own personal television studio. You control the camera, the lights, the set, the actors, and you don't have any unions to deal with! Layout was designed from a producer's point of view; you physically move a light in front of a subject the way you would in the real world. In the LightWave world, however, you have no cables, wires, or electrical bills to worry about. You never run out of videotape in your cameras, and you don't even have to worry about tripping over cables on the set. This chapter familiarizes you with Layout and some of its many possibilities. This chapter discusses the following topics:

- Understanding your goal

- Planning the scene

- Understanding keyframing

- Using the virtual camera

- Using LightWave's plug-ins

LightWave 5.5 is an exciting program. As you read on, you will hopefully want to find out more and more. You will also be eager to head on to more projects. Although your enthusiasm is a good thing, it is important to start with the basics and build on that understanding. Thus figure 5.1 shows the LightWave 5.5 interface upon startup.

FIGURE 5.1

The LightWave interface upon startup. LightWave 5.5 puts the default view at a upper-right perspective.

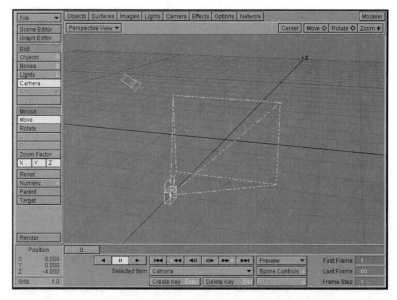

Understanding Your Goal

Your goal in Layout is to be as creative as possible. You must explore and never stop experimenting with the wide range of tools you now have at your fingertips. You can have fun.

Working toward a goal in 3D animation requires planning and preparation. To fully complete a project, the idea behind what should be included and what should not needs to be considered. Not only should you work out an animation on paper before you begin, you should also talk through ideas with co-workers and the client. A client or another animator's suggestions sometimes offer a different approach to the way an animation is created. Often, reaching your goal does not necessarily mean forging straight ahead. It can mean looking at all the information carefully surrounding your goal, and deciding on the best approach for you to take.

Your thought process while working on animations should encompass the entire project and your entire scene. What is the animation about and more importantly, where is it going? These are questions you should always ask yourself when entering LightWave's Layout for serious projects. You will inevitably produce a better animation and usually save time by paying attention to the entire scene. Chapter 3, "LightWave in Action," discussed planning. In this chapter, planning is stressed again. *Plan, plan, and plan!*

NOTE

Because you are such a Felix now after reading a few of these techniques chapters, you should be aware that having a great plan does not always mean you must stick to it. Sometimes the best work comes from variances in the plan.

Planning includes scene preparation and organization. The LightWave scene file can be used within other scenes as well. The section will take you through scene etiquette, if you will.

Using Existing Scenes

Existing scenes in LightWave are an asset to you. Scenes you have created, scenes freely distributed over the Internet, and scenes that ship with the LightWave software all contain something valuable. They contain elements and ideas that you can use for your current project. As an example, go to the File Requester and choose Load Scene from the drop-down menu. Locate your NewTek directory and load the Mustang scene from the Vehicles directory. This scene ships with your LightWave software and is included for more than just another animation to render. It is included for you to study and learn another way to set up an animation. Figure 5.2 shows the Mustang scene opened in Layout.

FIGURE 5.2
You can find the Mustang scene that ships with the LightWave 5.5 software in the Vehicles directory.

This scene can teach you many of LightWave's methods for setting up a proper scene. Take a look at the elements in this scene:

- Parenting

- Use of repeating motions

- Background image

- Pivot-point locations

- Three-point lighting

- Keyframing

Although the scene is relatively simple—when you break it down, you can study the many elements that comprise the scene. The blades, for example, are parented to the propeller. The propeller is set in motion 360 degrees only once, and the End Behavior is set to Repeat through the Motion Graph Panel. You can use this specific technique for many things, such as rotating globes, tires on a car, tires on a bicycle, chains on machinery, and anything else that needs a repeating loop. Repeating motion is better accomplished by loading an existing scene than fumbling through software manuals.

When you have time, explore the scenes in each of the directories installed with LightWave, paying special attention to those that use features new to LightWave 5.5. These scenes are there for you to learn from. Seeing is understanding. To familiarize yourself with any new tabs and features, take some time to click through the panels throughout LightWave 5.5.

Using Scenes from This Book's CD

As each chapter in this book was written, the objects, images, and scene files generated were saved for inclusion on the book's CD. Some scenes are ready to go for you; all you need to do is tell LightWave where to save the images and then press the Render button. Other scenes are included for you to follow along with certain exercises and to see what is being discussed. Just as you do with the NewTek system scenes, take some time and go through the accompanying CD and check out the scenes that have been included for you. You may find some of them useful in your next project.

Planning the Scene

Scene planning is exceedingly important for you and for your clients. Scene planning often resolves many troublesome issues before they arise—issues such as render times, allocation of objects, copyright on certain images, and so on. Could you imagine working through a project for two weeks, only to find out that the image you chose for a background color was the competition's color and not your client's? This is a far-fetched situation, but the idea is for you to plan your scene before you begin working on it. You should always keep the following few pointers in mind when planning:

- **Time frames.** How soon does this project need to be completed?
- **Length.** Can your system handle the rendering in time?

- **Output.** How does the client want the final product delivered? SVHS, BetaSP, D2, CD, U-Matic?

- Are the colors correct?

- Are objects such as client logos visible long enough?

- Does the client understand rendering time?

- Do all the objects need to be built from scratch?

- Is there a budget for purchasing pre-made objects?

These are just a few of the questions you should consider before starting a project. Standing up to these concerns can be a hassle, but doing so pays off during the course of the animation. You will have a road map for your project.

Setting Up Scenes One at a Time

After you have studied existing scenes and made a mental note of what scenes contain which techniques, select Clear Scene from the File drop-down menu. When you begin a project in Layout, you most often start with a clear scene. You then set up most scenes one at a time.

Animators take some standard steps when putting together an animation. Before the actual scene goes together, an object is loaded and the surfaces are set. It is much easier to surface an object when it is the only thing loaded in Layout. It is easier because there is less clutter and fewer surfaces from which to select. After an object has been surfaced (or whenever changes are made to the surface attributes), you need to save it. From there, objects can be loaded as the animator chooses.

Deciding what to load first depends on the scene. A bedroom scene's objects, for example, are all made and ready to be placed together in Layout to complete a scene. Which should be loaded first? Commonly, order of objects does not matter, but it helps with organization. For a bedroom, the room should be loaded first, and then the bed, dresser, and finally the knickknacks (pictures on the wall, objects on a dresser, and so on). In this situation, it is recommended that you load smaller elements last so that you have a place to put them.

In the following exercise, you make a truck drive down the road. In this situation, you load the ground, and then the road, and then the truck. This way, you can put each object into place accordingly. Loading objects out of order means loading, moving, loading again, and then putting the object back into place.

A Scene to Call Your Own

1. Load the Ground object (Ground.lwo) from the Chapter 5 directory of objects from the accompanying CD.

2. With the Ground and Road objects loaded, change views to place the road onto the ground. Go to the Front view by pressing 1 on the keyboard.

3. Move the Ground object down slightly so that it rests just above the ground. Press Enter to create a keyframe at zero for the object.

NOTE

LightWave defaults to Auto Key Adjust, instantly creating keyframes when an object is moved. Auto Key Adjust remains on unless changed by the user. Any changes to it are written to the LW configuration file upon quitting. Be sure to check in the Options Panel to see that this feature is turned off.

4. Now you can load the truck. From the NewTek Vehicles directory created when you installed LightWave, load the Monster Truck object. Place it on the road. The truck should load facing away from the camera (see figure 5.3).

5. The idea for this animation is to have the monster truck drive from the distance into the camera. Select the Truck object as the current object, and then select Rotate from the Mouse Function sub-menu. Turn off the Pitch and Bank buttons, leaving only the Heading or H highlighted.

6. Rotate the truck 180 degrees, and move it to the opposite side of the road. (You don't want to get a ticket, do you?)

7. Select Move and turn off the X and Y, leaving only the Z button highlighted. Move the truck back on the Z-axis to the very end of the road and create a keyframe at zero for it.

8. Perform a test render. You should see the truck all by itself at the end of the road.

FIGURE 5.3

The monster truck should load facing away from the camera when loaded into Layout.

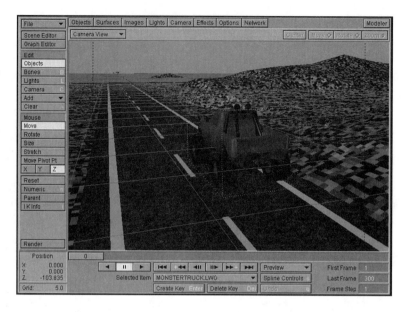

Adding fog here would really enhance the scene. A goal to keep in mind when creating scenes in 3D is to try and make the animation not look so clean. That is to say, computer animation has a tendency to look like it came from ... well, a computer. Adding fog through the use of 5.5's new Steamer plug-in adds more realism to the scene.

9. Enter the Effects Panel in Layout and select Gradient Backdrop. Here, you add a sky. Make the Zenith color a dark blue, the Sky color a sky blue, and make the Ground color exactly the same color values as the sky, and make the Nadir color a brownish-orange.

10. Enter a value of 5.0 for the Sky Squeeze, and a value of 15.0 for the Ground Squeeze. This brings the color spectrum closer together, giving more of a sunset feel to the scene.

11. Lastly, select Nonlinear 2 as the Fog Type, also within the Effects Panel. The Minimum Fog Distance should be 0, Maximum Fog Distance 220, Minimum Fog Amount should be 0, and the Maximum Fog Amount should be 100. Then, select the Backdrop Fog button. Close the panel, and go directly to the File drop-down menu and save the scene.

12. Perform a test render to see how your scene is coming along. You should see something like the image in figure 5.4.

FIGURE 5.4

A simple road, ground, and truck look pretty good with a little fog. The truck shouldn't be very visible. This is the idea; you want the truck to drive toward the camera out of the fog. The reason the fog is put in is to give some distance to the scene. Otherwise, you could see the road just end.

13. Move the truck forward on the Z-axis toward the camera. Continue moving it until it passes the camera's view. Create a keyframe for it at 300. Make a preview of the animation from the Preview drop-down menu.

14. Now you need to move the camera. With the camera in its original position facing the road, create another keyframe at 30. Now go to frame 30 by pressing f on the keyboard and entering the frame number **30**.

15. Press s to bring up the spline controls and set a value of 1.0 for the Tension. This tells the camera to ease out of the frame. Also, by creating a keyframe at 30, the camera will sit for one second before moving.

16. Go to frame 250 by again pressing f and entering the frame number **250**. Press Enter to go to the frame. Now move the camera down to ground level, and rotate it a bit so that it is facing directly down the road (see fig. 5.5).

17. Also at frame 250, create a spline tension of 1.0 so that the camera eases into the frame. When you make a preview, you should see the camera pan over and down, and the truck should drive right over it.

From this point, you should save the scene and the objects if you made any changes to the surfaces. The final thing you should do here is adjust the lighting. The default lighting right now is pretty good, but it could be better.

FIGURE 5.5

At frame 250, the camera is moved to the ground.

18. From the Lights Panel, change the Ambient Intensity to about 5%. Then, change the Distant Light to a Spotlight. Turn on Shadow Maps, and leave the rest of the values at their defaults.

19. Back in Layout, press the number 5 on the keyboard or numeric keypad. This changes your view to the Light view. This is what the light sees.

NOTE

If you have more than one light in the scene, you can use the up arrow to toggle through the different light views.

20. Position the light so that it looks down on the entire scene, slightly from the side, close to the ground. Figure 5.6 shows the view from the spotlight.

FIGURE 5.6

The default distant light is changed to a spotlight. The spotlight is set and angled from the Light view.

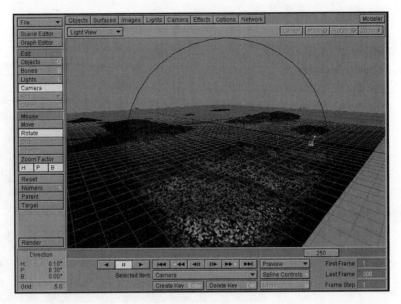

Perform another test render and see how you like your animation. Very simple, but this should give you a good idea of setting up a scene. Keep in mind the following few pointers:

■ Try to load the stationary objects first.

■ Load the larger objects before the smaller ones.

■ Objects that rest on top of other objects should be loaded after the base objects.

■ Set camera moves after objects have been animated.

■ Set lights as you see fit, either in the beginning or after all other elements have been set.

■ Save often.

Figure 5.7 shows the camera's position at frame 257. The monster truck is emerging from the fog and will pass right over the camera.

That scene was a basic scene setup. For larger projects, the methods are the same. In a more complex scene similar to this, you would add more cars, rotation to the tires, birds, clouds, and perhaps some road kill. Chapter 12, "Basic Animation Techniques," discusses animating scenes in more detail.

FIGURE 5.7
Frame 257: The monster truck driving out of the fog. Three objects, a little fog, and only four keyframes make up this easy-to-do animation.

Using Scenes Within Scenes

Using the previous animation, a situation may arise when you will want to add a bird, animal, or creepy-crawly thing. An animated bird would have repeat motions applied to each of its wings. Sometimes setting this up within an existing scene gets confusing when many other objects are loaded. Thus a good work technique is to set up the flying bird within a scene all by itself. Saving that scene enables you to reload it into another scene, such as the Monster Truck scene.

If you had made a bird's wings flap and finally got the motion just the way you wanted, for example, you could use that scene over and over. From the Objects Panel in Layout, clicking on the Load From Scene command enables you to load that scene into the current scene. You are asked whether you would like to load the lights from that scene as well. This decision should be based on how the lights are used.

TIP

A bird can be duplicated many times within one animation and made to look random, to create a flock of birds. Performing a Load From Scene and then cloning the object results in many birds performing the same moves. LightWave 5.5 enables you to move the motion paths for the birds by pressing Shift and Alt simultaneously and then moving the object.

If you have cloned the objects and want to add some randomization, you can enter the object's motion path and Scale All Keys. You can also create different flying bird scenes, for example, and adjust the entire scene from the Shift All Key within the Scene Editor. Save each scene variation, and then perform the Load From Scene.

Using scenes within scenes is good for many LightWave situations. As you work through projects and tutorials, you will find more and more uses for this feature.

Completing a Scene

Completing a scene is more than saving your work and rendering in good quality. Completing a scene also includes output to tape, audio elements, sound effects, and even editing. Later, in Chapter 16, "Output Options and Techniques," you will learn all kinds of fun things to do with your animation *after* the rendering.

Understanding Keyframing

The basis of animated movements in LightWave is keyframes. In a nutshell, a *keyframe* tells an element such as an object, light, or camera to "be here" at a specified frame. Contrary to popular belief, the fewer keyframes you have, the better (motion capture files excluded). Motion capture scenes are generated from rigs and have a large number of keyframes, usually one per frame. Scenes from motion capture rigs have many keyframes because they are created by sampling actual motions at short intervals.

Computer animation is different than traditional cell animation in many ways, one of which is keyframing. Traditional cell animators draw every frame of animation. In computer animation, artists create only a few frames, and the computer interprets the rest. The monster truck animated earlier, for instance, had a keyframe at 0. The next keyframe it had was at 300. That's all you had to set. The computer calculated the position of the truck from frame 0 to 300 and drew in it in. LightWave makes this process even easier with Auto Key Framing.

Using Auto Key Adjust

Under the Options Panel, within the General Options tab in Layout, you can find two buttons labeled Auto Key Adjust and Auto Key Create. These tools can be your best friends or your worst enemies.

After these settings are changed, LightWave uses them each time the program runs. You may not remember, however, and mess up one of your scenes. These tools can be beneficial when it comes to some projects, but they can also be the devil with others. Auto Key Adjust and Auto Key Create do exactly what their names imply: They automatically create keyframes. At times, Auto Key Adjust and Auto Key Create can prove helpful. It is a good idea to use some of the new 5.5 plug-ins, such as the Deformation, in conjunction with these tools. That way you can instantly see the effects the plug-ins have.

The downside to these tools being on is that it is easy to accidentally move an element within your scene that was set up perfectly. If the Auto Scene Adjust and Create keys were selected, you could reset many of your perfect keyframes—which took you hours to set up. Keep an eye on these and be careful when you use them.

NOTE

Those who are used to earlier versions have learned the hard way that this is a new method of animation. Previously, one could move an object, and then make a key for it at some frame. With these settings on, it is necessary to set the frame first, and then move the object. New users won't have this problem, and should prefer the more WYSIWYG approach.

Understanding Motion Graphs

You can access the Motion Graph Panel in LightWave by pressing m on the keyboard for an object, light, or camera. The Motion Graph Panel can prove extremely useful for precise element control within a scene. Figure 5.8 shows the Motion Graph Panel for the monster truck animation.

The Motion Graph Panel offers a wide range of control over Layout elements. Think of a bird flapping its wings, for example. The wings are flapping a bit too slowly. By entering the Motion Graph Panel and using the Shift Keys or Scale Keys, you can globally adjust the object's motion. The Motion Graph Panel also gives you the options to view Velocity of an object, the X, Y, and Z positions, the Heading, Pitch, and Bank Angles, and the X, Y, and Z scale of an object.

FIGURE 5.8
The Motion Graph Panel in LightWave 5.5.

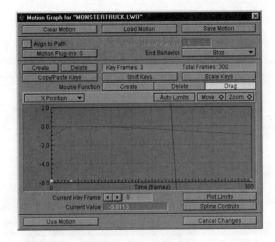

The Motion Graph Panel looks confusing at first. If you think of what you want to accomplish and what you are doing, however, the buttons will quickly make sense to you.

Applying and Editing Motion Graphs

Applying motion graphs is nothing more than making adjustments, scaling or shifting keys, and pressing Use Motion. You can save motion graphs, however, to be used for other things. Your animated car, for example, has a tire. Its motions needed to be modified slightly, which you did right from the Motion Graph Panel. Now you need to animate three more tires. Rather than resetting a new tire each time, you can click on the Save Motion button at the top of the panel, and reload it to be applied to the other tires.

Motion graphs are a blueprint to the motion of the selected item such as an object, light, or camera. You can edit spline tensions, add keyframes, or even modify the speed of an object's path right from the Motion Graph Panel. Chapter 12 provides much more information on using motion graphs.

Using the Virtual Camera

A wonderful part about LightWave is that the camera is your window to the world. As trite as it may sound, the camera in LightWave's Layout is truly a virtual camera. You don't need wires, cables, lens cleaner, or anything to get this camera up and shooting. What you do need are creative ideas and a vision.

A small camera-shaped outline represents the camera in LightWave (see fig. 5.9). The lens effect is represented by outward dotted lines. Should the camera's lens change, the size of the outward dotted line changes as well.

FIGURE 5.9

LightWave's camera.

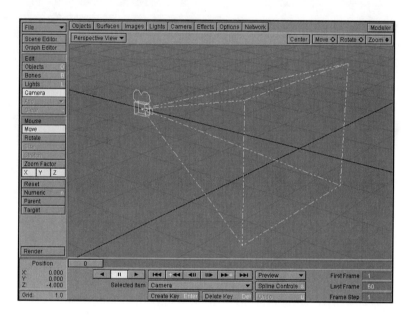

Angles

Camera angles are usually talked about when it comes to 3D animation. This book has dedicated an entire chapter to the camera because it is one of the primary elements in your animation. Chapter 11, "Cameras," will take you for a ride. Be sure to check it out!

The camera angle is more important to the animation than you may think. LightWave's camera offers many capabilities, including Pan, Rotate, Zoom, Dolly, and Truck—just like a Hollywood set. These camera terms are common in the video world as well. LightWave's camera can also mimic still cameras, however, in that certain lenses are available to help you achieve just about any look.

Creating Drama with Lenses

LightWave's camera lenses are representative of real-world equivalents to professional and pro-sumer cameras. Figure 5.10 shows the Camera Panel's Zoom Factor and Film Size.

FIGURE 5.10

LightWave's Camera Panel.

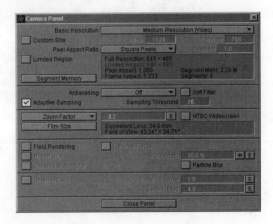

NOTE

The Film Size in LightWave affects only the Equivalent Lens readout and the strength of the Depth of Field.

Changing the zoom factor in LightWave is not a common thing for most animators. You should realize, however, the full creative freedom you have and the final look that you can achieve with a different LightWave lens. Figure 5.11 shows a scene where the camera is left at its usual default zoom factor of 3.2.

The second image has the camera banked to one side, panned in close to the calculator, and has a zoom factor of 1.6. The shot is much more dramatic. Think of an animation with this angle. It is, simply put, cooler to look at.

FIGURE 5.11
The default zoom factor is standard, but the image can look better.

FIGURE 5.12
A closer look at the desk with a zoom factor of 1.6 is more dramatic.

Of course, not all your animations will need to be dramatic. The point here is to not only experiment with textures, objects, and lights, but with the camera as well. Again, check out Chapter 11 for a thorough discussion on animating the camera and faking multiple cameras in LightWave, and for in-depth camera projects.

Understanding Lenses and LightWave

To make better use of the LightWave camera, it is good to understand how it works, and how a zoom factor envelope works. There is a good example of a technique you can use to simulate a scary movie camera technique. In this simple scene, the Skull object is floating above a hallway table. The camera is pulled out wide, but zoomed in close. As the camera moves in closer over five seconds or so, its lens zooms out to a zoom factor of 2.0.

NOTE

For Lenses and Zoom Factor equivalents, a reading is displayed within the Camera Panel in LightWave.

The result of this animation is a stretched background while the main object, the skull, remains about the same size in the camera's lens. This is a cool effect for scary "Oh no!" shots.

This common film move is easy to simulate in LightWave because you have the same controls at your fingertips. This way, however, you don't need to lay a track down on the ground and have someone push the camera dolly! Experiment with this technique on animated people and characters in long stretched hallways, corridors, and so forth.

Conveying Mood with Camera Perspectives

Camera perspectives share the same principles as camera angles: They can convey a feeling or mood for a particular shot. A wide-angle perspective can often give the feeling of a drug-induced situation, sort of a psychedelic mood. A long zoomed tight shot can bring about a feeling of closeness. Figure 5.13 shows a very wide angle on a bunch of cows.

The camera's zoom factor in conjunction with the camera's position is what makes up perspective. Add your own talent and creativity for placing the camera. These three elements—the zoom factor, the camera's position, and the animator's creativity—help to sell your animated message.

FIGURE 5.13
The camera's wide angle zoom factor enables you to make some strange animations.

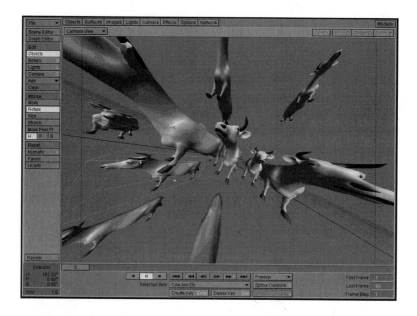

Creating a Different Feel

The camera's perspective helps to create a different feeling. You have probably seen photographs in which the camera is closer to the subject. In those photos, everything in the camera range is in focus. If the camera were far away and zoomed into the subject, the background elements would be out of focus. This is a much softer look, and really makes the target subject jump off the page.

In LightWave you can do the same thing. Assume, for example, that you have set up the scene, loaded all the objects, and now it is time to animate the camera. You want the background objects to be sort of just there. By moving the camera far away from the objects and zooming the lens in, you can create a blurry background. You must do one thing, however, to achieve this: turn on Depth of Field. In Chapter 11 you will use Depth of Field to set up a real-world camera situation.

Matching Real-World Cameras

Speaking of real-world camera situations, you may also come across a situation in which you need to animate a 3D character in the real world.

Chapter 15, "Compositing," examines the techniques and tricks to placing 3D elements into real-world environments. A key factor to good compositing is matching the camera.

Animators should be aware of the following things when matching cameras to the real world:

- The type of camera being used. Is it a home video camera, professional video camera, or film camera?

- The camera height and angle in the real shot.

- The camera lens used.

By mastering the camera in LightWave, you will also open your mind to new ways of putting together your animation. You should work hard to avoid the typical long, single camera shot for an entire animation. When you use LightWave, you will definitely come out ahead if you remember the real world and how video and film is shot when using LightWave's camera.

Extending Your Creativity with Plug-Ins

Layout, like Modeler, uses open architecture throughout for plug-ins. NewTek supplies LightWave with a variety of plug-ins, ranging from surface shaders to displacement plug-ins to image plug-ins. A number of Global Class plug-ins do their work behind the scenes. Other plug-ins are available for you to apply throughout the LightWave interface. The plug-in categories in LightWave can be found in many places. The primary plug-in classes in LightWave 5.5 are as follows:

- **Objects Panel.** Displacement and Object-Replacement plug-ins

- **Surface Panel.** Shader plug-ins

- **Effects Panel.** Pixel Filter plug-ins

- **Effects Panel.** Image Filter plug-ins

- **Options Panel.** Generic plug-ins

- **Motions Panel.** Motion plug-ins

- **Render Panel.** Animation Saver and Image Loader plug-ins

You can load each plug-in via a drop-down menu. Many plug-in classes enable you to use up to four plug-ins simultaneously.

A LightWave plug-in is often a small program that performs a difficult task. New to 5.5 are the Deformation plug-ins found within the Displacement plug-in class. Deformation plug-ins bring some of Modeler's Modify tools to Layout, applying them based on null objects in the scene. Without these plug-ins, a hefty bone structure and a lot of keyframes would need to be set to accomplish the same results.

The Pixel Filter plug-in class is where you can find plug-ins such as the new Volumetric plug-in called Steamer. This class holds plug-ins that manipulate the pixels of the image in some way. Similar to that are the Image Filter plug-ins that enhance or change the final rendered image—Blur, Emboss, Sepia Tone, and others.

The Options Panel plug-ins or Generic plug-in class is where you find plug-ins that are really separate programs to run with LightWave. Morph Gizmo, a new plug-in for LightWave 5.5, is technically a program all its own. It needs LightWave, however, to run. Figure 5.14 shows the Generic plug-in drop-down menu. Figure 5.15 shows the Morph Gizmo interface.

FIGURE 5.14

The Generic plug-in class found in the Options Panel.

FIGURE 5.15

The Morph Gizmo interface, a Generic class plug-in.

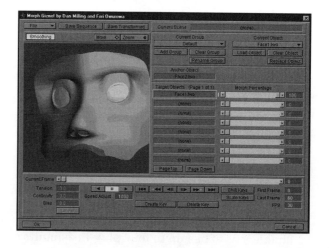

NOTE

Chapter 14, "Facial Animation and Morph Gizmo," provides tips and techniques to use with the Morph Gizmo plug-in.

Plug-ins prove extremely helpful in numerous animation situations. As you progress through this book, you will use certain plug-ins to perform particular tasks. Without many of LightWave's plug-ins, your job would be much harder. The right plug-in for the right job can sometimes be like an extra helper in your animation studio.

Choosing the Right Plug-In

As with many of the tools in LightWave, choosing the right plug-in depends on the job at hand. Some plug-ins will be used more than others; some won't be used at all. Often you will find yourself looking to third-party plug-ins, such as Dynamic Realities Particle Storm plug-in. This handy plug-in gives you particle power in LightWave. It is included with LightWave 5.5 to facilitate basic particle animation needs. Figure 5.16 shows the Particle Storm interface.

FIGURE 5.16

The Particle Storm plug-in interface.

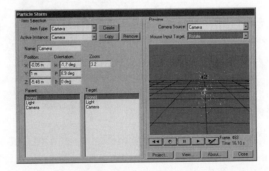

Choosing the right plug-in means knowing all the plug-ins available to you. This is when having the LightWave reference manuals by your computer is a plus. You could be working late and suddenly realize that the new Deform Shear plug-in from the Deformation class is exactly the tool you need to finish off your animation. There truly are so many plug-ins available to you in LightWave that it is easy to forget the exact operating procedure for some of them. Always refer to your LightWave reference and user guides for documentation.

Using Existing Plug-Ins

The plug-ins that come with LightWave also come with demo scenes. Look for the Deformation scenes in your LightWave directory. Sometimes looking at just a plug-in interface doesn't make much sense. When you see how the plug-in is set up within a scene, however, you will let out a big "Ooohhhh, I see ...."

Putting these existing plug-ins to use will enhance much of your work. Within the Effects Panel, for example, you can find Image Filter plug-ins that can take your animation to different heights. The Sepia Filter applies a sepia tone application to every rendered frame of your animation, giving it an antique look. The EmbossBW plug-in, on the other hand, can make your finished animation look as if an artist pressed it into a picture frame. Another plug-in that can enhance your scene is the Pennello Lite plug-in. With this plug-in, you can manipulate the rendered images as if you had a post-process unit processing the final images. Figure 5.17 shows the Pennello interface.

FIGURE 5.17
Pennello Lite interface,
an Image Filter plug-in.

Existing plug-ins are sometimes small and obscure. Looks can sometimes be deceiving, however. The Effector plug-in within the Displacement Map plug-in class, for example, looks insignificant enough in figure 5.18.

FIGURE 5.18
The seemingly simple
Effector plug-in
interface.

The Effector plug-in, however, enables you to drag an object through a space that it is not meant to be in. This is just one example of a plug-in being more sophisticated than it might appear at first glance. Figure 5.19 shows the Effector plug-in displacing a tube with a ball. When the ball travels through the tube's path, the sides of the tube are pushed away.

Another plug-in available from NewTek, though not included with LightWave 5.5, is Cyclist. The Cyclist interface is small and unassuming, but the plug-in itself is quite powerful. Cyclist enables you to create a single motion based on a parent object's movements. If you wanted to make a spider walk without Cyclist, for example, you would need to animate each little leg over the right amount of time, based on the spider's movements. In addition, you would have to move the spider. Animating this way often creates legs that are not moving in real time with the body. Cyclist enables you to move the spider, and have the legs follow. If the spider backs up, the legs walk backward. This plug-in is great for other animations such as spinning tires on a car or wheels on a bicycle, just to name a couple. Chapter 16 discusses Cyclist in more detail.

FIGURE 5.19
The Effector plug-in seems harmless enough, but is powerful enough to move a ball through a tube.

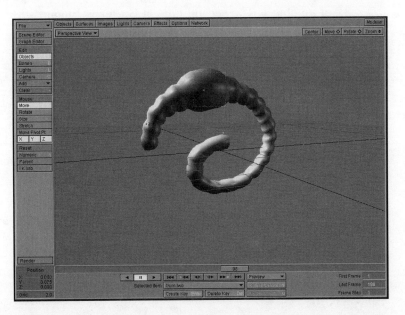

This tool can have many uses—medical, special effects, or even something fun such as a cartoon bullet spreading a gun's barrel as it shoots out.

As with the plug-ins in Modeler, take some time and go through the plug-ins in Layout. Experiment with them for a while and come up with some ideas and uses of your own.

Using Third-Party Plug-Ins

After going through many of the plug-ins in Layout, you may decide that there is something else you want to do, but don't have the tools for. You may want a plug-in created by a third-party developer just for LightWave.

Third-party plug-ins are anything from Surface plug-ins to Pixel Filter plug-ins to programs such as Particle Storm, mentioned earlier. These third-party developers generate plug-ins that fill a void within the LightWave environment. One of those plug-ins is Gaffer from Worley Laboratories. The Gaffer plug-in is a complex program that runs in two places. The Gaffer portion of the plug-in, which controls shadows, specularities, and lighting effects, can be found within the Surfaces Panel. This plug-in applies itself to the surface of an object. The second part of Gaffer is Bloom, which enhances the final image with specular glows. You find this plug-in within the Image Filter plug-in class. Figure 5.20 shows the Gaffer interface.

Look on the Internet for third-party plug-ins for LightWave; they are becoming increasingly common. These plug-ins range up in price from $10. The few plug-ins mentioned in this section only skim the top of the valuable resources available to you. Using third-party plug-ins means that your LightWave work will never get dull. There will always be a plug-in to add to your arsenal of effects and tools. The hardest part for you is finding the time to learn them!

As Part One of *Inside LightWave 3D* concludes, you should have a good understanding of LightWave's Layout and Modeler, and their uses. Part Two guides you through "LightWave Modeler in Action" in Chapter 6, "Character Modeling with MetaNURBS" in Chapter 7, "Textures and Materials" in Chapter 8, and much more.

FIGURE 5.20

The Gaffer interface is quite impressive to look at and offers quite impressive results.

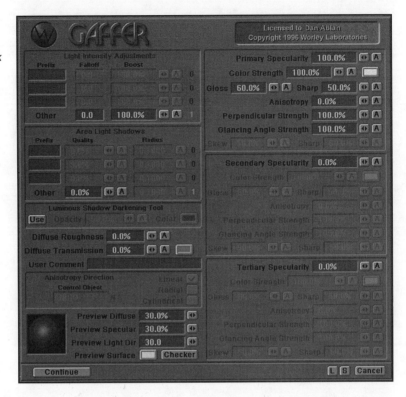

Summary

Learning and applying techniques in Layout is an ongoing process. You should never stop learning. Use the tools available to you often, and work toward enhancing your talents as an animator through different ideas and techniques. You should keep the following few things in mind when working in Layout:

- Have a goal and stay focused.

- Use existing scenes or parts of existing scenes in your current scenes to save time and effort.

- Plan out your scenes.

- Add drama and mood to your scene with interesting camera angles.

- Use different perspectives for various looks.

- Apply plug-ins for added effects such as post-process image enhancements.

Working in Layout is more than loading objects and setting lights. It is the techniques that you learn and develop on your own that make your animations shine. As you apply different techniques and understand their affect on your 3D animation, consider what other possibilities are available to you. Read on to Chapter 6 to enhance your 3D modeling skills.

Part II

BUILDING 3D SCENES

Chapter 6

LightWave Modeler in Action

In Chapter 4, "Modeler Techniques," you were introduced to the rudiments of Modeler, LightWave 3D's object creation engine. This chapter assumes that you have progressed beyond the basics and are ready to put Modeler into action in your graphic design and animation projects. This chapter covers the following topics:

- *Creating models*
- *Carving up your geometry: drilling and Booleans*
- *Generating text and logos*

Creating Basic Models

After basic preplanning (see Chapter 3, "LightWave in Action"), it is necessary to choose the best method for creating your model. There are many approaches that you can use during the modeling process:

- Building a model from modified primitives

- Extruding simple shapes into complex models

- Using Boolean modeling and drilling

- Using Metaballs

- Using Metaform

- Using MetaNURBS

- Spline patching

Each of these modeling methods has inherent strengths and weaknesses, depending on the type of model being created. For instance, Boolean modeling is great for less organic objects. Objects that do not need to be smoothly shaped can be created with Boolean operations by selectively adding or subtracting geometry to build complex shapes. It is often not the best tool for organic modeling, because the seams between joined parts are difficult to blend after a Boolean operation. Organic models need smooth flowing edges, and generally seams are limited.

Metaballs in LightWave are useful for creating simple organic shapes, such as hands for a character, but are generally too tedious for complete organic forms, such as a head-to-toe character. Metaball meshes often require a high degree of detail to look clean and can be difficult to animate with bones in Layout.

Metaform and MetaNURBS are often the all-purpose tools for creating organic models. There are times, however, when their inherent imprecision and "softness" can make it difficult to create exacting smooth forms that follow specific contours (such as a jet plane modeled to plans or an industrial-design appliance). In such cases, spline modeling and patching are good choices.

Don't become too comfortable with a particular method of modeling, ignoring other avenues that may be more suitable for a particular task. Experimenting with other modeling methods can expand your knowledge and talents.

Before getting to the "meat" of modeling, it is necessary to discuss some of the primitives available in Modeler, as these are the basic building blocks from which your models will be constructed. This next section will cover primary primitives you should be familiar with. To learn about additional primitives in Modeler, be sure to refer to your *LightWave User Manual and Reference Guide* from NewTek.

Modeler Primitives

Primitives are the basic forms from which other models are constructed. Modeler includes a relatively small set of primitives: points, simple polygons, spline curves, boxes, spheres, discs/cylinders, cones, and text. In addition to these, the LW_Primitives plug-in adds several more.

Points

The most basic element in Modeler is the point, out of which all other objects are derived. Points make up polygons. Follow along with this brief exercise to become familiar with the creation of points in Modeler.

The next few steps will walk you through creating points, selecting points, and making a polygon. Think of points as the fasteners that hold together objects. Even spline curves have points on either end or throughout controlling the curve. Points are very important to your LightWave Modeling.

MAKING YOUR POINTS

1. Create a disc in Modeler. From the Objects tab, select the Disc tool and press n on the keyboard to call up the Numeric Requester. Note that the default Sides in LightWave 5.5 is 24, and Segments is 1.

2. Change the Sides to 30, make Axis Z, Segments remain at 1, while the Bottom and Top values should be set to 0. Leave all other settings at their defaults. Click on OK.

NOTE

To be sure about the default settings, click the Reset button within the Numeric Requester.

3. Press Enter to make the disc. Notice that the disc is made up of 30 evenly spaced points around the exterior edge.

4. Select a few of the points (anywhere on the disc) with the left mouse button. Press the z key to delete them. You'll see the area of the polygon literally collapse without the points.

This example shows how important points are to 3D objects. They are the rivets that weld the object into a solid object. Now, read on to learn more about creating points for other Modeler primitives.

Clicking on the Points button under the Polygon tab, or pressing the + key shifts Modeler into Point-Creation mode (see fig. 6.1). You create a point under the cursor by right-clicking with the mouse in any view (except the OpenGL view). If you need to align the point in several dimensions, left-click-and-drag with the mouse to align the point; then press Enter or Return to create the point.

FIGURE 6.1

Use the Points tool to create a point in any view except OpenGL view.

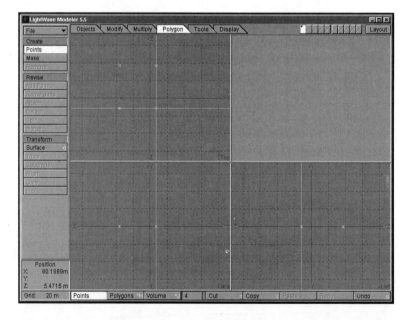

In addition to the Point creation tool, Modeler provides two more functions for the management of points: Weld and Merge. Both of these tools combine multiple points into one point. The Weld tool will take all selected points and move them to the location of the last selected point before combining them. The Merge tool will combine all points within a certain distance of each other.

The Merge tool gives you three options for merging: Automatic, Fractional, and Absolute. Automatic merges the points that are almost overlapping. Fractional will merge points that are 1/(10 to the power of n) or closer, compared to the full size of the selected geometry. (n equals the value you enter in the Merge Points dialog box.) Hence, a value of 3.0 means $1/10^3$ or 1/1000th of the size of all currently selected geometry. Absolute merges all points within the specified distance of each other.

In most cases, you can use the Automatic setting for merging points. Merging points is important to your models to eliminate points that occupy the same space. The next exercise will help you better understand the use of Merge Points.

Often when creating objects, there is symmetry involved. A complex character you might be building is identical on both the left and right side of its face, for example. With this, you model just one side of the face and then use the Mirror tool to create the opposite side of the face. When this happens, a noticeable seam appears at the point where the object was mirrored. Follow the next few steps to eliminate seams using the Merge Points command.

MERGING POINTS AND ELIMINATING SEAMS

1. Create a ball in Modeler using the Ball's default settings in its numeric requester.

2. Using the right mouse button in the Polygon mode, lasso around the right side of the ball to select just the polygons on the right half.

3. With only the right-half polygons selected, press the z key to delete them. You should now have a hemisphere.

4. Press q on the keyboard to enter the Change Surface Requester. Leave all settings at their defaults, but turn on Smoothing. Click on Apply to close the panel.

5. Select the Mirror tool from the Multiply menu. Here, you have two options: You can either manually set the mirror by clicking the left mouse on the proper axis, or you can set it numerically. Because you made a default ball, the center of the ball, which is now the right edge,

should be lined up with the 0 point on the X-axis. Press n on the keyboard, set the Plane to X, and the position should be 0. Click OK to close the requester.

6. Press Enter to mirror to the half sphere. Turn on the OpenGL Smooth Shaded Preview from the Preview Type selection within the Display Options Panel (d). Notice the seam down the middle of the sphere in the preview window?

7. Press m on the keyboard to call up the merge Points tool. Select Automatic and press OK to perform the merge. You'll see a message stating how many points have been eliminated. Click on OK, and you'll see the OpenGL Preview update to a smooth sphere without a seam.

Merge Points eliminates the points that are sitting on top of each other. In the previous example, a seam was created because a duplicate of the sphere was created beside the original. The intersecting areas shared the same points. Merge eliminated those unwanted points.

There might be a time, however, when you would want a seam and refrain from using Merge Points. In addition, you may have a situation in which a seam needs to be created. To do this, simply selecting the desired polygons, cutting, and then pasting in the exact same position will create additional points between objects sharing the same space.

Polygons

Without points, you can't have any polygons. Simply put, polygons do not exist without points. You can create a polygon from a selected set of points by pressing the p key. Pressing Ctrl+p will generate a spline curve through the selected points. Figure 6.2 shows a variety of different polygons and curves.

FIGURE 6.2
A collection of curves and polygons.

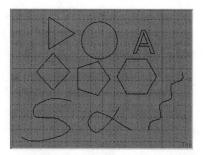

LightWave supports polygons with up to 32,000 points. Polygons with one or two points are special cases, forming point particles and three-dimensional line segments. Polygons of greater than two points have a distinct direction they face, called the *normal vector*. You can imagine the normal as a stick jutting out of the polygon perpendicular to its surface, as illustrated in figure 6.3. A polygon's normal plays a big role in determining its visibility to the camera or to raytracing. Polygons facing away from the camera or rays are termed *back-faces* and are usually ignored for the sake of expediency when rendering a scene (a process termed *back-face culling*). It is possible to give a polygon a double-sided surface, in which it faces both directions, but use this option with caution due to the increased render times for the back-faces.

FIGURE 6.3
The normals for a set of polygons.

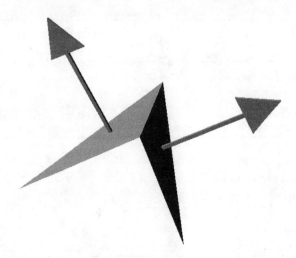

A polygonal normal is determined by the user when points are selected to create a polygon. Points must be selected in order from left to right in a clockwise manner. When this is done and a polygon is created, the normal will point out of the screen. Selecting points counterclockwise would result in a flipped polygon. Flipped polygons can be corrected using the f key to flip selected polygons so that they face the opposite direction. However, it's a good idea to get into the habit of selecting points in a clockwise manner.

Modeler includes a number of tools for managing polygons and spline curves in your models; tools for merging polygons, splitting them, adding to or removing points from them; and so on. All of these reside under the Polygon tab in Modeler.

In addition to the Polygon tools, Modeler has many tools specifically for use on spline curves. These tools include Make and Make Cl, Start CP and End CP, and others described in the following list. You can find these under the Tools tab in Modeler.

- **Make and Make Cl.** Create an open-ended and closed curve, respectively, from the selected points.

- **Start CP and End CP.** Convert the first and last point in the curve into a control point for the start and end of the curve. If you create a control point for a curve with this tool, it is possible to control the curve direction entering into or exiting from the first or last point.

- **Freeze.** Converts a spline curve into a regular polygon. If the curve is open ended, it will add an edge from the first to last point.

- **Smooth.** Assigns control points to smooth adjoining curves, as shown in figure 6.4.

FIGURE 6.4
The top curve in this illustration shows a curve with start and end control points. The center curves show two adjoining curves before smoothing (the join point is close to the axis). The bottom curves show the same curves with smoothing applied.

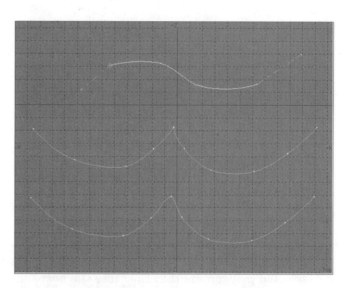

Boxes, Balls, Discs, and Cones

Modeler's basic primitives consist of boxes, balls, discs, and cones (see fig. 6.5). If you look at the world around you, most objects can be created using these four basic primitives. Look at a pop can, for example. You can create, extrude, and shape a disc to create the can. You can create and carve doorways from various boxes. The primitives are there for you as building blocks for 3D modeling. You can find all of these under the Objects tab in Modeler.

FIGURE 6.5

Primitives in Modeler, both in 2D and 3D form.

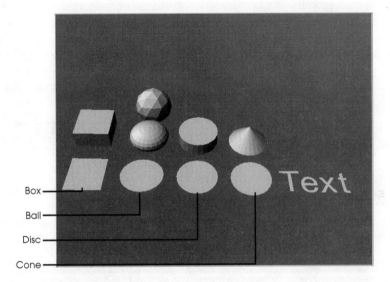

Using any one of these tools is as simple as activating the tool, left-clicking-and-dragging in any view to define two dimensions of the object, and then left-clicking-and-dragging the outline in another view to define the third dimension. For several of these tools in LightWave 5.5, pressing the right or left arrow keys will increase or decrease the number of segments, respectively.

As an alternative, you can press the n key or click the Numeric button to open the Numeric Options Panel, allowing you to set the dimensions of the primitive, as well as the number of sides and segments to be used to create it.

Following are some tips for using the Box, Ball, Disc, and Cone tools:

- If the shape is only dragged out in one view (for instance, only the Top view), the final shape created will be a single flat polygon (or a mesh of polygons) in the shape of a rectangle or ellipse/circle.

- Holding down the Ctrl key when you first begin dragging the outline of a box, ball, cone, or disc will create a perfect square or circle in that view.

- Using a low sides setting (such as 3,5,6) for the Disc tool can generate regular polygons (triangles, pentagons, hexagons, and so on) quite easily.

- If, for whatever reason, you are unhappy with the shape or orientation of the object being created, you can reset the tool by clicking in any empty region in the border area surrounding the view windows in Modeler. Such areas exist to the right of the tabs at the top of Modeler's interface, and below the buttons on the left-hand side.

Modeling with primitives often means creating complex objects out of many primitive shapes. You can create the interior of a museum with many boxes for walls, doors, windows, tiles, and pictures, for example. You can use discs for canister lighting, door knobs, and so on. You can create simple every day objects with primitives as well. This exercise will demonstrate how to use boxes, balls, and discs to create an everyday traffic signal.

CREATING A TRAFFIC SIGNAL

1. Enter Modeler and in a clean layer, create a box with the following settings:

	Low	High	Segments
X	-4.0083m	4.0083m	1
Y	-9.983m	12.025m	1
Z	-4.0083m	4.0083m	1

   Click on OK, and then press Enter to make the box.

2. Press c on the keyboard to copy this box to memory. Go to a new layer and press v to paste it.

3. Press Shift+h to call up the Size tool. Press n on the keyboard to enter the Size tool's Numeric Requester. Enter a value of 90% for the Factor. Click on OK to size the box down. This smaller box will help cut out an area of the traffic signal housing.

4. Select the Move tool and enter its numeric requester. Enter a Z value of -6.57m and click on OK to move the box forward. Place the smaller offset box in a background layer. Place the large centered box in a foreground layer.

5. Press Shift+b on the keyboard to call up the Boolean Operations. Select Subtract, and click on OK. Figure 6.6 shows the results of the Boolean Operation.

FIGURE 6.6

Simple primitives such as boxes begin to form a traffic signal.

6. In a clean layer with the Booleaned Traffic Signal object in a background layer, create a ball with the following settings:

Ball Type:	Globe	
Side:	32	
Segments:	16	
CenterX:	0m	
	Y:	1.021m
	Z:	-2.7643m
Radii	X:	3.3019m
	Y:	3.2507m
	Z:	972.6398mm

Click on OK and press Enter to make the ball. Your object should resemble a traffic signal lens.

7. Copy the ball and move it up to the top of the traffic signal box (which is in a background layer) for the red light. Paste the original, and repeat the step for the bottom lens for the green. Figure 6.7 shows the original ball copied twice for the traffic signal lenses.

8. At this point, it's a good idea to surface the lenses so that they each have separate colors. Select the polygons making up the top lens, and press q on the keyboard. This will bring up the Change Surface Requester where you can rename the selected polygons to Red_Lens. Deselect the red polygons, and repeat the process for the yellow and green lenses.

9. With the traffic signal box in a background layer and the balls in a foreground layer, press Shift+b to call up the Boolean Operations. Select Union and press OK. In a moment, the lenses will be joined with the traffic signal as one object.

10. From here, surface the different parts of the object as you like. To add a bit more to this, create an elongated disc for the pole holding the traffic signal in place. This pole can be attached from below for a street height

traffic signal, or the pole can be bent and attached to the traffic signal
from above. Figure 6.8 shows the traffic signal created from primitives.

FIGURE 6.7

*One ball is copied twice
making three traffic
signal lenses.*

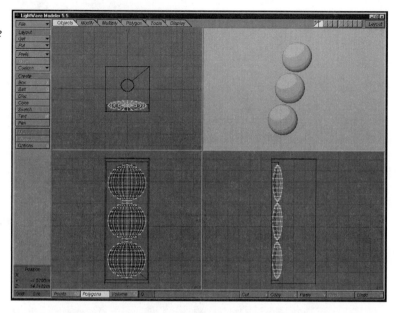

FIGURE 6.8

*You can build a useable
traffic signal in minutes
with primitive shapes.*

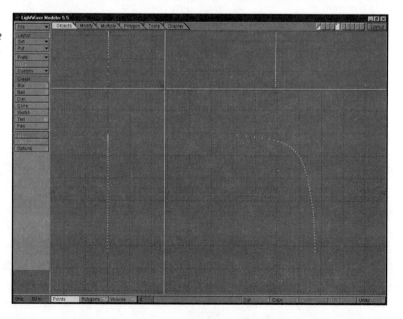

The traffic signal you just created is basic. You can see that within minutes, however, those simple balls and boxes begin taking shape into something else. Primitives are essential to building many types of objects and characters in LightWave.

Generating Higher-Order Forms from Primitives

Basic primitives are the building blocks to great models in LightWave. But you can progress beyond basic primitives for even greater creativity using higher forms of primitive shapes. Modeler contains many tools for generating more complex forms, from lathing and extruding to skinning and morphing. You can find all of the tools described in this section under the Multiply tab in Modeler. Each of them can give you the ability to create objects that are more complex than traffic signals or streetlights. These tools enable you to go beyond creating objects with basic primitive shapes.

Lathe

You can use Lathe to create a number of different rotational forms, depending on the starting shape and the options chosen in the Lathe Tool Numeric Requester.

You use the Lathe tool by simply clicking on the desired axis for rotation. You can also set values numerically through the Lathe Tool Numeric Requester. Examining the numeric panel shown in figure 6.9, the options for Lathe are self-explanatory. In this panel, you can specify specific angles, sides, axes, and offset values. Setting the offset enables you to determine how far up the axis the lathed shape will travel as it revolves. Use the offset to make objects such as springs or spiral staircases.

FIGURE 6.9
Use the Lathe Tool Numeric Requester to enter specific values that affect the outcome of the lathed shape.

Follow the next exercise to better understand how to use the Lathe tool. This exercise will show you how useful the Lathe tool is in Modeler. By making one simple curve, you can quickly make an intricate banister for a stairway.

MAKING A BANISTER

1. Enter Modeler, and in a clean layer begin clicking points from top to bottom in the Face view. Make the first point directly on the 0 X-axis. Continue creating points to the right of the axis and downward. Make about 30 points, and curve them randomly, as in figure 6.10. Be sure to add the last point directly on the 0 X-axis.

FIGURE 6.10

A line of points created in order to make a curve.

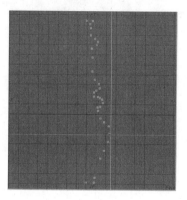

2. With the points still selected, press Ctrl+p to make an open curve. From here, smooth out any areas of the curve that seem odd. Figure 6.11 shows the final curve.

FIGURE 6.11

Once you make an open curve from selected points, you can drag or move individual points to smooth out the curve.

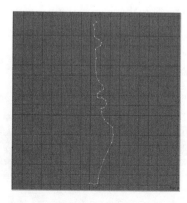

3. Once you have the curve completed, select the Lathe tool from the Multiply menu. From the Top view, click directly on the 0 Y-axis. A line will appear that represents the Lathe tool's rotational pivot point. As you place the Lathe tool's pivot point on the 0 Y-axis, the representational line will change from blue to red.

4. Once the Lathe tool is in place, press Enter to make the object. Figure 6.12 shows the lathed object.

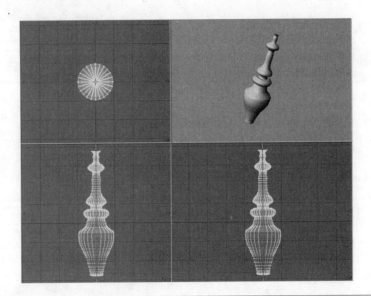

FIGURE 6.12

The original curve lathed around the 0 Y-axis to become a bedpost or banister.

This exercise showed you a basic working example of the Lathe tool. You can use this example for a countless number of objects such as bottles, cans, vases, flashlights, and more. Once you create a lathed object, you can manipulate further with bending and shearing, or use the Magnet tool for additional shapes.

Extrude

The Extrude tool enables you to quickly create an extruded shape along any of the primary axes. For more complex extrusions, see the Path and Rail Extrude tools detailed in the following section. To use this tool, simply click in the view of the desired direction of the extrusion.

A handle will appear in an opposite view indicating the depth of the extrusion. Click on the end of the handle to adjust the extrusion depth. The numeric panel, shown in figure 6.13, allows for precise specification of extrusion depth and the number of segments to extrude.

FIGURE 6.13
The numeric options for
the Extrude tool.

If, for example, you want to extrude a flat text object, click on the face of the object in the Face view. This will tell Modeler to extrude the object on the Z-axis. If you click on the Side view of the object, Modeler will think you want to extrude the object from the side. Try extruding a simple text object in different views and remember to use the Undo command. Figure 6.14 illustrates the Extrude tool on text.

NOTE

Sometimes, when clicking on the handle of the Extrude tool, you might accidentally reset the orientation of the extrusion. If this happens, simply click in the original view for the proper extrusion direction, and begin again.

FIGURE 6.14
Text after extrusion has
been applied.

Following are some tips for using the Extrude tool:

■ You can extrude three-dimensional shapes, provided they are not closed, such as a box or a sphere.

■ For the sides of the extruded object to face outward, the polygons to be extruded should face away from the direction of the extrusion or the direction of rotation for the lathe.

- It is possible to extrude spline polygons, but only edges will be generated. That is, the ends will not be capped. For lathing, this is not an issue.

- When extruding or lathing splines, the Curve Division setting on the Options Panel (under Objects) determines the fineness (and hence the polygon count) of the final object.

Path and Rail Extrude

Path Extrude is useful in creating an object that follows a motion path defined in Layout, such as a road that follows a car's motion, a tunnel that follows the camera's motion, and the like. To perform a successful path extrusion, you need a motion file, either saved out of Layout or converted from another motion format into LightWave's motion file format, and a shape to extrude.

Rail Extrude will extrude all currently selected foreground geometry (points or polygons) along one or more rails (spline curves) in the background layer(s).

The next exercise demonstrates how to use a path created in Layout to create an object in Modeler. This exercise shows you how to create a different type of extrusion on an object. Other objects, such as railings, tubes, or cables may need to be extruded along a specific path.

Included on the CD accompanying this book is a file Cameramot.lws with the camera moving along a simple arcing path. The motion of the camera has been saved to the file Cammot.mot, which will be the basis for your path extrusion.

CREATING AN OBJECT ALONG A PREDEFINED CAMERA'S PATH

1. Start both Layout and Modeler.

2. Load the Cameramot.lws file into Layout.

3. In Modeler, create a point centered at 0,0,0.

4. Now, activate the Path Extrude tool. When the File Requester appears, select the Cammot.mot file.

5. In the Path Extrude dialog box, leave the First and Last values unchanged, but set the step to **5.0**.

6. A warning dialog box will appear indicating that only points were generated. Click on OK. Notice that a series of unconnected points were created.

7. Select the points in order from the most negative in the Z direction to the most positive. Create a spline path by using the Tools, Curves, Make tool or pressing Ctrl+p. This will create a spline curve to be used for a rail extrude, as shown in figure 6.15. Be sure to save the scene at this point. Give it a name such as ExtrudTest.lws or something similar.

FIGURE 6.15

Spline path created by path extruding a point along a saved camera motion path.

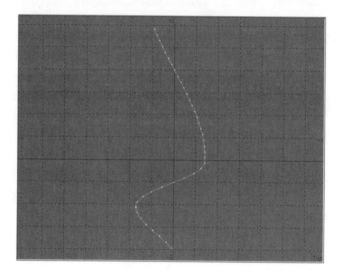

The next part of the exercise will use a rail extrude because the motion path had the Align to Path option checked in Layout. This option is not saved with a motion path file, so Path Extrude can't be used. Rail extrudes do have the option of orienting the extruded shape along the spline curve and are thus more desirable in this case. In other cases, the Path Extrude tool would have sufficed.

8. Make the layer containing the spline path created in step 7 the background layer.

9. Create a flat disc in the Face view, with a radius of approximately 200mm.

10. Move this disc to the beginning of the spline path in the background layer, rotating it in the Top view until it is roughly perpendicular to the direction of the spline path, as in figure 6.16.

FIGURE 6.16
Disc oriented at the beginning of the spline path in preparation for rail extrusion.

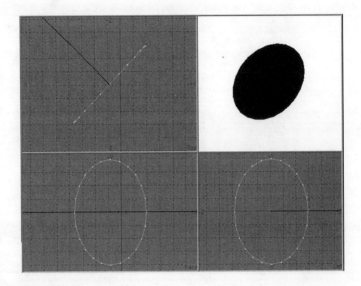

11. Select Rail Extrude. In the dialog box, set the Segments to Uniform Knots, and type **100** in the numeric field. Keep Oriented checked on and press OK.

12. The disc should now be extruded along the spline path in the background. Press the f key to flip all the polygons inside-out, as the camera will be traveling down the inside of the tube.

13. Use Objects, Put (Export in LightWave 5.0), and export the object into Layout. If all was done properly, the camera should now be traveling down the inside of the tube. Texture the tube to your liking. Your tube should look like the one in figure 6.17.

This simple exercise only scratches the surface of what Rail Extrude can do. It can also be used to extrude along multiple paths, each one controlling the extruded shape. Figure 6.18 shows objects extruded along multiple paths. The file Multirail.lwo on the accompanying CD illustrates the use of multiple spline paths to extrude a form.

FIGURE 6.17
The finished tube, ready for export to Layout.

FIGURE 6.18
Objects created with an extrusion along multiple paths.

Skin and Morph

The Skin and Morph tools enable you to build a model from a set of discrete contours. These contours can be either spline curves or polygons. Once the contours have been built, they can be connected by one of these tools.

Morph requires that the polygons have the same number of vertices. If this condition is not met, Modeler will display an error dialog box and refuse the operation. This means you must design the contour levels with the same number of vertices at the outset; fixing them later can become a laborious and time-consuming process.

TIP

You should use a single polygon as the basis for each layer when using the Morph tool. This shape can then be reshaped with the Drag tool.

Morph works better with standard polygons, as it ignores areas of spline curves in between vertices. It also has the capability to do a segmented transition between contours. It will automatically connect even the most disparate shapes together because it works with the point-order of the contour polygons.

Skin, on the other hand, does not require identical vertex counts and adds only one layer of polygons. Joining them together, therefore, is easy. Skin properly interpolates between vertices on spline curves, connecting the closest areas between contours. If you want to add a twist at a particular level, use Morph.

As an example, another use of Skin can be to digitize a physical model made out of soft clay, or from a photograph by shooting the successive contours with a video camera mounted on a stand and connected to a video digitizer. Using these images as a background image in modeler, trace over each, arrange the contours in order along an axis, and skin them.

This same technique can work for contours of a geological map. To do this, be sure that successive contour shapes do not greatly vary from each other. If so, you may need to add intermediate shapes to mitigate the skinning from one layer to another. Figure 6.19 shows a skinned shape from contours.

FIGURE 6.19
A skinned shape created from a series of contours traced from a contour map.

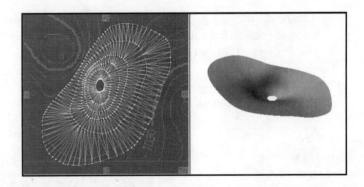

When you create an object in Modeler, you will use primitive shapes, as described earlier in this chapter. You may also use more advanced tools to create higher-order forms for more complex objects, as you just read. But there are other types of objects that require more curves and more intricacy. You can create organic objects in Modeler with numerous tools, as explained in the next section.

Creating Organic Models

LightWave's Modeler has three organic modeling tools: Spline Modeling (and Patching), Metaform, and MetaNURBS. You can use each of these tools to create smooth flowing shapes such as faces, bodies, stylized text, and more. This section introduces you to these tools and some of their uses.

Spline Modeling

Spline modeling and patching is perhaps the oldest form of organic modeling available in Modeler. Due to a combination of a general misunderstanding of how to use spline modeling effectively, not enough documentation in the LightWave reference manuals, along with the introductions of the newer organic tools Metaform and MetaNURBS, it may also be the least used of the organic modeling tools. However, this doesn't mean that spline modeling is ineffective.

The basis of spline modeling is the spline cage, which consists of a number of connected intersecting spline curves that represent a rough outline of the model.

The best starting point for spline modeling is to envision your model as a series of spline contours at various intervals, as shown in figure 6.20. Using the Polygon Points tool to lay down points and then make a spline curve through them creates each contour spline. If the contours are extremely similar, it may be possible to copy and paste one contour spline and then reshape it using the Drag tool.

FIGURE 6.20
Beginning the spline modeling process by laying down spline contours.

Once the basic contours are laid out, you can then cross-connect them with spline contours running perpendicular to the original contour splines.

It is important to select existing points, because you need to connect the splines in order to patch them. It is also necessary to ensure that only three or four spline curves surround each gap in the model, and that no spline curves intersect more than once with each other. In order to achieve this, you may need to create cross curves of only a few points each and then use the Curve Smooth tool to smooth them together, as shown in figure 6.21.

FIGURE 6.21

Creating cross-contours by selecting existing points and creating spline curves through them.

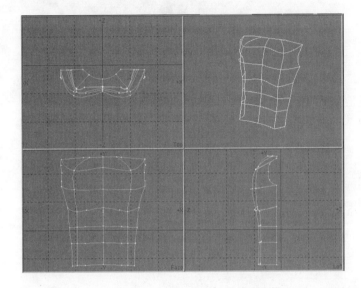

Once a basic shape has been fleshed out for a model, it may be necessary to go in and create additional points and possibly beginning and ending control points to force particular curves into the desired shape. It also might be necessary to add additional splines to create detail in critical sections of the model. Figure 6.22 shows the final spline cage after detail has been added to it. You can find this spline cage file, Beefyspline.lwo, on the accompanying CD.

Spline Patches

After the spline cage has been created, it needs to be patched. Spline patching refers to the act of creating a polygonal surface between selected splines. This will enable you to render the object in Layout.

FIGURE 6.22
*The final spline cage
after detail has been
added in crucial
sections.*

TIP

Think of a spline cage as the wire framing of a blimp, and think of patching as the fabric that wraps around the wire frame. You may want to check out the Spline Cage Primitive plug-in (LW_Primitives) from the Objects, Custom plug-in list. This plug-in creates an instant spline cage for you to work with.

To select splines for patching, you simply select the set of three or four splines in counterclockwise order surrounding a gap in the cage. Press Ctrl+f or click on the Patch button under the Tools tab to bring up the Make Spline Patch dialog box. Here, you enter the desired number of polygons you want to create in each direction. If you select the wrong number of spline curves, or they do not intersect properly, Modeler will respond with an error. If everything is selected correctly, a patch of polygons will be stretched across the selected splines.

TIP

One trick that you can employ when spline patching is to place the spline cage in a different layer in Modeler, select the splines for patching, and then multiple-select a different layer before patching. The patch will then be created in the second layer, leaving the cage layer uncluttered for selecting new sets of splines for patching.

Which curve you select first determines which direction is parallel and which is perpendicular in defining the polygon count for the patch. Parallel indicates the number of polygons created parallel to the first selected spline, and perpendicular indicates the number created perpendicular to it.

Triangular Spline Patches

Triangular patches are especially sensitive and require care in the selection order used. Because there are only three splines controlling the patch, one set of polygons created must end up as triangles in one corner. The corner between the first two selected curves is the one that contains the triangles. Figure 6.23 shows the selection order necessary to create a patch with the triangles in the upper-left corner.

FIGURE 6.23

This figure shows the order of curve selection needed to place the triangular polygons in the upper-left corner.

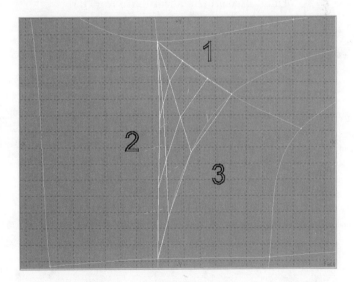

Once you create all the patches, selecting the layer with the patches only and merging points will connect adjoining patches. Because the quads generated from splines are likely to be nonplanar, it will probably be necessary to triple the polygons in your model. If, however, you want to do more detailing of your model in Metaform or MetaNURBS mode, you may want to leave the polygons as quads for now.

There are two approaches to spline modeling and patching. The first is to create a rough spline cage, patch at a low polygon count, and then add detail with other modeling tools. The second approach is to put the majority of work into the spline cage and patch at a medium to high polygon count. Either is an acceptable form of modeling, depending on the individual tastes of the modeler.

Metaform

Before the introduction of MetaNURBS in 5.0, Metaform was the method of choice for animators wanting to create organic models in LightWave. Figure 6.24 shows a rough cage object on the left before applying Metaform and afterward on the right. Note the extreme roughness of the cage as compared with the smoother Metaform object. You can find this object as file Mformobj.lwo on the accompanying CD.

FIGURE 6.24
Object before (left) and after (right) Metaform.

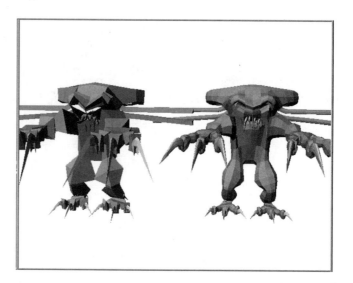

> **WARNING**
>
> Metaform can rapidly add unnecessary complexity to an object if used liberally. Although it is tempting to continue using Metaform on an object each time a new change is made to the cage object, polygon counts will quickly soar. There are occasions when it is necessary to Metaform an object once, even perhaps twice, to add necessary detail to certain regions, but use it sparingly.

Typically, Metaform modeling involves creating a rough cage object, Metaforming, checking the result, undoing the Metaform, and readjusting the geometry. Adjusting the geometry involves moving points or polygons around with the Move or Drag tools, adding detail, and so on. Eventually with practice, you can become proficient at predicting the shape of the Metaformed object, eliminating the need to constantly re-Metaform the object to inspect your changes. Even so, Metaform modeling can be time-consuming for complex objects.

One of Modeler's newer tools, MetaNURBS, introduced in 5.0, can dramatically speed up the time taken to create a smooth, organic-looking object.

MetaNURBS

MetaNURBS can be considered an interactive version of Metaform in which the cage object and the smoothed NURBS surface are visible simultaneously. Because manipulations to the cage object are immediately visible as changes to the smoothed surface, you receive instant feedback during the modeling process. Be sure to read Chapter 7, "Character Modeling with MetaNURBS," to see this feature in action.

MetaNURBS will only work with quadrangles (four-sided polygons) or triangles (triangle patches were introduced with 5.5). Triangular MetaNURBS may have smoothing problems and should generally be avoided.

The complexity of the frozen NURBS object is related directly to the Patch Division setting on the Objects, Options Panel. The higher the value, the more polygons will be generated from each original cage polygon. Using a patch division setting of 1 can be an interesting way to smooth out a rough object. Continually turning the object into MetaNURBS and freezing with a patch division of 1 will smooth out rough edges in your object fairly quickly without changing the polygon count.

More applications related specifically to MetaNURBS modeling can be found in the discussion of the Multiply tools later in this chapter.

Organic Modeling Tools

Although this section focuses on Modeler tools that relate most strongly to organic modeling, these same tools are useful in other situations. In fact, they have great use across the spectrum of modeling methods in Modeler. The tools covered in this section are the following:

- Mirror
- Knife
- Bevel
- Smooth Shift
- Smooth Scale
- DragNet

Mirror

The Mirror tool mirrors the selected geometry about a plane. You can specify the area to be mirrored using the mouse or by entering parameters on the Mirror numeric panel. You can also use the Mirror tool to create opposites of objects such as a shoe or glove. It is often much easier to design half of a character's face, mirror it, and then merge points rather than duplicating actions on either side of the face. Figure 6.25 shows a creature half-designed using MetaNURBS, mirrored, and then stitched together using the Merge tool.

FIGURE 6.25
Character stitched together from two mirrored halves.

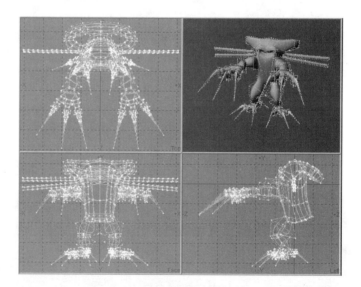

TIP

Although it is certainly convenient to stitch a character together from two halves, no creature is symmetrical. Take some time and imbalance things a little bit. Even subtle differences between the two halves can make for a more realistic character. Two identical halves can look artificial.

Knife

Knife is a new function introduced with Modeler 5.5, which works just like pulling a string through your model along the axis of choice. Knife's greatest usefulness is probably in splitting quad polygons into smaller pieces for detailing while in MetaNURBS mode. In addition, you can use the new Knife tool to break apart an object for an explosion. Use the Knife tool and randomly slice up an object into multiple segments. From there, select each area that has been cut by the Knife and save them separately. The objects will then load into the proper positions in Layout, but you can animate the individual pieces. Give it a try.

Knife will come in handy anytime you create a model and suddenly need to bend it, or need to smooth out a corner. Often when working with three-dimensional models, adding points for additional control and smoothness doesn't work. Using the Knife tool will evenly create new points and slice polygons on entire 3D objects. Knife also replaces the tedious task of making a background plane object to cut a foreground object using a Boolean Operation. As you can see, this is a useful addition to LightWave Modeler.

Bevel

Bevel takes each individual selected polygon and bevels it away from its original position, adding quad polygons along the beveled edges. Figure 6.26 illustrates the use of Bevel on some text.

FIGURE 6.26
Result of applying a bevel to a text object.

Beveling can add subtle edges that can promote a greater sense of realism to your models. For instance, it might be tempting to model a computer as a straight box with gadgets stenciled or Booleaned into the front. However, adding a slight beveled edge can give it a more true-to-life look.

Smooth Shift

Smooth Shift moves groups of polygons together along their respective normals, filling the gaps with quad polygons.

The real power of Bevel and Smooth Shift is unleashed when combined with MetaNURBS or Metaform. Both can easily add detail to an area or even extend a limb from a character's body. Work through the following exercise to see the effectiveness of this approach by creating a simple Squid object. You will use the Smooth Shift, Bevel, MetaNURBS, and Metaform tools to create one object.

CREATING A SQUID

1. Create a box, entering the following values into the numeric panel:

   Low X,Y,Z: -150mm,
   High X,Y,Z: 150mm,
   Segments: 1 for all values.

   Once created, press the a key to auto-size all views to the box.

2. Go to the Polygon tools, select Subdivide, and when the pop-up appears, click on the Metaform button and click on OK.

3. In the Top or Face view, select all of the polygons on the left half of the object.

4. Apply Multiply, Smooth Shift (F key). Change the Offset Value to 0 and click on OK (leave the Smoothing Angle unchanged).

5. Select the Move tool (press t). Move the polygons -200mm in the X direction.

6. Select the polygons on the right half and stretch (h) them to 0% (0.0 in older versions of LightWave) in the X direction, centering the stretch at 0,0,0.

7. Deselect all polygons and turn on MetaNURBS (Tab key).

8. In the Left view, select the four middle polygons, but deselect the ones toward the left end of the object. Stretch these polygons by 70% (.7 in older versions of LightWave) along the X and Z axes, centering the stretch at 0,0,0.

9. Again in the Left view, select all eight outside polygons, deselecting the polygons along the left end (negative X) of the object.

10. Select bevel (b). Enter 5mm for the Inset key, 100mm for the offset, and Edges set to Inner. Click on OK. Bevel with these same settings three more times. You should now have a set of eight arms. At this point, apply a surface name to the arms through the Change Surface requester (q).

11. Deselect all polygons and apply Metaform (d) again to the entire object. Figure 6.27 shows the object Metaformed.

FIGURE 6.27

Using the Bevel tool to create limbs for an organic MetaNURB creature.

12. This next step is slightly tricky. If you look at the arms in the OpenGL preview, you will notice two rows of polygons along the inside of each arm. Select all of these polygons.

13. Press the q key and change the surface for these polygons. In the name field, change it to Suckers and press Apply.

14. Select Bevel. Change the settings to a -1mm inset and a 5mm shift and apply the bevel.

15. Select Bevel again and change the settings to a 4mm inset and a 0mm shift. Apply the bevel.

16. Finally, apply a bevel with a 4mm inset and a -4mm shift. Once done, you should have a nice set of suckers on your creature's arms.

17. Use combinations of Smooth Shift, Bevel, Knife, and the like to finish detailing the squid's body. Your squid should resemble figure 6.28.

FIGURE 6.28

*Squid modeled in a
matter of minutes with
MetaNURBS and Bevel.*

You can see this entire project in the object file Squid.lwo included on the accompanying CD. The different layers in this file show the steps taken to create the squid object. Be sure to load them in Modeler.

You can also use Bevel or Smooth Shift to quickly create limbs, hands, and even fingers on your models while in MetaNURBS mode. This makes it possible to quickly create seamless organic forms, as opposed to the more traditional method of building up forms from several parts and then trying to stitch them together.

Smooth Shift, Bevel, MetaNURBS, and Metaform will perhaps be your most commonly used modeling tools. You will find that taking simple primitives and applying bevels and MetaNURBS functions on it can create all sorts of objects.

Smooth Scale

Smooth Scale is a new tool introduced with LightWave 5.5 that can be quite powerful. This tool shifts all points uniformly outward (or inward if the offset value is negative) along the normal to the surface at that point. Using the Smooth Scale tool, it is easy to thicken or thin out an object or a portion thereof. Figure 6.29 shows a Cow object "fattened" to a plush-doll thickness by applying the Smooth Scale tool.

DragNet

Another tool new to Modeler 5.5 is the DragNet tool. DragNet is a combination of the Drag tool and the Magnet tool and is useful for pulling areas of character faces into different expressions, especially when used in conjunction with MetaNURBS. When you click on a point to drag it, the surrounding area is dragged along with a Magnet region centered about the drag-point.

You can adjust the falloff from the drag-point from the Numeric Panel for this tool. Figure 6.30 shows the use of DragNet on the model file Face2.lwo included on the CD-ROM.

FIGURE 6.29
The cow "fattened" to plush-doll proportions using the Smooth Scale tool.

FIGURE 6.30
Using DragNet to pull a character's face into an expression.

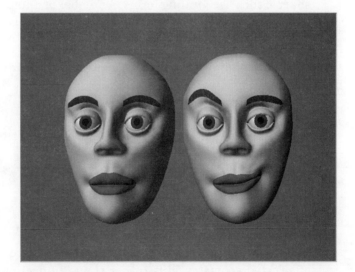

TIP

Using the DragNet tool with a very high radius (for example, 1km) enables you to drag connected pieces of geometry about easily, such as individual letters in a word or individual Metaballs, by clicking on a single point and dragging them.

To use DragNet, click on the right mouse button (Mac users, press the Command key and mouse button) to set an effective range the same way you would for the Magnet tool. Clicking-and-dragging with the left mouse drags the point and pulls the other points in the affected area along with it.

These tools enable you to create individual forms. The next set of tools in this chapter enable you to duplicate forms.

Duplicating Organic Geometry

This section will introduce you to the Clone and Array tools, which, rather than creating single geometric elements, duplicate existing geometry. The tools are under the Multiply tab in Modeler.

Clone

The Clone tool enables any number of duplicates of the current geometry to be created with specified translation, scaling, and rotation applied to each clone successively. Using the Clone tool, you can easily create many useful shapes, such as spiraling forms, a number of duplicates along a linear non-axial path, and so on. Figure 6.31 shows cloning used to create a nice graphic-design flourish using the scaling settings.

FIGURE 6.31
Using the clone feature with scaling to create a graphical flourish.

Array

The Array tool is similar to the Clone tool in that it creates multiple copies of selected geometry. But rather than duplicating the geometry along a simple set of transformations, array enables you to create grids or rings of duplicates in 1, 2, or 3 dimensions, with optional jittering of the placement of each element.

The Array tool is great for creating objects that repeat in a pattern. You can create a field of grass from one blade, for example. Figure 6.32 shows a colonnade created from one arch that was arrayed to complete the structure.

FIGURE 6.32

A colonnade created using the radial Array tool. The arches were radial-arrayed and then Boolean-subtracted into the walls. The columns were similarly arrayed.

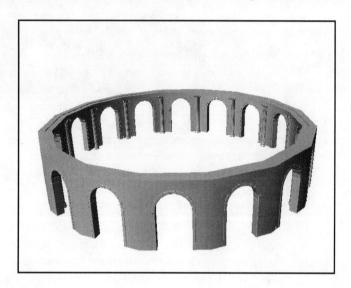

Path and Rail Clone

The Path and Rail Clone tools work like the Clone tool, except that the parameters for cloning are specified either with a motion path or with a spline curve (or possibly multiple spline curves). The results of Path cloning can best be described as making snapshots of your geometry as if they were keyframed in Layout at specific times; scaling, rotation, and movement are all preserved. Figure 6.33 illustrates Path cloning.

To familiarize you with the Rail Clone tool, follow the next exercise using the elements created earlier with both the Path and Rail Extrude exercises. This exercise will guide you through the use of Rail Clone. You can use it as an aid to your Layout setup in that multiple objects can be set up based on a path. These objects can be loaded into Layout virtually eliminating positioning.

FIGURE 6.33

*A familiar object cloned
with Path Clone.
Notice that rotation,
scaling, and translation
are preserved.*

FIGURE 6.33

*A familiar object cloned
with Path Clone.
Notice that rotation,
scaling, and translation
are preserved.*

CREATING MULTIPLE LIGHTS IN MODELER

1. Load the Lghtfixtureslayers.lwo object file from the accompanying CD into Modeler. Press a to fit all views. This file has three layers: one containing a spline rail, another containing a circular array of light fixtures, and the last containing a circular array of points registered with the light fixtures. The spline curve is the same as with the Pathtube.lwo file covered in the section on path and rail extrusion. The Light fixtures and points are registered to the circular polygon that was extruded into a tube in that exercise.

2. Put the first layer with the spline curve in the background. Put the fourth layer in the foreground.

3. Select and apply the Rail Clone tool from the Multiply menu. Set the Segments to Uniform Lengths and specify 15; click on Oriented and click on OK.

You should now have 15 clones of the light fixtures oriented so that they correspond cleanly with the camera path tube generated in the afore-mentioned exercise.

4. Apply the Rail Clone tool to the single point polygons in layer 5. Do this by placing the points in the fifth layer in the foreground and the spline curve (in layer 1) in the background. Run Rail Clone from the Multiply menu.

5. With the Cloned points in the foreground, run the LW_LightSwarm plug-in from the Objects, Custom menu. A Requester will appear asking you to make a scene. Here, you enter the scene file name that will be used for the LightSwarm. Point the directory to your NewTek/Scenes folders and then enter a file name of **Lights.lws** or something similar.

6. Next, another Requester will appear asking you for the Light Repository Scene. This is the scene the LightSwarm plug-in uses to create lights. Here, you need a preexisting scene with a light set up that will be used as the cloned light with the LightSwarm plug-in.

7. The plug-in interface appears, and here you can set the primary light, as well as a glow light. Glow lights will create duplicate lights for glows.

8. Figure 6.34 shows a rendering from the included file Camtube.lws where this process was used to light the tunnel through which the camera flies.

FIGURE 6.34
Creating cloned lights and light fixtures using Rail Clone.

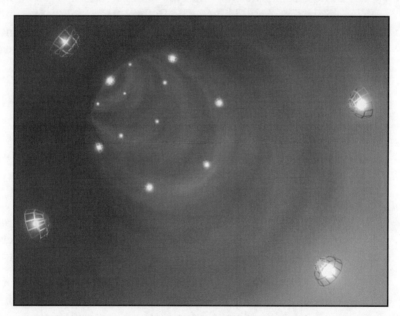

The creation of objects is not the only thing you can do in Modeler. Often, after an object is created, you may decide to modify it for additional detail, or for a new animation. You may also decide to modify existing objects for your own use, such as the ones supplied for you on the accompanying CD.

Modifying Objects in Modeler

Modeler contains many tools for modifying geometric forms. Most of these are grouped under the Modify tab. They can be broken into three groups: the Transformation tools, the Flex tools, and the Deformation tools.

- **Transformation tools.** Enable you to move, rotate, size, stretch, and drag points and polygons.

- **Flex tools.** Enable you to Shear, Twist, Taper, and Bend selected objects.

- **Deformation tools.** Enable you to apply an effect more strongly to the center of an object and have that effect face out toward the edge of the area.

The Transformation and Flex tools evenly affect all of the selected geometry in the foreground layer. The Deformation tools represent a different class of tools that can best be characterized as "soft-edged," in which the effect is applied most strongly in the center, fading out toward the edges of the affected area.

The Transformation Tools

The use of each of the Transformation tools should be clear to you, therefore, they will not be covered in very much detail. These tools include the following:

- **Move.** Moves the selected points or polygons along the axes in the active view window.

- **Rotate.** Rotates the selected points or polygons around the position of the cursor in the view where the mouse has been clicked. You can also adjust the center of rotation in the Numeric Panel.

- **Size.** Scales all dimensions evenly from the center of scaling. The center of the scaling is wherever the mouse is clicked in the current view. You can also adjust this using the Numeric Panel.

- **Stretch.** Works interactively on the two dimensions available in any one view panel. The center of the scaling is wherever the mouse is clicked in the current view. You can also adjust this using the Numeric Panel.

- **Drag.** Enables you to quickly move points around in the active view window.

Each of these tools only works on the currently selected points or polygons in the foreground layer(s). If no points or polygons are explicitly selected, then Modeler applies the operation to all points and polygons in the foreground layer(s).

Holding down the Ctrl key while performing Move or Stretch will restrict motion and scaling to one dimension only. Holding down the Ctrl key when Rotating restricts the rotation to 15-degree increments.

The Flex Tools

The Flex tools include the following. As with the Transformation tools, the use of these tools should be clear to you.

- **Shear.** Shears or skews the selected geometry along the selected axis.

- **Twist.** Twists the selected geometry around the selected axis.

- **Taper.** Tapers the selected geometry along the selected axis.

- **Bend.** Bends the selected geometry along the selected axis.

The default mode for applying these tools is Automatic, where the effect is automatically applied along the full length of the object. You can also apply the effect in Fixed mode, where the center and range of the effect is adjustable.

Modeler 5.5 introduces a new interactive Fixed mode that works by clicking-and-dragging using the right mouse button (Mac LightWave users can use the Option key while clicking on the mouse to simulate a right-mouse-button click).

The selected axis for the Flex tools is selected by a mouse click-and-drag in whichever view is looking down on the axis of the effect. A Shear along the Y axis, for example, would be controlled from the Top (X–Y) view. This may require some getting used to if you are migrating from another 3D package, such as 3D Studio.

Typically, the positive end of the model is moved along the effect axis. However, if you want to move the negative end of the model, bring up the Numeric Panel and change the Sense from positive to negative. If in Fixed mode, you can adjust the Sense by reversing the Low and High fields on the Numeric Panel, or you can interactively adjusted them using the right mouse button. In order to use the new Sense tool without applying the effect, press the Keep button to use the new settings.

All of these tools have an Ease In and Ease Out factor that causes the effect to be applied in a more curvy, organic way. Modeler 5.5 adds interactive slider adjustments to these values on the Numeric Panel for these tools.

Following is an exercise that illustrates a use of the Twist tool in combination with morphing and the Lathe tool. These tools can enable you to create a spinning tornado. This exercise will guide you through the steps needed to create a Tornado object in Modeler.

A TWISTY TORNADO

1. Enter Modeler. Using the Points tool (Polygon tab) and the Create Curve tool (Tools tab), create a curve in the Left view, similar to the one shown in figure 6.35.

FIGURE 6.35

A curve representing the profile of the tornado.

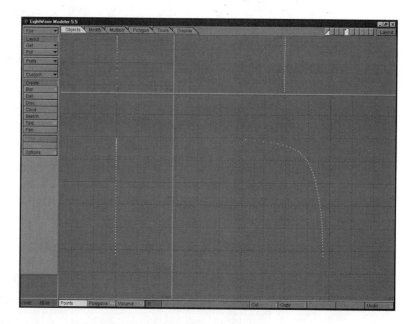

2. Lathe this shape around the Y-axis.

3. Triple all the polygons. This is a very crucial step for any object that you intend to deform, as the default quad polygons may become nonplanar during deformation.

4. Copy the contents of the foreground layer into an empty layer. Make the new empty layer the foreground layer.

5. Apply a twist with the following settings:

   Axis: Y
   Range: Automatic
   Preset: Ease Out
   Sense: -
   Angle: 720 degrees
   Center: 0,0,0

6. Save the twisted object as **tornado.lwo**.

7. Switch back to the layer with the untwisted tornado and save this object as **Tornadomorph.lwo**. You may optionally kill all polygons for this object before saving (by pressing the k key), as you are only interested in preserving the alternate point positions.

8. In Layout, load the two tornado objects, morph the Tornado object into the Tornadomorph object, and texture as you like. The texture will naturally twist around the tornado, following the direction of the morph. Your tornado should look similar to the one in figure 6.36.

FIGURE 6.36
Rendering of a tornado object, with the fractal texture spiraled using the Twist tool and surface morphing.

A sample scene, Tornado.lws, is included on the accompanying CD for your inspection. Take this scene and create your own variations and add enhancements to see what you can create.

The Deformation Tools

Up until now, the tools covered evenly affect all of the selected geometry in the foreground layer. The Deformation tools represent a different class of tools that can best be characterized as soft-edged, where the effect is applied most strongly in the center, fading out toward the edges of the affected area. Hence, these are most often used to move about regions of objects. These tools consist of the following:

- **Magnet.** Can smoothly push or pull regions of your model into the desired shape. The points closest to the center of the Magnet region will be pulled more strongly, with the pull falling off toward the edges of the Magnet region.

- **Vortex.** Creates forms spiraling inward toward the center. The amount of rotation varies from the center toward the outside edges of the effect.

- **Pole 1 and Pole 2.** Scaling with falloff. Portions closer to the center of the Pole region are scaled more strongly. Portions close to the edge of the Pole region are hardly scaled at all. Pole 1 applies the scale evenly in all directions from the center, while Pole 2 allows control over scaling along pairs of axes at a time.

TIP

Like the Twist tool, you can use the Vortex tool to create cloud vortices, such as hurricanes and wormholes. To achieve this effect, create a nonvortexed version of your object and a vortexed version. In Layout, dissolve out the vortexed version of the object, texture the nonvortexed version, and then morph the nonvortexed version into the vortexed one. If you've done your texturing properly, you should have a nice wormhole/hurricane type of effect.

Other intermediate-level tools, located under the Tools tab, include Point Jitter, which you can use to apply a random jittering to points; Quantize, which snaps all points to the nearest value specified in the Quantize dialog box; Smooth, which is used to smooth details, blending them into each other; and Set Value, which enables you to set the X, Y, or Z coordinate of a set of selected points.

Modifying objects enables you to create entirely new objects from existing geometry. You can take this process one step further by using Modeler's Drilling and Boolean functions to carve objects.

Carving Geometry: Drilling and Booleans

Tucked away under the Tools heading are three small buttons that add a good deal of power to Modeler: the Drill, S Drill (Solid Drill), and Boolean tools. Using these tools, LightWave Modeler can easily sculpt complex forms from simpler shapes, carve shapes into the surfaces of objects, and add detail to push the object toward photorealism. Whatever the use, these three tools will add a great deal of flexibility to the modeling process.

Drill

You can use the Drill tool to carve the shape of one or more two-dimensional polygons (in the background layer) into the geometry in the foreground layer. This can have a variety of applications, such as creating virtual street signs, applying two-dimensional logos to geometry, and lettering the hull of a spaceship, to name a few. Figure 6.37 shows the Drill interface.

FIGURE 6.37

The Drill tool options dialog box.

Drill is also extremely useful for adding polygon detail to a flat region. You can then modify this detail using Smooth Shift and Bevel to add surface detail to models.

To set up your geometry for the drill operation, the object you want to drill should be in a foreground layer and the object that will do the drilling in a background layer, as illustrated in figure 6.38.

TIP

You can restrict the polygons drilled in the foreground layer by selecting them. This is useful for instances where you may need to drill only one side of an enclosed object, or you may just need to optimize the time it takes to drill by eliminating extraneous polygons from consideration.

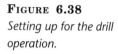

FIGURE 6.38

Setting up for the drill operation.

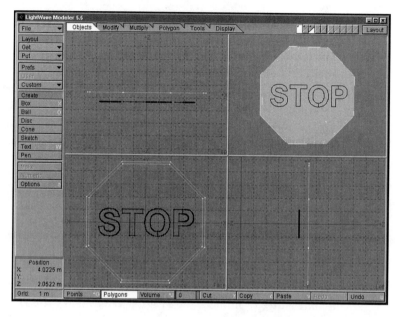

From the Drill Panel, you can choose from among several options. The first is the axis for the drill operation. Consider the drill object as being pulled along the axis specified, slicing everything in its path. So, for example, if you were drilling with a bit that stretches in the X and Y directions, the Z-axis would be your drilling axis of choice. Other panel options include the following:

- **Core.** Slices the geometry and leaves only the parts of the geometry that fall within the borders of the slicing polygons.

- **Tunnel.** Tunnels out the slicing polygons from the geometry, leaving a hole in place of the slicing polygons.

- **Stencil and Slice.** Both are a combination of the Core and Tunnel tools, leaving both the areas of geometry inside and outside of the drill polygon areas. The difference between Stencil and Slice is that stencil has the option of specifying a new surface for the drilled-in polygons, whereas Slice leaves the newly formed polygons with the same surface as the original polygons.

Figure 6.39 shows the four drill methods and their results.

FIGURE 6.39
*The four Drill methods
and their results.*

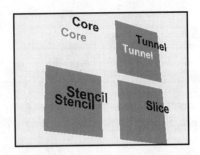

WARNING

As with other modeling methods, drilling 2D polygons into existing 3D geometry can generate nonplanar polygons.

Solid Drill

Solid Drill is similar to the Drill function, but it only works with 3D objects. Figure 6.40 shows the results of different Solid Drill operations.

FIGURE 6.40
*The results of the Solid
Drill options (in
clockwise order from
upper left): Core,
Tunnel, Slice, and
Stencil.*

Just as with the polygon Drill tool, the Solid Drill tool will not cap any of the sliced geometry, and therefore has the potential to leave empty holes in your geometry. To create solid shapes after cutting is done, you should use the Boolean functions available in Modeler.

Booleans

The Boolean tool is an extremely useful tool in Modeler. It enables you to quickly sculpt an object from its parts, combining them into a final object.

There are four types of Boolean Operations supported by Modeler: Union, Intersect, Subtract, and Add. Figure 6.41 illustrates the difference between these four methods:

- **Union.** The parts of each object that intersect each other will be removed.

- **Intersection.** The opposite of Union. Only the parts common to both objects will remain.

- **Add.** Cuts the geometry, adding additional points and polygon edges as necessary, but does not remove any polygons after the operation is done.

- **Subtract.** Cuts the geometry and removes geometry from the original object in the shape of the cutting object.

FIGURE 6.41

The four supported Boolean Operations in clockwise order from the upper left: Union, Add, Subtract, and Intersect. Note that the Union and Add objects have been slightly enlarged to reveal the ways their respective geometry has been cut.

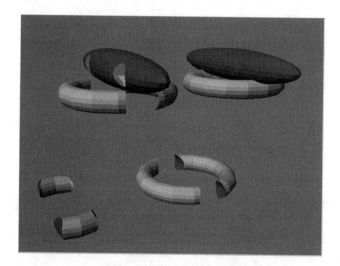

The resulting geometry of a Boolean Operation retains the surfacing of the original objects. It is helpful to name surfaces carefully ahead of time to allow for easy reselecting of those surfaces by using the Statistics Panel.

Boolean Operations can be prone to error if the objects consist of nonplanar polygons; the objects have double-sided polygons; or the objects have flipped polygons. If you encounter such problems, take appropriate steps to eliminate nonplanar, double-sided, or flipped polygons before applying the Boolean Operation.

TIP

There is a plug-in that can turn single-sided polygons into double-sided ones. If you're doing Boolean modeling, don't use double-sided polygons.

In the following exercise, you will create an ancient room, complete with Roman-style columns. Part of aging this room and giving a sense of it being a ruin involves breaking the tops off of one of the columns and placing it on the ground. This file can be seen in successive steps in the multilayered object file Colbool.lwo on the accompanying CD.

This exercise will show you one of the most practical uses for Boolean Operations. The Boolean Subtract command enables you to break apart objects. With this tool, you can carve objects rather than build them.

CREATING RUINS

1. Load the Column.lwo file into a layer in Modeler.

2. Put the column layer in the background, making an empty layer the foreground layer. From the Objects menu, select the Ball tool and press n on the keyboard to call up the Numeric Requester. Create a Level 2 Tessellation ball with a rather elongated shape in the Y direction. Set the X and Z Radii to 500mm, and the Y Radii to 800mm. This is done through the Ball tool's Numeric Panel. Click on OK, and press Enter to make the ball.

3. Position this ball so that its lower edge intersects one of the corners of the column. Give the polygons on this ball a surface named **Break**.

4. Select the polygons at the bottom edge of the ball that intersect the column, selecting only as many as necessary to completely cut through the column.

5. Perform two smooth subdivides on the selected polygons by pressing Shift+d. Set the fractal value to 1.0 in the Requester. Click OK. This should generate a nice, rough cutting edge.

6. Copy the column into two separate layers and the ball into two additional separate layers.

7. With one ball in a background layer and a column in a foreground layer, select the Boolean tools (Shift+b) and click Subtract to subtract one of the balls from one of the columns.

NOTE

It is important to remember that the object that is to be subtracted, intersected, unioned, or added should be in a background layer. The item to receive the Boolean Operation should be in a foreground layer. Think of the background layer object as the tool used to perform the operation.

8. Boolean Intersect the second ball with the next column. Delete the base of the column when done.

9. Merge Points to eliminate unwanted edges.

10. Because the ball was textured with the Break surface, the areas of the Boolean joins where the ball surface was originally will retain that surface. Use the Display, Polygon Statistics Panel by pressing w on the keyboard while Polygon Selection mode is enabled from the bottom of the interface. Here, you can select all the polygons with the Break surface. Once selected, perform a smooth subdivide on these again with a fractal value of 1.0. Your object should resemble Figure 6.42.

FIGURE 6.42
Using multiple Boolean Operations to break apart a column.

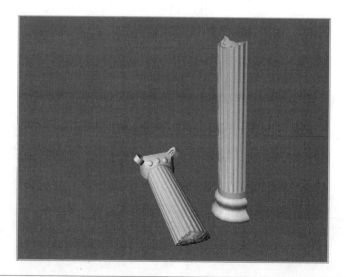

Boolean Operations are a powerful tool in Modeler. These functions let you "carve" objects rather than build them. Although the tools described here offer nearly unlimited modeling possibilities, a 3D artist's bread and butter is often creating 3D text and logos, which are detailed in the next section.

Generating Text and Logos

Perhaps the most popular computer-animated effect is the flying logo or other animated logo effects. Over a career in animation, you will undoubtedly encounter many logo animation projects. Although the rest of this section discusses the creation of 3D text and logos, some of the tools discussed here can apply to nearly all modeling tasks, not just to text and logos.

Converting a 2D Logo to 3D

Although there are occasions where you may be called upon to create a logo from scratch, most often, you will be asked to convert a logo from printed artwork into a 3D element. Before starting to model, insist that your client provide the artwork printed as neatly and as large as possible. The cleaner the original artwork, the better chance you will have of accurately reproducing it. Try to obtain the artwork in its original vector format (for instance, Adobe Illustrator, EPS, or DXF) if it exists. Electronic conversion of the logo from one or another format into LightWave is a much less painful route than hand-tracing it. Although, a hand-traced logo can be one of the cleanest forms of logo creation you can produce.

N OTE

An original EPS file can be converted to a 3D object through 5.5's new LW_Import_Illustrator plug-in. Read the Illustrator plug-in section coming up in this chapter.

Assume for the sake of the next exercises that all that you have access to is a printed version of the logo. Figure 6.43 shows a fictional logo designed specifically for these exercises. It consists of a relatively simple geometric shape, some moderately complex shapes, some freeform text, as well as simple, straightforward text.

Fictional logo to be converted into 3D.

Although many programs can auto-trace an image and convert it into a vector format that can then be converted into 3D, the traced files often require a fair amount of cleanup before they are ready to use in production. The time that would be spent cleaning up this data is roughly equal to what it would take to trace the object in Modeler from the start. This is the approach you will take in the following exercise.

Creating a 3D Logo: First Steps

1. Load the scanned artwork (Logo.tga) from the accompanying CD. Do this by going to the Backdrop Panel within the Display menu in Modeler. Load the image from the Z image loader.

2. Set the artwork as the background Z image in Modeler.

Modeler now enables three separate background images, one for each axis, which can be useful for tracing multiple shots of an object in three dimensions. For now, you need to trace only the one image in the X-Y (face) view. This will project the image along the Z-axis, keeping all settings at their defaults. Figure 6.44 shows the backdrop image projected along the Z-axis.

3. The horizontally sliced circle is easy to re-create in Modeler. First, use the Ball or Disc tool to overlay a circle over the background image.

4. In a separate layer, trace over the gaps in the circle using the Box tool, extending the edges of each rectangle/box beyond the edge of the circle.

5. Place the boxes in the background layer and the circle in the foreground. A simple drill using the Tunnel option completes this shape. Save the object as **Logo1.lwo** or something similar. Figure 6.45 shows the disc created over the backdrop image, with boxes in a background layer.

Next, you need to tackle the palm tree shape and custom text. In Modeler, there are several methods that you can use for this. Option one would be to use the Points tool, laying down points along the outline and connecting them into either a polygon or spline curve. Option two would be to use the Sketch tool to trace the outline of the shape and create either a spline curve or polygon. Option three would be to use Modeler 5.5's new Pen tool to directly create polygons point by point. Both of the latter two options will be explored in the following exercise.

TRACING THE PALM TREE FOR THE LOGO

1. Continue from the previous exercise.

2. To trace the palm tree, drag the view divider until the Face view is full-window. Center the palm tree in the Face view and zoom in using the (.) key until it fills the view.

3. Use the Sketch tool from the Objects menu to trace the palm tree outline by clicking on the left mouse button and dragging the mouse. If you have one, a drawing slate will give you more control than the mouse. As you sketch, don't worry about straying off the outline; you'll clean up the shape shortly.

4. After you have traced the shape using Sketch, press Enter to make the curve. You will then need to weld the first and last points of the sketch curve to close it. Do this by selecting the first and last points, and choosing Weld from the Tools menu (Ctrl+w).

5. The next step is to clean up the curve. Using the Drag tool, drag points around to make the curve adhere more tightly to the outline of the palm tree. In some cases, there may not be enough points in an area to accurately frame the palm tree image. If so, use the Points tool from the Polygon menu to create additional points, and then use the Add Points tool to add them to the curve. Figure 6.46 shows such a case.

6. Once the curve has been modified to fit the background image, use the Freeze (Ctrl+d) tool to convert it into a polygon. Note that the Curve Division in the Options Panel (o) will affect the number of points generated in the final polygon. A Curve Division of medium should work nicely.

FIGURE 6.46

Adding points to a curve to accurately frame a shape.

Simply tracing the outline of the palm tree is not enough to accurately represent the logo. There are holes in the palm tree that need to be accounted for.

7. To create these holes, switch to an empty layer and trace them using the Sketch tool. Modify these curves as necessary and freeze (Ctrl+d) the curves to create polygons.

8. Select the layer with the palm tree shape as the foreground, the hole polygons as the background, and do a drill operation to cut out the holes.

Note how detailed the palm tree is. This is because it's generated from a set of spline curves. Although this may be desirable in some cases, too much detail, especially around tightly curved areas, can be a headache to proper beveling. Higher than necessary polygon counts also can slow down rendering time. It is probably necessary to remove excess points, especially from the tightly curved areas where they tend to cluster.

9. To remove unwanted points, simply select the offending points and press the Delete key (or press z). For accuracy, zoom into the area in question with the Zoom command (Ctrl+z). Save your work as palmtree.lwo or something similar. Figure 6.47 shows the removal of extraneous points from a tightly curved area on the palm tree polygon.

FIGURE 6.47
*Removal of excess
points in the outline
polygon.*

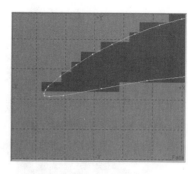

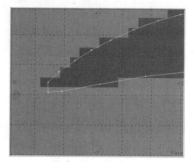

In this next exercise, you will generate the custom text for the logo. Rather than using the Sketch tool, you will use the new Pen tool to create the outline polygon directly.

USING THE PEN TOOL TO GENERATE CUSTOM TEXT

1. To use Pen, click on the Pen button from the Objects menu, and begin clicking on points using the mouse. As new points are added, the growing polygon is expanded to accommodate those points. Be sure when laying down the points to space them closely enough to keep the edges smooth.

2. Finally, trace the hole in the "e" in another layer and drill it into the Dreams outline (see fig. 6.48).

Finally, there is the Premiere Resorts text, which appears to be (and is) a fairly standard font. In this case, the client told us that the font used was CorelDRAW!'s AvantGarde Medium, which bears a striking resemblance to the PostScript font Avalon Book included with LightWave. This gives you a great opportunity to play with the Text tool in Modeler.

FIGURE 6.48
*Tracing the freeform
Dreams text.*

3. In Modeler, activate the Text tool and click on the Numeric button, or press n on the keyboard (in older versions of Modeler, the Text dialog box comes up automatically when the Text tool is invoked).

Modeler 5.5 adds a new level of interactivity to the placement of text. By simply typing the text desired, moving the text marker around, and resizing it with the sizing handle at the top, text can be quickly and accurately created. Press the Enter key and the outline will be converted into polygonal text. Figure 6.49 shows the Text tool being used to match the text in the logo. With that, the tracing phase of the logo design is complete.

FIGURE 6.49
*Matching the text to
the background image.*

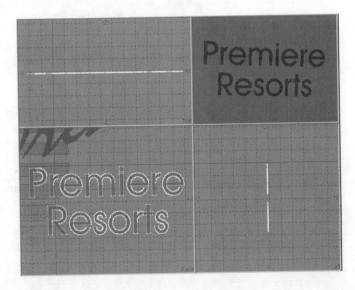

At this point, all you've done is generate two-dimensional polygons. Now comes the process of turning these polygons into 3D objects using the Extrusion and Bevel tools.

4. These tools will be applied by first extruding and then beveling. If beveling is done first, the back sides of the logo would also be beveled resulting in superfluous polygons in the logo object.

It may be necessary before extrusion to perform a bevel check to see if any points end up crossing each other, creating a degenerate polygon. Figure 6.50 shows a situation like this. In this particular case, welding (Ctrl+w) two almost coincidental points on either side of the polygon can clear up the problem. Another remedy for vertex crossing errors is to weld crossing points together after the bevel operation.

FIGURE 6.50
A misbeveled polygon caused by crossing vertices.

5. After performing a bevel check, undo the bevels on each polygon. Assign the name sides to the side surfaces of each polygon so that this surface will be automatically assigned to the sides during extrusion. Now, extrude the object with an Extent of 100mm.

6. After extrusion, lasso-select the front polygon and assign the surface name bevels.

7. After beveling, the front face should still be selected; assign a surface name to these selected polygons called **Faces**. Adjust surfacing in

Layout and animate to taste. A finished scene, Logo.lws, can be loaded for inspection from this chapter's projects directory on the accompanying CD. Figure 6.51 shows the finished 3D logo.

FIGURE 6.51
The finished Logo object ready to be animated.

TIP

When animating a logo such as this, save the elements separately and animate them independently in Layout. The resting frame in the animation would show the elements coming together to create the full logo.

Creating Chiseled Text

Another common logo type is text chiseled into an object, such as a beveled block of marble, metal, and so on. You can use Boolean Operations and Text creation to create your own Chiseled Text look. Load the Lasrlogo.lws scene file from the accompanying CD to begin on your own. This next exercise will guide you through creating text for a chiseled look and uses the Surface Effectors plug-in to generate a laser. You need the Surface Effectors plug-in to complete this exercise.

CREATING TEXT FOR AN ANIMATED LOGO

1. Create a box, approximately 3 meters wide and 1.5 meters tall. The depth is not crucial but should be deep enough to accommodate the text you are going to chisel into the front.

2. Bevel the front polygon to taste. Generally though, a bevel of about 100mm for both the Inset and Shift should work well. Also, turn off Smoothing in the Change Surface (q) Requester for the Box object.

3. Copy this object and paste it into another layer.

4. Use the logo you created in the previous exercise, or create your desired text in an empty layer. Bevel it (be sure to check for beveling errors) and extrude the beveled text.

5. Arrange the Text object so that it penetrates the front surface of the box and Boolean subtract it. Prior to Boolean subtraction, you may want to surface your respective objects. Do this through the Change Surface (q) Requester.

6. Take the original box, and offset it slightly in front of the copy with the Booleaned text. Give the front polygon a different surface (Box Mask is used in the sample file). Save the contents of both layers.

7. In Layout, surface the box and box mask surfaces identically. Quickly do this through the Surfaces panel. Select Surface Color for Current Surface for the surface names you assigned in Modeler. For the mask surface, use an animated transparency map to knock away the mask by using a plug-in called Surface Effectors from Prem Subrahmanyam Graphic Design. This plug-in enables animated trails of effect to follow a null object.

Figure 6.52 shows the laser logo animation being created using this plug-in. You can find this scene file on the accompanying CD as Lasrlogo.lws. (You will need Surface Effectors to see this scene in action.)

Animated 3D logos are very popular. It is up to you to think of new and exciting ways to animate your client's artwork. Using methods such as the one described in this section, you can take your logo animations beyond the ordinary look.

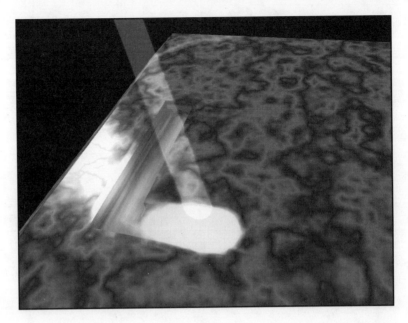

Summary

This chapter covered basic model planning, Modeler's tools, and modifying tools. Other chapters will cover more advanced modeling concepts, such as character modeling. You read about:

- Modeler primitives
- Generating higher-order forms from primitives
- Creating organic models
- Organic modeling tools
- Duplicating organic geometry
- Creating text and logos

Although all of these can provide the basic building blocks for successful modeling, only you can provide the main ingredients to successful modeling, and those are practice and patience. While a rich and powerful set of tools can ensure that you are not hindered from creating models housed in your imagination, only time and experience will bring the necessary skills to create models that truly stand out and work well in your animations.

Chapter 7

CHARACTER MODELING WITH METANURBS

The capability to create great character models has always

been a sought-after talent in the computer animation indus-

try. Most 3D artists believe that the creation and animation

of human characters, whether cartoon-like or realistic, can

be one of the most challenging and rewarding aspects of

modeling—it can be considered the Holy Grail of the field.

LightWave has several tools that you can use to achieve

realistic characters, a couple of which are splines and

MetaNURBS. The latter is the newest and most innovative

tool and can produce results equal to traditional spline

modeling in a fraction of the time. MetaNURBS gives you the flexibility to create seamless characters, and to make an entire library of body parts that you can weld together to create many different organic creatures.

The exercises that follow will arm you with organic modeling skills that include the following:

- Understanding basic MetaNURBS concepts

- Keeping the polygon count low

- Building a human character

- Preparing the object for LightWave Layout

- Creating Morph targets with MetaNURBS

Understanding Basic MetaNURBS Concepts

MetaNURBS is a fantastic tool for sculpting life-like objects in Modeler. NURBS, or Non-Uniform Rational B-Splines, at times can seem like sculpting with a piece of virtual clay. The technique is based on computer-created splines, made by transforming hard-edged geometry into smooth curves.

The model creation process consists of two modes in which you will work: Polygon mode and MetaNURBS mode. You can toggle between them with the Tab key. Polygon mode is where the basic object takes shape in the form of triangle- and quad-based polygons. The finished version does not reside here. The second mode (MetaNURBS) enables you to deform the splines derived from the original polygons. Both modes are important to each other.

The Two MetaNURBS Modeling Modes

When modeling with MetaNURBS, you will encounter two work modes. These modes, Polygon and MetaNURBS, are where the entire modeling process takes place. You switch between each mode constantly to build or check progress. You must understand the difference between the work modes before you can begin modeling with MetaNURBS. The following sections explain these modes in detail.

NOTE

To toggle between the MetaNURBS modes, press the Tab key. You can also do this by pressing Ctrl+i.

Polygon Mode

In Polygon mode, you create the basic object's geometry by traditional modeling methods. This object serves as a polygonal model to be used for the MetaNURBS patches, where each three- or four-point polygon makes a MetaNURBS patch. Whether built by using Modeler's primitives (Box, Cone, Circle, and so on) or by creating polygons point by point, the object is built in its simplest terms in this mode.

The object is usually box-like in its geometry, but it gives the character (which will be created with MetaNURBS) its fundamental shape. Often the object has many non-planar polygons, which are almost essential for making an interesting MetaNURBS cage.

NOTE

Non-planar polygons have four or more points not on the same horizontal plane, thus creating a non-renderable surface. They usually are avoided in conventional 3D modeling because of rendering errors that can occur when they are used. The non-planar polygons used here, however, will not be rendered, so you don't have to worry about errors.

Making MetaNURBS objects sometimes requires that the polygonal mesh be pulled to extremes. It's not unusual to see a very long pointy nose in the polygonal version of the object. After you switch to MetaNURBS mode, the curve created by this extreme point position can be subtle.

MetaNURBS (B-Spline) Mode

In this mode, the spline version of the object is drawn. The splines in this mode are unlike traditional splines in that the user does not draw them. The computer draws the curves, based on the point distance and polygon orientation in Polygon mode.

This version of the object is your representation of what the finished model will look like after you transform it into polygons with the Freeze command, found under the Tools tab. If you loaded the MetaNURBS object into Layout, the camera wouldn't see it because the object doesn't consist of polygons.

NOTE ──────────────────────────────

LightWave can't render splines; they are just used as modeling tools. The camera in LightWave Layout can see only objects consisting of polygons.

When working in this mode, the OpenGL view displays a bright blue outline around the shaded preview. These lines are the spline cage created in Polygon mode. If you switch back and forth between modes and watch the OpenGL view, the relationship between each mode becomes obvious. The blue outline around the MetaNURBS cage is in the exact shape of the polygonal version of the object.

NOTE ──────────────────────────────

You can turn the blue outline on or off for visibility purposes. Do this by pressing the d key to enter the Display Options Panel. Uncheck or check the Patch Polygon selection next to Visibility. This doesn't affect your model in any way, only its visibility in the view windows.

Make sure no polygons are selected when you switch between modes. LightWave performs operations on selected areas only. If nothing is highlighted in yellow, LightWave assumes that everything is selected. You don't want part of the object to be in Polygon mode while the rest is in MetaNURBS mode. This can happen when hiding part of the object but not remembering what mode you were in when you did it.

WARNING ──────────────────────────────

Try to use only four-point (quad) polygons when constructing a MetaNURBS object. If necessary, you can use three-point (triangle) polygons on occasion, mostly when you need to seal a hole in the model's geometry. If you accidentally create a two- or five-point polygon early in the building process and you don't check the progress in MetaNURBS mode until later, you must delete the illegal polygon. Then, you must reconstruct the adjacent area.

The MetaNURBS Theory

The single most important concept to remember about modeling with MetaNURBS is that polygonal geometry—whether quad- or triangle-based—equals smooth, flowing curves when transformed into MetaNURBS splines. These splines are not actually what the finished object consists of—they are just a framework for constructing a curved object interactively. Later, when the spline cage is frozen, it is re-created with as many polygons as needed to form the curves that make up the object. To get to that end, you can use several different means:

- Build shapes point by point and create polygons as you go.

- Start with a box and bevel key polygons in the appropriate direction to achieve limbs and facial features.

- Create a template of your object's shape and extrude it.

- Use a combination of all these techniques. This is usually the most effective way.

The well-known way of MetaNURBS modeling by beveling a box into different shapes is more time-consuming than the way you will construct the human character outlined in this chapter. Beveling is covered when adding detail to the object is discussed. The following section discusses the placement of points in space and how they affect the spline curvature.

Point Placement

When moving points in a MetaNURBS cage, overcompensation is normal—and sometimes necessary—to get the splines to curve properly. In the following exercise, you create a single polygon box to view a MetaNURBS spline patch at its most rudimentary level. Points are added to create extensions to the box and illustrate how the distances between points affect the spline curve between them. Points spaced farther apart make a much wider arc than those close together.

This exercise also gives you a basis for understanding how to create a MetaNURBS object point by point, as simple as it may be. A more 3D approach to this technique is discussed later.

THE EFFECT OF POINT SPACING ON SPLINE CURVATURE

1. Open Modeler and draw a simple, flat box in the Top view.

2. Press the f key to flip the polygon's surface facing up the Y-axis.

3. Press Tab to change to MetaNURBS mode.

Notice that the square has been transformed into a smooth oval (see fig. 7.1). The blue line around the object in the OpenGL view is called the *Patch Polygon*. It represents the actual polygonal shape created at the beginning of the exercise. This square polygon has no purpose except the use of its corner points as MetaNURBS control handles and to calculate surface normal orientation.

TIP

You can turn off the Patch Polygon by clicking on the Display Panel and selecting Options. At times, Patch Polygon can be useful for modifying hard-to-find points, but at other times it can obstruct your view.

FIGURE 7.1
When in MetaNURBS mode, this quad-based polygon is represented by a blue outline in the OpenGL view.

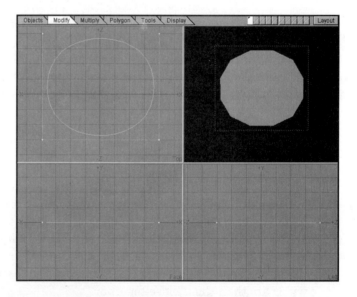

4. Press Tab to switch back to Polygon mode.

5. Click on the Polygon tab at the top of the screen and select Points. Right-click to make six new points in front of the box on the Z-axis.

NOTE

When adding points to a model, the Polygon mode should be selected (press the Tab key to switch to Polygon mode).

6. Select four points in a counterclockwise direction and press p to make a new polygon (see fig. 7.2). Repeat this procedure until you create three new polygons.

FIGURE 7.2

Create an extension to the box by selecting four points at a time and then pressing p to make new polygons.

Select these points

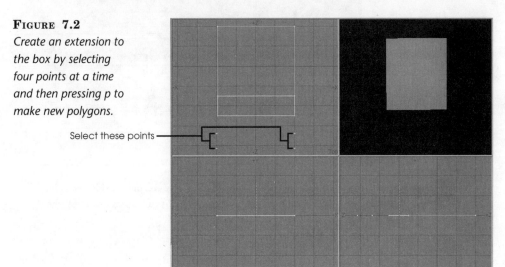

7. Press Tab to switch to MetaNURBS mode.

You should see something that resembles a bullet-head. Notice that the polygons with greater point distances have wider arcs on their curves.

8. Switch to the Modify menu and choose the Drag tool.

9. Start dragging points in any direction you want, even up and down on the Y-axis. Notice that the distances between points greatly affect how the curves behave (see fig. 7.3).

FIGURE 7.3

The distances between points in a MetaNURBS object greatly affect how the curves behave.

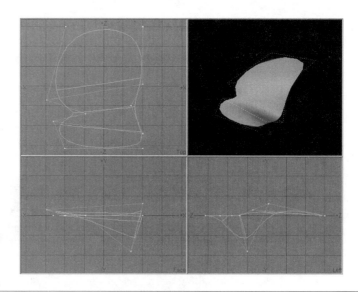

NOTE

When creating a polygon, the direction in which points are selected determines which way the polygon surface normals will face. These normals are the side of the polygon seen by the camera in Layout.

The preceding exercise might seem a bit basic, but it gives you an understanding of how MetaNURBS splines work. Easily created, hard-edged geometry generates smooth curves. The next section shows you how to apply these concepts to create objects with more dimension and depth.

Building a Human Character

This section takes the concepts and theories discussed earlier and puts them into practice in the creation of a male human character.

The construction of the character you model will be a smooth, efficient process if you follow the steps outlined in this chapter. You are, however, encouraged to experiment, especially when making final adjustments to the shape.

Instead of attempting to arrive at every detail at the outset of building, each complex section is fabricated as its own separate object, and then stitched together by welding points. Many sculpting techniques used in this chapter are not as calculated as normal modeling procedures. It may seem unconventional to start with the hand, for example, but don't think of it as the start of the human object. Think of it as a component in a group of body parts that will be comprised of a torso, feet, a head, and a hand. As separate objects, you could use each one of these parts to create any number of figures. During this chapter, however, they serve as your character's basic building blocks. The hand being created is not only a part of Biff, but could also be a part reserved for your next creation.

Maintaining an artistic frame of mind (as opposed to technical) is another key aspect to remember if you want a life-like character with personality. The nature of MetaNURBS's interactivity and quick feedback provides the capability to try wild and different things that you might not attempt with normal modeling methods. The stages you are guided through are as follows:

- Making the hand from a 2D template

- Making the foundation of the human body by employing the same techniques used in the hand-building exercise

- Scaling polygons and dragging points to sculpt the physique

- Attaching the hand to the wrist

This exercise also teaches you about the pitfalls of modeling with MetaNURBS. If you avoid a few simple, common mistakes early on, you will spend less time fixing errors and have much more fun.

Building the Hand

The right hand is used as a starting point in the creation of the model (whose name happens to be Biff) outlined in this chapter. After MetaNURBS becomes second nature to you, it really doesn't matter where you start modeling. You might, however, just be getting acquainted with it, so the creation of the hand will help get you started.

Even though the hand is a deceptively complex extremity, modeling it is easier than the main body (torso, legs, arms) because you can lay out its general shape with no mirroring or welding of sections. After the hand is completed, you can save it or copy it to another layer for safekeeping until you are ready to attach it to the body in a later exercise.

A common method for constructing a MetaNURBS hand is to make a segmented box and bevel it. This method is effective, but you have less control over placement of detail areas such as the knuckles. The object Hand_template.lwo (on the accompanying CD), was instead created by drawing a flat template of a hand, and arranging polygons in the correct places. Load the Hand_template.lwo object. The polygons are laid out in a way that enables beveling to create knuckles and other detail areas. The top image in figure 7.4 shows the arrangement of polygons in the hand template. This is only one of many different combinations that could work, depending on the shape the hand needs to be. By switching to MetaNURBS mode, the smooth contour of a hand can be seen even as a 2D template (see the bottom image in fig. 7.4).

FIGURE 7.4

The top image is the hand template in raw Polygon mode; the bottom image is the hand in MetaNURBS mode.

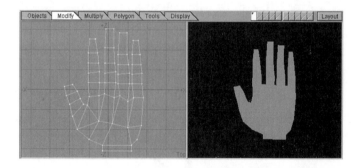

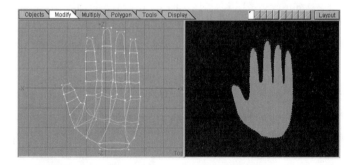

USING A TEMPLATE TO BUILD A HAND

1. Go to the Multiply menu and choose the Extrude option. Extrude the hand approximately 120 mm on the Y-axis to give it some thickness (see fig. 7.5).

2. Switch to MetaNURBS mode by pressing the Tab key. Your object should resemble a hand without cylindrical fingers.

FIGURE 7.5

Use the Extrude tool to apply a third dimension to the hand template.

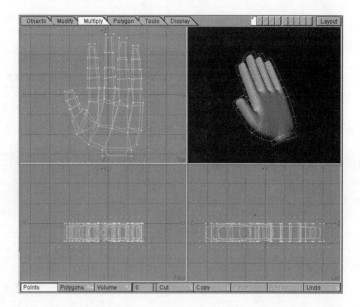

3. Select the polygons that make up the fingers and thumb and choose the Stretch tool under the Modify menu.

4. Using the Left or Front view as a reference, stretch the fingers inward along the Y-axis to help them take on a more cylindrical shape (see fig. 7.6). If they need to be thinner from the Top view, select each finger individually and use the Stretch tool.

FIGURE 7.6

Stretch the end polygons of the fingers to make their appearance more tapered.

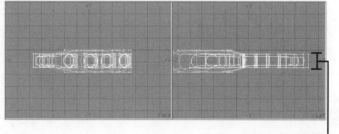

Scale inward

5. Deselect everything except the fingertips, and stretch these polygons in even further to avoid getting a blocky look.

6. Deselect the fingertips and select the polygons that make up the lower palm area.

TIP

To fit a selected group of polygons in the view, press Shift+a. You can also center a desired object area in the view by placing the cursor on that area and pressing Shift+g.

7. Move the palm polygons down along the Y-axis to give the lower part some roundness (see fig. 7.7).

FIGURE 7.7
Add some shape to the palm by moving the selected polygons down along the Y-axis.

Move selection down

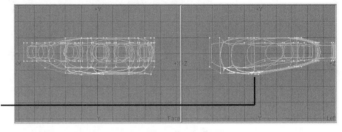

8. Select the four knuckle polygons by using the Top view. You can then deselect the ones directly beneath them in the Left or Face view.

9. Choose Bevel from the Multiply Panel (b on the keyboard) and enter an inset of **40 mm** and a shift value of **20 mm** (see fig. 7.8). This creates the knuckles on the hand.

FIGURE 7.8
Use the Bevel tool on the selected polygons to create knuckles.

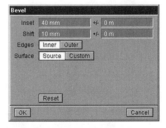

TIP

After beveling a selected group or single polygon, the new ones created are highlighted. Moving around the polygon itself can be easy, but finding individual points for dragging can be difficult. Now would be good time to turn on Patch Polygon. Choose Options from the Display Panel (press d on the keyboard). You can then see blue outlines of the polygonal version of the object. This makes tracking down its points much easier.

10. Choose Move from the Modify Panel (or press t), and bring the beveled knuckles upward along the Y-axis to your liking. Resize the new knuckle polygons individually to make them sharper or more round (see fig. 7.9).

FIGURE 7.9

Smaller beveled polygons result in sharper knuckles.

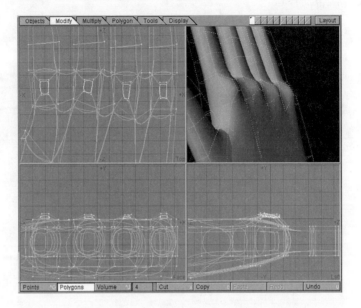

As you can see, selecting and pulling various polygons essentially sculpts your object. Another useful technique is to select individual points and drag them. Even dragging a point to extreme places has a subtle effect on the curvature of the splines. The traditional polygon version of the object could end up with many non-planar polygons this way. Because the polygons serve no purpose other than the use of their points, however, it won't affect the object.

11. Select the wrist polygon at the bottom of the hand and delete it. Think of it as the "cap" at the end of a jar, which needs to be removed (see fig. 7.10).

12. Go to File, Save Object As. Name the object **Hand_Biff.lwo** and save it for later use.

FIGURE 7.10
Delete the polygon at the wrist to prepare the hand for attachment to another object.

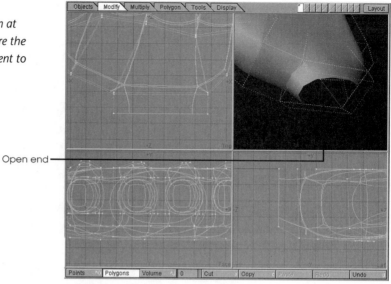

Open end

The amount of detail you add to the hand depends on your needs. The fingers on the hand in figure 7.11 have been slightly bent and garnished with another set of knuckles.

FIGURE 7.11
You can add extra details such as bending the fingers into a relaxed state and adding more knuckles, depending on your needs.

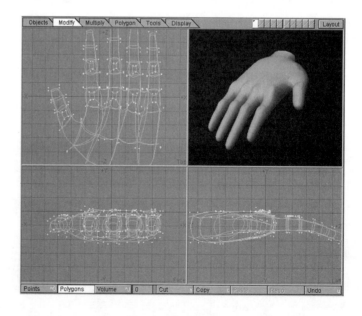

The polygon at the end of the hand was deleted to prepare the object for welding to an arm without visible seam. This step is absolutely necessary because when two cylindrical sections are attached to each other, the resulting weld cannot leave polygons inside the object. Picture the arm with the welded-on hand as if it were open at the end of the bicep. If you could actually pick up the arm and look into this open end as if it were a telescope, you could see all the way to the end of the fingers. If something inside the arm were obstructing your view, it would mean that the "cap" polygons were not deleted and are still inside the object. If this does happen, MetaNURBS won't calculate the new weld properly and hideous errors will be visible on the seam.

It is important to keep the welding area down to as few attachment points as possible to keep the building process moving smoothly. Rarely is it necessary to use more than four points in the attachment areas.

Building the Right Side of the Body

Even though the hand looks more complex, it is easier to construct because there is no need to mirror half of it or weld any points. You can model it as one shape and then extrude it. The basic shape of the human body appears deceivingly simpler, but much more is involved in its creation.

The accompanying CD supplies a simple template of the character to be built. You will extrude and modify the template to form a semi-cartoonish male. Biff will be a cross between a realistic, digitally scanned human and a round, simple character.

In addition to being a great figure that you can use in animations, the finished model also makes a useful generic figure that you can modify many different ways to create different characters—even female. After you learn the basics for creating Biff, it will be pretty easy for you to create his pal Buffy, provided you have reference of the female form. The following exercise goes through the step-by-step procedure for extruding a template and welding the halves together.

The shape of Biff's body has been laid out in Biff_template.lwo. The template is only one half of the object. Because the human body is symmetrical, you can develop it on one side, and then mirror and weld it.

EXTRUDING THE TEMPLATE AND SHAPING THE LOWER BODY

1. Load the object Biff_template.lwo from the accompanying CD.

2. Choose Extrude from the Multiply Panel to deepen the template approximately 160 mm along the Z-axis (see fig. 7.12). The exact amount is not important; just getting some thickness to the body is all that matters at this point.

FIGURE 7.12

Extrude the template of the body into a 3D MetaNURBS cage.

Extrude along the Z-axis

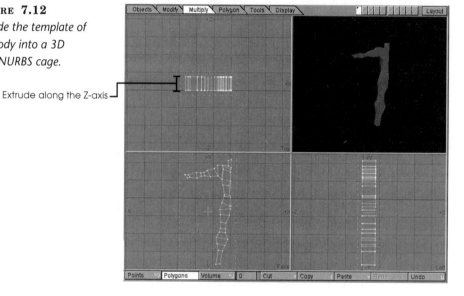

3. Switch to MetaNURBS mode. In the Front or Left view, select the polygons that make up the shin and knee area. There should be 17 polygons highlighted (see fig. 7.13).

4. Choose Stretch from the Modify Panel. Stretch and take away some of the thickness of the selected areas by using the tool in the Left view. Continue shaping the areas to your liking by dragging points. This gives the lower leg area some taper (again refer to fig. 7.13).

5. Select the polygon on the back of the model that will be the buttocks. Move it outward conservatively along the +Z-axis. To give it more roundness, you can also bevel and shape it further.

FIGURE 7.13
Use the Stretch tool on the knee and shin areas to give the leg some taper.

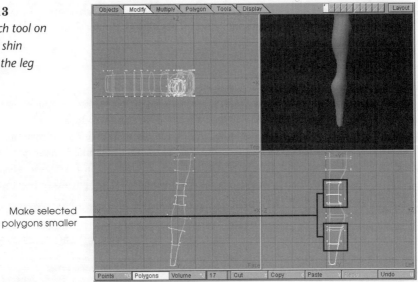

Make selected polygons smaller

6. Select the polygons in the crotch area and push them inward along the +Z-axis. You revisit this entire area for further shaping after the object has been mirrored and welded. Figure 7.14 shows the crotch and buttocks polygons highlighted.

FIGURE 7.14
By selecting the polygons of the buttocks and crotch, you can give some shape to the pelvic area.

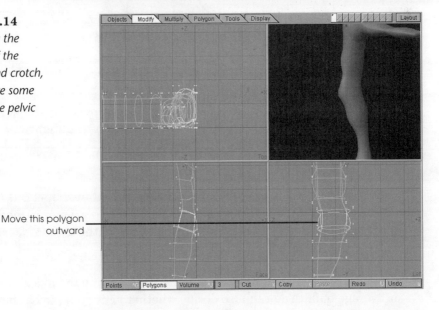

Move this polygon outward

Biff's contour is being kept simple at this stage because it's better to build a foundation and work on the fine details later.

TIP

A good idea is to set your Undo levels higher if system memory allows it. You can do this by choosing Options in the Objects Panel (press o). The maximum Undo level is 15. Remember that using the Tab key to switch to MetaNURBS mode counts as an undo, so the default setting of 3 could make it impossible to go backward if you've done something undesirable. With it set to 8 or more, you can do a bevel or a drastic point adjustment on a certain area just to see what it looks like, and then decide whether you will move forward or go back and try something else.

Copying (Ctrl+c) a crucial stage of your model-building process and pasting (Ctrl+v) it into an empty layer can help you go backward even further than setting a high Undo level. This could be considered an alternative to changing the default setting.

The front profile of the arm has already been shaped in the initial template (the X-axis). One advantage this technique has over the beveling method is that some of the shaping is finished even before the object has three dimensions. The following exercise shows how to give the body some shape in the remaining two dimensions: Z and Y.

SHAPING THE UPPER BODY

1. Fit the arm in the views by using Ctrl+z and zooming in, or by selecting it and pressing a.

2. Using the Top view, select the polygons that make up the wrist, elbow, and upper bicep. There should be 12 polygons highlighted.

3. Using the Stretch (h) tool in the Top view, make the polygons thinner so that they are to your liking (see fig. 7.15).

4. The arm probably still looks a little flat and unshapely. If the Patch Polygons (blue outlines in the OpenGL view) are not turned on, turn them on now. This makes it easier to tweak the arm further.

5. Deselect all polygons and drag the points inward (see fig. 7.16).

This is where you should decide whether Biff is going to have a muscular or average build. You can also decide whether he is going to be chubby or slim, and then select the midsection polygons and stretch them accordingly. Another option for adding more detail is to select the elbow polygon on the back of the arm and bevel it into a sharp end.

FIGURE 7.15

Modify the wrist and elbow polygons to give the arm a nice taper.

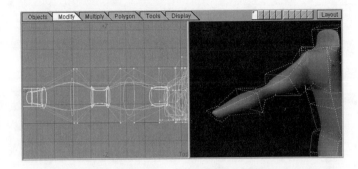

FIGURE 7.16

Use the Drag tool to put finishing touches on the arm.

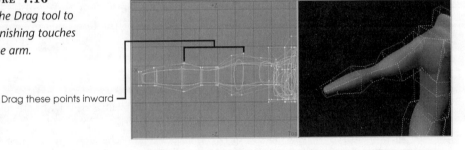

Drag these points inward —

TIP

The more complexity your object has, the more difficult it becomes to locate points. If you're trying to drag a single point and snagging others by accident, switch to the Polygon Edit mode and select the polygon that contains the point first. Then, no bystander points can be affected by the Drag tool. LightWave only operates on selected areas unless everything is deselected.

Now is a good time to check the progress of the character model you are creating.

Checking the Model's Progress

At times during the model creation process, you may want to know what your object will look like as a true polygon object ready for render in Layout (as opposed to a simple polygon object, also known as the MetaNURBS cage). At any stage during modeling, switch to Polygon mode and in the Tools Panel, select Freeze to convert the MetaNURBS object into polygons to check for imperfections (or press Ctrl+d on the keyboard). To take it a step further, from the Polygon Panel, select Triple to triple all the four-point polygons. This eliminates any non-planar polygons. Select Undo more than once to go back to the MetaNURBS cage if everything looks all right.

Using Metaform to Check Progress

Another method that gives the same results is to select Transform, Subdivide from the Polygon Panel, and then select Metaform in the Requester box. Metaform is somewhat like an early version of MetaNURBS. It takes simple, boxy geometry and calculates smooth curves from the orientation and point distances. The main difference when using Metaform is that you can only see the smooth, organic object after the simple geometry is finished. It is like a finishing touch that you perform to transform the simple polygonal object into its final, curvy state. With MetaNURBS, real-time feedback is available while adjusting the spline version of the object.

NOTE

Sometimes the OpenGL view draws the spline version of a MetaNURBS object with flaws (brown patches or unusually dark spots), especially in the areas that contain sharp corners and three-point polygons. Usually, the object integrity is fine, but you can check on it by using one of the methods previously mentioned.

Attaching Separate Body Parts

Because of the complexity of the human form, it is a good modeling approach to build each component separately, and then attach them to each other later. The simplistic nature of splines makes welding parts together without a seam quite easy. The ends of most appendages on a Human object have four points at the welding areas. Try welding an object with a high polygon count to another—not only is the location of points difficult, but making it appear seamless takes lots of tweaking.

The hand has already been built. Although its construction helped build a working knowledge of a MetaNURBS modeling technique, it also serves another purpose in this chapter: Biff needs a hand. Rather than waiting until the body half is mirrored, it is a good idea to attach the hand now, using the steps outlined in the following exercise.

WELDING THE HAND TO THE WRIST

1. Select the single wrist polygon at the end of the arm and delete it to prepare for the hand attachment.

2. Put the body in the background of the layer, then hold Shift and select the next empty layer.

3. Load Hand_template.lwo into the layer and note its position and size compared to the body.

4. Choose Modify, Size, and stretch the hand to the appropriate dimensions. Use your judgment while scaling the hand so that it is proportionally correct to the entire body.

5. Switch to Polygon mode (press Tab) to line up the seams for welding.

6. Orient the hand with the Rotate (y) tool and the Move (t) tool until the ends of each object line up correctly (see fig. 7.17).

FIGURE 7.17
Position the hand to align it for a clean weld to the arm.

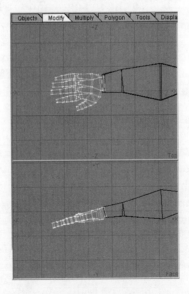

7. Drag points until the four corners on each open end are in close proximity to each other, as the closeup on figure 7.18 illustrates.

FIGURE 7.18
Using the Drag tool, position the open holes on the end of each object so that their points overlap.

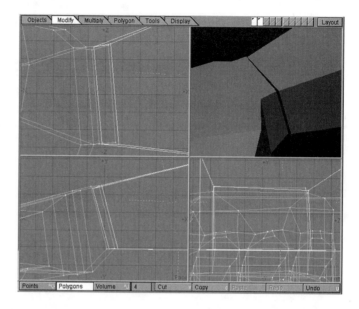

Use the apostrophe (') key to switch between layers as you line up points to be welded. It is also a good practice to use Polygon mode when you weld unless you have the Patch Polygon turned on. Otherwise, points appear to be floating in space and are hard to associate with polygons.

8. Cut (x) the hand from its layer and paste it into the body's layer.

9. At the bottom of the Modeler interface, press the Points Mode button. Select two overlapping points (one from the wrist, and one from the hand), and then go to Tools, Points, Weld. Alternatively, press Ctrl+w to weld the points together.

The point selection process can be difficult if the object is a complex one. Sometimes it can appear that you are selecting only two points. Others might get selected too, however, giving you three or more selected points. When this happens, use another view to deselect the excess points. The Weld command is only useful to you at this stage if points are being joined two at a time.

10. Repeat the process for the remaining pairs of points, and then press Tab to view the seamless weld of the wrist in MetaNURBS mode.

To attach a foot to the body before the mirroring process takes place, just load Foot.lwo and repeat the preceding steps. It is the same procedure, just performed in a different area of the body.

TIP

Locating pairs of points to be welded can be like finding the proverbial needle in a haystack. Selecting all the polygons not related to the weld and hiding them with the minus key (–) can make the area appear much less populated. When its time to unhide, use the backslash key (\).

You could have also used the Merge command to connect the hand to the arm. With the four end points from each object selected (to isolate the Merge tool to that area alone—if no points are selected, the Merge tool does its thing over the entire object, creating a mess), choose Tools, Merge, and instantly create a seamless wrist.

Finishing the Right Side of the Body

When all modeling work is finished, you will notice that it is the little details that make the model look interesting. For a male figure, slight shifts in body proportions and musculature can make or break the figure design. When building a female figure, the subtlest curvature of the hips, small of the back, or thighs in either direction can make a big difference. An average figure is just the slightest bit off from being a great figure, and vice versa.

Biff is an athletic-type guy, so he should have developed pectorals. Because there is a polygon conveniently located in the chest area (placed there during the creation of the template), the method best applied here is to select this polygon and bevel it.

The following set of steps shows how you can use the Bevel tool to add musculature if needed.

BEVELING THE CHEST

1. Select the chest polygon and use the Bevel tool under the Multiply Panel. Type in an inset of **20 mm** and a shift value of **10 mm**.

2. Drag points on the resulting end polygon to shape the chest to its final state. Try pulling points to extreme places to get different effects (see fig. 7.19).

FIGURE 7.19

You can use the Bevel tool to create new geometry to add detail to the chest.

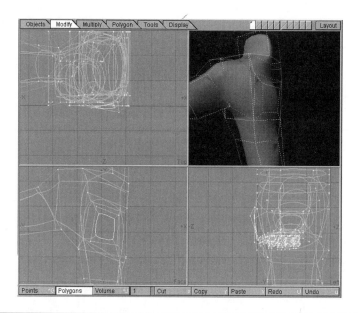

When beveling a single polygon, four new ones are created. That can add a little more detail than required, depending on the area being worked on. To get rid of this unwanted detail, deleting a polygon(s) might be necessary. The hole can then be sealed by welding points.

Mirroring Symmetrical Objects

Whenever an object is being created, take into account the detail it contains, location of those details, and whether they are exactly the same on both sides. Many objects, human or inanimate, are symmetrical—both sides are exactly alike. Objects of this nature take half the time to build than non-symmetrical ones do because you can mirror your work.

Now that the basic details of Biff's body are sculpted, the next step is to mirror the half and weld the seam down the middle. You have a couple of different ways to weld halves of MetaNURBS objects together:

■ Match up points perfectly and weld a single seam.

■ Create a bridge between the halves, one polygon at a time.

For the purposes of this exercise, the second method is employed because a new row of polygons at the center of Biff's body would be nice to have. These detail polygons are used to shape out the crotch, back, and abdominal areas. The steps outlined in the next exercise describe the process of using the Mirror tool and stitching seams.

MIRRORING THE BODY AND WELDING THE SEAM

1. Select the seven polygons down the center of the object that have surface normals pointing in the +X direction (see fig. 7.20).

FIGURE 7.20
Delete these polygons or unwanted geometry will be inside the object and ruin the seam on the mirroring process.

Delete ——

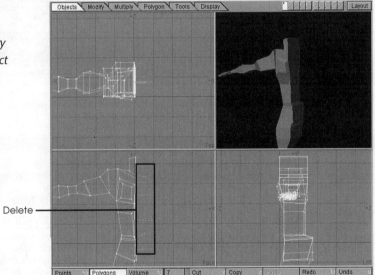

2. Delete the selection. No polygons can be inside the object. Otherwise, problems will occur with MetaNURBS's calculations.

3. Select the polygon at the very top of the neck and delete it. The neck needs to be open to attach a head later.

4. Choose Multiply, Mirror, and then press Enter to make the opposing half of the body (see fig. 7.21). When using Mirror, the points on the inside can end up directly on top of each other, or with a space between them depending on where the tool is placed.

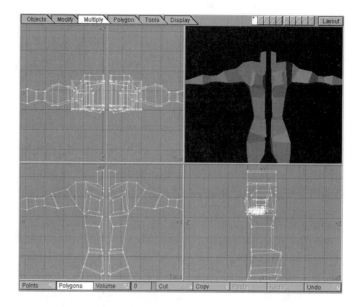

5. When welding the front seam, the points on the back become very distracting. To avoid this distraction, select all the polygons on Biff's back and use Display, Visibility, Hide Sel (or press the hyphen key [-]). Having Polygon mode (press Tab) in effect makes the process much easier also.

6. Make sure that MetaNURBS mode is off. Select four points in a counter-clockwise direction, and press P to make a polygon. Think of it as a bridge between the halves.

7. Repeat the polygon creation procedure all the way down to the crotch area until the body has no seam in the middle (see fig. 7.22). If you happen to create a polygon with surface normals facing in the wrong direction, just Flip (F) it.

8. At the bottom of the seam, there is an open four-point hole. Select these four points and create a new polygon facing the –Y direction.

9. Press the backslash key (\) to Unhide the back polygons and view the entire object. If you have created a smooth seam, select the polygons of the entire front area of the body, including the chest, stomach, and any other area that might block the open back seam.

FIGURE 7.22
Create a bridge of polygons to connect the halves of the body.

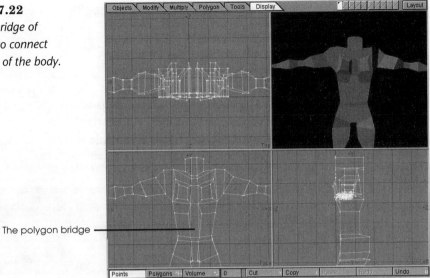

The polygon bridge

10. Repeat steps 6 and 7 for Biff's back seam until the object is totally enclosed where the Mirror operation was performed. The only open area should be at the top of the neck.

You may find that using a whole new column of polygons to connect the body halves is not necessary. A less intricate body might only need to have the points overlapped by dragging them into position and welded (or merged). If more precision is needed, use the Set Val tool to align all points on the inside to one value along the Y-axis. After the object is mirrored on the value that the points were set to, the correct points overlap and are instantly ready for welding.

Shaping the Remaining Unrefined Areas

Biff is almost a complete man, except for the fact that he is headless and his general shape could use a little fine-tuning. Shaping the body into its final form is the next step in the building process, and can also be the most fun. This is where the character gains a little personality. Is Biff going to be a scrawny stick figure, an obese, stocky guy, or maybe a muscular athlete? At this point, his physique's contour could go any route that you want. Save the figure at this stage and name it **Male_body.lwo** to keep it as a generic model that you can modify into an entire cast of different characters (as long as the MetaNURBS geometry is maintained).

You can shift the template for Biff around until it has a feminine shape, or you can modify the generic male model until it has the look of almost any type of female. The model in figure 7.23 is a character (Buffy) sculpted from the same template used for Biff. You have the template and the skills—you supply the inspiration and imagination.

FIGURE 7.23

This female character was created from the same body template used earlier.

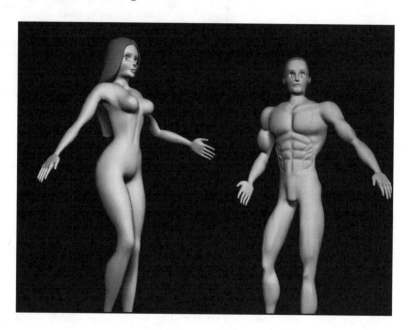

The little details are going to help give Biff his physical persona. The remainder of the exercise is dedicated to refining the body and covers the following areas:

- The midsection is very boxy and needs some attention. It should definitely have a rounder appearance. The polygon bridge, which was created to stitch together the body halves, is helpful in tweaking this area.

- The neck is far too wide when viewed from the side perspective. It will be stretched into a more cylindrical shape to accommodate a head more easily.

■ The buttocks area has already been formed correctly if you followed earlier steps, but a little advice is offered on how to make it look better.

■ Biff's pectorals (chest muscles) have too much space between them. Some simple suggestions are made concerning the sculpting of them.

The torso doesn't have much detail at this stage of development, but how far that aspect goes is entirely up to you. The following exercise provides a few ideas for improving the midsection.

MODIFYING THE MIDSECTION

1. Using the Tab key, set the screen to Polygon mode.

2. Select the polygons adjacent to Biff's stomach (the love handles). Their surface normals face opposite directions along the X-axis.

3. Stretch (H) the selection inward along the Z-axis, using the Left view. This takes the square edge away from the middle of the body (see fig. 7.24).

FIGURE 7.24
You can stretch the sides of the torso to rid Biff of the boxy look in that area.

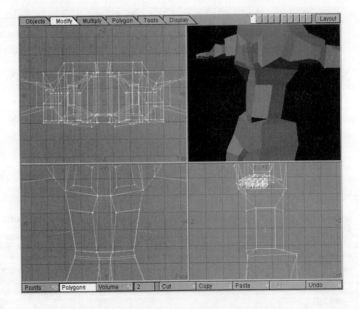

4. Select the polygon in the center of the stomach and the one directly behind it (middle of the back). Using the Front view, place the Stretch

tool in the center of the highlighted area and stretch the polygons until they are very thin. These two thinned out polygons serve as the separation of the stomach muscles and the dip, which appears in the spinal region.

TIP

Depending on the shape desired for the character being created, you can use different tools under the Modify menu for deformations. In addition to Stretch, Move, and Drag, you can also use Magnet, Smooth Scale, Dragnet, Taper, and Bend—even Twist can be useful if your character's design requires it. Consult your LightWave user and reference guides for details on how to use these tools.

After the midsection has been shaped appropriately, you can add details if so desired. These additions could include abdominal muscles or a rib cage. Alternatively, the model can be kept simple and a bump map can be applied in Layout to give the illusion of muscles. There is no need to go into further details on Biff's torso if clothing will be added later.

At this stage, Biff's neck is the same width as his torso when viewing him from a side perspective. This next step in the refining process shows how to modify the square-looking neck, still using the same techniques utilized earlier.

SHAPING THE NECK

1. Select all the neck polygons. There should be eight of them.

2. Using the Stretch tool in the Left view, decrease the width of the neck until it looks more symmetrical all the way around its circumference.

3. It is now the correct size, but it still looks too square at the corners. Deselect all the neck polygons, except the ones on the sides, and decrease their width even further (see fig. 7.25).

TIP

To quickly zoom in on an area that you want to modify, select the desired polygons and press Shift+a. The selection fits itself into the view perfectly. Additional zooming in and out can be done with < and >.

FIGURE 7.25

Manipulating the polygons on the side of the neck can bring a more cylindrical appearance to it.

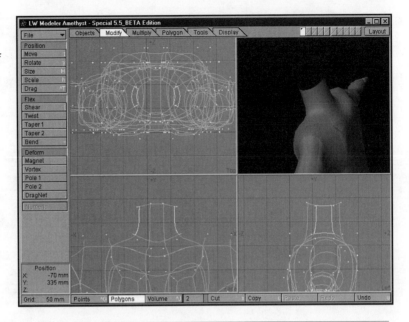

Another option in the refining stage is to refine the buttocks area. If you followed earlier steps in the building process, you did make some adjustments to the buttocks when making initial adjustments to the lower body. If you are willing, you can perfect it by making the polygon in the middle of the buttocks thinner and moving (T) it slightly along the –Z-axis (toward the front of the body).

The chest muscles could use some work, because they are supposed to be part of a muscular character. The following exercise gives a couple of suggestions for shaping the chest region.

SHAPING THE PECTORALS

1. Hide the polygons of the back by selecting them and pressing the hyphen key (-). You want to hide these polygons because they obscure the chest area and make working on it more difficult.

2. Select the polygons of the inner chest and stretch them toward the center until they are very thin (see fig.7.26). This brings the pecs a little closer to each other and puts a crease between them.

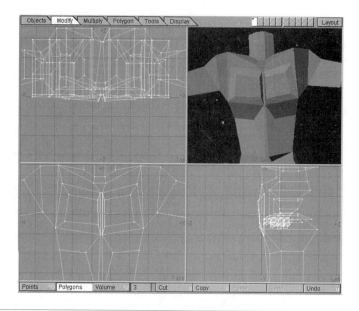

Altering the chest further is just a matter of using methods described earlier in this chapter. Experiment with different looks by scaling polygons and dragging points. Even making extreme modifications will have a subtle effect on the object's shape. You should now possess the knowledge for modifying any part of the body.

One of the main concepts that this chapter has stressed is the fact that building a complex MetaNURBS object is easy if the process is taken one step at a time. A human model is actually one complex object made up of several object subgroups. Most of these objects can be drawn into a two-dimensional template, extruded, sculpted, and then prepared for welding to another body part by making an open hole at the area of attachment. Creating Biff would have been far more difficult if you had tried to create every detail at the outset—that is, an entire human shape with hands, feet, and a head. Take advantage of the simplicity MetaNURBS affords. Model sections separately that will form a synergy when put together.

Because most people in the real world have a head, Biff will not be complete until he, too, has one. The next step is to load the Biff_hea.lwo object from the accompanying CD and weld it to the end of his neck.

Attaching a Head to the Shoulders

Although it is definitely pleasing to see a head on Biff's shoulders, you can also learn an important technique while connecting it. The Biff_hea.lwo object contained on the accompanying CD happens to have a four-point opening at the bottom of the neck. Attaching this object to the neck on the finished body would be no problem if the same number of points resided on the other side. So the question arises: How do you weld a four-point section to an eight-point section? In previous exercises, sometimes a polygon bridge needed to be created to fill a gap between sections. The same principle applies here, except one side has twice as many points as the other. Because both sides to be connected are an even number, it should not be too difficult to figure out how to attach the head. The following exercise guides you through the process.

ATTACHING THE HEAD

1. Select the eight points at the top of the neck and move them down along the negative Y-axis. Or, select all the neck polygons and use the Stretch tool on them to make them shorter—as long as the end result is a neck that can barely be seen protruding from the shoulders.

2. Load the object Biff_hea.lwo and position it above the shoulders with a space of about 20 mm. If necessary, size it to the correct proportions (see fig. 7.27).

3. Select the four corner points of the opening at the bottom of the Head object.

4. Select the four points in the center of the neck (two in front, two in back). In the Front view, use the Drag tool to bring them upward until they overlap the four points that make up the opening at the bottom of the Head object (see fig. 7.28).

FIGURE 7.27

Bridging a gap between two ends with a different number of points can be tricky.

A polygon bridge will fill this gap

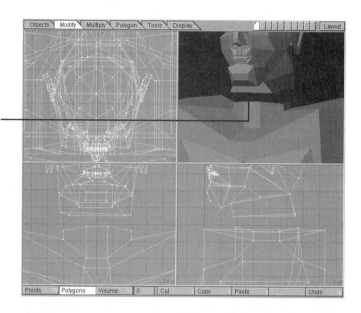

FIGURE 7.28

After these eight points are close together, you can merge or weld them.

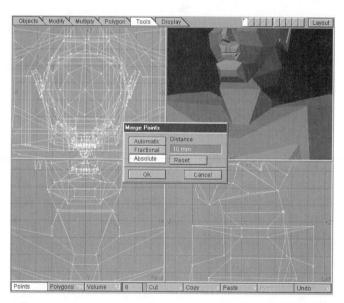

5. Make adjustments in every view until the points appear to be directly overlapping each other. Under the Tools menu, select Merge (M). Click on the Absolute button and enter **10 mm** in the Distance field. This ensures that all selected points within 10 mm of each other merge together. In this case, four points are eliminated.

After the points are merged, two holes are left on each side of the neck. Stitching up these holes is easy if previous exercises were followed.

6. Seal up the two remaining holes on the neck (one at a time) by selecting four points and pressing the P key (see fig. 7.29). Make sure the new polygons' surface normals are facing the correct direction. If not, press the F key to flip it (them).

FIGURE 7.29

The seamless neck is complete after the remaining two holes are sealed by creating new polygons.

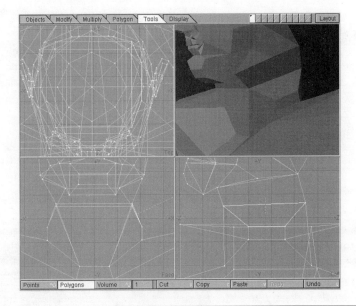

The head might have been more difficult to attach if there were an even number at one opening and an odd number at the other. Triangles (three-point polygons) would need to be employed to accomplish this kind of attachment. In previous versions of LightWave, triangles weren't available in MetaNURBS modeling. You can imagine how much easier the building process has become!

Other elements can make MetaNURBS modeling easier, but these are more abstract concepts. Try to keep a non-technical frame of mind while building a MetaNURBS object. If you usually put an exact numerical entry in the Bevel tool, try just putting in an estimate instead. You can then adjust the object from there as opposed to having the exact dimensions laid out at each and every step. Calculating every action precisely as if you were modeling architecture can put a ceiling on your creativity and make your character evolve into something that looks less like a person and more like the Lincoln Memorial.

Another concept to keep in mind is that a low polygon count on your MetaNURBS cage can keep your objects manageable. This is a very important concept to remember and will save you plenty of time if modifications are needed later.

Keeping the Polygon Count Low

Remember that using fewer polygons for organic MetaNURBS objects is usually the best approach. Fewer polygons mean less control points, which makes it less likely to get bumps and dips in your object where it should be smooth.

Look at the legs, which are side by side in figure 7.30. They both look exactly the same. The one on the right, however, contains a higher number of polygons. The leg with fewer polygons is more efficient because its splines are longer and smoother due to the greater distances between its control points.

FIGURE 7.30

The key to a manageable MetaNURBS object is to be conservative with the polygon count.

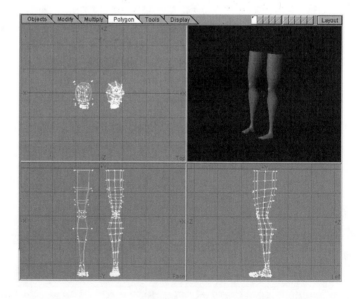

If you wanted to change the shape of the high polygon leg, it would be far more difficult because there are many more points to pull. If you wanted to change the sweep of the thigh, tweaking several points would be necessary on the more complex Leg object. The simple object is far easier to manipulate and it furnishes smoother results.

The human body is comprised mostly of cylindrical shapes. A MetaNURBS cylinder is much easier to manage if fewer (preferably four) polygons make up its circumference. Doing this keeps longer distances between spline control points, thus generating wide, smooth arcs. Excessive subdivisions beyond the basic box are usually unnecessary unless you are sculpting highly detailed areas such as kneecaps, elbows, and noses.

The level of polygons in your MetaNURBS spline cage also determines the number of polygons in the finished (frozen) object, depending on the Patch Division setting in the Object Options Panel. The next section discusses freezing the object and ending up with a polygon count that works in any situation that arises.

Preparing the Object for LightWave Layout

Now that the modeling of the object is finished, you should save it for future projects, whether to be modified into an entirely different character or cannibalized for its parts. You can accumulate many different models to form a character graveyard folder on your hard drive. Just think of yourself as Dr. Frankenstein when the time comes to raid the folder for body parts. After you have modeled a perfect hand and foot, it's safe to assume that you won't need to do it again, unless the character you're working on is a mutant, demon, or some other inhuman creation. Various appendages are at your disposal in the graveyard, waiting to be copied, pasted, and welded to another model.

Another option to consider is that the MetaNURBS geometry can be useful for creating Morph targets to be loaded into Morph Gizmo. You can copy one object into several layers, each one being edited in a different way, perhaps to achieve facial expressions. (See Chapter 14, "Facial Animation and Morph Gizmo," for more details about the Morph Gizmo.) Because of the low number of polygons in a MetaNURBS object, you can use all the Modify tools to reshape it, and extreme modifications are possible without severely deforming its integrity.

When the simple, boxy, polygonal object is saved, all the MetaNURBS spline information is retained along with it, assuming that the object consists of triangle and quad polygons only.

Freezing the MetaNURBS Splines into Polygons

As mentioned previously, the camera in Layout can't see a MetaNURBS object because it is just a spline-based reference object to aid you in the creation process of your model. The smooth MetaNURBS curves must be transformed into polygons to make the object render ready. The command used for this operation is Tools, Curves, Freeze. The splines are converted into as many polygons as needed to make the object look exactly like the MetaNURBS version you are seeing in the OpenGL view.

The number of polygons created from the Freeze command depends on the Patch Division setting under the Objects, Options dialog box. The default setting is 6, but that can produce an unusually high number of polygons, especially when they still need to be tripled. A setting of 3 in the Patch Division check box is more conservative, and you will still have the option to subdivide the polygons further if you require a smoother look.

TIP

If the figure is to be set up with a bone structure in Layout, model the arms and legs halfway between their range of motion. The arms should be outstretched to the sides like open wings, for example, and the elbows slightly bent. The legs shouldn't be perfectly straight either. This spread-eagle type modeling prevents creasing at joints when boning the object—especially in the hip area.

After the MetaNURBS cage has been turned into a polygon-based object (don't confuse the render-ready object with the initial, simple polygonal object you used as a spline cage), the polygons can be tripled to make the joints more receptive to bending without creating non-planar surfaces. Every quad created from freezing is turned into a triangular polygon. Now, bending the model's joint with bones will not cause ugly rendering errors; no matter which way a triangle's points are moved, it can always be seen as a flat surface.

Refining the Object to Its Full Potential

As with everything, there is always room for improvement in the model. Any model created with MetaNURBS can be worked on until it eventually looks quite realistic; it is just a matter of how far you're willing to take it. Always keep the MetaNURBS geometry saved so that it can be modified again. It could serve many uses, including the following:

- Spare parts for other characters

- A complete character to be loaded into Layout and set up with a bone structure

- An ongoing project that you can always get back to later and turn into a perfect 3D model

Now that the major modeling work is finished, you can begin the process of bringing Biff to life. To help accomplish this task, you can employ MetaNURBS to create Morph targets by manipulating limbs. One of the most common jobs morphing takes care of, however, is creating lip movement and general facial deformations to give your character personality. The next section discusses this topic.

Creating Morph Targets with MetaNURBS

Animating interesting facial expressions can bring a character to life in a much different way than just body movements alone can. Lots of emotion can be conveyed by simple hand gestures, head movements, walking style, and so on. Sometimes, however, your character must have a voice. To bring speech into the picture, building morph targets using MetaNURBS should be considered for moving the lips and making facial gestures.

Because they are spline based, MetaNURBS enable you to model facial expressions easily and save them as morph targets, whether they're to be used in a long chain of targets for traditional LightWave morphing or imported into Morph Gizmo.

MetaNURBS comes in very handy for the task of facial animation when used to create morph targets. The addition of Morph Gizmo to LightWave 5.5 enables you to load several morph targets and adjust sliders corresponding to each object, thus blending several different targets and getting much more complex facial expressions than previously available. The next exercise focuses on the creation of this target, using an object that has already been constructed. The exercise in the following section guides you through the following procedures:

- Making a copy of a head as many times as needed to accommodate all the expressions in your character's acting range

- Modifying the copy in each layer by moving points and scaling polygons to achieve different facial expressions

- Saving each head as a separate morph target to prepare them for Morph Gizmo

Modifying a Head to Generate Morph Targets

The first step in this process is to load an object that suffices for a simple facial animation. To animate facial expressions on a single Skin object by morphing, an entire body needs to be used. Even though the only part being modified is the face, the entire object must be saved as a target, because morphing depends on all targets having the same number of points. For the purposes of this exercise, you use Biff's head. It is already at your disposal and was created with morphing in mind (that point is expanded on later). The head will be animated with Morph Gizmo in another chapter, but the creation of the targets can happen right here. The following exercise gets you started.

CREATING FACIAL EXPRESSIONS VIA MetaNURBS

1. Start with a clear set of layers in Modeler. Choose File, Clear if needed.

2. Load Biff_hea.lwo into the first empty layer.

3. Copy (C) the head and Paste (V) it into the next empty layer. Repeat this operation for the next few layers, until you have multiple copies of the same expressionless head in several layers.

4. Go to the second layer and begin by modifying the brow. Select the three polygons above the eyes and pull them down to create a mean, disgruntled look.

This may seem like a small step to take, but it is all the modification needed for this object. Each target should represent every separate aspect of the facial expression you want to convey.

5. Select the polygons of the mouth.

6. Choose Modify, Deform, Magnet. Set the tool's spherical influence area over the left end of the mouth by using the right mouse. Then, drag the area upward with the left mouse button to create a smile. Repeat this for the other end of the mouth, unless you want to make the face appear to smirk. When using the Morph Gizmo to animate, a combination of a smirk with the furrowed brow could produce a sinister looking character.

When all facial modifications are made, and you are happy with the results, freeze and save each object. Try to keep in mind that using an organized naming convention can help you keep track of things in Morph Gizmo, especially when you have a lot of targets to deal with. Morph Gizmo can deal with objects as groups. Thus by naming every variation of the mouth targets with file names such as Mouth_smile, Mouth_closed, and so on, you will make the job less complicated. Make sure the original that you started with is also saved; it serves as the Anchor object for Morph Gizmo.

TIP

When making your Morph Targets, a good memory saver is to remove the polygons from the object before saving it. When LightWave calculates a morph from one object to another, points are all that are needed to complete the operation. In addition to saving memory, you also save time, because no Dissolve setting is needed for the morph targets to make them invisible—they're all ready to go as a point-based object. If the Morph Surfaces button is checked, the polygons need to stay with the object. This trick can only be used under the Object Panel in Layout, because Morph Gizmo accepts only polygon-based objects.

In addition to the expressions created in the preceding exercise, you can sculpt an entire set of phonetic mouth shapes to simulate speech. You can synchronize the morphing with a voice track, bringing an extra bit of life to the animation. Also, the nostrils could be flared out, eyes open and shut, or whatever facial expressions are needed to give your character the capability to act. A great source of facial expressions is right on your shoulders. Make faces in a mirror (preferably not in public) to use as references for your morph targets. Hopefully, the exercises in this chapter have given you the ability to achieve any facial expression imaginable.

NOTE

For some great training on creating and animating faces, check out Susan Ishida's Characters videotape available at Joe's Digital Bar and Grill on the Internet (www.mindspring.com/ ~surferjoe). The tape covers every aspect of creating a human head, point by point (which is the most controllable way to model in MetaNURBS). It is a very valuable resource. You can also contact Joe's Desktop Bar & Grill, PO Box 1665, Westminster, CA 92684. Thanks, Susan!

Summary

This chapter gave you the tools to make the most of LightWave's organic modeling capabilities. If it seems hard to grasp at first, just remember that the only thing that will make you a good character modeler is to practice and experiment. Try pulling a point in an extreme fashion just to see what happens. Sometimes the best qualities of a 3D model (or anything, for that matter) arise from experimentation, or even from "mistakes."

Think about how much personality and emotion a 3D object can convey even before it is textured and animated. Look at what you're creating and ask the question: Does my object have those qualities?

Chapter 8

TEXTURES AND MATERIALS

Textures and materials can make your models appear very realistic. They make the difference between an image that looks 3D and one that is convincingly real.

Creating compelling surfaces requires a thorough study of real-world objects. Reality is chaos and, therefore, you need to create subtle nuances in your surfaces to mimic reality. No surface is perfect. There is always some form of chaos on the surface.

This chapter will explain LightWave 5.5's textures and materials and how you can use them to create the chaotic surfaces of real objects. You'll learn about:

- Understanding surfaces and texture and parameters

- Determining your surfacing needs

- Using procedural textures

- Using image maps

- Using advanced texture effects

- Animating procedural textures

- Using Photoshop to create image maps

- Scanning textures

- Additional resources

As with every aspect of LightWave, understanding textures and materials will have a profound impact on the speed and quality of your work. Don't just stop where the tutorials end. Continue to explore the depth of LightWave's textures. There are literally thousands of texture possibilities within LightWave.

Understanding Surfaces and Texture Parameters

Before you start to surface an object, you need to know where the surfaces are edited. Figure 8.1 shows the Surfaces Panel where you edit all of the objects' surface properties. A surface's properties are the values that determine the surface appearance. These properties are also commonly referred to as surface attributes.

Use the properties in the Surfaces Panel to control all of the surface attributes for your models. You'll find these properties covered in the *LightWave User Manual* and *LightWave Reference Guide*. There is a second layer to the Surfaces Panel where you edit specific texture properties. This layer is called the Texture Panel and you access it by clicking on the T button located on the Surfaces Panel. Figure 8.2 shows the Texture Panel.

FIGURE 8.1
The Surfaces Panel in Layout.

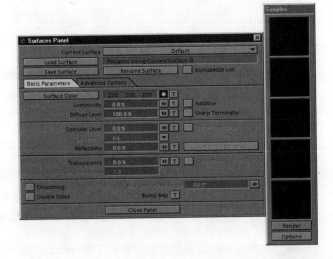

FIGURE 8.2
The Texture Panel in Layout.

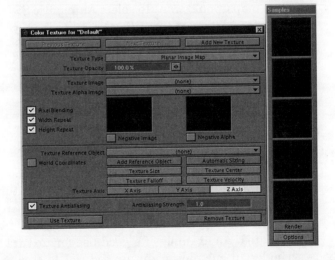

The Texture Panel properties are more detailed than the Surfaces Panel so they require more explanation than the LightWave manuals offer. The following sections cover each of the specific properties for surface textures.

Texture Size

The Texture Size property controls the physical size of the texture you are applying. This property applies to both procedural and image map textures. This setting is usually edited when using procedural textures and tiled image maps. Determining the proper texture size is easily handled by using the Automatic Sizing feature.

Automatic Sizing

The Automatic Sizing feature is only available when an image map method is selected from the Texture Type list. You don't need to have an actual image selected to use this feature. Automatic sizing determines the physical size of the surface along all three axes. This is an invaluable tool for determining the size of your procedural and image map textures. Typically, when using image maps, you'll want to select Automatic Sizing to fit the image map to the surface. When you are tiling an image map, you'll want to use Automatic Sizing to determine the surface size; then use Texture Size to resize the image map. When using procedural textures, you need to determine the surface size with Automatic Sizing; then select the procedural texture and enter the desired Texture Size.

Texture Falloff

Texture Falloff is the point at which the texture falls off and becomes nonexistent. The values are represented with percentages. The percentage of falloff for every unit of distance moving away from the Texture Center is calculated. An example of a good use for texture falloff would be creating wrinkles in curtains using procedural bumps. You want the top of the curtains to be smooth and the bottom to be bumpy. If the curtain is 2 meters long, you would use a falloff of 50% for the axis where you want the bump to fade. For every unit, the texture would fade 50%. Because the curtain is 2 meters tall, the bump texture would fade to zero at the top of the curtain.

NOTE ───────────────────────────────

A unit in LightWave equals 1 meter.

Texture Center

The Texture Center value is set by the Origin Point in Modeler. The point where the axes meet in Modeler is the Origin Point. This is the Texture Center of the surfaces on the object. Texture Center is where all procedural textures and repeating image map surfaces start. If you move the Texture Center, the texture will move accordingly. You can move the texture off the surface by exaggerating the Texture Center values. This setting can be manually changed but it's rarely required. It's important to note that moving the pivot point in Layout will have no effect on the Texture Center.

Texture Velocity

Velocity is used to move textures across the surface. These are best used with procedural textures. The values represent the distance moved per frame. To determine the texture velocity, perform the following formula:

1. Divide the distance to travel by the time it will take to move the given distance.

2. Divide the result by the animation's FPS rate.

Simply put, the Texture Velocity formula is: (Distance/Time)/FPS.

If, for example, you want a procedural fog texture to move 5 meters over 10 seconds at 30fps, the Texture Velocity would be: (5/10)/30=.0166

Good uses for Texture Velocity would be animating smoke, fog, clouds, fire, water, and so on. You will be using Texture Velocity to animate smoke later in this chapter.

Texture Axis

Texture Axis is one of the most critical settings for a texture. It is the axis to be used when mapping the texture. Mapping is based on the default position of the object when it's loaded into Layout. If you are mapping a planar image map on a surface that is facing the Z-axis, you need to select the Z Texture Axis to accurately map the surface. If you are cylindrically mapping a texture vertically around an object, you need to select the Y Texture Axis. If you are interested in exploring Texture Axis in more detail, you'll find a bounty of information in the *LightWave Reference Manual*.

TIP

When creating your surfaces in Modeler, it's a good idea to include the mapping axis in the surface name. This is usually done by including the axis in parentheses at the end of the name, for example: Cigarette Box Back (z).

Texture Antialiasing

Use this feature to soften the image map appearance and to remove artifacts that occur in surfaces that have detailed patterns. Also use this feature to prevent scintillation, which is the flashing pixels that appear during animations that incorporate pattern in their image maps. You can also use Texture Antialiasing to soften bump maps to make them appear more natural. The amount of Texture Antialiasing is controlled by the value in the Antialiasing Strength field. The higher the value, the softer the image will appear.

WARNING

Avoid using high Texture Antialiasing values on color maps. It will add an undesirable blur to the image maps. It is best only to use antialiasing for color maps when there is a small pattern in the image. Under these circumstances, a setting of .5 is recommended as the maximum value.

Now that you have a basic understanding of the surface and texture parameters, you will learn how to put these parameters to work for you.

Determining Your Surfacing Needs

You need to determine the resources you'll need to complete the surfacing project before you start. There are two major resources you will draw upon to texture surfaces: procedural textures and image maps.

Procedural textures are mathematical algorithms. Simply put, they are fractal images painted over the surface in 3D space. These textures are computer-generated, which makes them an essential tool for creating photorealistic surfaces. Image maps, on the other hand, are actual illustrated or painted images that are mapped to the surface of the object. Because these textures are created with illustration or painting programs, they are much more flexible for creating detailed photorealistic textures.

You need to identify which surfacing technique, or combination of techniques, is best for each object before you begin to texture your scene. Look at figure 8.3, for example. You can see that there are a large number of surfaces in the scene. The cigarette and cigarette box will need image maps because they are highly detailed textures that can't be created with procedurals. However, the ashes, smoke, and glass are easily created using procedural textures. A solid understanding of the capabilities and limits of procedural textures and image maps will make it easy to effectively surface an object or scene.

Of course, there are cases where you will want to combine procedural textures and image maps to create photorealistic surfaces. You can, for example, use procedural texture bump maps to add surface detail to a plastic bottle, which has an image map label texture. More often than not, you'll be combining the two surfacing methods to achieve the best results.

FIGURE 8.3
Determining your surfacing needs.

Procedural textures and image maps are discussed in more detail in the following sections. You will be performing several exercises that will give you insight into how you can make the most of procedural textures and image maps.

Using Procedural Textures

The main advantage to procedural surfaces is that they are truly 3D. They conform to irregular objects without pinching or stretching the surface, which is a common problem with image map textures. Figure 8.4 shows the advantage a 3D procedural has over a 2D texture when surfacing objects of irregular shape. The image map texture stretches across the surface of the object, whereas the procedural map is evenly distributed over the surface of the object. The image map is also limited to 3D space so there is no variance in the texture. The procedural is completely unique on all axes of the object. Procedurals are best used to apply continuous detail to an irregular-shaped object such as a molded plastic pager.

FIGURE 8.4
Procedural textures versus image maps.

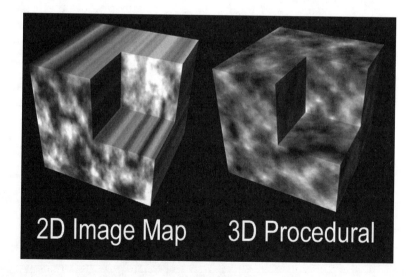

Creating Realistic Surfaces with Procedurals

LightWave 5.5 has several procedural textures. These textures come in two forms: surface color and bump. Fractal Noise is the most commonly used surface color procedural texture. This is typically used to add dirt to objects. It can also be used to add specular irregularities to object surfaces.

There are a variety of bump procedural textures. There are unique ones such as Bump Array and Crust. Although these are interesting textures, they are rarely used in photorealistic surfacing. The most popular bump procedural textures are Fractal Bumps and Crumple. These are very important procedural textures for creating surfaces such as plastic, metal, and rubber.

The scope of this chapter covers how to create the three most common real-world surfaces using procedural textures. You will learn how to create the following surfaces:

- Plastic

- Rubber

- Metal

You are encouraged to experiment with the procedural textures to discover your own special tricks and techniques. Take some time to experiment on your own to discover new uses for the procedural textures. They can save you a lot of time you might normally spend trying to create the same effect with image maps.

WARNING

Procedural surfaces will significantly increase your render times. The more you add, the longer the render time. You should avoid excessive procedural textures when photorealism isn't required.

Creating Plastic with Procedurals

The most commonly used procedural texture is Fractal Noise. This texture is usually used to add dirt and specular highlights to objects. The two most important textures for photorealism are Fractal Bumps and Crumple. These textures are typically used to add subtle surface distortion (texture) to make an object appear photorealistic. Every real-world object has a surface texture with some level of roughness on the surface. Although it may be so small that it can't be felt to the touch, it will certainly have an impact on the specularity of the object. To make photorealistic objects, you must add a procedural bump texture to your surfaces.

The following exercise will show you how applying a simple Fractal Bump can make your models take on the appearance of photorealistic plastic.

DID YOU PAGE ME? PART ONE

1. Open LightWave's Layout and load the Beeper.lws scene from the accompanying CD. You should have a scene with single beeper, as shown in figure 8.5.

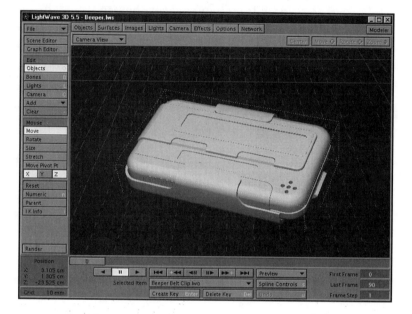

2. Open the Surfaces Panel and click the Options button in the Samples Panel. You will be working with dark surface colors so you need to add a background pattern to the rendered sample that will make the darker surfaces easier to see. Select the Background Pattern check box and click the OK button to save the changes.

3. Select Beeper Body from the Current Surface list.

4. Enter the following settings for Basic Parameters:

Surface Color	10,10,10
Luminosity	0
Diffuse Level	60
Specularity Level	80
Glossiness	16
Reflectivity	5
Transparency	0

TIP

Hold Shift down while clicking the Surface Color button to bring up the original RGB Color Requesters, which are faster to set than trying to pick a color in the color scratch window.

Polished plastic is a rather soft material, so the glossiness has been set relatively low so the light will wash out on the surface of the object.

5. Click on the Reflection Options button. Under the Reflection Type list, select Ray Tracing and Spherical Map. Now select the ReflectionMap.iff image from the Reflection Image list, and click the Close Panel button. Plastic has a very small level of reflectivity that is important to achieve for the realistic look. The ReflectionMap.iff image is designed to mimic the natural reflection of a room on the object's surface.

6. Click the Bump Map button on the Surfaces Panel and select Fractal Bumps from the Texture Type list. Now enter the following properties for the fractal bumps:

Texture Opacity	100
Texture Size	.00001,.00001,.00001
Texture Amplitude	40
Frequencies	10

This will add a very small bump texture to the surface, which is an element of chaos that helps to make the beeper case appear real.

7. Click the Add New Texture button and select Crumple from the Texture Type list. Now enter the following properties for the crumple:

Texture Opacity	100
Texture Size	.0002,.0002,.0002
Texture Amplitude	40
Number of Scales	4
Small Poyour	.75

This bump layer is added to break up the continuity of the first bump layer. The surface on a beeper case is slightly rough so the addition of the Crumple bump adds to the realism.

8. Click the Use Texture button and select the Render button in the Samples Panel. You should see a black ball with a bumpy surface and soft specularity in the first preview box, as shown in figure 8.6. It should have a checkered pattern behind it that is the background pattern you added to make the sample render visible.

FIGURE 8.6

The Surfaces Panel showing the preview rubber surface.

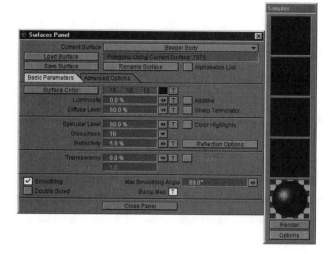

9. Now that you have created a realistic plastic, you should save it for use on future models. Select the Beeper Body surface from the Current Surface list and click on the Save Surface button on the Surfaces Panel. Give it the name **Polyurethane_Plastic.srf** and press the Save button. To use this surface in the future, simply select the Load Surface button and select it by name.

The surface you have just created is a photorealistic polyurethane plastic texture, the common material used to manufacture pagers. To see the actual result on the model, press your F9 button to create a quick render. As you can see, there are many other plastic surfaces you need to create to finish the scene. Because you have already created the basic plastic surface, you can simply copy the surface settings to the other surfaces.

Copying surface settings from one surface to another will save you a lot of time that would normally be consumed by replicating identical settings.

COPYING SURFACES

1. Select the Beeper Body surface from the Current Surface menu. This is the surface you want to copy.

2. Click the Render button on the Samples Panel to render a preview of the surface.

3. Select the Beeper Logo Background surface from the Current Surface menu. This is the target surface for the copy function.

4. Click on the rendered sample in the Samples Panel. You will be prompted with a Requester that asks if you want to Copy surface settings from this sample to the current surface? Click Yes.

You have now copied the beeper body surface parameters to the Beeper Logo background. Because the Beeper Logo background is a different type of plastic, you need to make a few changes:

1. Change the Basic Parameters.

Surface Color	35,35,35
Luminosity	0
Diffuse Level	60
Specularity Level	30
Glossiness	16
Reflectivity	5
Transparency	0

2. Click on the T next to Bump Map and change the Fractal Bump Texture Amplitude to 20%. Click on the Next Texture button and change the Crumple Texture Amplitude to 10%. This will create a smoother surface but still retaining the texture of plastic.

3. Copy this surface to the Beeper Logo Text and Beeper Power Button surfaces.

4. Select the Beeper Logo Text surface from the Current Surface list and change the Surface Color to 250,250,250.

5. Select the Beeper Power Button surface from the Current Surface list. This surface is a smooth, polished plastic so a bump map isn't necessary. Deselect the Bump Map by clicking on the T button.

6. Change the Basic Parameters to the following:

Surface Color	0,0,0
Luminosity	0
Diffuse Level	80
Specularity Level	90
Glossiness	256
Reflectivity	5
Transparency	0

You have now surfaced all the plastic parts on the beeper. Next, you will create a photorealistic rubber surface.

Creating Rubber with Procedurals

Rubber is one of the most common surfaces found in real-world objects. It's also one of the more complicated surfaces to create because of the specularity of rubber. Rubber is soft and porous so it tends to absorb light. When light shines on it, it actually represents specularity using its own surface color. This is the attribute of rubber that makes it appear soft and porous. Creating rubber is very similar to creating plastic with a slight difference in specularity.

This exercise will show you how to finish the scene you started in the previous exercise, by creating the rubber surface. You apply a simple fractal bump, while lowering the specularity and glossiness, to make your models take on the appearance of photorealistic rubber.

DID YOU PAGE ME? PART TWO

1. Select the Beeper Rubber Button surface from the Current Surface list.

2. Enter the following settings for Basic Parameters:

Surface Color	30,30,30
Luminosity	0
Diffuse Level	80
Specularity Level	30
Glossiness	16
Reflectivity	0
Transparency	0

Rubber has a soft and porous surface so the diffuse level will be higher to show the surfaces color, whereas the Specularity and Glossiness are low to spread the light out over the surface.

3. Click the Bump Map button on the Surfaces Panel and select Fractal Bumps from the Texture Type list. Now enter the following properties for the fractal bumps:

Texture Opacity	100
Texture Size	.00001,.00001,.00001
Texture Amplitude	50
Frequencies	3

This will add a very small bump texture to the surface that will make the rubber surface porous.

4. Click the Use Texture button and select the Render button in the Samples Panel. You should see a black ball with a bumpy surface and soft specularity in the first preview box.

5. Copy this surface to the Beeper Rubber Button Arrows and change the Surface Color to 250,250,250.

All the rubber surfaces have been created. There are just two more surfaces you need to create to complete the photorealistic beeper: the beeper readout and clear plastic that covers the beeper readout.

The following exercise will show you how to make the beeper readout surface appear like an actual digital readout by using fractal noise in the surface color.

GOING DIGITAL

1. Select the Beeper Readout surface from the Current Surface list.

2. Enter the following settings for Basic Parameters: The surface has been given a luminosity value because the digital readout is self-illuminating.

Surface Color	126,125,102
Luminosity	20
Diffuse Level	80
Specularity Level	30
Glossiness	64
Reflectivity	0
Transparency	0

3. Click on the T button next to the Surface Color and select Fractal Noise from the Texture Type list.

4. Enter the following settings, which create a very small dark spot on the surface to give the surface the appearance of a digital readout:

Texture Opacity	50
Texture Size	.0001,.0001,.0001
Texture Color	43,43,28
Frequencies	3
Contrast	1
Small Power	.5

5. Select the Beeper Readout Clear Plastic surface from the Current Surface list and enter the following Basic Parameters:

Surface Color   255,255,255
Luminosity   0
Diffuse Level   95
Specularity Level   35
Glossiness   64
Reflectivity   5
Transparency   0

6. Click on the Reflection Options button. Under the Reflection Type list, select Ray Tracing and Spherical Map. Now select the ReflectionMap.iff image from the Reflection Image list and click the Close Panel button.

You have now completely surfaced the beeper. Press the F9 button to render a preview of the scene. For best results, open the Render Panel, select the Trace Shadows and Trace Reflections buttons, and render the scene. You should have a scene of a photorealistic beeper, as shown in figure 8.7.

FIGURE 8.7
The beeper with plastic, rubber, and digital surfaces applied.

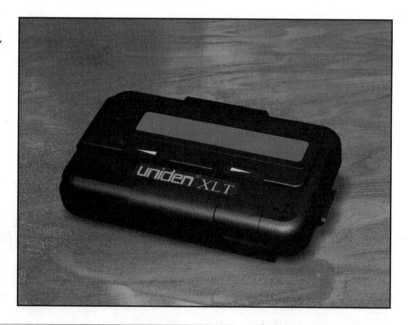

You can modify this basic rubber surface to create a variety of different rubber surfaces. Be sure to save the surface before you continue to the next exercise.

Now it's time to take a look at the last of the three most popular procedural surfaces: metal.

Creating Metals with Procedurals

Another excellent use for procedurals is to create photorealistic metal surfaces. Metals are easy to create, yet they have a profound impact on the realism of the scene.

This exercise will show you how applying a simple fractal bump and reflectivity can make your models take on the appearance of photorealistic metal.

LOCKED OUT: BRASS AND CHROME

1. Open LightWave's Layout and load the Padlock.lws scene from the accompanying CD. You should have a scene that looks like figure 8.8.

FIGURE 8.8

Making a photorealistic padlock with procedural metals.

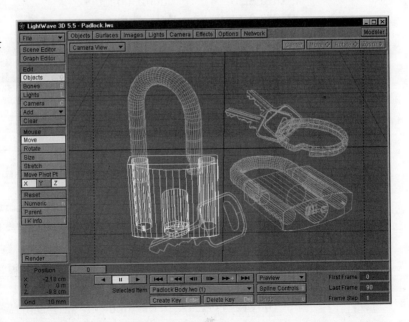

2. On the Surfaces Panel, select the Lock Body surface from the Current Surface list. Enter the following settings for the Basic Parameters.

Surface Color	191,173,111
Luminosity	0
Diffuse Level	40
Specularity Level	40
Glossiness	64
Reflectivity	40
Transparency	0

You are making a polished brass surface. Like all metals, brass has a low Diffuse Level and a medium reflectivity. Typically, brass would have a lower Specularity level but the brass is polished so its Specularity is slightly higher.

3. Select the Color Highlights check box. Brass is a colored metal so you need to have color highlights for photorealism.

4. Click on the T button next to Bump Map and select Fractal Bumps from the Texture Typelist. Now enter the following properties:

Texture Opacity	100
Texture Size	.0002,.002,.0002
Texture Amplitude	20
Frequencies	1

This adds a brushed texture to the surface. To make brushed surfaces, you need to make the texture size of one axis dramatically larger than the others, which will stretch the bump along that axis. In this case, the bump is stretched along the Y-axis that creates vertical brushing. Now click the Use Texture button.

5. Click on the Reflection Options button. Under the Reflection Type list, select Ray Tracing and Spherical Map. Now select the ReflectionMap.iff image from the Reflection Image list and click the Close Panel button. Metal has a high level of reflectivity that is important to achieve the realistic look. The ReflectionMap.iff image is designed to mimic the natural reflection of a room on the object's surface.

6. Click the Render button on the Samples Panel and you will see a brass ball with a brush texture.

7. Copy the brass texture to the following surfaces: Lock Body Back, Lock Body Front, and Lock Key Hole.

The keyhole is a smooth brass so you need to deselect the Bump Map and change the color to 204,190,140. The keyhole is manufactured in a different process so there isn't a perfect color match. It's subtle nuances like this that make an object appear realistic.

The body of the lock is now surfaced with a realistic brass texture (see fig. 8.9). The next step is to surface the lock bolt with a chrome texture.

FIGURE 8.9
Photorealistic brass surface created with procedural textures.

8. On the Surfaces Panel, select the Lock Bolt surface from the Current Surface list. Enter the following settings for the Basic Parameters:

Surface Color	220,230,240
Luminosity	0
Diffuse Level	15
Specularity Level	40
Glossiness	64
Reflectivity	50
Transparency	0

Chrome is a highly reflective metal so it has a low Diffusion Level and a higher Reflectivity.

9. Click on the T button next to Bump Map and select Fractal Bumps from the Texture Typelist. Now enter the following properties:

Texture Opacity	100
Texture Size	.0002,.002,.0002
Texture Amplitude	20
Frequencies	1

This adds a brushed texture to the surface. Because this is chrome, which tends to slightly warp the reflection, it's a good idea to add a slight Ripples texture.

10. Click on the Add new Textures button and select Ripples. Enter the following properties:

Texture Opacity	100
Texture Size	.0003,.0003,.0003
Texture Amplitude	10
Wave Sources	3
Wavelength	.0003
Wave Speed	0

Ripples is an animatable texture but because the Wave Speed is 0 and there is no Texture Velocity, the texture will not animate.

11. Click on the Reflection Options button. Under the Reflection Type list, select Ray Tracing and Spherical Map. Now select the ChromeReflectionMap.iff image from the Reflection Image list, and click the Close Panel button. It's best to use a grayscale reflection map for all highly reflective surfaces to prevents the surface from reflecting too much color.

12. Click the Render button on the Samples Panel and you will see a very reflective chrome ball with a brush texture.

13. Copy the chrome texture to the Lock Bolt Face surface.

There are still two remaining metal surfaces in the scene: chromed alloy and aluminum alloy. The keys are aluminum alloy and the key ring is chromed alloy—most commonly used for tools. These surfaces are already generated. They are located in the Current Surface list. Take a look at them and see how they differ from the other surfaces. It's also a good idea to save all of these surfaces for later use.

The lock is completely surfaced—or is it? There is still one element of photorealism missing. There aren't labels on the locks or keys. This is where procedurals are no longer an option. To create very detailed and specific surfaces such as labels, you must use image maps. Save this scene because you will be applying texture maps later in the chapter.

Creating Surface Transparency with Procedurals

Although the surface color procedural textures can be used to add color, they can also be used to remove it. These textures can be applied to the luminosity and transparency properties to make portions of the surface transparent.

Marble is a surface color procedural texture that you can use to create marble textures, but it's also very handy for creating electrical effects. The following exercise shows you how to create an electorplasmic door using the marble texture.

PLASMA DOOR

1. Open LightWave's Layout and load the Plasma_Door.lws scene on the companion CD.

2. Open the Options Panel and select the Layout View tab.

3. Deselect the Use OpenGL and OpenGL Textures boxes. These are of little benefit when working with procedural textures. Now press the Close Panel button.

4. Open the Surfaces Panel and click the Options button in the Samples Panel. You will be working with transparent surfaces so you need to add a background pattern to the rendered sample that will show the effects of the transparent surface.

5. On the Surfaces Panel, select the Plasma Door surface from the Current Surface list. Enter the following settings for the Basic Parameters:

Surface Color	0,255,0
Luminosity	0
Diffuse Level	0
Specularity Level	0
Glossiness	0
Reflectivity	0
Transparency	0

The Diffuse Level has been set to 0 because you are going to use the marble texture to make green lightning-type plasma veins. You don't want the object color to be visible.

6. Click on the T button next to Luminosity and select Marble from the Texture Typelist. Now enter the following properties for marble:

Texture Opacity	100
Texture Size	.1,.1,.1
Texture Axis	X
Texture Value	100
Frequencies	5
Turbulence	.5
Vein Spacing	.1
Vein Sharpness	5

7. Now click the Use Texture button. This will create veins of plasma that run vertically along the X-axis of the surface.

8. Select the Additive check box. This will cause the object color to be added to the objects behind it. Because the diffuse was set to 0, there will be no color added to the objects behind the door. The area where the surface color would normally be shown will be transparent. This saves you the effort of creating a procedural transparency map.

9. Click the Render button on the Samples Panel, and you will see an image with several vertical green veins over a checkered pattern.

10. To see the surface on the model, press your F9 button to create a quick render. You have just created an electoplasmic door. You can use the same technique to create a variety of energy effects.

As you can see, you can use the procedural textures for a number of different concepts that aren't related to the texture name. Take some time to experiment to discover new uses for the procedural textures. They can save you a lot of time you might normally spend trying to create the same effect with image maps.

Using Image Maps

As stated earlier, image maps are actual illustrated or painted images that are mapped to the surface of the object. Because these textures are created with an illustration or painting program, they are much more flexible for creating detailed photorealistic textures. After you have decided to use image maps, you need to identify the best possible mapping method: planar, cylindrical, spherical, or cubic. The mapping method is critical when using image maps. The most common problem with 3D images is the presence of texture stretching. This will make even the most promising scene look terrible. The following sections cover some guidelines for the image-mapping methods.

Planar Mapping

In planar mapping, images are projected on the object in the direction of the X-, Y-, or Z-axis. Planar maps are typically used on surfaces that are flat. If used on round or cylindrical objects, the texture will stretch undesirably.

Now that you understand planar image maps, you can load the Padlock.lws file and complete the bump map surfacing of the locks.

LOCKED OUT? BUMP MAPS

1. Continue from the padlock scene you worked on earlier in the chapter.

2. Open the Images Panel and load the following images from the CD:

   PadlockBottomBump.iff
   PadlockBackBump.iff
   PadlockFrontBump.iff
   PadlockBoltBump.iff

3. Select the Lock Body Front surface from the Current Surface list, and click on the T button next to Bump Map.

4. Click on the Add New Texture button and select Planar Map from the Texture Type list.

5. Load the PadlockFrontBump.iff image from the Texture Image list and select the Z Texture Axis. Now press the Automatic Sizing button.

6. Deselect Pixel Blending, Width Repeat, and Height Repeat.

7. Set the texture Antialiasing Strength to 5% and the Texture Amplitude to 200%. This will create a prominent bump on the surface. Now press the Use Texture button.

8. Repeat steps 2–6 for the following surfaces: Lock Body Back, Lock Body Bottom, and Lock Bolt Face. Be sure to use the correct mapping method and bump maps as indicated in the surface name.

The lock scene is now complete. Open the Render Panel and select the Trace Shadows and Trace Reflections options. Now press the F9 key to render a preview of the image. Your render should look like figure 8.10.

FIGURE 8.10
Raytraced procedural metals.

TIP

To achieve a photorealistic render when using reflective surfaces, you must have objects in the scene to be reflected on the surface. A surfaced ground plane works well for testing the reflectivity of an object's surfaces.

The following exercise will show you how to create a photorealistic cigarette box by applying planar image maps to its X, Y, and Z surfaces.

KICK THE HABIT: PART ONE

1. Open LightWave's Layout and clear the scene.

2. Open the Options Panel and select the Layout View tab.

3. Click on the Use OpenGL and Enable OpenGL Textures boxes.

4. Select the 128 option in the Texture Resolution list and press the Close Panel button. You will use quite a few image maps so you want to keep the Texture Resolution low to preserve memory. Using the OpenGL Textures viewing mode makes it possible for you to see how the textures are being mapped to the surface without having to test render.

5. Load the Cigarette_Box_Bottom.lwo object from the accompanying CD.

6. Click on the Add button and select Load Object File. Load the Cigarette_Box_Top.lwo object from the accompanying CD.

7. Select Cigarette_Box_Top.lwo from the Selected Item list. Click the Parent button, select Cigarette_Box_Bottom.lwo, and press OK. This will parent the top of the box to the bottom so you can rotate them together.

8. Open the Images Panel and load the following images from the CD:

CigBoxBackTop.iff
CigBoxBottom.iff
CigBoxBack.iff
CigBoxFront.iff
CigBoxRight.iff
CigBoxLeft.iff
CigBoxRightTabTop.iff
CigBoxLeftTabTop.iff
CigBoxFrontTop.iff
CigBoxTop.iff
ReflectionMap.iff

You will be mapping these images to the surfaces on the cigarette box.

9. Open the Surfaces Panel and click on the Alphabetize List check box. This will sort your surfaces alphabetically, which will make it easier to find them. Surfaces are usually listed by the object, in the order the objects were loaded in the scene. This can be useful if you want to edit the surfaces on an object you just loaded. If you are looking for a surface by name, it's better to use the Alphabetize List function.

10. Select Cig Box from the Current Surface list. The box is made of coated paper that has a soft and shiny surface that is slightly reflective. This slight reflectivity is important for making the object photorealistic. Enter the following settings for Basic Parameters:

Surface Color	235,235,235
Luminosity	0
Diffuse Level	90

Specularity Level   30
Glossiness   64
Reflectivity   3
Transparency   0

11. Click on the Reflection Options button. Under the Reflection Type list, select Ray Tracing and Spherical Map. Now select the ReflectionMap.iff image from the Reflection Image list, and click the Close Panel button.

12. Click the Render button in the Sample Panel and copy this texture to all the other surfaces.

TIP

When copying surface sample settings to many surfaces, press the up/down arrow keys with one hand to cycle through the surfaces and use the other hand to click the surface sample thumbnail and the Yes button.

13. Select the Cig Box Back (z) surface from the Current Surface list.

14. Click on the T button next to Surface Color, and select Planar Image Map from the Texture Type list.

15. Select CigBoxBack.iff from the Texture Image list. An image will appear in the first display window. Select Z Axis under Texture Axis. The surface normal for this surface is facing the Z-axis. You want to project the image map along the Z-axis to map it correctly.

16. Click on the Automatic Sizing button. You will be asked if you want to proceed; click on Yes.

17. Select the Texture Aliasing box, enter .5 in the Aliasing Strength field, and click the Use Texture button. Normally, you wouldn't want to alias a color image map but because there is a tight pattern on the object, it will be necessary to avoid artifacting in the render.

18. Deselect Width Repeat, Height Repeat, and Pixel Blending. These settings are not necessary for this surface.

You have just surfaced the back of the cigarette box. To preview the texture, close the Surfaces Panel and rotate the Cigarette_Box_ Bottom.lwo object on its Heading. You'll notice the image map is backward, as shown in figure 8.11.

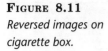
FIGURE 8.11
*Reversed images on
cigarette box.*

This is because images are mapped from the positive (front) side of the
axis. The image map is reversed because the surface normal for the back
of the box is on the negative side of the axis. To remedy this, you can edit
the image map by flipping it horizontally in a paint program, but this is
not the best method. The easiest way is to change the Texture Size of the
axis that is flipped to a negative value. In this case, it's the X-axis that
needs to be a negative value.

19. Open the Surfaces Panel, and click on the T next to Surface Color.

20. Click on the Texture Size button, place a minus (-) in front of the X value,
    and press OK. Click on the Use Texture button and close the Surfaces
    Panel. The image on the back of the box is now facing the right direction.

TIP

Image maps that are mapped to a surface on the negative side of the axis will be flipped. To
correct this, use a negative value for the Texture Size of the axis that is flipped.

There are several surfaces left to be textured. Repeat steps 13–20 for
each of the remaining surfaces. The surface names indicate the image
mapping axis. When you finish, you should have a cigarette box that
resembles the one in figure 8.12. Press the F9 button to render a preview
of the model.

FIGURE 8.12
*Cigarette box surfaced
with planar image
maps.*

Cylindrical Mapping

Cylindrical mapping wraps the image around the selected axis. The default setting wraps the image a single time around the surface so the image meets on the other side. The image can be wrapped around the object an unlimited number of times. This value is set in the Image Wrap Amount field at the bottom of the texture window. There are many cases where you will want to wrap a repeating texture around an object several times, for example: a tree trunk, metal pipes, or even a pumpkin. In these cases, you'll save on memory by creating a smaller, repeating, image map and wrapping it multiple times.

The following exercise will show you how to create a photorealistic cigarette by applying several cylindrical maps.

KICK THE HABIT: PART TWO

1. Open LightWave's Layout and load the CigNaked.lwo object from the companion CD.

2. Open the Images Panel and load the following images from the CD. You will be mapping these images to the surfaces on the cigarette.

   CigColor.iff
   CigBump.iff
   TobaccoColor.iff
   TobaccoBump.iff

3. Select Cigarette Butt from the Current Surface list and enter the following settings for Basic Parameters:

Surface Color	235,235,235
Luminosity	0
Diffuse Level	70
Specularity Level	5
Glossiness	16
Reflectivity	0
Transparency	0

The cigarette is made of a soft paper that has a dull surface so the Specularity level and Glossiness are low.

4. Click on the T button next to Bump Map and select Crumple from the Texture Type list. Now enter the following properties for the crumple:

Texture Opacity	100
Texture Size	.0001,.0001,.0001
Texture Amplitude	10
Number of Scales	4
Small Power	.75

The cigarette wrapper is slightly crumpled due to the tobacco inside. The crumple texture makes the cigarette appear more realistic. Click the Use Texture button.

5. Click on the T button next to Surface Color and select Cylindrical Image Map from the Texture Type list.

6. Select CigColor.iff from the Texture Image list. An image will appear in the first display window. Select Y-Axis under Texture Axis.

7. Click on the Automatic Sizing button. You will be asked if you want to proceed; click on Yes. The Width Wrap Amount should be left at 1 because you only want to wrap the texture around the surface once.

8. Deselect Height Repeat, Pixel Blending, and Texture Antialiasing. These settings are not necessary for this surface. Now click the Use Texture button.

9. Close the Surfaces Panel. The cigarette now has a visible texture map. The next step is to add a little reality to the cigarette texture with a bump map.

10. Open the Surfaces Panel and click on the T button next to Bump Map. Click on the Add New Texture button and select Cylindrical Map from the Texture Type list.

11. Select the CigBump.iff image from the Texture Image list and select the Y Texture Axis. Now press the Automatic Sizing button.

12. Enter the following surface properties:

Antialiasing Strength   1
Texture Amplitude   100
Width Wrap Amount   1

The bump map will create creases along the body of the cigarette and wrinkles at the end where the tobacco is visible. The antialiasing strength will soften the bump map so it looks more natural.

13. Deselect Pixel Blending and Height Repeat. Now press the Use Texture button.

Your cigarette is complete and should look like the cigarette in figure 8.13. The Cigarette Filter and Tobacco surfaces have already been textured using the planar mapping technique discussed earlier. Close the Surfaces Panel and rotate the cigarette's pitch 90 degrees. You'll see the tobacco texture at the end of the cigarette. Now rotate the cigarette to back, and press the F9 key to see a render of the cigarette. You can see how the bump map has added significantly to the realism of the object.

FIGURE 8.13
The completed photorealistic cigarette.

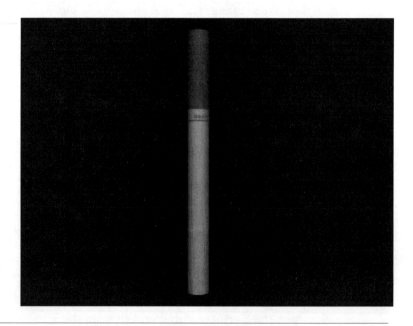

This cigarette exercise has shown the advantage of using cylindrical mapping on tubular shaped objects. Surfacing cylindrical objects would be very difficult with any other mapping method. You can use cylindrical mapping to surface a variety of tubular objects such as tree branches and metal pipes. It is also very useful when mapping organic shapes such as bananas and hot dogs. Now it's time to take a look at spherical mapping.

Spherical Mapping

Spherical image maps wrap a flat texture around the surface. It can be described as trying to gift wrap a basketball; you end up with too much paper at the top. This is exactly what happens with spherical mapping. Because a sphere tapers at the top and bottom, there is more texture map information than space available, so the texture is pinched. This is very undesirable. Spherical image maps work best when there is a solid color at the top and bottom of the image map. This prevents the stretching from being visible.

If you have a round object with detail, you are usually better off using a planar map for the top and bottom of the sphere and a cylinder map for the middle. This will eliminate the texture pinching and stretching. Seamless alignment of the textures can be difficult but a little perseverance and you'll be greatly pleased by the results.

There are occasions where spherical mapping is very useful. If you only need to decal something such as a logo onto a round object, for example, you can create a spherical image map with the logo and use an alpha map to clip the area outside the logo.

Figure 8.14 shows how a spherical image map was used to add a logo to a volleyball. The figure also shows the actual logo image map.

Cubic Mapping

Cubic image maps are similar to planar maps with one exception: You cannot select the mapping axis. The cubic map projects the image from all three axes at the same time. This is useful when you want to surface cubic objects that need the same surface on all four sides. It's also invaluable for surfacing walls and buildings where the texture is the same on all the walls.

FIGURE 8.14
The completed photorealistic volleyball.

The following exercise will show you how to use cubic image maps to quickly surface walls.

SURFACING WALLS

1. In Layout, clear the scene and load the Display_Box.lwo object from the companion CD. All the object's surfaces have been textured except the Box Walls surface. You will be applying a cubic image map to this surface.

2. Open the Surfaces Panel and select the Box Walls surface.

3. Click on the T button next to Surface Color and select Cubic Image Map from the Texture Type list. Then select Wall.tga from the Texture Image list.

4. Deselect Pixel Blending and Texture Aliasing.

5. Set the Texture Size to 1.75,1.75,1.75 and press the Use Texture button.

6. Click on the T button next to Bump Map and select Cubic Image Map from the Texture Type list. Then select WallBump.tga from the Texture Image list.

7. Now click on the Negative Image check box under the image. This will invert the image colors. Because the lines between the panels repre-

sents a weld, they need to be embossed. The image map must be white to emboss the weld so you need to invert the image map's colors.

8. Deselect Pixel Blending and enter the following texture properties:

Texture Size   1.75,1.75,1.75
AntiAliasing Strength   1
Texture Amplitude   100

Because cubic image maps are not represented with the OpenGL Texture settings, you need to render the scene to see the results. Press F9 to render a quick test. Your image should look like figure 8.15.

FIGURE 8.15
The display box with the walls surfaced using cubic mapping.

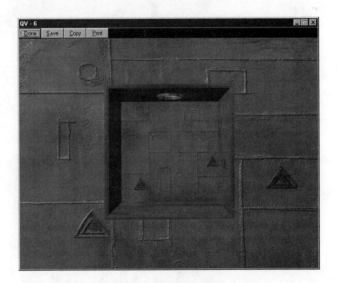

NOTE

The OpenGL Texture view mode will not show cubic image maps, so you need to render the scene to view the mapping results.

Your main goal in using image maps is to select a mapping method that will not stretch the image map. You need to carefully examine the surface to ensure you are using the proper method. There will be cases where you will want to use multiple mapping methods on the same surface. You may want to surface a pumpkin with photorealistic textures, for example. The pumpkin is almost spherical, but you don't want to use a spherical map for the color texture, because it will pinch at the top and appear unnatural. Instead, you need to use a cylinder map for the sides of the pumpkin, and a planar map for the top. To create the grooves in the pumpkin, you can use a spherical bump map because the grooves naturally come together at the top. Finally, to create the appearance of surface distortions, you can use a cubic bump map over the entire surface of the pumpkin. Here you have used all four image mapping methods on the same object to create photorealistic surfacing. Take a look at figure 8.16 to see a rendered pumpkin using all four mapping methods.

FIGURE 8.16
A photorealistic pumpkin using all four image mapping methods.

Now that you have an understanding of the image mapping methods, take a look at how you can use them to create advanced surfacing effects.

Using Advanced Texture Effects

Advanced texture effects take the standard surface properties a step farther. There are cases where the standard color and bump maps just won't do the job. This is where the advanced texture effects become necessary. Advanced texture effects include Transparency, Luminosity, and Reflectivity. You can use these three image map properties to create very complicated surface effects, without taking any more time than the traditional methods. The main advantage of these advanced effects is that you can affect only parts of the surface rather than the whole surface.

You need to use advanced texture effects to create surfaces such as a burning piece of wood or a cigarette. In these examples, you need to make only parts of the object luminous. This is where you need to apply a Luminosity image map. All three advanced texture effects use the same principles as a bump map. The magnitude of the effect is determined by the values of gray in the image map. White represents the maximum effect whereas black represents no effect. To make a piece of wood luminous where the fire is burning, you can use a Luminosity map with white areas under the fire, fading to black on the tips of the wood that are farthest from the fire. As you can see, there are some very exciting possibilities when using advanced texture effects. In the next section, you will explore the Luminosity and Transparency image map effects.

Luminosity and Transparency Image Maps

Luminosity and Transparency image maps are two of the most powerful advance texture effects. Luminosity maps are used to create glowing effects on surfaces like burning wood, LED screens, and computer monitors. Transparency maps are often used to make parts of surfaces transparent. This can be very effective for making light beams and rocket trails look gaseous. Transparency maps are also useful for making irregular edges on objects by making edges of the object transparent.

The following exercise will show you how to create a photorealistic burning cigarette by applying Luminosity and Transparency image maps.

KICK THE HABIT: PART THREE

1. In Layout, clear the scene and load the CigBurntNaked.lwo object from the companion CD.

2. Open the Images Panel and load the following images from the CD:

   CigBurntLume.iff
   CigBurntFilter.iff

3. In the Images Panel, select the CigColor.iff image from the Current Image list. Then Click on the Replace Image button and select Replace Image With and choose the CigBurntColor.iff from the companion CD.

4. Open the Surfaces Panel and select Burnt Cigarette from the Current Surface list.

5. Click on the T button next to Transparency, and select Cylindrical Image Map from the Texture Image list. Chose CigBurntFilter.iff from the Texture Image list. Click on the Negative Image box to invert the image map. This image will make the burnt tip of the cigarette transparent.

6. Set the Texture Axis to Y-Axis and press the Automatic Sizing button.

7. Deselect Pixel Blend, Height Repeat, and Texture Anitialiasing. Click the Use Texture button and press the T button next to Luminosity.

8. Select Cylindrical Image Map from the Texture Type list, and choose CigBurntLume.iff from the Texture Image list. This will add a nice glowing edge to the burnt cigarette wrapper.

9. Set the Texture Axis to Y-Axis and press the Automatic Sizing button.

10. Deselect Height Repeat and press the Use Texture button.

The burnt cigarette wrapper is now fully surfaced. Close the Surfaces Panel, and you'll see the end of the paper burnt with a red glow on the edge. Render the scene by pressing F9 to get a better look at the object. You should see a photorealistic burnt cigarette as shown in figure 8.17.

FIGURE 8.17

A burnt cigarette created with Luminosity and Transparency maps.

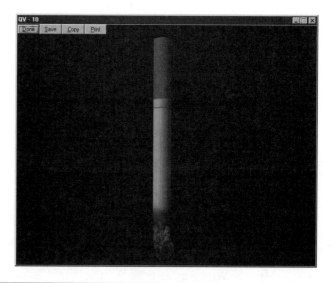

NOTE

The cigarette ashes were created using the Array tool in Modeler. A three-point polygon was created and cloned using the Array tool. Three layers of surfaces were selected to create the different burning stages of the tobacco. The burnt ashes look was created by layering three layers of Fractal Noise in the Surface Color. The size, color, and frequency of each Fractal Noise layer was set to a different value. The result was very convincing photorealistic ashes.

As you can see by the burning cigarette example, the advanced texture effects such as Luminosity and Transparency image maps can create impressive and photorealistic surfaces. Whereas Transparency maps are perfect for a dull object such as cigarette paper, they do have their shortcomings when an object is specular. Now would be a good time to discuss the clip maps and you can use them to make parts of specular objects transparent.

Clip Maps

Clip maps are very similar to Transparency maps, except the clip map works on the entire object whereas Transparency maps work on the individual surface. You assign a clip map in the Objects Panel on the Appearance Options tab. There are a number of reasons to use clip maps, but image mapping is the most common.

There are situations where it is desirable to use a clip map instead of a Transparency map. One advantage of a clip map is that the clipped area will not render in the scene. If you use a Transparency map with a specular surface, the transparent areas will still show specular highlights (even if 100% transparent), as shown in figure 8.18. A clip map will completely remove the clipped area from the render. Clip maps are great for clipping the fins on fish, edges of leaves, or any other object that is specular and needs an irregular edge or hole.

Glass and Index of Refraction

One of the most difficult real-world surfaces to replicate is glass or any other transparent surface. Although it's possible to create settings that mimic glass, you need to consider the most often forgotten aspect of glass: air. Air is a critical part of the index of refraction formula. Index of refraction is the degree at which light is bent as it passes through a transparent object. Glass will bend light as it passes through the surface but the light needs to be corrected on its way out. As light exits the glass surface, it enters air that has a neutral index of refraction. Therefore, to create photorealistic glass, you need to have both glass and air surfaces in the object.

FIGURE 8.18

A Transparency map versus a clip map.

The following exercise will show you how to create a photorealistic glass ashtray by using transparency and index of refraction.

KICK THE HABIT: PART FOUR

1. In Layout, clear the scene and load the Ashtray.lws scene from the companion CD.

2. Open the Surfaces Panel and select Ashtray Glass from the Current Surface list. Enter the following settings for Basic Parameters:

Surface Color	128,128,128
Luminosity	0
Diffuse Level	100
Specularity Level	60
Glossiness	64
Reflectivity	10
Transparency	90
Refractive Index	1.333

This will make the surface transparent like glass. The Refractive Index will bend the light as it enters the glass surface. This is a very important attribute for making realistic glass.

3. Click on the Reflection Options button. Under the Reflection Type list, select Ray Tracing and Spherical Map. Now select the ReflectionMap.iff image from the Reflection Image list, and click the Close Panel button.

There is still one half of a refraction formula missing: air. As light enters the glass, it is refracted at a value of 1.333, but as it exits the glass, it enters the air that is a refraction of 1.0. To make truly photorealistic glass, you need to add an air surface to the ashtray.

4. Click on the Modeler button in the upper-right corner of Layout. In Modeler, press the Get button and select the Ashtray.lwo object. This will import the model from Layout.

5. Copy the Ashtray object and paste it in layer 2. Now press the F button to flip the polygons, and name the surface Glass Air. The Air object should look like figure 8.19.

FIGURE 8.19

The glass ashtray air surface.

6. Select both layers 1 and 2, and press the Put button. Select the Ashtray.lwo object. This exports the model back to Layout.

You have just created the air polygons for the ashtray. Now you need to surface them.

7. Open the Surfaces Panel and select Glass Air from the Current Surface list. Enter the following settings for Basic Parameters:

Surface Color	128,128,128
Luminosity	0
Diffuse Level	0
Specularity Level	75
Glossiness	64
Reflectivity	0
Transparency	95
Refractive Index	1

Now select the Smoothing check box, and enter a value of 89.5 in the Max Smoothing Angle field. You now have the makings of photorealistic glass. Click on the Render button in Layout and select Trace Refraction; then press F9 to see the render scene (see fig. 8.20). For best results, select the Trace Reflections option. It takes a bit longer to render but the result is truly photorealistic.

FIGURE 8.20

A photorealistic glass ashtray created using both a glass and an air surface.

Now there is just one element missing in your smoking scene: the cigarette smoke, which you create with an animated procedural texture.

Animating Procedural Textures

All of LightWave's procedural textures can be animated by placing values in the Texture Velocity parameters. Animatable procedural textures are a cool feature of LightWave, making it possible to create effects that might otherwise be impossible with image maps. You can use animated procedural textures to create realistic gaseous surfaces such as clouds, fog, and smoke. You can also create the other natural effects such as fire and flame. There is no limit to the number of awesome effects you can create using animated procedural textures. One of the easiest and most useful procedural textures to animate is the Fractal Noise texture.

The following exercise will show you how to create photorealistic smoke for the burning cigarette you created in an earlier exercise.

KICK THE HABIT: PART FIVE

1. Open LightWave's Layout and load the Cigarette_Smoke.lws scene file from the companion CD. A smoke object has been parented to the Burnt Cigarette. The shape of the smoke object is critical to making the smoke effect realistic. As the fractal noise travels over the surface, it will change shape simulating wind currents.

2. Open the Images Panel and load the CigaretteSmokeFilter.iff image from the CD.

3. Open the Surfaces Panel and select Cigarette Smoke from the Current Surface list. Enter the following settings for Basic Parameters:

Surface Color	110,110,110
Luminosity	100
Diffuse Level	0
Specularity Level	30
Reflectivity	0
Transparency	100

The Diffuse Level has been set to 0 because you are going to use the Fractal Noise texture for Luminosity to make a wispy smoke. You don't want the object color to be visible—only the smoke. Now select the Double Sided option.

TI P

When surfacing smoke, clouds, or other gaseous objects, you need to use the Double Sided option so the texture is visible on the other side of the object.

4. Click on the T button next to Luminosity, and select Fractal Noise from the Texture Type. Now enter the following properties for Fractal Noise:

Texture Opacity	100
Texture Size	.008,.05,.008
Texture Velocity	.00001,.0005,.00001
Texture Value	0
Frequencies	310
Contrast	1
Small Power	.5

Now click the Use Texture button. This creates a wispy smoke surface that moves upward but travels slightly on the X and Z axes to give it a realistic motion.

5. Select the Additive option. This will add the color of the smoke to the objects behind it.

6. Click on the T button next to Transparency, and select Cylindrical Image Map from the Texture Type list. Choose the CigaretteSmokeFilter.iff image from the Texture Image list and select the Y Texture Axis.

7. Press the Automatic Sizing button. Deselect Height Repeat and Texture Antialiasing.

The image map filters the surface so the smoke is visible closer to the cigarette and fades off as it goes farther away.

8. Press the Add New Texture button and select Fractal Noise from the Texture Type list. Enter the following properties for Fractal Noise:

Texture Opacity	100
Texture Size	.008,.05,.008
Texture Velocity	.00001,.0005,.00001
Texture Value	100
Frequencies	310
Contrast	1
Small Power	.5

This texture will break up the smoke to give it a more natural dissipation.

9. Click the Use Texture button and open the Render Panel. Then select Automatic Frame Advance.

10. Click on the Save Animation button; enter the name **Smoke.avi**, and press Save. Now select Newtek AVI from the Animation Type list and press the Render button. This will create a 60-frame animation of the burning cigarette.

You have just created a photorealistic smoking cigarette. You can adjust the velocity values of the Luminosity and Transparency Fractal Noise to create different effects with the smoke. You can see a raytraced render of this animation in the Smoke.avi file on the companion CD.

You have now completed all the elements in the smoking scene illustrated in figure 8.1. You can load the full smoking scene from the companion CD to see how all these elements come together to make a photorealistic scene.

The following brief exercise will show you what all the elements you have created in the smoking exercises look like when combined in a single photorealistic scene.

KICK THE HABIT: PART SIX

1. Open LightWave's Layout and load the Cigarette_Cigarettes.lws scene file from the companion CD. You'll see a scene such as the one in figure 8.21.

FIGURE 8.21
Fully staged smoking scene.

2.   Press F9 to render a quick test. Your image should look like figure 8.21. You can render the entire scene with the animated smoke by continuing to step 3.

3.   Open the Render Panel and select Automatic Frame Advance. Now Click on the Save Animation button; enter the name **SmokingScene.avi** and press Save. Now select Newtek AVI from the Animation Type list and press the Render button. This will create a 60-frame animation of the burning cigarette in the photorealistic smoking scene. It will take quite a bit of time to render this scene because a great deal of math is involved with interpreting the index of refraction for the ashtray.

As you can see, animated procedural textures can save you a tremendous amount of time you might otherwise spend trying to create animated effects with image maps. This, of course, is just one of the many thousands of possibilities for animated procedural textures. Although it can take a bit of time to test animated procedural textures, the result is well worth the time invested. Another great use for animated procedural textures would be adding animated specularity and reflection to a metal surface to simulate movement in the environment. Be sure to invest some time in experimenting with animated procedural textures.

Using Photoshop to Create LightWave Image Maps

As discussed earlier, image maps are very powerful tools for creating realistic surfaces. Because these maps will need to be edited on your computer, you need a painting program. Photoshop is the first choice of most 3D artists because of its extensive feature list.

Photoshop offers a broad range of tools and capabilities that are fundamental to creating quality image maps. One of the most important features of Photoshop is its capability to manage multiple layers. This is very useful, because it is likely you will need to create layers for diffusion, specularity, and bump maps.

TIP

You should make it a habit to create your texture maps as large as possible. This will make them easier to paint and provides you with a texture for close-up shots. You can resample the image smaller to save memory when the object is not the focal point of the scene.

Creating a Painting Template

To create detailed image maps you need to have an accurate template. Although there are many ways to acquire a template, the most accurate method is to do a screen capture from the Modeler. The Modeler's Edit windows don't add perspective to the view of the mesh, which makes them perfect for capturing the best template for the surface. The following steps show you how to create an image map template.

CREATING PAINTING TEMPLATES WITH PHOTOSHOP

1. Open the Modeler and load the Oil_Can.lwo object from the companion CD.

2. Enlarge the Z-axis Edit window until it occupies the full screen, as shown in figure 8.22.

FIGURE 8.22
Capturing texture templates from Modeler.

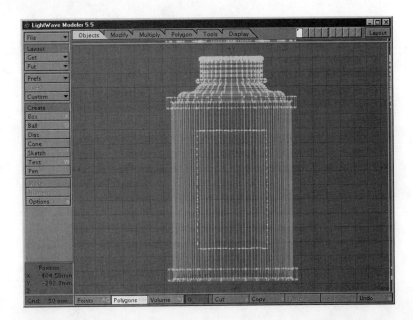

3. Press the Print Screen button, which captures the image to the Clipboard.

4. Load Photoshop and create a new image. (The image size is automatically set for the image on the Clipboard.)

5. Select Paste and your image is added to the background layer in the
Photoshop image.

6. Crop the image around the mesh so it looks like figure 8.23 and add a
new layer.

FIGURE 8.23
Creating texture
templates in
Photoshop.

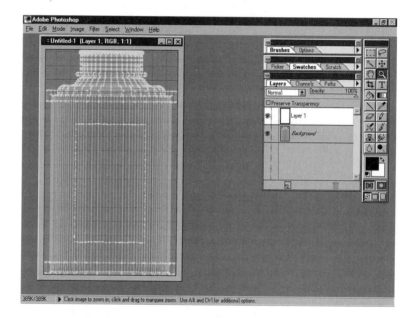

In some cases, the Print Screen feature will fail due to conflicts in Windows
memory management. Another option is to use a screen capture utility.

TIP

For all other platforms (Mac, Amiga, UNIX), I highly recommend you locate a screen capture
utility and use it to capture surface templates.

Because the template created in the previous exercise will be used for a
cylindrical image map, it needs to be sized to the correct width. The following
exercise shows you how to resize the image.

CREATING CYLINDRICAL MAP TEMPLATES IN PHOTOSHOP

1. Select Image Size from the Image menu item.

2. Deselect the Proportions check box. You only want to make the template wider, not taller.

3. Select PERCENT for the Width Value Mode.

4. Enter 325% and press OK. Cylindrical image maps are 325% of the object's diameter.

Now you have an accurately sized cylindrical image map template, which is ready for painting.

TIP

When creating cylinder maps in Photoshop, the width of the map should be 3.25 times the width of the object in your Modeler view.

You can use this same technique to capture templates for all your image map surfaces. Image map templates for the cigarette box in the smoking exercise were captured using the print screen technique. Be sure to resize your screen capture to at least twice its size, so you have an adequate image map for relatively close renders. You should try to make your image maps as large as possible for the master image. You can resample it smaller for renders that don't require close-ups. It's important to note that you can't resample a smaller image to a larger size. This causes pixelation in the image. You always want to resample images smaller.

Another great use for Photoshop is creating bump maps from color images.

Creating Bump Maps in Photoshop

The Layers feature in Photoshop is a wonderful tool for creating bump maps, enabling you to create the bump map and color map in the same file. This makes it significantly easier to keep track of your source files. The strength of the bump effect is determined by the gray values in the bump map image. Because the bump map is based on the color image, it's a good idea to use the color image as the foundation of the bump map.

Photoshop provides you with several tools for creating bump map images from color maps. The main tools are Brightness and Contrast, with Contrast being the most important of the two. Use Contrast to sharpen the difference between the light and dark colors in the bump map. This is important because a color map usually has minimal contrast between the high and low points in the image. Increasing the contrast amplifies the bump effect. This makes the rendered image appear to have a natural 3D surface texture.

In the following exercise you'll use Photoshop to create the bump map from the cigarette tobacco color map used in the smoking scene.

CREATING BUMP MAPS FROM COLOR MAPS

1. Open Photoshop and Load the TobaccoColor.tga image from the companion CD.

2. Duplicate the color layer in Photoshop and rename it Bump Map.

3. Open the Hue/Saturation Tools Panel from the Image, Adjust menu. Reduce the Saturation level to -100 as shown in figure 8.24 and press OK. Because bump maps use gray tones to represent values, the bump maps should be gray. This will also make the file size significantly smaller, which saves memory.

FIGURE 8.24

Creating bump maps in Photoshop.

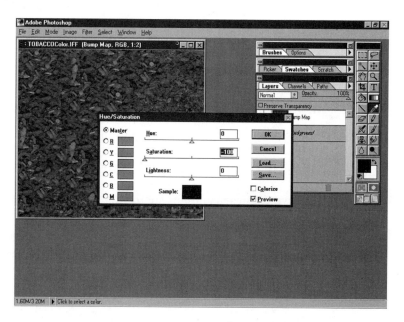

4. Open the Brightness/Contrast Tools Panel from the Image, Adjust menu. Set the Brightness to +13 and the Contrast to +60, as shown in figure 8.25. This will sharpen the contrast between colors, which makes the bump more prominent. Because the source image was dark, you needed to increase the brightness. Typically, you'll want to increase the contrast by a value of 20–30 and reduce the brightness by 10–15.

FIGURE 8.25

Adjusting the contrast of bump maps.

To save only the Bump Map layer, select Save Copy from the File menu. This will save a copy of the image as you see it in the view window. It's always a good idea to save the layered Photoshop file in case you need to make changes in the future.

NOTE

You can create diffusion, specularity, reflection, and transparency maps using the same technique.

As you can see, it's fairly simple to create bump maps from existing color maps. But where do you get the color image maps? Well, there are a number of possibilities. You can find them in texture libraries, photo libraries, and even on the World Wide Web. Of course, there are times when you can't find the perfect texture in these resources so you'll need to use the final method: scanning.

Scanning Textures

Another powerful tool in your texturing arsenal is a 24-bit scanner. A scanner enables you to scan images from pictures and books to use as a painting template in Photoshop, or possibly a source of sampling textures for cloning. Frequently, you can use the texture from one object to surface a completely different object. Figure 8.26 illustrates how a crab shell texture makes a wonderful photoreal fruit skin. The most important tip for textures is to use your imagination. Don't limit yourself to assuming that a driftwood texture is only good for driftwood when it actually makes a great surface for dead palm leaves.

FIGURE 8.26

Photorealistic fruit from a crab shell texture scan.

In the case of the cigarette box, images were scanned from an actual box and then retouched in Photoshop to make them unique. The same technique was used to capture the image map for the cigarette. You need to be creative when finding solutions for your surfacing needs. The image map for the tobacco showing at the end of the cigarette was created by spreading the tobacco from several cigarettes on a scanner. You can apply the same technique to scanning many other surfaces that can be difficult to illustrate.

T I P

When scanning loose objects for surfacing such as tobacco and dirt, you must avoid closing the scanner door. This will flatten the loose objects and it will look artificial as an image map.

Additional Resources

Creating realistic surfaces requires an abundance of quality source material, including the following:

- *Ultimate Visual Dictionary*
  Publisher: Dorling Kindersley
  ISBN: 156458640

  Over 5,000 color photographs of everything from the inside of a golf ball to the surface of the sun, from the skeleton of a platypus to the anatomy of an elephant. This book is an awesome visual reference.

- *The Eyewitness Book Series*
  Publisher: Dorling Kindersley

  There are 84 books in this series that are saturated with high-quality photos of objects. Each book in the series covers a different subject, such as Fish, Pirates, Reptiles, Oceans, Plants, and more.

- *The Macmillan Visual Dictionary*
  Publisher: Macmillan Publishing
  ISBN: 0-02-528160-7

  This book features over 3,500 full-color illustrations covering a wide variety of objects.

Summary

You now have a basic understanding of the powerful texture and material tools in LightWave 5.5. You've created procedural textures, image mapped surfaces, animated textures, and created several advanced special effects with textures. The following topics were covered in depth:

- Procedural textures
- Images maps
- Advanced texture effects
- Animating procedural textures
- Using Photoshop to create image maps

Now it's just a matter of experimentation to unleash the surfacing possibilities. Remember, textures and materials can make your models appear very realistic. They make the difference between an image that looks like it was generated in a 3D program and one that is convincingly real.

Chapter 9

MANAGING TEXTURES AND MATERIALS

LightWave 5.5 has many advanced features for animating textures and materials. There are cases where static textures won't do the job. This is when you need to unlock the power of animated textures and displacement maps.

This chapter will explain the advanced texture animation and displacement map features in LightWave 5.5. You'll learn the following:

- Animating textures with Reference objects

- Creating surface morphing effects

- Animating texture alpha masks

- Using displacement maps

- Incorporating image sequences in your animations

- Using the Effector Displacement plug-in

As with every aspect of LightWave, understanding how to animate textures and materials is essential for producing high-quality work. The tutorials in this chapter will touch on several uses for animating textures and displacement maps, but there are literally thousands of possibilities. You are encouraged to experiment with the techniques described and modify them to create your own unique effects.

Animating Textures with Reference Objects

One of the best new features in LightWave 5.5 is the Reference object. As described in Chapter 8, "Textures and Materials," the Reference object is a null object (or any other object) that is used as a point of reference for modifying image map textures. In effect, the texture is parented to the Reference object. Because the textures are parented to an object, you can animate the object, and the textures will mirror the changes made to the object. With Reference objects, you can move, rotate, size, and stretch the image map texture interactively. To properly use this feature, you must have the Preview mode set to OpenGL textures.

The following exercise will show you how to use a Reference object to move a cartoon character's eyes.

WHICH WAY DID HE GO? PART ONE

1. Open LightWave's Layout and clear the scene.

2. Open the Options Panel and select the Layout View tab.

3. Click on the Use OpenGL and OpenGL textures boxes.

4. Select the 128×128 option in the Texture Resolution list, and press the Close Panel button.

5. Load the Crazy_Cat_Eyes.lwo object on the companion CD. You should have a scene with a cat character in the center as shown in figure 9.1.

FIGURE 9.1

Animating textures with Reference objects.

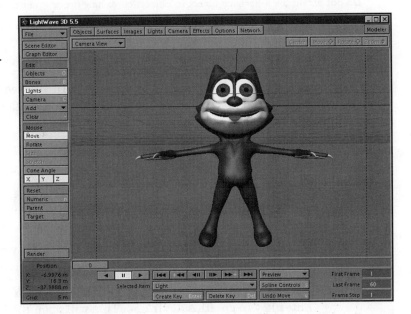

6. Open the Surfaces Panel and select Crazy Cat Eye Right from the Current Surface list. Then click on the T button next to the Surface Color indicator.

7. Click on the Add Reference Object button. This will add a null Reference object for the eye texture. Press the Use Texture button and repeat the previous steps for the Crazy Cat Eye Left surface.

8. Close the Surfaces Panel. The Reference object should be selected. If not, select it from the Selected Item list at the bottom of the screen.

9. Click on the Move button, hold down the right mouse button, and drag the Reference object up slightly. Holding down the right mouse button contains the movement to the Y-axis. When the screen refreshes, the eyes should have moved up.

10. Hold down the right mouse button again and drag the Reference object down. The eyes have moved down. Take a moment to move the Reference object along the X and Y axes to get a feel for the eye movement.

WARNING

Do not parent the Reference object to objects containing the referenced surfaces. This will cause the referenced textures to move whenever the object is moved.

Parenting your textures to a Reference object is a very quick and effective means for animating textured eye movement. To see this technique in action, perform the next exercise. This exercise will show you how to use a Reference object to animate the character's eyes.

WHICH WAY DID HE GO? PART TWO

1. Make sure you are in frame 1 of the sequence. The numbered bar, under the display window, indicates the current frame.

2. Drag the Reference object until the iris is in the lower-left corner of the eyes.

3. Press the Create Key button to create a keyframe. You can also press the Enter key to create a keyframe. This will open the Create Motion Key Panel. This is where you determine the keyframe and which objects you want to keyframe. The number in the Create a Key at box will automatically have the frame number entered for the current frame selected. The Selected Item button should automatically be selected but, if it isn't, go ahead and click on it. You can create a keyframe for all the objects, but that wouldn't be necessary because you are only moving the Reference object. Press the OK button.

4. Drag the Frame Number bar to the right until it reads frame 10. You can also press the f key to bring up the Go to Frame Panel where you can enter the target frame.

5. Move the Reference object until the iris is at the top of the eye. Press the Enter key and select the OK button in the Create Motion Key Panel.

6. Press the f key, set the frame number to **20**, and press OK. Now move the Reference object until the iris is in the lower-right corner of the eye and press Enter to create the keyframe.

Because you will be making a looping animation, you'll want the first and last frames to be the same position. The fastest way to do this is to go back to frame 1 and press Enter. Then enter **30** in the Create a Key at field and select the All Items button. Now press the OK button. This will copy the frame 1 settings to frame 30.

It's now time to render the animation to see the results.

7. Click on the Render button. Make sure the Render First frame value is set to 1 and the Render Last Frame value is 29. You don't want to render frame 30 in the animation since it is the same as frame 1.

8. Select the Save Animation button, chose the target directory for the animation, and enter the name **Eyes.avi**. Press OK.

NOTE

You must enter the .avi extension after the file name on PC systems. The program will not do it for you. If you do not enter the extension, the file will still be saved but you won't be able to open it until you add the extension.

9. Select LW_NewTek-AVI from the Animation Type list. This will save the animation as an AVI file. AVI files are good for previewing a test animation. When you are ready for the final animation, you should output the file as single frames. This assures you that the output is editable and decompressed.

10. Press the Begin Rendering button. This will open the Video Compression Panel. Select Full Frames (UNCOMPRESSED) and press OK. LightWave will begin rendering the frames. It will take a couple minutes to complete the render. When it's done, you will have an animation of the cat's eyes rolling around in circles. You can load the CatEyes.avi file on the companion CD to see a rendered animation of this exercise.

This was a simple example of using animated textures with a Reference object. The next section talks about how to create surface morphing effects.

Creating Surface Morphing Effects

Surface morphing morphs the surface attributes and textures between two objects. Because it's an object morphing option, you need to create morph targets. If you are just planning to morph the surfaces, you can use a copy of the same model. Be sure to change the surface names on the morph target model. If the surface names remain source models, surfaces will be changed to the target object's surfaces when it's loaded.

To create surface morph targets, load the object in Modeler, and select and rename all the surfaces. It's best to start the surface name with the word Target. For example, Crazy Cat Head would be renamed to Target Head. This will help you identify the surfaces in Layout. It will also put them all together when you sort the Current Surface list alphabetically. When you are done changing the surfaces, save the object with a different name.

Surface morphing can produce some very exciting effects, which would be difficult to create any other way. One excellent use for surface morphing is to transform a mild-mannered character into a super hero.

The following exercise will show you how to use surface morphing to transform Crazy Cat into the super hero PAWN, as shown in figure 9.2. To make the transformation more interesting, the target object's mesh was modified so there would be a change in the character's physique.

FIGURE 9.2
Surface morphing the cat into the super hero PAWN.

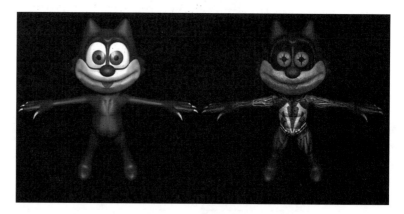

THE BIRTH OF PAWN! PART ONE

1. Open LightWave's Layout and Load the Crazy_Cat.lwo object on the companion CD. You should have a scene with a cat character in the center.

2. Open the Objects Panel and load the Pawn_Surfaced.lwo object from the companion CD by clicking on the Load Object button. It will take a minute to load all the image maps for the object.

3. Select the Crazy Cat object from the Current Object list. Now select the Pawn Surfaced object from the Morph Target list in the Deformations tab. This indicates that you will be morphing the Crazy Cat object into the Pawn Surfaced object.

4. Click on the Morph Surfaces check box. If this isn't checked, only the mesh will morph.

5. Click on the E button next to the Morph Amount field. This opens the Morph Envelope Panel. Envelopes are used to modify the effects over time. In the case of the morph, you will be creating keyframes for the morph transitions.

6. Set the Current Value to 0. Click on the Create button, enter **20**, and press OK. This creates a key at frame 20. Now set the Current Value to **100**.

7. Repeat step 6 and create the following key frames and values:

Key Frame	Value
40	100%
60	0%
80	0%

This envelope gradually morphs the Crazy Cat into Pawn Surfaced from frame 0–20. Then reverses the morph from frames 40–60. The result is a looping animation of Crazy Cat morphing into Pawn Surfaced and back again.

8. Press the Use Envelope button and select Pawn Surfaced from the Current Object list.

9. When morphing objects, you want to make the target object invisible so it doesn't render in the scene. You do this by setting the Object Dissolve value to 100%. Click on the Appearance Options Panel and enter **100** in the Object Dissolve field. Now press the Close Panel button.

You are now ready to test the animation. Because you are morphing surfaces, you will need to render the test animation. The Preview mode will only work on wireframe and solid shaded tests.

10. Click on the Render button. Make sure the Render First frame value is set to 1 and the Render Last Frame value is 59. You don't want to render frame 60 in the animation because it is the same as frame 1. Select the Save Animation button, chose the target directory for the animation, and enter the name **Morph.avi**. Press OK.

11. Select LW_NewTek-AVI from the Animation Type list. This will save the animation as an AVI file.

12. Press the Begin Rendering button. This will open the Video Compression Panel. Select Full Frames (UNCOMPRESSED) and press OK. LightWave will begin rendering the frames. It will take several minutes to complete the render. When it's done, you will have an animation of the Crazy Cat character morphing into his super hero counterpart PAWN. You can load the Morph.avi file on the companion CD to see a rendered animation of this exercise.

The morphing effect is impressive because you not only see the surfaces morph, but there is a distinct model morphing as well. You can stop here but you can make it even more impressive by adding a laser beam, which initiates the transformation.

To create the laser beam, you can use a light source with a shadow map to create a narrow beam, but the effect on the model will not be very distinct. The best way to create the laser beam is to actually map the effect to the model's surfaces. This is done by using texture alpha masks.

Animating Texture Alpha Masks

Texture alpha masks act as a transparency channel for the texture. They make the texture transparent based on grayscale values in the image. White would be opaque and black would be completely transparent. Alpha masks affect only the texture for which they are assigned and have no impact on the other textures for the surface. You assign a texture alpha mask in the Texture Panel where you select the Texture Image. A popular use for alpha masks is applying decals to objects such as labels and signs. You can also use alpha masks when creating animated texture effects.

LightWave 5.5 makes alpha mask animation simple through the use of Reference objects. You assign a Reference object to an alpha mask texture the same way you did with the Crazy Cat eyes in the first exercise. In effect, the alpha mask texture is parented to the Reference object. Since the textures are parented to an object, you can animate the object and the alpha mask texture will mirror the changes made to the object.

The following exercise will show you how to use alpha masks and Reference objects to create an animated laser beam signature, which prompts the morphing of Crazy Cat into the super hero PAWN. This is an advanced effect that requires a bit of repetitive work but it's well worth the time. You will be adding a light beam texture to all the surfaces so it can be animated.

THE BIRTH OF PAWN! PART TWO

1. Open LightWave's Layout and load the Pawn_Morph_with_FX.lws scene on the companion CD. You should have a scene with a cat character in the center. This scene is identical to the one you created in the previous exercise.

2. Open the Images Panel and load the Lit001.TGA image from the companion CD by clicking on the Load Image button. Now open the Surfaces Panel and select Crazy Cat Body from the Current Surface list.

3. Click on the T button next to Surface Color and select Planar Image from the Texture Type list. Chose the Lit001.TGA image from the Texture Image list and select the Z-Axis as the Texture Axis. Now select the Lit001.TGA image from the Texture Alpha Image list. The alpha texture is used to filter the Texture Image. In this case, you only want the light beam to be visible on the object's surface.

4. Click on the Add Reference Object button. You will be animating this texture so it needs a Reference object.

The key to making this effect work is sizing the light beam texture so it covers the width of the body. The Crazy Cat Body surface represents the full height and width of the object, so it makes sense to add the texture to this surface first so you can determine the proper size for the Lit001.TGA texture.

5. Click the Automatic Sizing button and then click on Texture Size. Because you will be entering these values a number of times, you should round them off. Change the settings to **13.5**, **12.9**, and **8.5**. Now write these numbers down because you will use them frequently.

6. Deselect Width Repeat, Height Repeat, and Texture Antialiasing. Press the Use Texture button.

7. Click on the T button next to Luminosity and select Planar Image from the Texture Type list. Chose the Lit001.TGA image from the Texture Image list and select the Z Axis as the Texture Axis.

8. Click on the Texture Size and enter the settings you wrote down from the previous texture: **13.5**, **12.9**, and **8.5**. Press the Use Texture button. This will make the light beam 100% luminous on the surface.

9. Now select Ref Obj from the Texture Reference object list. You want the luminosity texture parented to the same Reference object as the image texture so they move together.

10. Add the Lit001.TGA texture to the Surface Color and Luminosity of ALL the surfaces. Be sure to include the Alpha Texture in the Surface Color and always set the Texture size to 13.5, 12.9, and 8.5. As you add the textures, you need to select the Ref Obj as the Texture Reference object. All the surfaces need to have the same texture so the beam appears to move across the body as it's animated. Some surfaces already have a texture in the Surface Color so you'll need to click on the Add New Texture button to add a texture layer.

11. Once you have applied the texture to ALL the surfaces, click the Close Panel button. The Reference object should be selected and located in the middle of the head where the Object origin is located. The Lit001.TGA texture was created so it would line up with the Object origin. This makes it easier to key frame the animation.

12. Press the F9 key to render a preview of the scene. You should have an image of Crazy Cat with a white beam across his face as shown in figure 9.3. Now it's time to keyframe the animation.

13. Drag the Frame Indicator to frame 1. Select the Move button and drag the Reference object just below the cat's feet by holding down the right mouse button. Press Enter to create the keyframe (assuming auto-key adjust is off).

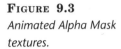

FIGURE 9.3
Animated Alpha Mask textures.

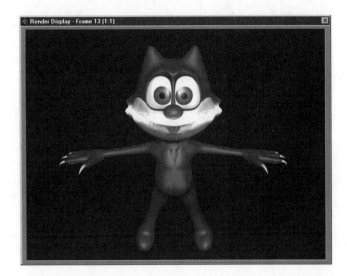

14. Press the f key, enter **20**, and click on OK. Drag the Reference object up to a position just over the cat's head, and press Enter to make the key-frame. This will move the beam up Crazy Cat's body while he morphs into PAWN.

15. Press the f key, enter **40**, and click on OK. Press Enter to create a key-frame. You want the light beam to pause for a few frames before it moves down to transform PAWN back into Crazy Cat.

16. Click on the Graph Editor button. This will open the Motion Graph Panel for the current object selected, which is the Reference object.

17. Click on the Copy/Paste button. In the Copy/Paste Keys Panel, enter **1** for the Low Frame, **1** for the High Frame, and **60** for Paste Frames at. This will copy the settings in frame 1 to frame 60 for a seamless looping animation. Press the OK button and then press the Use Motion button.

18. Press the f key, enter **80**, and click on OK. Press Enter to create a key-frame. This will create a pause at the bottom, before the beam heads back up and changes Crazy Cat into PAWN. Now it's time to preview the animation.

19. Click on the Render button. Make sure the Render First frame value is set to 1 and the Render Last Frame value is 79. You don't want to render frame 80 in the animation because it is the same as frame 1. Select the Save Animation button, chose the target directory for the animation, and enter the name **MorphFX.avi**. Press OK.

You can load the MorphFX.avi file on the companion CD to see a rendered animation of this exercise.

It took a bit of time to stage the laser morphing beam effect but the result is worth it. As you can see, animating alpha masks can be a very effective method for creating effects that might otherwise be impossible to create. You can use animated alpha masks to create a number of surface effects such as plasma weapon blasts on a starship. The most popular use for animated alpha masks is compositing explosions into 3D scenes. This is accomplished by using an explosion image sequence combined with an alpha mask image sequence that crops the area around the explosion. The alpha mask ensures that only the explosion will be seen, and not the rest of the area in the image map. You'll learn more about how to use image sequences later in this chapter.

You've just used several techniques for animating an object's surface attributes. Now it's time to take a look at techniques for animating the object's physical shape. The most common technique for animating the objects mesh is displacement maps.

Using Displacement Maps

As with bump maps, the grayscale values in a displacement map determine the height of the effect. The advantage of a displacement map is that it actually alters the physical shape of the object by moving the points. Bump maps affect only the surface of the object, which makes them inadequate for creating major physical changes in an object.

Figure 9.4 shows how displacement maps and bump maps compare. The first image shows how a displacement map was used to depress the land under the rock. It's a very convincing effect because the mesh is actually deformed. The second image shows the same effect using a bump map. Even though the bump setting was set to 2,500%, it still doesn't come close to the natural look of the displacement mapped image.

Displacement maps are the best choice for situations where you need a dramatic change in the appearance of objects such as ocean waves, terrain, or something as common as curtains blowing in the breeze, which you will create in the coming exercise.

FIGURE 9.4
Displacement maps compared to bump maps.

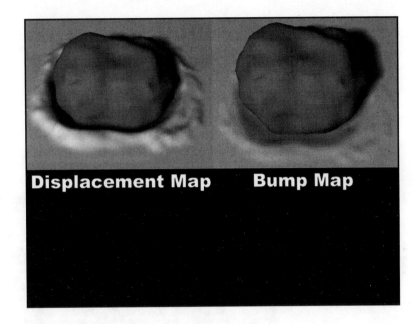

TIP

Since displacement maps alter the shape of the object, it's necessary to use objects with a large number of points and polygons. You will also need to triple the mesh to prevent nonplanar polygon errors that can occur when the mesh is displaced.

Animating Displacement Maps

Displacement maps are useful tools for animating the mesh of an object. There are many situations where a simple bump map cannot create the realistic depth needed for an effect.

With the OpenGL display mode selected, load the Curtain.lws scene on the companion CD. You should have a scene with curtains, as shown in figure 9.5.

ANIMATING THE CURTAINS

1. Open the Objects Panel and click on the T button next to Displacement Map in the Deformation tab.

2. Select Fractal Bumps from the Texture Type list and enter the following
    properties:

Texture Opacity	100
Texture Size	.35,.35,.35
Texture Falloff	0,110,0
Texture Center	0,-1,0
Texture Velocity	.001,.001,.2
Texture Amplitude	.2
Frequencies	3

FIGURE 9.5

*The Curtian.lws scene
ready to be animated.*

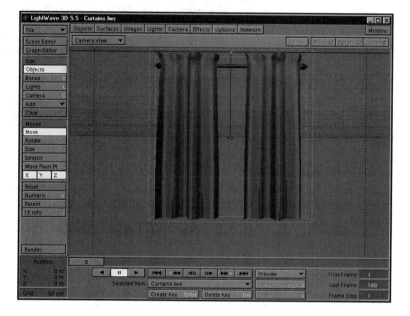

The challenge of animating the curtains with fractal bumps is to prevent
the top of the curtains from moving. To do this, you set the Texture
Falloff, which determines the point at which the texture falls off and
becomes nonexistent. This value is expressed as the percentage of falloff
for every unit of distance moving away from the Texture Center. A unit
in LightWave is one meter. Because the curtains are 1 meter tall, the
Falloff was set to 110%. The extra 10% was used to move the falloff well
below the curtain bar.

Because the object's origin is at the top of the curtains, the Texture
Center was set to -1 on the Y-axis to move it to the bottom. If you had not
done this, the falloff would have occurred above the object because falloff
is applied in a positive direction from the Texture Center.

Texture velocity was applied to animate the Fractal Bumps. A greater value was used for the Z-axis to simulate the wind blowing the curtains away from the wall (toward the camera). Small X- and Y-axis values were used to randomize the movement slightly for a more natural effect.

The Texture Amplitude determines the intensity of the effect. This value is measured in meters. Because the curtains are only 1 meter tall, the Texture Amplitude is set low to keep the curtains' shape from being moved too far.

3. Click the Use Texture button and close the Objects Panel. The lower part of your curtains are now deformed, as shown in figure 9.6.

FIGURE 9.6

Curtains with Fractal displacement map applied.

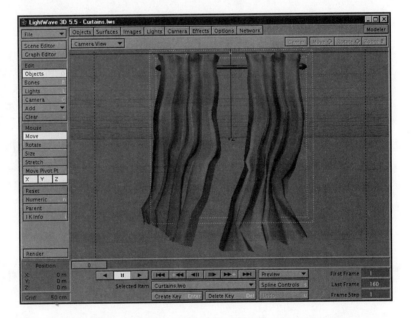

Now that you have animated a displacement map, you need to preview it to make sure you have created the desired effect. This is accomplished by making a preview of the animation.

4. Click on the Preview button in the lower right of the Layout screen and select Make Preview. The Make Preview Panel will appear in Layout. This panel is used to set the frame sequence you want to preview and the viewing mode to use. There are three modes for previewing animations: Bounding Box, which shows only a bounding box for the objects; Wireframe, which shows a wireframe view of the models; and OpenGL

Color Preview, which shows a color-shaded preview of the models. It's best to use Wireframe when previewing displacement animations because you will need to see the changes in the mesh.

5.   Select the Wireframe button and press OK.

NOTE

You should always use Wireframe mode when creating previews of displacement map animations. The Bounding Box mode will not show the model and the OpenGL mode will likely cause your system to crash because of excessive memory use.

It will take about a minute to generate the animation. You should see the wireframe in the view window changing. When the program is finished generating the preview, it will display the Preview Playback Controls Panel. This panel is used to play the preview. You can set the playback speed by clicking on the numbered buttons. The speed is automatically set to the Frames Per Second setting for the scene as indicated in the Scene Editor.

Press the Forward arrow to play the preview. You should see the lower part of the curtains blowing in the wind while the top remains unchanged. You can see a rendered animation of the curtains by viewing the Curtains.avi file on the companion CD. You can adjust the Texture Velocity and Texture Size to create different wind effects. Remember, the higher the velocity, the faster the curtains will move.

Displacement maps, like texture maps, can animate a Reference object. This Reference object can be animated to create some amazing effects.

Animating Displacement Maps with a Reference Object

You can parent a displacement map to a Reference object like any other texture. This makes for some powerful possibilities, particularly when you need an object in the scene to interact with another.

The following exercise will show you how to use a Reference object to animate a displacement map. In the exercise, you will be using the displacement map to literally lift a carpet up so a motorized mouse can crawl underneath. While the mouse is underneath, the carpet will deform to the shape of the mouse. Figure 9.7 shows a frame of the animation you will be creating in this exercise.

FIGURE 9.7
Animating displacement maps with a Reference object.

CATCH THE MOUSE! PART ONE

1. Open Layout and load the Rug.lws scene from the companion CD. You should have a scene with a carpet and robot mouse in the middle.

2. Open the Images Panel and load the following image from the CD-ROM: MouseDis.iff. You will see an image like the one in figure 9.8.

You can see the variations in shades of gray take on the shape of the robot mouse. The tips of the ears are full white because they need to be the highest point of the displacement so the mouse's ears can move under the carpet. The map is also a little chaotic so the displacement looks natural.

3. Open the Objects Panel, select the Carpet.low from the Current Object list, and press the T button next to Displacement Map in the Deformations tab.

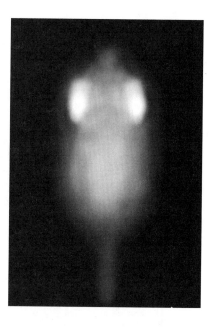

4. Select Planar Image Map from the Texture Type list, and chose the MouseDis.iff image from the Texture Image list. Choose the Y-Axis for Texture Axis and enter the following parameters:

Texture Opacity	90
Texture Size	1.25,.514,2.18
Texture Center	0,0,0
Texture Amplitude	.5

This will create a displacement that is the size of the robotic Mouse object. The amplitude has been set to .5 so the displacement is the height of the robotic mouse.

5. Press the Add a Reference Object button, and deselect Width Repeat and Height Repeat. Press the Use Texture button.

6. Close the Objects Panel. The screen will take a moment to refresh, and you'll see a displacement in the middle of the carpet that takes on the form of the robotic mouse. The Mouse object should be hidden under the carpet deformation, as shown in figure 9.9.

7. Select Mouse.lwo from the Selected Item list. Press the Parent button on the left side of the screen, select Ref Obj from the list in the Parent Object Panel, and press OK. This is a very important step. In effect, it locks the displacement map to the Mouse object. To see the benefit of

this step, select Ref Obj from the Selected Item list, and move it around the carpet in the X and Z axes. As you move the mouse, the carpet mesh is deformed to the shape of the mouse underneath. Now move the Ref Obj to the edge of the carpet. You'll see the back side of the mouse protruding from under the carpet as in figure 9.10.

FIGURE 9.9
The carpet deformed with the Mouse displacement map.

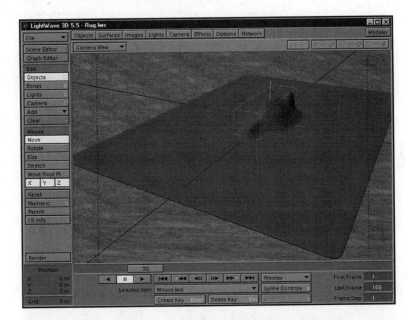

FIGURE 9.10
Carpet deformed with Reference object–controlled displacement map.

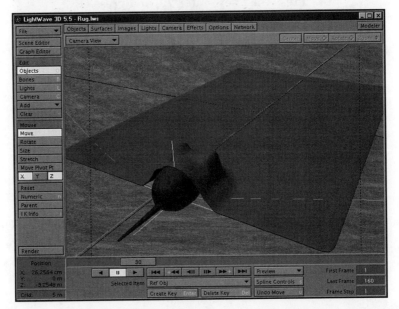

This is the key element to making the effect believable. As you move the Reference object over the carpet, the carpet mesh is actually lifted up so the mouse can go underneath. Now it's time to animate the Reference object to make the scene come to life.

8. Select frame 1 by moving the numbered frame bar to the right. Click on the Move button, and then press the Numeric button. This will open the Object Position Panel.

9. Enter the coordinates **-4.5,0,-1.65**, and press OK. This will move the mouse off to the left side of the screen.

10. Now press the Rotate button and press the n key on your keyboard. This is another way to open the Objects Panel.

11. Enter the values **90,0,0** in the Object Direction Panel and press OK. This will rotate the mouse so it faces the carpet. You are going to move the mouse under the carpet from left to right. Press the Enter key to create a keyframe.

12. Press the f key, enter **60**, and press OK. This moves the animation to frame 60 where you will create another keyframe.

13. Click on the Move button and press the n key. Enter the coordinates **3.31,0,-1.65**, and press OK. This moves the mouse to the right side of the carpet. Press the Enter key to create a keyframe.

14. Press the f key, enter **70**, and press OK.

15. Click on the Move button and then press the n key.

16. Enter the coordinates **-3.65,0,10.72**, and press OK. This moves the mouse to the far side of the carpet.

17. Now press the Rotate button and press the n key. Enter the values **180,0,0**, in the Object Direction Panel and press OK. This will rotate the mouse so it faces the camera. You are going to move the mouse under the carpet from the far side to the near side.

18. Press the f key, enter **160**, and press OK.

19. Click on the Move button and press the n key.

20. Enter the coordinates **-3.65,0,-5.72**, and press OK. This moves the mouse to the near side of the carpet. Press the Enter key to create a keyframe.

21. Now it's time to preview the animation. Press the Preview button and select Preview. Make sure the First Frame is 1 and the Last Frame is 160.

22. Chose Wireframe and press OK. It will take several minutes to render the preview. When it's done, rendering the Preview Playback Controls Panel will appear.

23. Press the Forward arrow to preview the animation. You'll see the mouse move from left to right under the carpet and then from the far side to the near side. Notice how the mesh of the carpet deforms to the shape of the mouse as it moves. Now it's time to render the animation so you can see the full effect of the displacement.

24. Click on the Render button. Make sure the Render First Frame value is set to 1 and the Render Last Frame value is 160.

25. Select the Save Animation button, chose the target directory for the animation, and enter the name **Rug.avi**. Press OK.

You can load the Rug.avi file on the companion CD to see a rendered animation of this exercise.

As you can see, animating displacement maps with a Reference object can create very impressive effects. There are a number of uses for displacement maps animated with Reference objects. You can use them to make creatures crawl under your character's skin, a gopher hole pop up in the grass, or even creatures slither under the sand. There are countless uses for displacement maps animated with Reference objects.

While animated displacement maps are great for creating major deformations of an object, you just can't create fine details with them because the mesh would need to be unbelievably dense. You'll encounter situations where you want smaller details to accompany the major ones you created with the displacement map. In these situations, you'll want to use a bump map that is animated with the same Reference object you used for the displacement map.

Using Bump Maps with Displacement Maps

Displacement maps are best for creating large effects, but bump maps are better for creating the smaller details. In the previous carpet animation, the displacement map is perfect for making the mouse-shaped deformation, but there is something missing from the scene that's essential for making it appear realistic. The deformation in the carpet is too smooth. The carpet would actually wrinkle a bit as the mouse moves. This is where a bump map is the perfect choice.

The following exercise will show you how to use a bump map with a Reference object to create small wrinkles in the carpet.

CATCH THE MOUSE! PART TWO

1. With the Rug.lws scene open, load the CarpetWrinkle.iff image from the companion CD.

2. Open the Surfaces Panel and select Carpet from the Current Surfaces list. Now press the T button next to Bump Map and press the Add New Texture button.

3. Select Planar Image Map from the Textures Type list and choose the CarpetWrinkle.iff image from the Texture Image list. Select Y-Axis for the Texture Axis and enter the following properties:

Texture Opacity	100
Texture Size	2,1,3
Texture Amplitude	500

This will create a bump map slightly larger than the mouse.

4. Select the Ref Obj from the Texture Reference object list. This will link the bump map to the displacement map and mouse.

5. Deselect Width Repeat and Height Repeat. Press the Use Texture button. Now you are ready to render the animation to preview the new effect.

6. Click on the Render button. Make sure the Render First Frame value is set to 1 and the Render Last Frame value is 160. Select the Save Animation button, chose the target directory for the animation, and enter the name **Rug2.avi**. Press OK. Make sure you change the file name so you don't overwrite the previous animation.

You can load the Rug2.avi file on the companion CD to see a rendered animation of this exercise.

As you can see, there are some very amazing effects you can create with displacement maps. Now that you have used displacement maps to animate, you are ready to explore their second use: modeling.

Using Displacement Maps as a Modeling Tool

One major advantage of displacement maps is that they change the physical mesh, which makes them ideal for modeling organic shapes such as terrain. Most of the time, displacement maps are used to create terrain, but they can be used to create other organic shapes that would be more time-consuming to create in Modeler. One example of a good use of displacement map modeling would be creating a flowing fabric look for a super hero's cape.

The following exercise will show you how to create a natural flowing super hero cape using a Fractal Bump displacement map.

Up, Up, and Away!

1. Open Layout and load the Pawn_Cape.lwo object from the companion CD. You should see a flat cape, as shown in figure 9.11.

FIGURE 9.11
Modeling PAWN's cape with displacement maps.

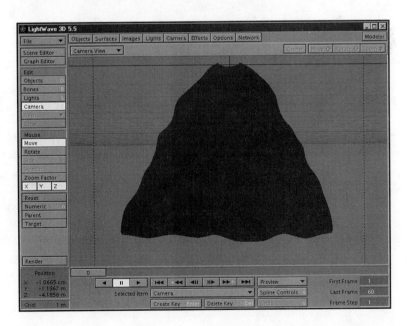

2. Open the Objects Panel and click on the T button next to Displacement Map in the Deformations tab. Now select Fractal Bumps from the Texture Type list and enter the following properties:

Texture Opacity	100
Texture Size	.5,.5,.5
Texture Falloff	0,50,0
Texture Center	0,-2,0
Texture Velocity	.1,.1,.2
Texture Amplitude	.2
Frequencies	3

This effect is very similar to the Curtain exercise. You want to make the lower part of the cape billowing and the upper part unaffected. The Texture Falloff is set to 50% on the Y-axis because the cape is 2 meters tall. You want the texture to fall off 50% for every meter, which makes it vanish at 2 meters. The texture Center is moved to -2 on the Y-axis so the texture will fall off at the top of the cape.

3. Press the Use Texture button and close the Objects Panel. You should see a deformed cape, as shown in figure 9.12.

FIGURE 9.12

Super hero cape modeled with displacement maps.

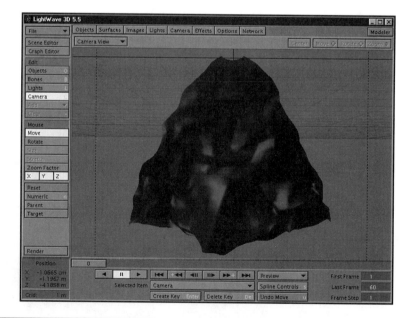

This effect would have taken much longer to create in the Modeler. Now you need to save the new cape. Open the Objects Panel and click on the Save Transformed button. This will save the displaced object. Be sure to enter a new name or you will overwrite the original cape file.

WARNING

When saving a transformed object, be sure to enter a different file name or you will overwrite the original object.

There are unlimited uses for displacement map modeling. You can use it to create depressions in the ground where a spaceship has landed, footprints for a T-Rex, the area of impact for a meteor, and so on. Take some time to experiment with displacement map modeling. You'll find it can be a real time-saver.

Now that you have created a super hero cape, it's time to put it to good use. In the next section, you'll learn to animate the cape effect with the PAWN super hero character.

Incorporating Image Sequences in Your Animations

Image sequences are basically an animation that has been saved in sequential frames. Image sequences can add a great deal of depth to an animation. To load an image sequence, open the Images Panel and press the Load Sequence button. You can click on any image in the sequence to load the whole sequence. The sequence must end in digits, for example: Fir0001.tga. Once you have loaded the sequence, you can press the Loop Sequence button, which will automatically loop the sequence if your scenes' frame counts exceed the number of images in the sequence.

Image sequences are commonly used to add clouds, smoke, fire, explosions, and other natural effects to scenes. You can create a realistic TV by placing an image sequence on the screen to simulate a TV show. While image sequences are most often used as animated backgrounds, they are very useful as animated reflection maps. An animated reflection map adds realism to a scene by simulating motion in the environment.

The following exercise will show you how to use image sequences as an animated background and a reflection map. You will be creating the animated logo for the PAWN super hero character shown in figure 9.13.

FIGURE 9.13

Using image sequences to create powerful visuals like the PAWN scene.

CREATING THE PAWN LOGO

1. Open Layout and load the PAWN_Logo.lws scene from the companion CD.

2. Open the Images Panel and load the Fir001.tga sequence from the companion CD.

3. Open the Effects Panel and select the Compositing tab. Select Fir (sequence) from the Background Image list. This will place the animated sequence in the background of the scene. Close the panel.

4. Open the Surfaces Panel and select the Logo Back surface from the Current Surface list. Click on the Reflection Options button next to Reflectivity and select Fir (sequence) from the Reflection Image list. This will create an animated reflection of fire on the back of the PAWN logo. A small level of luminosity was added to the surface to make the object appear as if it is being illuminated by the fire. A color blend texture was added to make the surface appear to reflect the colored light of the fire. Close the panel.

TIP

When working with image sequences that would appear to emit light, such as fire, it's necessary to apply a subtle color texture to the reflective objects. This will simulate the reflection of the colored light being emitted by the image sequence.

Now it's time to animate PAWN's cape with a Fractal Bump displacement map.

5. Click on the Objects Panel and press the T button next to Displacement Map in the Deformations tab.

6. Select Fractal Bumps from the Texture Type list and enter the following properties:

Texture Opacity	100
Texture Size	.5,.5,.5
Texture Falloff	0,50,0
Texture Center	0,-2,0
Texture Velocity	.001,.001,.2
Texture Amplitude	.5
Frequencies	3

This will create the effect of wind blowing the cape that is similar to the curtains effect you created in an earlier exercise. The Texture Velocity settings have been set so the cape moves at the relative speed of the fire flames. This will make the cape appear to move from the wind generated by the fire's intensity.

7. Press the Use Texture button. Because the cape is metallic, you'll need to apply the fire image sequence to the Reflection Options of the cape surface to make it blend with the elements in the scene.

8. Open the Surfaces Panel and select Pawn Cape from the Current Surface list. Press on the Reflection Options button next to Reflectivity, and select the Fir (image sequence) from the Reflection Image list. Press the Close Panel button. Now you are ready to render the Pawn Logo animation.

9. Click on the Render button. Make sure the Render First Frame value is set to 1 and the Render Last Frame value is 207. Select the Save Animation button, chose the target directory for the animation, and enter the name **PawnLogo.avi**. Press OK. Make sure you change the file name so you don't overwrite the previous animation.

You can load the PawnLogo.avi file on the companion CD to see a rendered animation of this exercise.

As you can see, incorporating image sequences can have a profound impact on the quality of your images. There are many uses for image sequences. You can create bump map sequences to create some very interesting effects. Using image sequences as a specularity map for metal will help to add realism to the objects. Spend time experimenting with ways to use the fire image sequence on the companion CD. You'll be surprised at the number of ways you can use a single sequence.

Using the Effector Displacement Plug-In

Effector is a displacement map plug-in that attracts or repels points in the affected object. The displacement of the Effector object is always spherical, regardless of the effector objects shape. The Effector object can be any object in the scene but it's best to use a Null object. If you use a Mesh object, you cannot vary the size of the displacement effect without resizing the object.

TIP

It's best to use a Null object as the Effector object. You should avoid using Mesh objects because they will exaggerate the effect and limit your ability to control the displacement value.

The size of the Effector object determines the maximum range of its displacement. This is a useful attribute because you can animate the size of the Effector over time by using an envelope. If the object size is a positive value, the Effector object will repel points; a negative value will attract points. If you want to suck a baseball through a garden hose, you would use a positive value to repel the points in the hose.

To use the Effector plug-in, select the object you want displaced from the Current Object list on the Objects Panel. Then click on the first Displacement Map Plug-Ins list on the Deformation tab. Select LW_Effector. Now click on the first Options button to select the Effector object. The default object name is Effector. You can change this to the name of the object you want to use as the Effector. In most cases, it will be a Null object. Do not enter the .lwo suffix.

WARNING

You can use multiple Effector objects as long as they begin with the same prefix. There are two settings for the Effector object: Core Radius and Falloff Distance. The Core Radius determines the size of the area in which all objects are equally affected. Simply put, everything within the range of the Core Radius receives a displacement value of 100%. The Falloff Distance uses the same principle as Texture Falloff. It represents the range where the displacement value becomes nonexistent. The displacement effect will gradually diminish between the Core Radius and Falloff Distance. It is best to use a low Core Radius to create a gradual, and more natural, displacement effect.

The following exercise illustrates how you can use the Effector plug-in to pull a golf ball through a curved metal pipe.

GOLF BALL FACTORY

1. Open LightWave's Layout and clear the scene.

2. Load the Golfball.lws scene from the companion CD. You should see the scene shown in figure 9.14.

3. Select the Null object from the Selected Item list. You will see a large number of keyframe indicators following the path of the metal pipe. The Null object is used to deform the pipe to the shape of the Golf Ball object. The Golf Ball object has been parented to the Null object so they move together. To make the effect more interesting, elbow joints have been added to the pipe. Since they are stronger than the pipe, the deformation effect will be minimal as the ball passes through the elbow joints. To achieve this effect, the Null object size is reduced at keyframes before and after the elbow joints.

4. Press the Size button in Layout. The Information Display in the lower-left corner of the screen displays the X, Y, and Z size of the currently

selected object. The values should read .035 meters. Press the Shift+right arrow keys to advance to the next keyframe. You'll notice the values in the Information Display stay the same. Now press the Shift+right arrow keys several times until the Frame Indicator reads 26. You can see the deformation present at the top of the pipe.

FIGURE 9.14

Using the Effector displacement map.

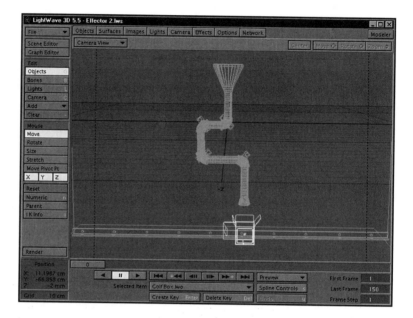

5. Press the Shift+right arrow keys several times until the Frame Indicator is at 31. The values in the Information Display are now reduced to .012 meters. This will reduce the displacement effect as the golf ball approaches the first elbow joint. You can see the displacement of the pipe is smaller.

6. Advance the Null object to frame 41. This places the Null object in the middle of the first elbow joint. Here, the Null object is a very small value of .003 meters. This reduces the displacement effect to a level which can't be seen.

7. Continue to advance the Null object through its keyframes to see how the size values change as the Null object enters and exits the elbow joints.

8. Now it's time to make a preview animation to see the displacement effect in action. Click on the Preview button in the lower right of the Layout screen, and select Make Preview. The Make Preview Panel will appear in Layout.

9. Select the Wireframe button and press OK.

It will take about a minute to generate the animation. You should see the wireframe in the view window changing. When the program is finished generating the preview, it will display the Preview Playback Controls Panel. Press the Forward arrow button to play the preview animation. You should see the golf ball moving through the pipe, deforming it along the way. Figure 9.15 shows a single-rendered frame of the golf ball animation.

FIGURE 9.15

Golf ball displacing a metal pipe.

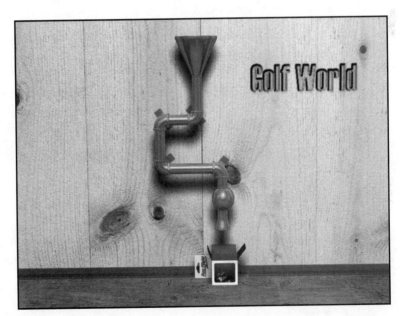

You can render the animation to see the final effect or you can load the Golfball.avi file on the companion CD to see a rendered animation of this exercise.

The Effector displacement map can be a very useful tool for animating spherical displacements. Typically, it's better suited for cartoon effects because of the exaggerated nature of the displacement. You might consider using it to create the effect of something being sucked through a vacuum hose or possibly an item falling though a drainage pipe. No matter which effect you're after, you'll find the Effector plug-in to be a useful tool in your 3D arsenal.

Additional Resources

There are several excellent resources for image sequences to use in your animation efforts. Artbeats, Inc., donated the Inferno sequence used in the PAWN Logo exercise. Below you'll find resources for animated image sequences.

Artbeats Software, Inc.
www.artbeats.com

- **Reel Explosions1, Reel Fire1:** Both products contain over thirty broadcast-quality, royalty-free sequences in 720 × 486 pixel Apple QuickTime format or Targa image sequences, with images digitized from 35mm and 16mm film. Reel Explosions1 contains zero-gravity explosions, ground explosions, three high-resolution shockwave rings, seven in-frame film resolution blasts, and more. Reel Fire1 contains over 30 fire, smoke, fireworks, and propane mortar sequences. Most of the fire sequences are seamless loops.

Visual Concepts Entertainment
www.vce.com

- **Pyromania:** A royalty-free collection of fire and explosion effects. Originally photographed on 35mm motion picture film. Scanned at 2048 × 1536 and sampled to 640 × 480. The CD contains many explosion and fire effects.

Summary

This chapter has touched on only a few of the thousands of possibilities for animating textures and displacement maps. The following is a recap of what you learned in this chapter:

- You can parent a texture to a Reference object so the texture can be animated.

- You can use surface morphing to morph the surface attributes and textures between two objects.

- Displacement maps are used to create major deformations to the object's shape.

- You can use images sequences to add depth to your animations.

- The Effector displacement plug-in is just one of the several displacement map plug-ins.

You have seen several examples of how to apply these effects for professional animation; now it's up to you to tap the unlimited potential of these powerful LightWave assets. You are limited only by your imagination.

Chapter 10

LIGHTING AND ATMOSPHERES

With so many elements to consider in your animations, worrying about the lighting and atmosphere in your scene is not always a priority. Yet the lighting you choose can make all the difference in the overall quality of your animation. Many animations are on the verge of being incredible, but lack one major thing: proper lighting. Working with the right lights in the proper manner can be the difference between amateur-looking animations and professional ones. This chapter walks you through exercises in lighting and atmospheres, using LightWave 5.5's new light sources and atmospheric tools. This chapter helps you change the entire look of your animations. Lighting in LightWave is powerful, and Version 5.5 offers even more control. This chapter covers the following topics:

- Lighting in Layout
- Lighting your projects
- Imitating natural light

Light, and sometimes the lack of it, is as important to 3D animation as air is to your body. Think about your animations. Although you may not do much with the lighting, it must be there or you would not see a single image. Lighting for 3D animation is based on real-world principles, but there are many subtle differences that you need to be concerned with in the computer that you would not be concerned with in the real world. These are differences such as bounced light (radiosity effects) or lights for light-emitting objects, because bright objects in the computer do not generate light. As you read through this chapter, you will find that the lights available in LightWave can truly make a difference in even the simplest of animations. When you follow along with the volumetric projects, you will really see what good lighting can produce.

Lighting in Layout

When you open LightWave, three objects appear. A grid for axis representation, a camera outline representing the camera, and a light representation. Figure 10.1 shows the default light source as it looks in Layout.

LightWave's default Distant Light looks like a Spotlight, but is in actuality very different. The default light generates light from an infinite source, whereas a Spotlight generates light from the light's specific location. LightWave 5.5 offers you the following five light sources:

- Distant Light
- Point Light
- Spotlight
- Linear Light
- Area Light

Along with these five light sources, the following sections discuss intensity falloff, ambient lighting, and shadows.

FIGURE 10.1

The default light in LightWave looks like a Spotlight, but is really a Distant Light.

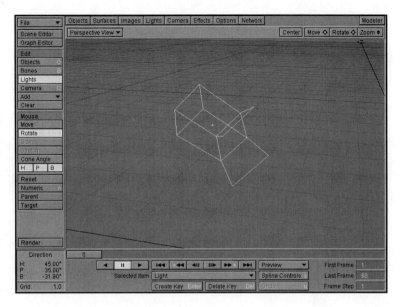

> **NOTE**
>
> LightWave always has one light in Layout. You can turn it off to cast no light in the scene, but LightWave always has at least one light.

Distant Light

The Distant Light is confusing in that its position has no reference to your scene. Only the angle in which the light is facing affects the scene. Figure 10.2 shows an object with only one light in the scene, a Distant Light. Notice that the light is placed to the upper right of the Pegasus. If you look at the Pegasus, however, you see that it is lit from the left side, as if the light was off in a distance. This light is useful for sunsets, daytime, or general lighting conditions.

A Distant Light's effect on an object is based on its rotational direction, not its position in Layout. That means that if the light is to the right of the object, pointing to the right, the object is lit from the left side as if the light is set in the distance (see fig. 10.2). Essentially, a Distant Light is like the sun: It lights everything and lights objects within its line of sight.

FIGURE 10.2
LightWave's default light, a Distant Light, only casts light based on where it is angled, not where it is positioned.

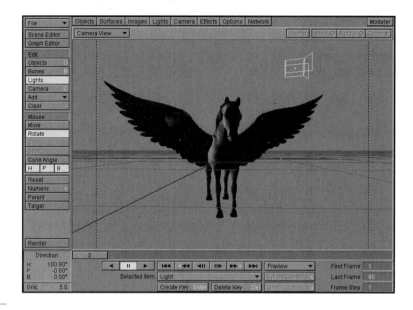

Point Light

The Point Light in LightWave can be thought of as a light bulb. This light type is useful for bulbs, candles, bright sunlight in a specific location such as over a horizon, street lamps, and more. Figure 10.3 shows the same Pegasus with a Point Light. Notice how the light acts like a bright bulb. You would use Point Lights in fireplaces, electronic consoles, or perhaps for special effects. Point Lights represent omni-directional lighting. Light sources that emit light in all directions are omni-directional. Point Lights are great for adding color to a scene from off camera, or for creating general room light for architectural scenes. Point Lights are also very useful when applying lens flares to scenes, as well as special effects lighting.

Spotlight

A Spotlight in LightWave is commonly used for controlled lighting situations. Spotlights work like they do in the real world, and emit light unidirectionally. Spotlights in LightWave create a beam of light to create effects similar to stage lighting, headlamps on a car, or recessed lighting in an architectural situation. You can direct the beam of light from a Spotlight through the use of animated cone angles in LightWave's Lights Panel. This beam can be as wide or as narrow as you would like, and the edge of the Cone angle can be adjusted to create soft- or hard-edge light falloff. Figure 10.4 shows the Pegasus with a Spotlight casting down from above.

FIGURE 10.3

A Point Light casts a general light from all directions. Take note of the light's shape, similar to a star.

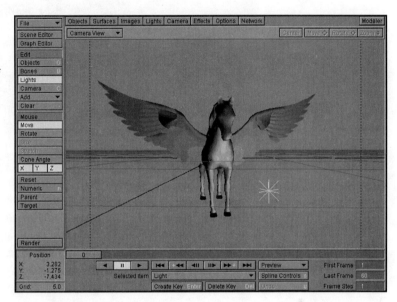

NOTE

Soft Spot Edge angles are not visible through OpenGL previews. They appear when rendered.

You may find that Spotlights are the most versatile of lights in LightWave because you can use them for so many things. You can use a Spotlight for track lighting simulations, canister lighting, a desklamp, street lights, and so on. Spotlights are also used for shadow mapping. *Shadow mapping* is a shadowing method that simulates soft-edged shadows. These types of shadows create more realistic shadowing effects, but take up more RAM.

NOTE

Only Spotlights can be used for shadow mapping. You can use all lights for ray traced lighting.

FIGURE 10.4

You can control the size of the light's cone for accurate lighting.

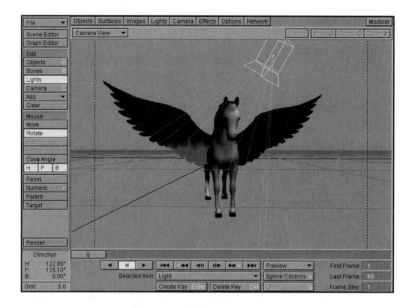

FIGURE 10.4

You can control the size of the light's cone for accurate lighting.

LightWave 5.5 includes two new lights, Linear and Area Lights. These lights cannot be used for shadow mapping, but you can use them for soft-edged ray traced shadows. This method of shadowing is the most accurate but does add rendering time. Read on to learn more about these two new light types.

NOTE

In figure 10.4, notice that the spotlight representation in Layout looks very similar to that of the Distant Light. A Spotlight shows dotted lines emitting from it, however, representing the Cone angle, or area of light specified.

Linear Light

New to LightWave 5.5 is a Linear Light. The Linear Light enables a single light to operate somewhat like a string of Point Lights. Unlike Point Lights, however, the direction of the light is generally perpendicular to the linear light and not omni-directional. Linear Lights do not generate a string of Point Lights; they only appear as such. Think of a fluorescent tube in your office or school. This is what a Linear Light can simulate. This light is ideal for fluorescent or neon lights. What's great about this new light type is that you can achieve soft-edged ray traced shadows and also generate cool specular highlights in your objects.

TIP

Before Linear Lights, specular highlights on surfaces appeared round. Objects in the real world don't always have round specular highlights, such as the hubcaps of a car's tire. The specular highlight would be elongated. Linear Lights can produce this type of effect, among others.

The Linear Light appears in Layout as a single line. It can be difficult to see in Layout given its thin representation, but it is very functional nonetheless. Figure 10.5 shows the Pegasus with a Linear Light added.

FIGURE 10.5
LightWave 5.5's new Linear Lights can duplicate fluorescent lighting. They are represented by a straight line in Layout. Notice that the light casts soft, realistic shadows.

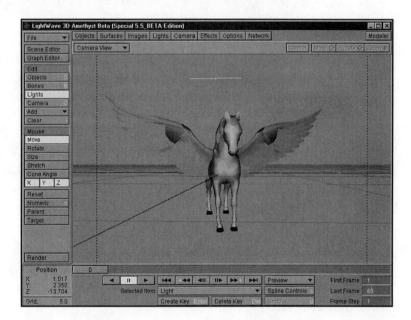

Area Light

LightWave 5.5's other new light is an Area Light. Area Lights appear as a large, flat square in Layout. These can be used similar to a studio light used by photographers to cast a large general light, hence the name Area Light. New to LightWave 5.5, the Area Light can also generate a soft-edged ray traced shadow, but it can do more, like a Linear Light. In reality, shadows are sharp from the start, and become blurry as the shadow travels farther from the object. Area Lights can help achieve this effect. An Area Light is essentially a 2D version of a Linear Light, with light generally emitted perpendicular to its surface.

Intensity Falloff

Light in the real world does not travel forever. Lighting in LightWave, however, travels infinitely unless an intensity falloff is applied. Intensity falloff is set to tell LightWave to have light fall off with a set range. Using this allows the light to look more realistic; otherwise, it goes on for infinity. Using LightWave's Intensity Falloff setting (via the Lights Panel), you can set the range of light intensity.

You can set intensity falloff based on the grid square size of your scene. If, for example, your scene has a 1 m grid, an intensity falloff of 2 m would make the light fade after two grid squares. Taking it one step further, if you have a scene of a computer desk, set up with a monitor, desk, papers, books, and so on, the scene could be using a grid size of 2m. Setting the desklamp falloff to 3m or so would enable the lamp to light just the desk area.

Setting intensity falloffs for all your lights can dramatically add to your scenes. Gaffers on movie and television sets work not only with lights, but the falloff of a light as well. Using falloffs also enables you to control how a light works over a distance. Traveling headlights on a car illuminate a road only so far. Setting the proper intensity falloff helps re-create the look of real lighting.

Ambient Light

Ambient light surrounds you in the real world. In LightWave, you can control ambient light to generate different moods and contrasts within an animation. Ambient light is the area within a scene not directly affected by a light source. Think of a car on a road, for example, under bright sunlight. The area underneath the car can be darker or lighter depending on the Ambient Light Intensity (Lights Panel). LightWave 5.5's default value for Ambient Light Intensity is 25 percent. In most animations, you can lower this value to around 10 percent. For more dramatic and contrasting lighting conditions, set the value even lower. Outer space, for example, usually has an Ambient Light Intensity value of 5 percent or so.

TIP

For best lighting results, set Ambient Light Intensity to 0 percent. Use intensity falloff on light sources, and add more lights to effectively control all lighting within a scene.

Producing Shadows

LightWave 5.5 offers new forms of shadowing with the addition of two new lights, Linear and Area Lights. Shadows are produced by light, therefore the mention of shadow types in this chapter is important. Shadow creation in LightWave can vary depending on which light source you choose.

Before 5.5, the option of hard-edged ray traced shadows or soft-edged shadow mapping were the available options. Now, you have the choice of shadow mapping, hard-edged ray tracing, or soft ray traced shadows with Linear and Area Lights.

Ray Tracing

Ray tracing is a method of generating realistic 3D images by tracing paths of light rays. The tracing of the paths of light are reproduced based on real-world properties to simulate natural lighting effects such as reflection, refraction, and shadows. Ray tracing is a method that enables you to create stunning photo-realistic images in LightWave. Many software packages offer ray tracing tools, LightWave being one of them.

Real shadows are not soft on all sides, but rather have sharper edges nearer the object and softer edges farther away. True shadows are only produced through ray tracing routines. Until 5.5, LightWave's ray tracing was limited to hard-edged shadows. With the addition of Linear and Area Lights, soft-edged ray traced shadows can be produced, resulting in the most realistic shadowing.

Shadow Mapping

As an alternative to ray tracing, LightWave offers *shadow mapping*, a form of shadowing that produces soft-edged shadows and takes up little extra render time. Shadow maps can only be applied through the use of a Spotlight, and require more RAM for adequate results. LightWave softens the edges of a shadow evenly on all sides.

NOTE

Although shadow maps are not completely accurate in form, they are the most common form of shadowing in LightWave. They can be used in most day-to-day animations because they require less rendering time.

Lighting Your Project

It would be misleading to tell you the best type of light to be used in all situations. Each light in LightWave is the best light depending on the project. It is important for you as an animator to understand what differentiates the five light sources in LightWave. Each has a different purpose and can be used alone or in conjunction with other sources. Along with each light comes different shadowing variables, either ray traced, soft-edged ray traced, or shadow mapped. Each variable of a light, such as its shadows, color, intensity, direction, and angle all play a role in your animations. Practice setting up scenes with each light type and mix them up as well.

TIP

Remember that lighting in LightWave is additive. If, for example, you have a light that casts on an object with 80-percent intensity, and you add another light at 70-percent intensity directly on the same surface, most likely, the object will be overlit. Use light intensities to equal a total value of 100–110 percent if all lights are cast directly on an object. Setting various light intensities works well when using the falloff edge of a light source to add dimension to a scene.

If you have a nicely modeled living room, using a bright Point Light in the middle of the room is not your best choice. You need to consider what the animation is about, and how you want the final images to look.

What is just as important as deciding what lights to use for your project is deciding how and where to place them. From there, you need to decide what colors the lights are, how bright they will be, and whether they cast shadows or have lens flares. The projects in this chapter guide you through different lighting situations in two different animations.

Combining Lights

It is important to note that you can use any combination of lights in any scene. It is up to you to decide where and when a particular light is appropriate. Don't be afraid to experiment with lights. After you have set up a scene with a lot of Spotlights, for example, perhaps replace those lights with Area Lights or Point Lights. Although the examples in the previous sections mentioned ways each light could be used, you have the creative freedom to find new and cool ways to use all the lights in LightWave.

The next section talks about light color. Very important to your animations and the objects within them, the light color you choose can make many differences. By combining the different variables of a light such as the color, intensity, and falloff, for example, you can improve the look of your images.

Light Color

The color you can choose for your lights is wide ranging. Using the standard RGB color scale, you have over 16 million choices. Light is never pure white, and although LightWave defaults at 255,255,255 RGB (white), you should get in the habit of giving even just a basic light a variance in color. Basic white light makes your images look washed out and unrealistic. The lights around you are all different colors and intensities. By practicing matching even just basic room lighting, you can add much dimension to your animations. You can choose different light colors through the Light Color button within the Lights Panel.

Assume, for example, that you are creating an animated logo. Instead of leaving just one plain white light up to the left, try lighting the logo from above with an amber or off-white colored light. Then, add a sky-blue colored light off the bottom right to simulate a cast of daylight. You can even add a bright orange-red light from behind and above for added depth.

The light color you choose can change the look of your entire animation. This next project takes you through lighting a living room in an evening setting.

CREATING EVENING INDOOR LIGHTING

1. Load the Room.lwo from the Chapter 11 directory on the accompanying CD. This is a good example of an object that has many different lighting possibilities. First, you will light this for evening.

2. Position the camera inside the room so that you have a decent perspective of the fireplace area (see fig. 10.6).

FIGURE 10.6

The Room object as seen through the eye of LightWave's camera.

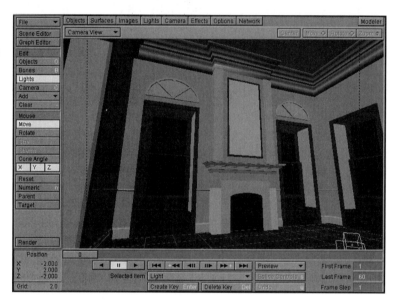

TIP

Remember that you may want a wider camera angle to see the entire fireplace area of the room. Change the camera Zoom Factor to approximately 2.0, from Layout's Camera Panel. You can also change the Zoom Factor directly from the main Layout interface.

Evening light is warm and inviting. To achieve this look, you use Spotlights to re-create the look of canister or track lighting in a unidirectional manner.

3. From the Lights Panel, change the default Distant Light to a Spotlight. Change the light color to a value of 250,245,215 RGB.

4. Set the shadow type for the light to Shadow Map, and lastly, set the Ambient Light Intensity to around 5 percent. Don't worry about the

other light settings or additional lights just yet. Setting an Ambient Light Intensity to 8 percent or lower creates a more dramatic scene. This also requires the use of more controlled lighting, the end result being a more realistic scene.

With a room like this, set up one light first, to get a feel for the environment. After the right ambiance has been set, you can clone the lights. This saves you the hassle of changing every value for every light.

5. Load the Tracklight.lwo file from the accompanying CD as well. Notice that it loads directly in place, on the ceiling. This is because when it was created in Modeler, it was saved in that position relative to the room. Saving objects in Modeler so that they load directly in place when imported into LightWave is helpful, especially for stationary objects. When you have an object that will be animated, it is better to save it centered around the Origin (0,0,0).

From here, you need to place lights in the track light unit on the ceiling. Earlier you changed the default light from a Distant Light to a Spotlight. You will use Spotlights for the four lights in the track.

6. Position the light so that it sits nicely inside the track. Changing views in Layout helps accomplish where the light is going. Figure 10.7 shows the light in place from the Side (ZY) view.

NOTE

If your light is much larger than the Track Light object, your grid size is too large. Use the bracket keys [and] to size the grid down. This enables you to position the lights more accurately.

7. At this point, you might think of adding more lights. Before you do this, however, test the color, shadow quality, and other light properties first. Figure 10.8 shows a render with the single light from the original camera angle.

8. The Spotlight is obviously not enough to light the entire room. But you need to set the Spotlight's properties before you can add more light to the scene. Back in the Lights Panel, change the Ambient Light Intensity to 70 percent. Change Spotlight Cone Angle to 50 percent, and match Spot Soft Edge Angle with 50 percent.

NOTE

The Spot Soft Edge angle cannot be larger than the Spotlight Cone angle. The Spot Soft Edge angle determines the fuzziness on the projected edge of the Spotlight.

9. After you have changed the Spotlight's properties, rename the light **Tracklight**, and then clone the light three times, one for each additional track unit. You will see four lights, named Tracklight(1), Tracklight(2), and so on. In Layout, place the lights into position with the other Track Light objects. Figure 10.9 shows the wireframe lights in position with the Track Light object. Note that you must check the Top, Side, and Front views when setting lights. What might look good in one perspective may not look good in another.

FIGURE 10.9

The original light was cloned three times for each additional track light.

10. Now render the scene. The scene is much warmer. Notice the soft shadows on the fireplace. The few track lights will do the trick for the time being. Save the scene, and then go to the Surfaces Panel.

The surfaces in your scene are very important to how the lighting looks. You may decide to paint the room dark green rather than white. Darker surfaces require more light to appear in an animation.

11. Load the Atrium1.tga image from the accompanying CD. Do this through the Images Panel in Layout.

12. Go to the Surfaces Panel and select the picture surface as the current surface. Click on the T button next to Texture Color to enter the Texture

Map Panel. Select Planar Image as the Texture Type, and place the Atrium1.tga image as the Texture Image. Select the Z-Axis, and click on Automatic Sizing. Turn off Texture Antialiasing. Figure 10.10 shows the Texture Map Panel.

FIGURE 10.10

The Texture Map Panel where image maps can be applied.

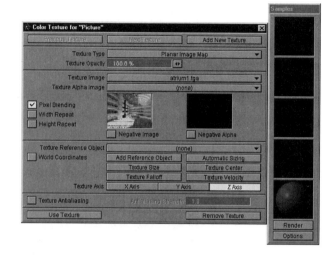

TIP

If you plan to use LightWave's antialiasing routines when performing your final render, you should turn off Texture Antialiasing within the Texture Map Panel. Antialiasing your image both in the Texture Map Panel and during rendering results in a blurred image.

If you render the image now, you see the room beginning to take shape. The atmosphere is being set, and what is left is up to you. You can place furniture, plants, even draperies in the room to add to the atmosphere. Each element you add can enhance the look of your render. Plants, for example, cast additional intricate shadows. Certain draperies add a finished look to an animated room, both within an animation and in the real world. As mentioned earlier in step 11 of the exercise, even the surfaces within your animation are important to the lighting conditions in your scene. Certain surfaces, such as metals, glass, or wood, pick up or reflect light in different ways. A wood texture, such as a flooring, draws light in. A brass desklamp, on the other hand, reflects light in the room. Consider what surfaces you plan to use when setting up lights in any of your scenes. Experiment on your own with the setup here for different results.

Applying Colored Lights to a Scene

Generally when you have an evening scene with a fireplace in the room, lighting a virtual fire is appropriate. When a warm fire is added to a scene, the mood is changed. The atmosphere in the room becomes warm and inviting. Lights are added to a fire to cast a soothing glow over the entire room. Added with the track lights created in the previous exercise, the fireplace puts a finishing touch on a warmly lit room. This section takes you through adding a fireplace and the lights required to do so. You will add colored lights to a scene, use an envelope, and work with displacement maps.

ADDING FIRELIGHT TO A ROOM

1. Load the room scene if you don't still have it loaded. If you have made changes to the lighting in the room, or added objects of your own, feel free to use that scene. From the accompanying CD, load the Fire1.lwo file from the Chapter 11 project directory. Like the Track Light object you loaded earlier in the evening lighting section, the Fire object loads directly in place.

2. Load the Fire2.lwo file and parent it to the Fire1.lwo object.

If you render the scene now, you would not see much of a fire going. You need to add light to the fire. Three Point Lights will do the trick.

3. Go to the Lights Panel and select Add Light to place the first fire light into the scene. Make this light a Point Light, and set the RGB value to a bright orange, somewhere around 252,170,33, and the Light Intensity to 20 percent.

4. Rename this light **Fire_Light_Bottom**, or something similar. Move this light to the bottom area of the Fire objects.

5. Clone the fire light two times, and rename one clone for the middle of the fire and the second clone for the flickering light the fire will give off. Move the middle light to the middle of the Fire objects, along with the flickering light. Also give these lights a bright orange color. Vary them a bit with a tint of yellow. Create a yellow tint by adjusting the green and red color parameters. Move the second Point Light to the middle of the Fire objects and the third Point Light to the top of the Fire objects. Figure 10.11 shows the lights in place.

FIGURE 10.11

Three Point Lights are added at 20-percent intensity, and placed at the bottom, middle, and top of the fire.

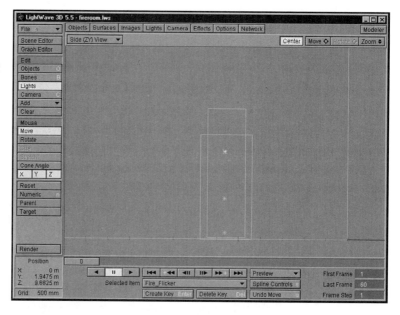

6. Now do a quick render of the scene. It is probably a bit bright. Go back to the Lights Panel, and make sure that Ray Trace is selected for each light. Close the panel. From the Render Panel, turn on Trace Shadows. Now render the scene.

NOTE

Ray tracing increases rendering times. To perform quick tests of the scene you are working on, change the resolution to LightWave's Low or Super Low settings. Don't turn on antialiasing until the final render.

If you notice, the scene is not as overlit as it was before. Without ray tracing turned on, the Point Lights in the fire cast light everywhere. Turning on shadows blocks the light, similar to real-world instances. You can also use intensity falloff to limit the effect of each Point Light.

Because of the fireplace, the room itself may be overlit. Typically when someone lights a fire to create a warm mood, the surrounding lights are brought down.

7. Change each of the track lights' intensities to around 20 percent. Figure 10.12 shows the render at this point.

8. You can create the flickering firelight by setting the Light Intensity envelope. Be sure to read ahead through the section titled "Animating Intensities" to create a flickering firelight.

FIGURE 10.12

The evening room with dimmed lights and a warm fireplace.

You can add more colored light to the scene for added moods. A bluish light cast from a window could give the feeling of daylight. An orange light cast from the windows could give the appearance of a sunset or sunrise. Following are other ideas for colored lights:

- **Animated photography darkrooms.** Use red lights.
- **Night vision.** Use green lights.
- **Psychedelic.** Use a rainbow of colored lights.
- **Staging.** Use red and blue lights in combination with white lights.
- **Mars animations.** Use reddish-orange lights.

Often the color of the light in a scene can do more for the final animation than the surfaces on the objects. Best results, however, come from good objects, good surfaces, and good lighting. Of course, good animation goes without saying. But what if you wanted to animate your lights? It is easy to do with LightWave's envelopes.

Animating Intensities

As you animate more often, you will find yourself wanting more control over the elements within your scene. LightWave can handle the task with its many envelopes throughout the program. The envelopes in the Lights Panel are no exception. If you look in the Lights Panel, you will see a small button labeled E next to a few other light control buttons. This is LightWave's standard envelope, and it can be applied to the following:

- Ambient intensity
- Light intensity
- Lens flares
- Cone angles
- Edge angles

This enables you to animate these features over time.

To add to this scene on your own, make the top Point Light of the fire flicker randomly between 20-percent intensity to 30-percent intensity every 7 or 8 frames. The following tutorial shows you how to create a flickering fire.

CREATING A FLICKERING FIRE

1. Continue from the previous exercise. Make sure the Fire Light is the current light. Click on the E button next to the Light Intensity button within the Lights Panel. Figure 10.13 shows the Envelope Panel for the light intensity of the flickering firelight.

2. Create a keyframe every 7 or 8 frames. Do this up to about 120 frames, or 4 seconds.

3. From the End Behavior drop-down menu, choose Repeat. Next, go to each keyframe within the Envelope Panel and vary the intensities. Your first frame should be 20 percent, the original intensity of the light. The next keyframe should ramp up the value about 10 percent, and the next keyframe should drop below the original setting to about 16 percent. Repeat this throughout the envelope, and click on Use Envelope to apply the envelope and close the panel.

FIGURE 10.13

The envelope for creating a flickering firelight.

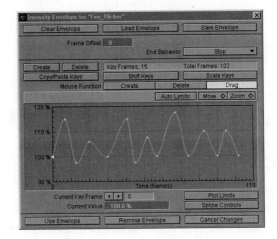

When you render a preview of the animation, the fire will be flickering. Added to this is the object's transparency texture, which is animated as well. The Fire objects Fire1.lwo and Fire2.lwo on the accompanying CD have the texture velocity already set.

TIP

To learn more about animated textures, visit Chapter 8, "Textures and Materials."

Animating light intensities is more helpful than one would think. An animated light doesn't always mean random flickering or dim lights slowly getting brighter. You can apply the envelope for light intensity just explained to many situations. A quick envelope from 0 percent to 100 percent over two frames, for example, simulates a light turning on, and a fast envelope setting simulates lightning. Also, animating light intensities is great for special effects such as bullets, laser beams, rockets, and so on.

TIP

You can instantly generate a random envelope in LightWave's Modeler. From the Objects, Custom drop-down menu, choose the LW_Envelopes plug-in. You can select from either a Linear, Oscillator, Exponential, Gaussian, Random, or Custom envelope. Figure 10.14 shows the values you can set to create a Linear envelope. This plug-in is great for animated light intensities.

FIGURE 10.14
The LW_Envelopes
plug-in in Modeler can
generate a number of
envelopes in varying
lengths.

Radiosity

Radiosity is a complex real-world property that goes unnoticed by the every-day person. Simply put, *radiosity* is bounced light. LightWave 5.5 cannot render bounced light; you can, however, fake the effect by using colored lights. A desklamp with a green lampshade, for example, casts white light on a desk. In the real world, the color of the green lampshade is softly cast onto its surroundings. LightWave cannot duplicate this automatically. Using a colored green light, you can generate the bounced lampshade light.

NOTE

LightScape Technologies, makers of Lightscape, a program that calculates and renders radiosity images, has a working agreement with NewTek, Inc., makers of LightWave. You can find sample images from Lightscape on the accompanying CD, as well as more information about their product.

To create the effects of bounced light, take a look at figure 10.15 as an example. This image from LightScape technologies shows how radiosity effects can make a rendered scene look very real. Load the image from the accompanying CD (Fig11_15.tga) to view in full color.

Notice that many areas of the walls and ceilings in figure 10.15 are colored. This color comes directly from the surface of the object near it, which is reflecting light. Notice the ceiling above the pool table, for example. As the light above the pool table hits the green felt, the color is reflected onto the ceiling. Although LightWave 5.5 can't render images like this automatically, you can fake it without much effort.

Load the Desklamp.lws from the Chapter 11 project directory on the accompanying CD. Be sure to save your existing work before clearing the scene.

FIGURE 10.15
This image from Lightscape Technologies was rendered with radiosity.

Render the frame. A simple table top with a lamp appears. Two lights are in the scene, one room light and one light for the lamp. Figure 10.16 shows the rendered image.

WARNING

Due to the ray traced shadows in this scene as well as the bump maps, you will encounter long render times at higher resolutions. To test-render a frame, use LightWave's Low or Super Low resolution settings.

After you finish clicking around and test rendering the scene, load the Fakradi.lws from the Chapter 11 projects directory. Render again, but this time note the difference in the back wall. The green tint is just a Spotlight set to an 80-degree angle, and a deep green color. It is aimed at the back wall from behind the desklamp. The appearance in the final render looks as if the green lampshade was casting a green light. The desklamp still casts white light from its opening. Figure 10.17 shows the faked radiosity image.

In addition to the green lamp on the back wall, you can add a brown/orange colored light aimed at the bottom of the wall closer to the desk. This light can simulate the color of the wood being bounced onto the walls.

FIGURE 10.16
The Desklamp scene is nice, but could use some radiosity effects.

FIGURE 10.17
A green Spotlight is cast on the back wall behind the desklamp to simulate radiosity effects.

Radiosity effects are easy to re-create. Although very subtle at times, using them can truly enhance your scene.

TIP

Try bringing Ambient Intensity to almost 0, and add more lights for precise control of a scene's illumination.

Adding lights to your scene can always improve your look. There are times, however, where you need to take away light from a scene while still keeping it lit.

Dark Lights

LightWave 5.5 gives you added control over your lighting conditions with the capability to add Dark Lights, or Negative Lights, to your scene. In essence, a Dark Light actually subtracts light from the area in which it is cast. Assume, for example, that you have a few characters dancing around on stage and everything is lit exactly the way you want. You add the last element, a backdrop of a nicely painted piece of art your niece drew. Suddenly, you realize that the image is incredibly overlit. You can't lower the diffusion level on the image because that will reduce the clarity. You can't reduce the lights in the scene because that will take away from the characters on stage. What do you do? Enter Dark Lights.

Here are some ideas of how you can use Dark Lights:

- Cast traveling shadows.

- Use with projected images.

- Create a mysterious black hole for cartoon characters without modeling a thing. Adjusting the Spot Soft Edge angle can change the edge of the hole.

- Create a storm cloud blocking the sun.

- Create an eclipse.

Setting a Dark Light is very simple. You load a light—a Spotlight works well—point it at the area you want to darken, and set a negative light intensity value—instant Dark Light. Load the Dark Lights scene, Darklight.lws, from the Chapter 11 project directory on the accompanying CD, and render a test frame. You should see a big black hole on the desk (see fig. 10.18).

The color of a Dark Light plays a role in its effect. The brighter the color of the light, the darker the affected area will be.

FIGURE 10.18
Dark Lights can take away light from a scene. Here, a black hole is easily created with a –200 percent Spotlight.

The amount of light intensity you use, or the lack of it, determines how much light is taken away from the affected area.

Applying a Dark Light to a scene is easy. Think of applying Dark Lights as adding lights to a scene. You will add a light to an area within a scene so that you can "suck away" light by setting a negative value.

Applying Dark Lights is as easy as adding lights. This feature can prove very beneficial in that you now have even greater control over the look and feel of your animations. Using a Dark Light in your animations offers many solutions to lighting problems. But the biggest challenge to an animator is re-creating natural light.

Follow along this brief tutorial to set up a Dark Light. You can use Dark Lights to add contrast to your scenes or control lighting conditions. This exercise uses the living room scene created earlier in this chapter to demonstrate how Dark Lights can black out the corners of a room.

APPLYING DARK LIGHTS

1. In Layout, load the Room.lws scene file from the accompanying CD.

2. From the Lights Panel, load an additional light. Make it a Spotlight, and change its Spotlight Cone Angle to 60 percent, as well as its Spot Soft Edge Angle.

3. Set the Light Intensity to –80 percent, and close the Lights Panel. Back in Layout, aim the light into one of the bottom corners of the room. Test-render the scene. You will see that you have just dimmed the lighting in just that particular corner.

You can adjust the color of the light and the negative intensity to create various effects. Be sure to experiment with this powerful feature on your own. Load the DarkLightRoom.lws scene from the *Inside LightWave 3D* CD for a headstart.

Imitating Natural Light

Without question, the re-creation of natural light and natural elements is the most difficult task an animator can encounter. The tools in today's software packages make the job a bit easier, but the animator still needs to make a believable image.

Imitating natural light means paying close attention to the world around you every part of your day. It means understanding light color—how it brightens and how light falls onto objects. Here are a few key things to keep in mind when imitating natural light:

- Know the general brightness of a light you are re-creating.

- Know the light's real color.

- Fog and atmosphere play an important role in natural light.

- Shadows and ambient light are as important as the light itself.

The next project re-creates an outdoor lighting situation. The object is composited over the image. For more detailed information on compositing, see Chapter 15, "Compositing."

CREATING NATURAL LIGHTING

1. Open the Chapter 11 project directory and load the TrafficCow.lws scene file into Layout.

2. Notice that the scene looks sparse. But, there's more to this scene than meets the eye. Go to the Options Panel, and turn on BG Image to show the image of the highway traffic. This image is placed as a background image within the Effects Panel. You want to add 3D elements to the 2D background image. Your biggest hurdle is matching the lighting conditions.

3. Look at the second right lane in the image. Notice what the color of the light is—a pale yellow or slightly off-white color. Now notice the shadows in the real image. These are the two key elements you need to duplicate in LightWave. Go to the Lights Panel and change the Ambient Light Intensity to 0 percent. Because the shadows are dark, and the lighting is hard sunlight, a lower Ambient Light Intensity helps duplicate the real-world lighting.

4. You can add more to the look of a scene with shadows. A tree above can cast shadows onto the objects, adding more realism, for example. In this particular scene, the Cow object needs to cast a long soft shadow, just as the cars do.

5. In the Lights Panel, change the default Distant Light to a Spotlight. Make the Spotlight Cone Angle 40 degrees, and make the Spot Soft Edge Angle 40 degrees.

6. Move the light to the right of the cow on the X-axis, about 400 mm or so. Move the light up about 170 mm or so on the Y-axis. This light position does not have to be exact, but it does need to cast a shadow that matches the background image. Test render your scene to see how the shadow is being cast on the ground.

NOTE

The Ground object is already surfaced using LightWave's Front Projection Image Mapping function. Read about compositing in Chapter 15.

7. The bright sunlight in the composited image is somewhat yellow and orange in color. Set the Spotlight's Light Color to 252,241,214 RGB to match the sun's color of light.

8. Lastly, set the Light Intensity to 150 percent to make the light bright and hot, similar to the sun. Test render again.

9. Load the TrafficCow2.lws scene to see the final light position and color to make the cow appear to be standing in the middle of the road.

Creating natural light is nothing more than setting the proper Ambient Intensities, Colors, and Light Intensities. The right combination of the three proves effective in imitating nature. To add even more realism to a naturally lit scene, you can use LightWave 5.5's atmospheric settings, described throughout the upcoming pages.

Imitating natural light is a tough part of animating in any 3D package. There are no tricks or secrets to matching real-world light. As mentioned in Chapter 2, "Concepts and Theories," your eyes are the judge when the final image is rendered.

Two new LightWave 5.5 features can help you in your natural lighting efforts, however. Those two new elements are Pixel Filter plug-ins called SkyTracer and Steamer. SkyTracer generates awesome looking clouds with a cool colored sky. Steamer creates fantastic volumetric lighting. The next two sections walk you through these new plug-ins.

Atmospheric Lighting

Atmospheric lighting is a new term to many 3D animators. LightWave added a plug-in to 5.5 called SkyTracer. What SkyTracer does automatically used to take an animator hours to do. Figure 10.19 shows the SkyTracer plug-in found under the Effects, ImageProcessing, Pixel Plug-ins tab.

SkyTracer's interface looks scary at first, but makes good sense when you begin using it. Although the interface for this new plug-in can be intimidating at first, its functionality and results make it simpler to use. Figure 10.20 shows an image that was instantly created with SkyTracer.

With the SkyTracer plug-in active and the SkyTracer's Instant Preview activated (this is the Refresh key), you can see an image that was not built in LightWave's Modeler or Layout; it was generated by SkyTracer.

FIGURE 10.19

The SkyTracer plug-in found within the Pixel Filter plug-ins.

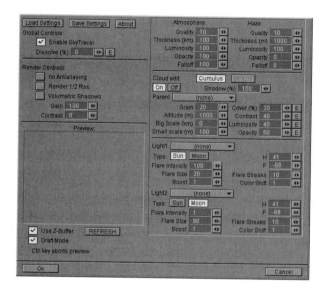

WARNING

SkyTracer eats up rendering time! Be careful using it because it may add significant time to your renders. The final image, however, is worth the wait.

FIGURE 10.20

Instant previews from the SkyTracer plug-in. This plug-in adds instant sky and clouds to your scenes.

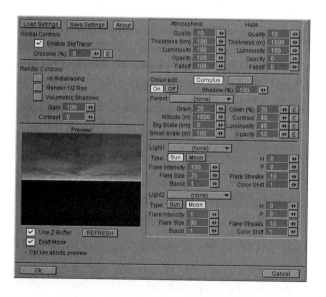

SkyTracer is beneficial because it can save you hours of work by generating beautiful atmospheric images such as sunsets and sunrises at the push of a button. What is a plus is that the generated image can look different every time. It also generates a sky around LightWave's 3D universe. By using SkyTracer, wherever the camera is pointed in Layout, there will always be a sky viewed from a different angle. Using a background image of a sky, the image is always the same regardless of where the camera points. In the following quick SkyTracer tutorial, you can set up your own image through SkyTracer.

NOTE

Remember that you don't need to clear a LightWave scene to load a new one. LightWave automatically dumps the existing scene for the new one unless told otherwise. You can load a scene into an existing scene by selecting the Load From Scene command within the Objects Panel.

USING SKYTRACER

1. Load LightWave, or save and clear any existing work.

2. Go to the Effects, Image Processing, Pixel Plug-ins tab. Select SkyTracer as the current plug-in, and click on the Options Panel to open the SkyTracer interface. Before you do anything else, click on the Refresh button at the bottom of the screen. What do you see?

3. This good-looking image is only the start of your creative control. Go to the top right of the panel under Atmosphere. Change the values to the following:

Setting	Atmosphere	Haze
Quality	22	25
Thickness	60 km	600 m
Luminosity	180	30
Opacity	80	10
Falloff	45	5

These values change the default sunset sky to something more dark and surreal. The Atmosphere settings are different elements of the clouds, which are stacked one on top of each other. The Quality settings for both Atmosphere and Haze determine how accurate the results will be. A value of around 20 is acceptable. You shouldn't go above 30; otherwise your render times significantly increase.

Each of the parameters within SkyTracer can be adjusted for varying cloud strengths and brightness. You can instantly see results from adjustments by clicking on the Refresh button. Figure 10.21 shows a different tone within the clouds and sky.

FIGURE 10.21

A few parameter changes to SkyTracer, and a different look is achieved.

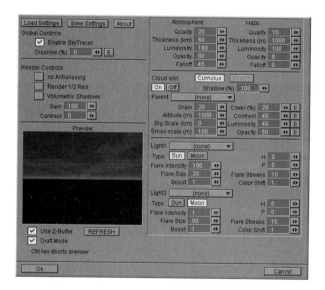

NOTE

Refer to your *LightWave Reference Guide*, page 17.25, for specific details on the SkyTracer plug-in.

You can incorporate SkyTracer into your scenes in a few ways. First, you can generate a sky and add the rest of your objects to the scene. Because SkyTracer requires long rendering time, using it to generate a sky on a frame-by-frame basis is not always practical.

The other option is to use SkyTracer to generate a single sky image. From there, the image can be rendered, saved, and mapped onto a large dome-shaped object covering Layout. Use SkyTracer to generate a beautiful image map, and map it onto a large sky object. Your render times drop significantly, and you can still gain different perspectives when the camera moves.

The third way in which you can use SkyTracer is to generate a single image, and reload it into LightWave as a background image. Although the image is always stationary no matter where the camera and objects are, the SkyTracer image is a beautifully rendered image and it enhances your scene.

SkyTracer can create stunning 3D clouds and beautiful background images. Adding Volumetric Lighting to your animations, however, brings your work one step ahead.

Volumetric Lighting

A long awaited addition to LightWave has finally arrived in Version 5.5. Volumetric Lighting comes to you in the form of a Pixel Filter plug-in called Steamer. *Volumetric Lighting* refers to lighting that has physical volume. The combination of light scattering and absorption is the basis for Volumetric Lighting effects. Other variables play a role in Volumetrics as well, such as volume shape and size, density distribution inside the volume, surrounding lighting conditions, and the behavior of the light itself. LightWave 5.5 has included Steamer to compute and calculate these computational issues to enable the rendering of more realistic atmospheric lighting conditions. Figure 10.22 shows the Steamer interface.

FIGURE 10.22
The Steamer plug-in interface found in Pixel Filter plug-in section.

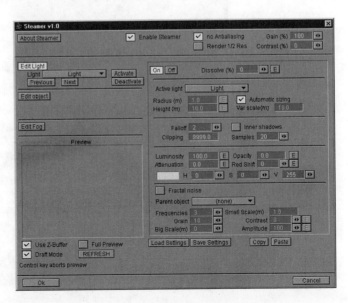

Steamer is actually two plug-ins in one. The main Control Panel is found under the Effects, Image Processing, Pixel Filter plug-ins section. The other is found under the Objects, Displacement Map plug-ins section. Figure 10.23 shows the second plug-in associated with Steamer for particles.

FIGURE 10.23

Steamer's second plug-in within the Objects, Displacement Map plug-ins is a great tool for making steamy particles.

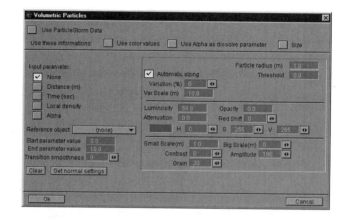

Steamer has a wide range of uses, from special effects to realistic atmosphere. A common use for Steamer is the glowing light behind the logo animation. This effect can help enhance even the simplest logo animation (see fig. 10.24).

FIGURE 10.24

Even with a simple logo, Steamer creates a very cool looking animation. And it is easy to create.

This cool Steamer look is described in detail on page 17.23 of the *LightWave 5.5 Reference Manual.*

You can take this same effect and apply it to other elements such as a door opening in the darkness with light spilling out. Alternatively, you can re-create Batman and Robin running toward the camera with a bright light streaking from behind them.

Adding Steamer to real-world environments, however, is also a useful way of maximizing the plug-in's power. The following exercise adds rays of light, often seen in movies, to a simple hallway.

Because Volumetric Lighting reacts with the objects in a scene, a person running or an object passing through breaks the beam of light. Before Volumetric Lighting, a Light Cone object (a fake beam of light) could be used to simulate a light beam. Objects passing through the beam, however, actually break the polygon with the transparent surface. Volumetric Lighting creates real beams of light that interact with other objects in a scene.

USING STEAMER

1. Load the Hallway object (Hallway.lwo) from the accompanying CD's Chapter 11 project directory.

2. Make the existing scene light a Spotlight, and change its color to a soft blue, something around 110,230,240 RGB. Bring it to the back of the hallway and point it toward the camera.

3. In the Lights Panel, add another Spotlight.

TIP

As an alternative, you can use LightWave 5.5's new Add feature directly from Layout. From the Edit group of buttons on the left side of the interface, select Lights as the current Edit item. The Add menu changes just below it to enable you to add any light type. Click on and select Add Spotlight from the drop-down menu (see fig. 10.25).

FIGURE 10.25

*The new Add function
in Layout enables you
to add any light type to
the scene, without
going into the Lights
Panel.*

4. With the newly added Spotlight, move it above and just outside the hallway ceiling.

5. Move and point the Spotlight down at a slight angle. For this, press the number 5 on the numeric keypad to select Light View. This enables you to see what the light is seeing, allowing greater ease of placement. Make sure you select the new Spotlight as the current light after selecting the Light View mode. Figure 10.26 shows the light in place.

FIGURE 10.26

*The Volume Light in
place above and
outside the hallway, as
seen through the eye of
the light.*

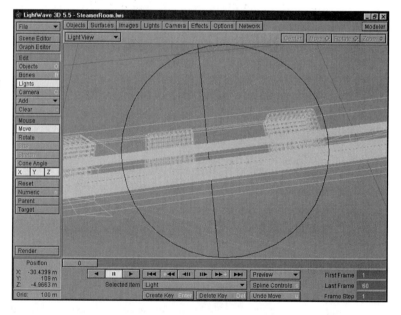

6. Press the number 6 key to return to Camera view. Move it inside the Hallway object. (You will become used to the numeric keypad before long because of switching views in Layout so often.) As a note, the numeric keypad view selection is much faster than clicking and selecting from the drop-down menu with the mouse.

7. Render a frame of the scene. Don't worry, you won't see much of anything yet. Go into the Effects Panel and select the Steamer plug-in from the Pixel Filter plug-ins. Click on the Options tab to enter the Steamer Options Panel.

8. From the Lights Panel, you should take a moment to rename the lights to help you organize your scene. Name the first light **Room Light**, and the second light **Volume Light**.

9. In the Steamer Options Panel, select Edit Light. Choose Room Light as the current light, and click on Activate. You should see the set of controls turn on at the right side of the screen. Set the Active Light to Room Light. Set the following:

Automatic Sizing	Off
Angle	75
Height	1000
Falloff	1
Clipping	9999
Sample	30
Luminosity	10
Opacity	0
Attenuation	5
Red Shift	0
H	0
S	0
V	255

This produces that "light at the end of the tunnel" look often seen in movies. Figure 10.27 shows the scene with Steamer set to the Room Light.

Render out a low-resolution frame to take a look. Adjust the settings a bit if you want to see what other looks you can come up with. After you have something you like, save the scene and go back into the Steamer Options Panel.

FIGURE 10.27
A Spotlight is placed in the back of the hallway and the Steamer plug-in is applied to give a "light at the end of the tunnel" look.

10. Again, select Edit Light, but this time choose the Volume Light as the current light. Click on Activate. Enter the following values:

Automatic Sizing	Off
Angle	50
Height	500
Falloff	2
Clipping	9999
Sample	30
Luminosity	10
Opacity	0
Attenuation	10
Red Shift	0
H	0
S	0
V	255

Each of these settings controls various parameters for Volumetric Lighting. Many of the values are what they appear as, such as Luminosity, Height, Angle, Falloff, Clipping, and so on. Some, however, need a brief description.

- *Attenuation* controls the interior behavior of the light. From the point in which light is scattered, it is attenuated depending on the length of the travel.

- *HSV* is the Hue, Saturation, and Luminosity for the overall effect's colors. This includes background colors, light color, and red shift.

TIP

For complete definitions of each control in Steamer, refer to page 17.5 of NewTek's *LightWave Reference Manual*.

This is just a starting point for you to use Steamer. Follow along some of the tutorials in the LightWave manual. With all this information, you are well suited to creating your own volumetric scenes. The question remains, though: When do you use Volumetrics?

Volumetrics are definitely cool. As a brand new feature to LightWave 5.5, you will probably want to use them often. But should you? Of course you should! Use all your tools in LightWave all the time. It is how you use the tools that could be a potential downfall of your project.

When lens flares were introduced in LightWave 3.0, animators went crazy, adding flare to every light in the scene. In time, the overuse subsided, and people learned how to effectively and creatively use lens flares. The same situation can be applied to Steamer and SkyTracer. In time, people will use them more effectively to enhance their scenes. Volumetrics do hog rendering time. For certain animations, however, the final output is worth the wait.

Using Volumetrics will become a regular routine in your work, if it already isn't. Simple things such as creating lens flares without actually turning on a flare are possible, as well as creating beams of light without an object or generating a cool-looking ground fog. Take a look at the next two images, figures 10.28 and 10.29, which are samples of some things you can do with Steamer and Volumetrics.

Refraction

In the real world, refraction is a key property when it comes to light. Refraction can easily be taken for granted because it is so common. In LightWave, however, you need to assign refraction properties to your scene. On page 4.11 of the *LightWave 5.5 Reference Manual*, you will find a refraction index. This table tells you different refractive properties for various surfaces such as water, glass, liquid, and so on.

Refraction in LightWave is very simple. You need to know a few basic rules, and you can be up and running. The following are just a few ideas of how to put refraction into your animations:

■ A magnifying glass truly magnifies with refraction turned on.

■ Objects such as fish, sharks, or logos under water bend with the waves.

■ A glass, empty or full, on a countertop looks even more realistic than a glass without refraction.

■ Special effects can be created with warped refraction.

These are just a few ideas for using refraction. To set up an object that will use refraction, it helps to understand how light travels. A glass of water, for example, has interesting surface properties. A basic glass of water has at least five surfaces in which you could apply refraction:

1. The light travels into the glass on one surface and refracts.

2. It travels out of that surface and refracts (because the glass has thickness).

3. Next, the light hits the water inside the glass and refracts.

4. From there, the light hits the glass again and refracts.

5. Finally, the light travels out the backside of the glass and refracts again.

Each of those areas can have varying refractive properties. The differences might be so subtle, however, that you can get away with the glass and just the water refracting.

To use refraction, set the Refractive index from the Surfaces Panel. You need some level of transparency set for each surface to use refraction. After the surface is told to refract and a value has been set, be sure to turn on Trace Refraction from the Render Panel.

Experiment on your own with refraction and see what you can come up with.

TIP

Any types of ray tracing, whether they are shadows, reflections, or refraction, add time to rendering. Do your test renders in Low or Super Low resolutions.

Summary

Lighting is a fun part of setting up an animation. At times, you will need to tweak again and again to get just the right look. The results, however, can be overwhelming. Here's a few last reminders when working with lighting:

- An object's surface affects the lighting results.

- Judicious use of ambient intensity is important to lighting a scene.

- Shadows play a key role in lighting in the real world. They should also do so in the 3D world.

- The use of atmospheric conditions such as fog and Volumetric Lighting significantly enhances a scene.

- Try changing the ambient color to match the scene.

- Don't overuse lens flares.

- Light a scene as if it were being set up in the real world.

- Avoid default lighting settings.

- Always change the light color, even if to a simple off-white.

- There is no need to set a light intensity higher than zero when using flares by themselves.

- Animate lights over time, both in movement and intensity for different effects.

- Be willing to experiment. Try to reproduce real-world lighting situations.

As you read through the next few chapters on animation, take into account how light plays a part of each scene. Try using the animation techniques for objects on light sources. Now, with your newfound lighting information, bring your mind over to Chapter 11, "Cameras."

Chapter 11

CAMERAS

LightWave's camera is a powerful tool that you can use to add significantly to the look and feel of your animation. You may not think of the camera as an animation tool, but used properly, it is a powerful tool. This chapter will guide you through camera uses and techniques that can boost the look and feel of animations.

You can animate the camera in LightWave over time, changing lenses so it can zoom, dolly, rotate, pan, tilt, and perform other camera moves sometimes not so easy to do in the real world. LightWave is limited to one camera at this time. However, you can easily create cuts between what appears to be different cameras in the same scene. You can use this technique with LightWave's one camera. This chapter takes you through several exercises that explore the following topics:

- Generating action with the virtual camera
- Using multiple cameras to animate the action
- Working with LightWave's lenses
- Understanding and applying depth of field
- Animating the camera

Generating Action with the Virtual Camera

The virtual camera is fraught with possibilities. With it, you can travel anywhere, rotate to your heart's content, or even move the camera faster than a blink of the eye. The virtual camera enables you to generate virtual worlds. Figure 11.1 shows the wireframe representation of LightWave's camera.

This camera is your window to LightWave's render. Although you have six different views to choose from in Layout, when you push the Render button, you see the images through the camera. Upon entering Layout, LightWave puts the view to Perspective. Get in the habit of setting up your scenes from the Camera view. It's easy to set up an entire animation from a Perspective or Side view, for example, and then see something entirely different when rendered.

You can animate LightWave's camera similar to animating objects within a scene. The camera also has a motion graph, as shown in figure 11.2, like an object does. This Motion Graph Panel enables you to repeat motions, set keyframes, tweak spline controls, or scale keyframes among standard Motion Graph tools.

The virtual camera in LightWave gives you complete control over movement and timing, unlike any camera in the real world. There are no cables, no batteries, no tripods or steady cams, and your shoulder won't even get tired.

FIGURE 11.1

The wireframe representation of LightWave's camera.

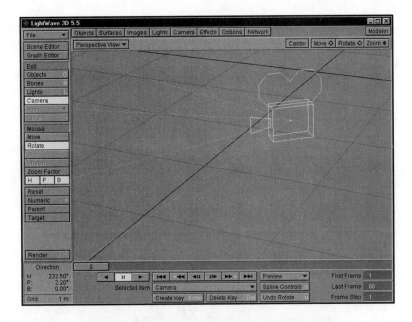

FIGURE 11.2

LightWave's camera has a Motion Graph Panel like an object. Here, you have control over the camera's motion paths, scaling, shifting keyframes, and more.

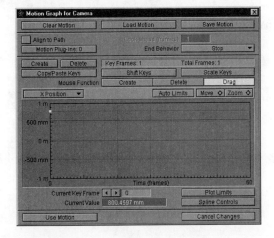

Using Multiple Cameras to Animate the Action

LightWave has the capability to use multiple camera shots. Although there is only one camera in LightWave, you can change the camera shot within the same animation by moving the camera to a new position, rotation, or angle. Too often, animations generated are from one perspective, with the exception of a slight camera move. Sometimes animations have one camera with too much movement. LightWave is a virtual set, enabling you to create an entire scene, set the lights, and then position the camera. The following project takes you through an animation that recreates the cameras at a Formula One race, using multiple cameras.

CREATING MULTIPLE CAMERAS

1. Enter Layout and save any work you may have. Load the RaceTrack.lwo object from the Chapter 11 project directory on the CD accompanying this book. Then load the Land.lwo file.

2. Close the Objects Panel and look at the layout. Go to the Camera view by pressing the number 6 key on the numeric keypad. You should see something like the layout shot in figure 11.3.

FIGURE 11.3

LightWave's layout from the Camera view once the Land and Racetrack objects are loaded.

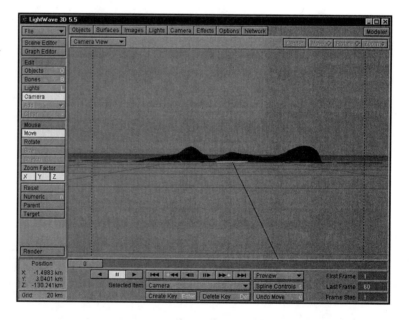

This view makes the ground and the racetrack look very small. Actually, they're not. The grid size is simply too large. Right now, the grid size is set to 50Km, quite large. Press the number 3 key to view the layout from the side. Notice how big the camera is in relation to the Land object? Figure 11.4 shows the Side view.

TIP

If you can't see the camera and object when changing to a Side view, press the comma key (,) a few times to pull out the view.

FIGURE 11.4

Because of a large grid size, the camera overpowers the Land object.

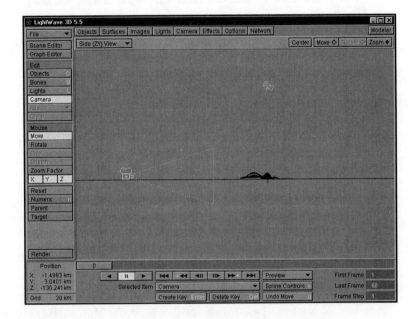

You need to change the grid size so that the camera is more easily managed. That is to say, with a large camera such as the one in figure 11.4, you will have a hard time maneuvering it around the racetrack. This makes sense because the camera right now is the same size as the track.

3. Continue pressing the left bracket ([) key until the grid size is 20m. You can see the grid size in the Information Panel at the bottom left-hand side of the screen, as in figure 11.5. You can also numerically change the grid size through the Options Panel. Changing the grid size does not affect the render or the view of the camera.

FIGURE 11.5

The Information Panel at the bottom left-hand side of the screen shows the current grid size.

Direction	
H:	-48.60°
P:	8.70°
B:	0.00°
Grid:	200 m

4. Switch back to Camera view (push 6 on the keyboard) and move in toward the racetrack. You'll notice now that moving the camera takes many more mouse movements. The smaller the grid size, the more precise the movements will be, and vice versa.

5. Instead of manually moving the camera, you can numerically move it. Select Move for the camera's Mouse function, and press n on the keyboard to call up the Numeric Requester. Enter the following values:

    X   32m
    Y   10m
    Z   -13m

This will position the camera in the middle of the racetrack. Rotate the camera down and to the left until the racetrack is in view. Create a keyframe to lock it in place.

6. Next, load the Racecar.lwo object. Its default position is 0 X,Y,Z. The car is not on the track, but instead of moving the car around the track and making a number of keyframes, the Path To Motion plug-in was used to create a motion path around the racetrack. You can load this motion path through the Motion Graph Panel.

7. With the Car object selected as the current object, press m on the keyboard to bring up the object's Motion Graph Panel. Select Load Motion at the top of the screen and load the Track.mot file from the Chapter 11 Motions directory on the CD. Figure 11.6 shows the Motion Graph Panel with the new motion loaded.

8. Select Align to Path in the Motion Graph Panel and then click on Use Motion and Repeat for the end behavior and return to Layout. You'll now see the car lined up on the track. If you make a wireframe preview, you'll see the car move along the track. Press the number 4 on the keyboard to make a preview from the Perspective view.

NOTE

Align to Path in the Motion Graph Panel enables the Car object to follow the motion path. It aligns the object's Z-axis to the path. Without this setting, only the car's pivot point follows the path.

FIGURE 11.6

The Motion Graph panel for the race car. You can use a pre-existing motion to animate the car.

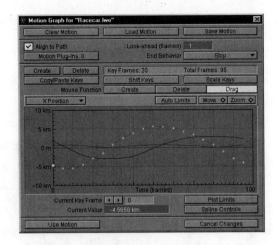

You can use motion paths for both objects and cameras. If you want to match the camera's path to the car's path, you can load the same motion path in the camera Motion Graph Panel. If you loaded the same motion file, however, the camera will be in the exact same position as the car. You can use the Shift Key function to move it from there.

9. For this first camera setting, all you need to do is create an establishing shot. Move the camera to a general area shot to position of about:

Move
X   21.6485m
Y   23.8m
Z   34.4643m

Rotate
H   -115.6
P   30.7
B   0.0

Figure 11.7 shows the camera overlooking the racetrack.

Save the scene as **track_wide.lws**. This is the scene in which the camera will cut from different stationary locations around the racetrack.

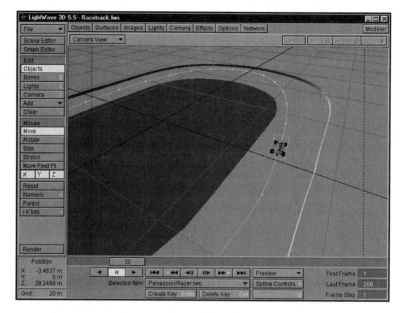

Varying Camera Angles

With the camera in stationary position and the car moving around the track, you now have the freedom to play with the camera angles. LightWave's camera angle can range from 0.0001, the equivalent of a 0.0mm lens with a field of view at 179.99×179.99, to a lens equivalent that makes the field of view unrecognizable within LightWave's Layout. When talking about camera angles in LightWave, you need to consider the camera's zoom factor. The zoom factor can be animated over time, as can the camera itself. The correct combination of the zoom factor and camera angles in Layout can create great-looking results.

The camera's zoom factor in LightWave defaults at 3.2, the equivalent of a 24mm lens on a 35mm film camera. You can adjust the film size through the Camera Panel, which affects only the equivalent lens readout and the strength of the depth of field. If you are working with depth of field in your animations, different film sizes vary the depth of field effect.

TIP

Your personal preference for a default zoom factor may be the original setting of 3.2, or perhaps something higher or lower. When you find a zoom factor you like, you can set it as the default zoom factor by editing the LW.cfg file. Do this by opening the LW.cfg file from the NewTek/Programs directory into a text editor. Change the zoom factor to the desired number and resave. Be sure to quit LightWave if you decide to edit any part of the configuration files.

For the main camera in the racetrack animation, a zoom factor of about 1.8 works well. Set this value in the Camera Panel. You can also set the zoom factor from the Interface button in Layout, found under the Mouse menu items.

The next animation exercise, Quick Camera Cuts, is designed to show you how to animate the camera as a real-world element. If you watch a race on television, there are a few key camera locations and angles. Some camera angles are standard, and some are exaggerated.

Using Standard Angles

Unfortunately at this time, LightWave's parenting capabilities are limited. Even though you can parent anything to anything in LightWave, the particular item is either parented or it's not. Because one camera needs to be parented to the car for the traveling shots, and the other for stationary shots, two scenes can be created. The elements within each scene are identical, except for the camera positions. You can render out the two scenes and then cut between them in your Personal Animation Recorder, Perception Video Recorder, Targa Board, or even a video tape editor.

TIP

If you generate still images, make a note of where the camera position should change, and piece together the individual frames before converting them to an animation recorder. This way, you won't need to edit finished animations.

The first scene, the Track_wide.lws, will have three camera shots. A shot on one side of the track will capture the car spinning around a turn. The next shot will be close to the ground, watching the car zip by close to the camera. The third shot will be above the track with a quick pan following the car around another turn.

QUICK CAMERA CUTS

1. Load the Track_wide.lws scene from your hard drive, or use the one on the book's CD. With the camera's zoom factor set to 1.8 (a 13.5mm wide-angle lens), go to frame 90 and create a keyframe for the camera. At this point, change the last frame of the animation to 600 to make a 20-second animation.

2. Press the s key on the keyboard to call up the camera's spline controls and select Linear. This will lock the camera in place at this frame. Now move the camera to a wide shot of the end of the track and create a key at frame 91. Also select Linear from the Spline Control Panel.

3. With the camera in the same position as it is in frame 91, create a keyframe for it at frame 120. You can quickly create a keyframe by pressing Enter. You can also jump instantly to a particular frame by pressing f on the keyboard and entering the frame number. Set a spline of Linear as well.

4. At frame 121, move the camera to a shot close to the ground on the other side of the track. Use the following values to help place the camera:

    Move
    X   -39.2722m
    Y   2.7m
    Z   -30.8058m

    Rotate
    H   -23.1
    P   20.7
    B   0.0

5. Create a keyframe (press Enter) at frame 121. Set Spline Controls to Linear.

This will cut the camera to the other side of the track. The car quickly shoots past the camera, over about 30 frames.

6. At frame 138, create a keyframe in the same position. Again, set Spline Controls to Linear.

7. Go to frame 139, and move the camera to above the track, somewhat centered. This last shot will follow the action from an Aerial view. Where the other two cameras held their positions, the third camera is going pan slightly. Use the following values to help you place the camera:

Move
X   -25.6806m
Y   11.7m
Z   -22.3993m

Rotate
H   49.8
P   26.2
B   0.0

Figure 11.8 shows the aerial shot at frame 139.

FIGURE 11.8

*The third camera shot
is from above the
racetrack, ready to
catch the action.*

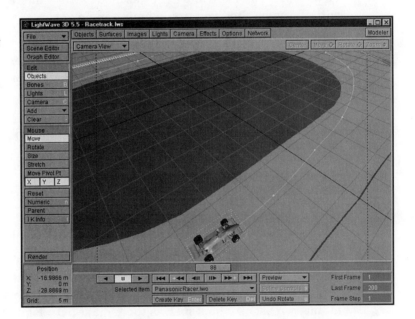

NOTE

The camera positions for Move and Rotate do not have to be exactly matched to the number
listed here. These are simply a reference for you to create your own cool camera moves. Of
course, you can use these if you prefer.

8. With the camera at keyframe 139, create another key in the same
   position at frame 145. Also lock it down with Spline Controls set to
   Linear.

9. Now, rotate the camera's heading to about –297 at frame 170. Create a
   keyframe there. Press the s key and enter a spline tension of 1.0.

This last shot lets the car enter the frame and pans quickly to the left, watching the car drive around a turn as it leaves the Camera view.

In video and film, editors like using shots in which a subject, (in this case the race car) enters and leaves the frame before cutting to a new shot. The same rules should apply in your animations. Avoid *jump cuts*, shots in which the subject in view is in the same perspective in two different frames. For example, if a news anchor was perfectly centered as a head shot in a Camera view from slightly left, and a cut was made to the camera slightly to the right with the same shot, you would have a jump cut.

Each camera should have a varying shot. So one camera can be a tight shot, whereas the other is a wide shot. In the case of animating around the racetrack, letting the car enter and leave the frame before cutting eliminates the need for tight or wide shots.

Save this animation but don't clear the scene. After you save it as **Track_wide.lws**, save it again, but this time name it **Track_car.lws**. This will let you work with a new scene without accidentally saving over the first one. You set keyframes in the first scene up through 170. You can pick up from here to create closeups of the car.

Enlivening the Action with Exaggerated Angles

If you've seen a race televised, you are familiar with the cool, fast-moving shots from ground level next to the race car, or the shots from the driver's point of view. These extra wide and exaggerated shots translate well into 3D for many reasons. Shots such as these make 3D a lot of fun. You don't need to worry about camera mounts, cables, wireless transmitters, and the like. Simply move the camera into position and render.

The car is already set in its motion around the track. You simply need to move the camera into key positions as you did with the stationary camera. This camera will follow along with the car. The shots will be close up, as if the different cameras were clamped onto the car. In order to fit the whole shot into the camera's lens, the view needs to be slightly wider. Before you start this exercise, however, go to the Camera Panel and change the zoom factor to 1.4, the equivalent of a 10.5mm lens.

CREATING A DRIVERS POINT OF VIEW

1. Select the Camera as the edit item. Press m on the keyboard to enter its Motion Graph Panel. Select Clear Motion. This will reset the camera's move and rotational keyframes. Using Clear Motion works for objects as well. This saves time rather than going through the scene and deleting each keyframe.

2. With the camera's position reset, parent it to the car. Move the camera to the driver's side, slightly above the back wheel looking down the track as in figure 11.9. Create a keyframe at 0 for the camera's initial position. You may need to adjust the grid size to make the car fully visible to the camera this close. Change the grid size to 5m. This will also allow for more precise movement of the camera.

FIGURE 11.9

With the camera parented to the car, anywhere the car moves, the camera will follow.

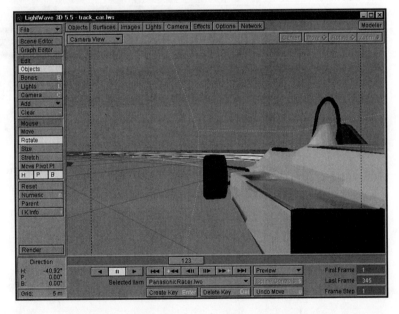

3. Make a quick wireframe preview and you'll see the camera move along with the car around the racetrack. In the first scene you put together with the camera stationary shots, you created keyframes through 170. The car left the frame at around 200. Based on that, you want to cut in this shot at around frame 200. Change the first frame of the entire animation to 201 and the last frame to 700. Create a keyframe at 290. This will hold the shot for three seconds.

4. At frame 290, select Spline Controls and choose Linear to lock the camera down. Go to frame 291, and move the camera to the hood of the car as in figure 11.10. Create another key. Again, select Linear from the Spline Controls.

FIGURE 11.10

The shot at frame 291 shows the driver's point of view.

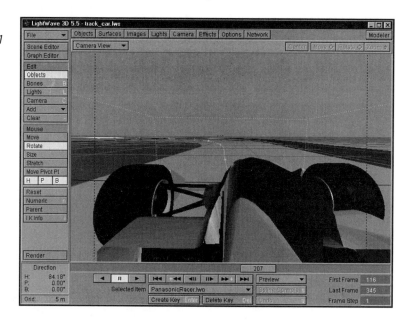

5. You want to hold onto this shot for about five seconds, so create another keyframe at 440. Again, select Linear from Spline Controls. At frame 441, move the camera to:

Move
X   675.148mm
Y   824.9999mm
Z   4.776m

Rotate
H   -529.6
P   -3.4
B   0.0

This shot is in front of the car as if the camera were mounted on a car ahead. Create a keyframe at 441 for the camera and set Spline Controls to Linear. Your shot should look like the one in figure 11.11.

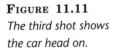

FIGURE 11.11
The third shot shows the car head on.

6. Create a keyframe at 700. Spline settings should be set to Linear; save the scene. Make a wireframe preview and watch the shots you just made.

You can use the techniques in these exercises for any animation in which you want to cut to different cameras. Because one frame of video travels past the eye so fast, the result looks like a cut. In actuality, the camera is moving positions faster than you can see it. Changing camera angles and positions is a great way to add a different look to your animations. Changing the perspective can also add to the scene.

Shooting from Different Angles

It's easy to add different angles to your scenes, to change or enhance the appearance of objects and images. Changes in angles are not typically found in animation. Figure 11.12 shows an angle in which the camera is set very close and very wide onto the Stratocaster object found in the NewTek directory of objects. This camera's zoom factor is set to 0.4, the equivalent of a 3mm lens. This makes the guitar look long and tall.

Different angles don't necessarily mean wide-angle shots either. Using different angles in your animations can create or accentuate a different feel or mood. When shooting real video, many videographers don't take the camera off of their shoulders. In animation, many animators don't get the camera off of their shoulders either. That is to say, the camera is sometimes ignored, and camera angles from the floor, from above, or even Dutch angles, can help the overall look and feel of the finished animation.

Varying the Scene with Dutch Angles

Applying a Dutch angle to your animation offers a different way of looking at things—literally. Simply put, a Dutch angle is a banked camera. Figure 11.13 shows a lizard monster with a closeup shot at ground level. The camera is banked about 40% to give the feeling of something odd and uncomfortable.

Try using Dutch angles on architectural renderings, characters, or logos. Move beyond the standard shots and try something more fun and creative whenever you can.

Angles and shots can be anything you want. Remember to watch your television and movie screens carefully. Pay attention to all the aspects of the film, not just the computer animation. Consider how the lighting was set up, and consider how the angle of the camera and the shot at hand affect the current scene. In the next section, you will work with a critical element of the camera, the lens. You should always be aware of the camera lens. Is it zoomed in, is it pulled back, wide angle, or something else?

FIGURE 11.13
A Dutch angle added to the camera set to ground level, creating a more ominous feeling.

Working with LightWave's Lenses

LightWave's camera lens is a tricky thing. It can generate entirely different looks with the click of a button. You can adjust the lens settings for LightWave's camera to match any real-world lens. Figure 11.14 shows the lens information area within the Camera Panel.

The information here can change the entire look of your animation.

Deciding When and How to Use Different Camera Lenses

You know that LightWave's camera can be adjusted to varying camera lenses. The question is: When should you use different camera lenses? As with any part of LightWave, the tool and methods you choose to create an animation all depend on the project at hand.

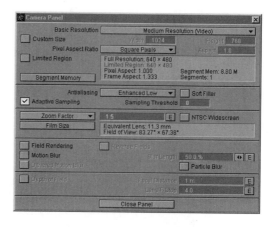

What should be a standard lens for everyday animations such as 3D logos? That depends on your taste or your client's needs. The default lens of 24mm (zoom factor of 3.2) is common in most situations. However, you might find that a lens of 15mm is more appropriate (zoom factor of 2.0). A wider lens on a 3D logo can bring the 3D element more to life. For example, load the Logo.lwo file from the Chapter 12 project directory on the CD accompanying this book. Move it in toward the camera. Figure 11.15 shows how the object looks with the default lens of 24mm.

FIGURE 11.15

A default lens of 24mm makes the logo look ordinary.

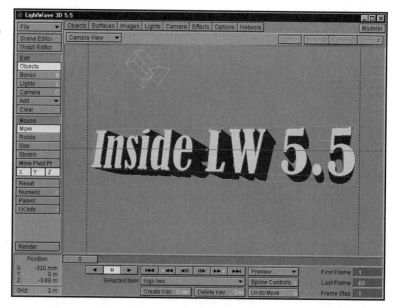

Now, go to the Camera Panel and make the lens 7.5mm. Do this by changing the zoom factor to 1.0. Figure 11.16 shows how the logo looks now. It has a bit more punch to it.

FIGURE 11.16

The logo has more punch with a wider lens.

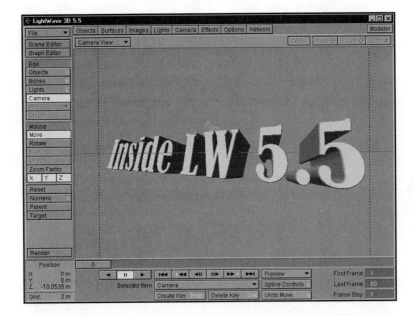

The lens on a logo can change the look and feel of an entire scene. Try different lenses on different logo jobs. Making a powerful corporation's logo look gigantic by widening the lens can help make a better animation.

If you work with real video, LightWave's lens control will play an important role in your animation. Compositing a character, for example, would require you to match LightWave's lens with the real lens used to shoot the video or film. Without the proper lens setting, the character's perspective will not match up to the real-world perspective. See Chapter 15, "Compositing," for more details on matching lenses.

Animating the Camera Lens

If you watch television or music videos, you notice that they are full of the popular slice-of-life look. This is the look in which the cameraperson can't seem to keep the camera steady on the subject. There are quick pans and tilts, with some quick zooms in and out. For whatever reason, this look is hot, and you can duplicate it in LightWave. Later, in the Dollys and Pans sections, you can read about steady camera movements. Follow along now to make your own slice-of-life animation.

CREATING A HAND-HELD CAMERA LOOK

1. Load the toys scene from the NewTek/Games directory on your computer. This scene came with your LightWave software. If you didn't load it into your system, simply find the scene on your original LightWave CD.

2. Press 6 on the keyboard to view the scene through the camera's point of view.

TIP

Remember to get into the habit of setting up your animations through the Camera view. The Camera view is what will be seen when the animation is rendered.

The toys scene is a good scene to work with for setting up a camera animation because it has many objects, and the camera at startup has only one keyframe at 0.

3. The camera has a default keyframe at 0. Move the camera about 1 meter in on the Z-axis. Select Move and push the camera in toward the toys. Select Rotate, and with the right mouse button (Mac users—use the Control key), bank the camera about 8 degrees to the right. Then, create a keyframe at 10 for the camera. If the camera won't bank, check to see that the B control button next to the H and P buttons is turned on at the left-hand side of the screen.

4. Move the camera to the left on the X-axis about 20mm. Move it down on the Y-axis about –15mm, and bank it to the right another 8 degrees. Create a keyframe at 16.

TIP

You can use the numeric requester for Move to quickly enter a value of +20mm, for example, and click on OK. This will move the selected item to the precise value instantly.

5. Move the camera back on the Z-axis about 500mm, and then move it to the right on the X-axis about .5m. Create a keyframe at 23. The Tricycle object should now be partially out of Camera view, as in figure 11.17.

FIGURE 11.17

An offset Camera view yields a slice-of-life look when added to the rest of the scene.

6. Move the camera in about 1m. Create a keyframe at 30. Then, move the camera to the left and up so that the objects in the scene are partially out of the camera range to the bottom right of the screen. Create a keyframe here at 35.

7. Move the camera back about 1m on the Z-axis. Create a keyframe at 40. Then, rotate the camera on its pitch about 10 degrees and move the camera slightly to the left. Create a keyframe at 46.

8. Repeat this idea for another 100 frames or so. Create keyframes every 4–7 frames. Try making a wireframe preview and see how it looks. Be sure to set the last frame to something like 100 or so. Save the scene as **Slice.lws**.

TIP

If you want, load the Slice.mot motion file from this book's CD-ROM and apply it the camera through the Motion Graph Panel (m) for the Toys.lws scene. The Toys scene came with your NewTek files when you installed LightWave. Look for it in the Games directory with the NewTek folder. Figure 11.18 shows the Motion Graph Panel for the camera moves in this animation.

FIGURE 11.18

The Motion Graph Panel for the camera. Here, the motion for the camera can be adjusted, scaled, and saved for use on other camera moves or object moves in the future.

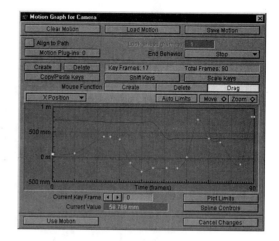

This look is very common in television commercials, and you can use it in your 3D animation. Try turning on Motion Blur from the Camera Panel for more realistic effects. But to quickly take this look one step further, read the next section to learn how to add a zoom envelope to it.

Creating and Modifying Zoom Factors

The zoom factor in LightWave's Camera Panel was discussed earlier in this chapter. This section deals with creating and modifying the zoom factor to enhance the look of your animation.

Although there is a tendency to think of zooming the camera and moving the camera as the same thing, they are not. Moving the camera into a subject simply changes the position of the camera. Zooming in on a subject changes the focal length of the lens, and therefore, changes the look of the animation. The combination of moving the camera and zooming truly enhances your shot. Load the Slicelife.lws and render a small QuickTime or AVI of it, and you'll see that zooming in the camera creates a different feel.

Figure 11.18 shows the camera's Zoom Factor Envelope. The Zoom Factor Envelope adjusts the zoom on the camera over time at various keyframes.

TIP

When using fast zooms in your animation, render the scene with motion blur for an added effect.

FIGURE 11.19

*The zoom factor for
the camera shows how
the lens can be quickly
zoomed in or out
through an envelope.
You can adjust each
keyframe for variance.*

FIGURE 11.19

*The zoom factor for
the camera shows how
the lens can be quickly
zoomed in or out
through an envelope.
You can adjust each
keyframe for variance.*

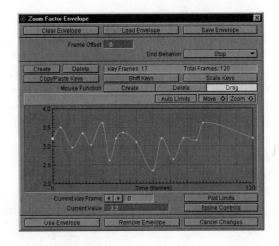

The zoom factor in LightWave can really help your animation look better. Animating the zoom factor through its envelope window gives you complete control over what the camera sees and how something is seen. This, in combination with the subject of the next section, depth of field, can turn simple animations into professional animations.

Understanding and Applying Depth of Field

Depth of field has been a feature in LightWave for years. However, due to slow processors, many animators could not afford the luxury. But even today's inexpensive Pentium 100s can handle a small animation with depth of field applied.

NOTE

Depth of field requires that you use at least Medium antialiasing to activate.

Depth of field is not complicated. A camera in the real world has focus. The computer camera does not. Because the real-world camera focuses on different parts of a scene and has an aperture, images in view can go out of focus. This look can be simulated in LightWave through the Camera Panel. Figure 11.20 shows the Camera Panel's Depth of Field settings.

Depth of field is the size of the area in which objects are in focus in a scene. The depth of field depends on the size of the aperture, the hole in the lens through which the camera records the scene. The smaller the aperture, the more objects will be in focus. For example, take a scene with a woman seated at a table. In front of her on the table is a bowl of fruit. Behind her on the wall is a painting. With a small aperture, the entire scene could be in focus, even though the camera is actually focusing on the woman's face. But as the aperture becomes larger, perhaps to compensate for low light, the woman may be in focus and the fruit and the painting would be blurred. How much or how little of the scene you want in focus depends on what you want to emphsize. In LightWave, you need to set the aperture or f-stop and the focal length to simulate depth of field.

FIGURE 11.20

LightWave's Depth of Field controls.

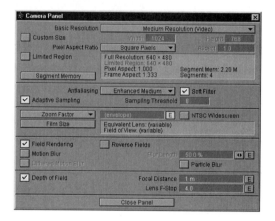

Setting up a depth of field shot is easy. First, you need to set your Anti-aliasing level to Medium (or higher). This will activate the Depth of Field button in the Camera Panel. Selecting the Depth of Field button turns on the Focal Distance and Lens F-Stop entry boxes. Here, you can set the values to tell LightWave how much or how little focus you want in your scene.

Save your work from Layout, and load the Toys.lws scene again from NewTek/Games directory on your hard drive. From the Camera Panel, with Medium antialiasing set, enter a focal distance of 5 m, and an f-stop of 2.0. Close the panel and render the scene.

NOTE

Even though you need Medium antialiasing set, you can render the image in low resolution for speedier tests.

Your rendered image should look like the one in figure 11.21.

FIGURE 11.21
A rendered image using Depth of Field. The Chessboard scene from NewTek was used with a focal distance of 200mm and a lens f-stop of 4.0. The focal distance is set to the center of the chessboard, making objects in front of and behind it out of focus.

Animating Depth of Field

Animating the depth of field to achieve a rack focus is not much more difficult than creating a simple envelope. A *rack focus* shot is when the camera's focus changes from viewing a distant object to a close object, or vice versa. If you look next to the focal distance and f-stop settings, you'll see the familiar E buttons. These envelopes can be set to animate either the f-stop or focal distance over time. An example of this would be a shot of a flower, in focus, although the background is out of focus. Then the camera changes focus, almost reversing the view to an out-of-focus flower with a sharp background.

TIP

An easier way to animate a rack focus and depth of field is with Unlimited Potential's WaveFilter 2.0. With this LightWave plug-in, you can animate depth of field by moving a Null object in Layout. Also, WaveFilter doesn't require you to have a minimum Antialiasing level of Medium.

If you happen to be animating a shot in which the camera is slowly panning a scene, you may want to add depth of field. Typical shots in video and film often are focused on something in the middle of a set, whereas the objects close to the camera are blurred. Setting up your animations like this can add more depth to your scenes and give you a more realistic look. Take a look at the LightWave-generated M&M commercials next time you are flipping through the TV channels. You can see Depth of Field techniques used often. Real-world cameras have depth of field. Perfect focus for everything in a shot is nearly impossible other than on a computer.

Animating the Camera

Adding motion to the camera for smooth, fluid shots can soften the look and feel of your animations. Even slight, subtle moves of the camera take your animations to a new level. Complete the following exercise and the ones following it to create an animation using dollys, pans, tilts, and a boom effect.

CREATING A DOLLY SHOT

1. Load the Dollyshot.lws scene from the book's CD. This will load one large object with a few simple buildings and a street.

2. Select the Camera and press Delete for frame 25 and frame 300. This existing scene already has a camera motion set up. You will set up your own motions for the camera in the next few steps.

3. The camera is in a position at the side of the road in front of the tree on the X-axis, similar to figure 11.22. This frame should be already set at 0. The camera should be looking at the first building, while still in the street. This means that the tree on the sidewalk is between the camera and the building. Here's a good place to use depth of field, by the way.

4. This is the starting point for the camera. You want the camera to sit for almost a second before it begins to move. Create a keyframe at 0 for the first camera position. Then, without moving or rotating the camera, create a keyframe at 25.

5. Next, make sure the X, Y, and Z controls are on for Move functions and move the camera down the street on the Z-axis, with the camera's focus on the buildings. When you get to the end of the buildings, create a keyframe at 300.

FIGURE 11.22

The initial shot for the camera. This is what the camera will see when the animation begins.

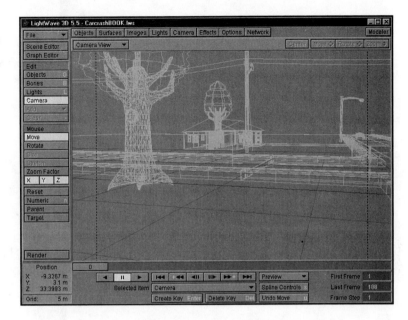

6. Make a preview of the animation. The camera holds for almost a second and then moves slowly down the street.

This is quite basic. Camera moves do not need to be fast moving or too advanced. Often, a basic slow pan or dolly such as the one in this exercise is subtle, but classy. It will add movement to a scene without taking away from the subject on camera. To go further, you can spice this animation up with a few more camera moves and spline controls.

Spline Controls

If you look at the preview shot you just made, you'll notice that the camera might drift a little before it begins moving down the street. You might also see that the camera stops abruptly at the last keyframe. Cameras, like most things in the real world, don't necessarily move like this. A camera in motion in the real world will slowly ramp up to full speed and then slow down for its resting position. This next exercise will demonstrate how to accomplish this movement with LightWave's spline controls.

TIP

Pressing f on the keyboard calls up the Go To Frame Requestor, enabling you to quickly type in the desired frame number. Also, if you press s on the keyboard and the spline controls don't pop up, you probably don't have a keyframe. A keyframe must be set for an object, light, or camera to activate spline controls.

WORKING WITH SPLINE CONTROLS

1. Go to frame 25 for the camera. Press s on the keyboard to call up the Spline Control Panel.

2. In the Spline Control Panel, enter a value of 1.0 for the Tension. Click OK to close the panel. Go to frame 300, and also enter a Spline Tension of 1.0. Click OK and make a preview of the animation. Notice how much more subtle the movements are.

You can apply spline controls to many elements in LightWave. The camera can benefit from splines, as can objects, envelopes, motion paths, and lights. The spline controls consist of four items: Tension, Continuity, Bias, and Linear. Linear can be either on or off. When Linear is turned on, any values given to Tension, Continuity, and Bias are overridden. The values in each range from 1.0 to 1.0. The following list outlines the job function of these three spline controls:

■ **Tension.** Controls the "ease" in and out at a keyframe of a selected item. A value of 1.0 tells the item to ease in as slowly as possible. The opposite of that would be the item slamming into a keyframe with a value of –1.0. Note that the length of the animation affects the results of Tension settings.

■ **Continuity.** Creates a break or emphasizes a motion path. Setting a Continuity value of –1.0 can be useful for making an object ricochet off of another object. Using a positive 1.0 value would make an item overcompensate a keyframe. This is not extremely useful, except for things such as animated characters.

■ **Bias.** Controls the slack of an item around a keyframe. A value of 1.0 creates slack on the back side of a keyframe while a value of –1.0 creates slack on the front side of a keyframe. You can use Bias for animating things such as a zero-g airplane. As the airplane reaches the top of its arch (keyframe), it slows down. As it passes over the arch, it speeds up.

You can adjust the Bias controls and see their effects through the Motion Graph Panel. Figures 11.23 and 11.24 show the differences in a Motion Graph with a Bias spline control of 1.0, and without.

FIGURE 11.23

A Motion Graph Panel for the camera has a Bias spline control of 1.0 set at frame 60 of 120.

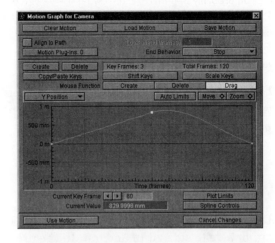

FIGURE 11.24

The same motion path without any spline controls set.

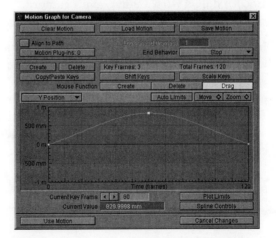

You can set spline controls from the Layout window as well and not use the Motion Graph Panel. Pressing s on the keyboard calls up the spline controls for Tension, Continuity, and Bias for the current frame. Experiment with the spline controls on all of your elements in LightWave. Tension will be your most widely used spline control, so get into the habit of setting it up often. Here's why: Have you ever set an object in one place for a certain number of keyframes and then set it in motion frames later? Does the object not stay still? Does it just sort of float around before it begins moving to the next keyframe? If you've seen this, that means you need to set a spline control on the last keyframe before the motion. For example, your first keyframe is 0. The next is 30, and the third keyframe is 90 at the back of the layout. The first two keyframes are in the same location. At frame 30, you would enter a Tension of 1.0 in the Spline Control Panel (press s on the keyboard) to lock the item in place at the frames from 0 to 30, and also have the item "ease out" of the keyframe at 30.

Understanding how spline controls can enhance the movement of your camera can help you set up more interesting shots, such as dollys, trucks, pans, or tilts, which are discussed in the next sections.

Dollys and Trucks

Dolly and truck are terms used to describe the movement of the camera either side to side, or in and out. In the previous two exercises, you created smooth dollys with LightWave's camera. Use the same technique to truck the camera from side to side.

In LightWave, you can always dolly and truck on the proper axis no matter which angle the camera is set to. If, for example, the camera is banked to the right, moving on the X-axis would simply move it on the X-axis. By holding down the Ctrl key, you can dolly the camera on its rotation relative to the camera's axes as opposed to the world axes, which can be different if the camera is rotated. The same rule applies to the heading or pitch of the camera when attempting to truck the camera.

Pans and Tilts

A panning shot is a left-to-right or a right-to-left sweep of the camera from a stationary position. A pan used in combination with an animated zoom can be a true representation of a real-world camera. Think of tilting the camera up or down, similar to moving your head up and down to look around. Rotating a camera on its heading will produce a panning shot, whereas rotating the camera on its pitch will create a tilt shot.

Use these basic video and film camera principles anytime you are setting up an animation. Remember that you don't have to worry about power cords, tripods, steadicams, or the like; just animate the camera.

Booms

Major television programs and films often use boom shots to introduce a set or segment. A boom is a rig that enables the camera to shoot from high up. A typical shot where you've seen a boom used is a scene of a neighborhood street. The camera starts out up in the trees and slowly moves down to street level to reveal a car moving into the frame. Shots such as these add real style to your animations and can give them a personality.

Summary

The camera in LightWave has always been quite powerful. In this chapter, you read that the camera is a tool that can add depth and dimension to your LightWave scenes. This chapter covered:

- Working with the camera
- Creating multiple camera shots
- Working with depth of field effects
- Using camera lenses

Using the camera along with good lighting while adding proper motions to objects within your scene will add the finishing touches to your animation. Chapter 12, "Basic Animation Techniques," will discuss using animating background elements, OpenGL textures, refraction, reflection, and more.

Part III

ANIMATION SCENES

BASIC ANIMATION TECHNIQUES

"Animation Techniques" might seem to be a misleading title

for a chapter such as this one—at first. The topic of anima-

tion techniques is broad enough to be an entire book. As a

LightWave animator, you will use different animation tech-

niques to accomplish your tasks. Animation techniques

mean more than just motion, they mean object organization,

layout design, ray tracing, and the other elements that bring

an animation to life. This chapter explains many of the ne-

cessary ingredients that complete a LightWave animation.

Animation techniques in this chapter will guide you through:

- Working with objects
- Motion paths
- Refraction
- Refraction and reflection
- Rendering animations

This chapter discusses many techniques you might use every day with LightWave. How you use these techniques is up to you. As an animator, you have a blank canvas on which you can create anything you want—real worlds, imaginary worlds, cartoon worlds. Whatever you choose, the techniques will remain the same. In this chapter, we will set the foundation for basic animations.

In the first exercise, you will create two scenes that will become one animation. The first part involves creating an animated background element, whereas the second part uses that animation as a background image sequence. Later in the chapter, when talking about refraction, you'll create animated objects that appear to be under water.

Working with Objects

Loading an object into Layout requires that you know two important factors: object size and object position.

An object's size is important because you will most likely animate that object with other objects. If you design objects on different scales, you'll run into problems and delays. Each object will have to be resized before it is animated. If you model or adjust your objects in Modeler according to a real-world scale, your objects will load properly in Layout. The alternative to modeling to the real world is modeling to the computer world. That is to say, if you create a planet surrounded by spaceships, use the size of the planet as a reference in a background Modeler layer.

An object's position is very important to its motion in Layout. If your object is created and saved off of its center of rotation (off of the X, Y, and Z axes), it will rotate and move in odd ways. Be sure that your object has its position set properly before you load it into Layout. Do this through Modeler and the Center plug-in. For more Modeling and orientation information, refer to

Chapter 6, "LightWave Modeler in Action." In addition, refer to your LightWave Reference Manual for a discussion on pivot points in Modeler.

You can load objects in Layout through the Objects Panel and the Load Object button. LightWave 5.5 enables you to load an object into Layout without entering the Objects Panel. Using the Add drop-down menu on the left side of the Layout interface, 5.5 enables you to load an object or add a null object instantly. You can also select Load From Scene to load objects from other scenes. Additionally, the Replace Object button enables you to replace a current object with a new one. However, be sure to note that different object orientations will also be replaced.

NOTE

Using Load From Scene actually adds a scene to the existing scene. LightWave 5.5 does not have the option to select which objects to load when using Load From Scene; it loads them all.

Using Null Objects

Null objects are single points that LightWave uses to control many different parameters such as grouping, parenting, or Inverse Kinematics. A null object doesn't do anything by itself, nor does it appear in a render. It does, however, offer more control and functionality to many of LightWave's features. You can use null objects for Inverse Kinematic control points called Goals (covered in Chapter 13, "Bones and Character Animation"), as parent objects for different groups, and more. You can use nulls to control groups of Lights and for reference objects in 5.5 to control texture placements on objects. Null objects are very useful throughout Layout, and you will call upon them often as you progress with LightWave.

You can use a null object to parent two objects. Each object moves independently, but the null object can move both objects globally. As an example, think of a mother trying to control two children, each trying to play with the other. If the children's mother puts them in a stroller built for two, she can control them with one effort, although both children are still absorbed in their individual actions. Without the stroller, the mother would have to move one child, then the other, and movement would disrupt the children's actions or motions. Think of a null object as the mother for whatever objects are assigned to it.

In the following exercise, you will add elements from the book's CD to create a scene. You will add a null object to control the different elements, although they maintain their own independent actions.

CREATING A BACKGROUND ANIMATION

1. Open LightWave's Layout, and load the Advncd.lwo file from this book's CD. You should see the word Advanced in Layout. Then load the Comm.lwo file to see the word Communications, also in Layout.

2. These two words will slowly drift by the camera, blending slightly with the background, one faster than the other. Move the camera in to close up on the word Advanced so that only about three letters of the word show. Create a keyframe for the camera at frame 0. Figure 12.1 shows the Camera view.

FIGURE 12.1
The camera moved in close to the letters.

From here, you can either load the rest of Layout's elements or begin moving the objects. Typically, the more complex a scene is, the slower the response time will be. In such a case, loading and setting up a few scenes at a time works well. Here, however, you can load all of the elements.

3. From Layout, select the Objects button under the Edit menu at the left-hand side of the screen. Then, click and hold the Add button to add a null object. You can also add a null object through the Objects Panel.

4. Move the null to a central point between the two word objects. Create a key for it there. Be sure to check the position from all views.

The next step is to parent the objects and set them in motion. The moving objects will stay close to each other during their movements.

5. Select the Advanced word object as the current object. From the left-hand side of the screen, select the Parent button. From the drop-down menu, select the Null object as the parent for the Advanced word.

TIP

Although only one null object will be used in this animation, you can rename the null object to better organize your scene. From the Objects Panel, with the null object selected as the current object, choose Save Object. You can't save a null object the way you do a regular polygonal object, so you'll only rename it. Enter a new name when the requester asks what to save the null as. See figure 12.2.

6. Now that the Advanced word is parented, parent the Communications word to the null as well. Once that is complete, save the scene as **AdvWords.lws** or something similar. Select the null object and move it around. You'll see the parented object move with it. If you create motion files for the objects, they will retain their motions while the null object moves, rotates, or scales them. These are the objects you will use for the final scene. Now, you need to add the images.

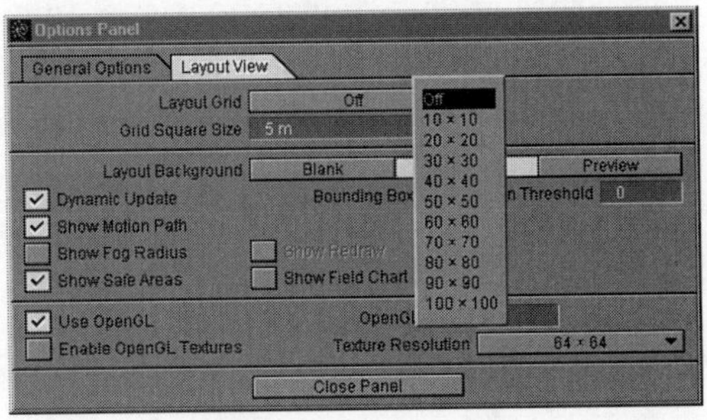

FIGURE 12.2

You can turn off the Layout Grid in the Options Panel to help remove clutter from the Layout view. This doesn't affect the scene, however.

Assigning Image Maps to Objects

You'll find that one of the most useful features for loaded images is image maps. Image maps are images that are loaded into LightWave from various sources. These can be scans of photographs, stock photography from a CD, or images from a digital camera, for example. Once an image is loaded into LightWave through the Images Panel, they can be mapped onto surfaces of objects in various ways. Image maps apply to many areas of LightWave, such as:

- Surface color
- Luminosity
- Diffusion
- Specular level
- Reflectivity
- Transparency
- Bump maps
- Clip maps
- Displacement maps

Image maps are essential for creating great-looking animations. Using a good 2D paint package in conjunction with LightWave is a must for animators.

As you become proficient in LightWave, you will inevitably begin using images throughout your animations. Images can be used for backgrounds, reflections, or for surfaces. This exercise will show you how to load an image and apply it to text objects in Layout.

USING IMAGE MAPS

1. From the Images Panel, load the Cloud.tga image from the projects directory on the CD that accompanies this book.

2. Load another image from the CD, Bluebkd.tga, and then close the Images Panel. Next, go to the Effects Panel, and under the Compositing tab, place the Clouds.tga image as the Background Image, as in figure 12.3.

FIGURE 12.3

The cloud image selected as the background image.

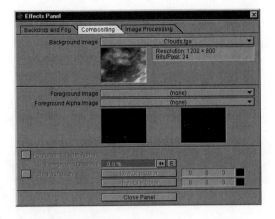

TIP

If your system can handle it, you can show the background image in Layout from the Options Panel. Click on BGImage and the image will appear in the background. Remember that nothing can be done to this image in Layout. Textures, lights, motions, and such won't affect the image. While you're in the Options Panel, you may want to turn off the visibility of the Layout Grid, as shown in figure 12.2. This helps clear up the Layout view.

3. Close the Effects panel. Often, animators use different contrasting images between their object textures and background images. Here, however, you are going to use the same image for both the background and object texture. From the Surfaces Panel, select the Advanced surface. Next to the Surface Color selector, press the T button to enter the Texture Panel.

4. Select Planar Image map as the Texture Type, and place the Clouds.tga image as the Texture Image. Turn off Width and Height repeat, set the Texture Axis to Z, and click Automatic Sizing. Turn off Texture Antialiasing and click Use Texture. Figure 12.4 shows the Texture Map Panel for Surface Color.

The same texture will also be applied to the Communications word. Even though the objects will be surfaced exactly the same way, separate surface names were given to them so that the image map applies to each object independently. With both objects named the same, the image would travel through both objects at once.

5. Because the same image will be applied to the Communications word, you don't have to reset the entire surface again. From the Surfaces Panel with the Advanced word as the Current Surface, click the small

Render button under the texture preview windows, as shown in figure 12.5.

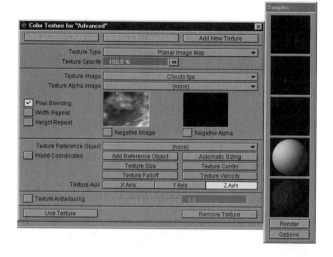

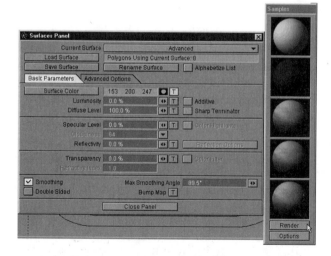

6. By testing the surface here, you can get a quick preview without rendering. You can also paste this surface to another, which is what you'll do for the Communications word. Select Communications as the Current Surface, and click on the Texture Sample in the preview window. A Requester like the one shown in figure 12.6 will appear

asking if you want to copy these surface settings to the current surface. Click Yes to copy the surface settings. Pressing s while in the Surfaces Panel will create an instant sample surface.

FIGURE 12.6

When you click the sample surface, LightWave asks if you want to copy the surface settings in the preview window to the current surface.

7. Your surfaces are now set. From the Objects Panel, remember to Save All Objects to keep the current surface settings. Additionally, you can Save Surface from the Surfaces Panel to apply this surface to other objects. Note, however, that only saving the object locks the surface to it for later use.

Render the image; it should look like figure 12.7.

FIGURE 12.7

The rendered image shows the words blending with background, almost indistinguishable.

The words in this image look somewhat washed out, or blended too much with the background. For this current project, that's the effect you are after. You can enhance this and separate the objects from the background slightly with the Glow feature.

8. From the Surfaces Panel, under the Advanced Options tab, find the Glow Effect area. Here, enter a value of 100% to the current surface. Add the glow to the other word's surface as well.

To use Glow, it must be turned on. Simply adding a 100% glow value in the surfaces Panel does nothing, unless you also turn on Glow from the Effects Panel's Image Processing tab.

9. Click on Enable Glow Effect. Leave the Glow Intensity and Glow Radius at their defaults. Close the panel, and in the Layout view, make another preview. Does the text stand out from the background? The glow adds a subtle but effective outline around the words. Remember that this is only the background animation. Only a slight representation of the words Advanced Communications needs to be seen; it doesn't need to be blatant. Figure 12.8 shows the rendered image with more defined objects.

FIGURE 12.8
LightWave's Glow Effect makes the letters stand out slightly from the background.

The results of using the same image as both the background and texture map, along with the glow effect, create an elegant, unusual look for the animation. When the letters are animated, the texture map cloud will move along with the letters, whereas the background cloud image will remain stationary.

TIP

For an added look, you can make the objects move through the texture, rather than having the texture stay attached to the objects. From the Surface Color Texture Panel, click on World Coordinates for the texture map. Do this for both the Advanced and Communications words.

OpenGL Texture Placement

LightWave 5.5 offers a new feature that can enhance your scene and object setup time tremendously. The OpenGL texture placement enables you to assign a null object to the actual image map on an object. In Layout, you can move, size, stretch, and rotate the image in real-time before rendering. Long gone are the days of guessing a texture's exact size, rendering a test frame, and repeating the process until it looks right.

LightWave 5.5 offers Texture Reference objects applied from the Surfaces Panel. By clicking the Add Reference Object button in a Texture Map Panel, LightWave adds a null object that is assigned to the texture at hand. This exercise will guide you through the setup and use of Reference objects.

USING REFERENCE OBJECTS FOR TEXTURES

1. With the Advanced objects loaded and the scene saved as AdvWords.lws, go back to the Surface Color Texture (T) Panel. In the middle of the texture panel, click the Add Reference Object button. You'll see the Texture Reference object added to the drop-down menu of Reference objects.

2. Return to Layout, and the RefObj should appear highlighted. If not, select it as the Current Object. In order to fully maximize OpenGL Texture placement, you need to perform a few steps. Go to the Options Panel and turn on the OpenGL display; also turn on OpenGL Texture. Depending on your system, set the resolution to 128×128. Usually, you don't need to go higher than this for simple setups.

TIP

If you've placed an image map on a texture and have turned on OpenGL Textures in the Options Panel but still can't see the texture on the object, you forgot one step. From the Scene Editor, remember to show the particular object (or all objects) as a Textured Solid, as in figure 12.9.

FIGURE 12.9

Be sure to tell
LightWave how to
display an object, such
as a textured solid,
from the Scene Editor.

3. Back in Layout, select the RefObj as the Current Object. Select Rotate from the Mouse commands. From the Camera view, with the right mouse button (mouse button and Ctrl for Mac), click and pull to the right. You'll see the image rotate on the surface of the object. This is a great new feature.

Without 5.5's Reference objects in Layout, angling an image such as this on an object would mean rotating the image itself in a paint program, and then reapplying to the object. Now, it's as easy as a click of the mouse.

4. Once you like how the image looks on the object, create a keyframe for the RefObj to lock it in place.

Because a null object controls the image, you can animate that null, in essence, animating the texture map on the object. This would include Size, Stretch, Move, or Rotate.

Using Reference objects is a real time-saver for creating more accurate images on textures. Later in the book in Chapter 14, "Facial Animation and Morph Gizmo," you'll use Reference objects to line up a human face onto a 3D head. Using Reference objects can be good for:

■ Rotating images on objects for a different look.

■ Applying image maps of faces to 3D heads.

- Applying image maps to space ships, tanks, and robots.

- Accurate placement of decals on cars or other objects.

- Sizing and positioning any image map on any object.

Working with Motion Paths

Motion paths in LightWave are instantly generated anytime an element is put into motion. In this animation, the camera will remain stationary with only one keyframe at zero. The Advanced word and the Communications word will move left to right of each other. The motion path can be edited later in the motion graph panel.

CREATING A MOTION PATH

1. Continue from the previous exercise. With the camera close on the objects, select the Advanced word object and turn off the Y and Z Move commands. With only the X-axis available, select Move from the Mouse menu on the left side of the Layout.

2. Move the Advanced word off to the right of the screen, just beyond the camera's range. Set a keyframe for it at 0.

3. Move the Communications word to the right-hand side of the screen and create a keyframe at 0. The Layout view should be free of objects except for null objects. You can also turn off the Y and Z Move commands.

4. Now, move the Advanced word to the left and off of the screen, and then create a keyframe at 350.

5. Select the Communications word, and move to the left and off of the screen. Change the Last Frame field (at the bottom right of the Layout interface) to 650.

6. With the word moved off screen, create a keyframe at 650. This will make the objects begin moving right to left, with the Communications word moving slower.

7. Make a wireframe preview and see how it looks in motion. You can find a wireframe preview on the CD accompanying this book. Depending on how much RAM your system has, the preview playback may not be in

real-time. If you are working with 64 MB of RAM or more, the preview should play well.

You can press the m key to enter the current object's Motion Graph Control Panel, as in figure 12.10.

FIGURE 12.10

The Motion Graph Panel for the CommIMG word. Here, spline control adjustments, keyframes, and scaling or shifting of frames can enhance and better control an object's motion.

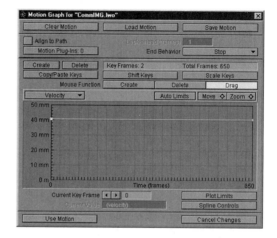

The Motion Graph panel enables you to add or delete keyframes in a particular motion. You can also make adjustments to any motions, such as spline controls. For the Advanced word object and Communication word object, you don't need to make any adjustments here. However, if you have added more keyframes to the object, a spline tension of 1.0 enables even greater control of motion of the object. The tension control would help the objects "ease-in" and "ease-out" of their respective keyframes.

Using the Motion Graph Panel allows you to see a graphical depiction of motion while giving you quicker access to keyframes. You can create, edit, and delete keys faster and easier in the Motion Graph Panel.

Make adjustments to objects, even the camera, through the Motion Graph Panel when you can. This area offers more precise control and can help you achieve the exact look you want. You can easily shift or scale an object's motion here as well.

Enhancing Animation with Background Elements

Background elements can significantly enhance the look of your animation. Instead of a plain-colored backdrop, you can add motion and various elements to the background for any type of scene. In this current example, you can use a background element for animated company logos.

Once you follow all of the steps on the previous pages, you should be ready to render the animation. Rendering this animation produces a sequence of images that can be loaded back into Layout as a background sequence. This sequence requires very little rendering and eliminates the need for LightWave to recalculate motions, glows, and other Layout instructions. You've set the background image as the clouds and set the objects in motion. Now you need to render the animation to be reused in another animation.

SETTING UP RENDERING

1. Go to the Camera Panel and set the Basic Resolution to Medium. Set the Pixel Aspect to D2, set Antialiasing to Enhanced Low, and select Soft Filter. Also turn on Adaptive Sampling with a setting of about 16.

2. Turn on Field Rendering, and then close the panel. The Rendering Mode should be Realistic.

3. Select the right value for your machine for multithreading: 1 Thread for 1 system processor, 2 Threads for 2 system processors. Turn off Show Rendering in Progress as well as Data Overlay. You don't need a render display, and the Render Last Frame value should be 400. The Render First Frame should be set to 1. Click on Automatic Frame Advance, and then select Save RGB Images.

When the Requester appears asking where to save the RGB images, find a secure place on your drive, and perhaps create a new folder for them. If you have a Personal Animation Recorder, Perception Video Recorder, Targa board, or some other playback device, save to that particular drive. Save the frames as BKD or similar. The RGB Image Format works well as a 24-bit TGA. Set this from the drop-down menu of selections. Lastly, click Begin Rendering.

You can now use your rendered animation as a background element in another animation.

Image Sequences

If your animation has finished rendering and you want to see what it looks like, compile it into a video recorder, such as a Personal Animation Recorder (PAR), Personal Video Recorder (PVR), or perhaps your nonlinear editing system. Playing back the animation can show you what the background animated image will look like.

Background sequences are useful for many applications such as compositing, rotoscoping, image manipulation, or simply time saving. The sequence you rendered out from the previous exercise can now be loaded into Layout and more elements can be added on top. This animation technique helps free cluttered Layout workspaces and saves time by allowing LightWave to not re-render background elements, but rather, only display an image.

In Layout, save all your work and clear the scene. Go to the Images Panel and instead of loading an image, select Load Sequence. The next exercise will guide you through the steps needed to use a background sequence in Layout.

USING BACKGROUND SEQUENCES

1. Press the Load Sequence button and select the first frame of the sequence of images you just rendered. You won't see an image in the Current Image window, but it will read filename (sequence). As the new animation is rendered, the sequence will be called up one frame at a time.

2. Close the Images Panel and then open the Effects Panel. Press p on the keyboard to open and close panels. As a note, you can instantly close panels by clicking on another panel.

3. Enter the Compositing tab, and select the loaded sequence as the Background Image. Figure 12.11 shows what your compositing window should look like.

4. Close the panel and return to Layout. If you go to frame 35, for example, and press F9 to render the current frame, you'll see that LightWave finds and renders frame 35 of the image sequence.

FIGURE 12.11
*Loading a sequence
and selecting it as the
background image
does not initially show
an image.*

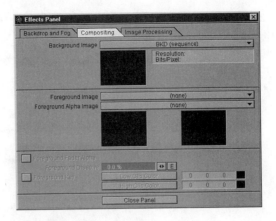

From here, you can load different elements to animate over the background.
However, you may want to add some effects to the background for an added
look. One way to do this is to process the images in a paint package such as
Adobe Photoshop, or a compositing and special effects tool such as Digital
Fusion. If you want to stay in LightWave and process only the background
images, you can do this through WaveFilter 2.0. Figure 12.12 shows the new
WaveFilter interface.

FIGURE 12.12
*WaveFilter from
Unlimited Potential
enables you to blur the
background images
without affecting the
other objects in the
rendered scene.*

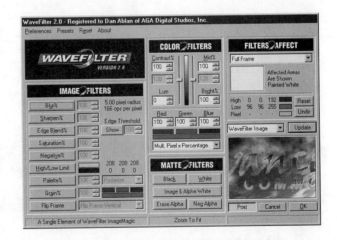

With WaveFilter, you can add many effects to your rendered images such as
Sharpen, Negative, High and Low Limits, Contrast, Grain, Blur, and many
other image processing capabilities. You can apply any effects to any part of
the rendered image. For this particular scene, Blur has been turned on and
set to affect the background only, as in figure 12.13.

FIGURE 12.13

WaveFilter's power enables you to blur only the background image sequence.

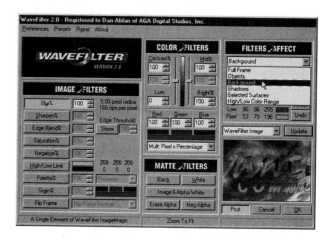

From here, you can add the rest of the elements to your scene. The original animation is set as a background image sequence and will be blurred for added softness in the background. Figure 12.14 shows the blurred image when rendered. Load a few more objects to complete the scene. You can load the same letters, Advanced and Communications, and animate them coming into position over the backdrop, for example. With these sets of letters, however, you can take off the cloud surface and leave the letters white, for example.

FIGURE 12.14

WaveFilter blurs the background image upon rendering.

With background sequences, you can change lighting, add shadows, and set reflections without any affects. Background sequences appear in an infinite plane, and no object light or other element can disrupt them. This exercise will demonstrate the use of background sequences in a scene with added objects and motions.

CREATING ANIMATIONS WITH SEQUENCES

1. Load the AdvncdIMG.lwo file and the CommIMG.lwo file into Layout with the background image sequence still in place. These are the same two-word objects you used to animate the background image sequence, yet with different surfaces.

2. Move the Advanced word behind the camera, and rotate it on its bank about –30 degrees or so, as in figure 12.15.

FIGURE 12.15

The Advanced word with a white surface is loaded and moved behind the camera to begin its motion into the frame. Note that this is a Perspective view of Layout.

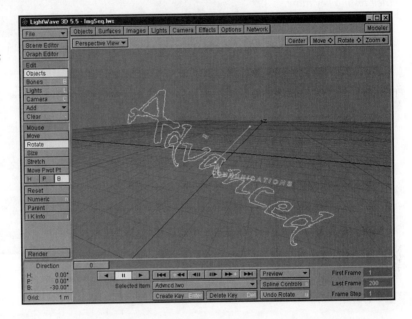

3. Now move the Communications word into the frame so that it's fully visible from the Camera view (press 6 on the keyboard). Then, move the word down on the Y-axis by selecting Move and using the right mouse button from the Camera view. Move the word so that it sits just outside of the frame. Create a keyframe for it at 0.

4. Now that the objects are in their initial starting positions, move the Advanced word into the frame from behind the camera. Set the bank rotation back to zero and create a keyframe for the Advanced word once it's in full view at frame 200.

5. Select the Communications word, and while it's still at frame 0, create a key for it at 180. This will hold it in place for 180 frames before it begins

moving. Note that you may want to add a spline setting of Linear to frame 180 to lock the object in place.

6. Move the Communications word back up on the Y-axis so that it is resting just under the Advanced word. Create a key for it at 240. Figure 12.16 shows the objects in their resting positions.

FIGURE 12.16

The two objects are in their resting keyframe positions centered on screen. Remember that when rendered, the background image sequence will appear.

NOTE

Unless an offset is specified for the background sequence within the Images panel, frame 1 of the animation will use frame 1 of the image sequence. Generally, rendering frame 0 will not show a background image. Render from frame 1 and up.

The last element to take care of is setting spline tensions of 1.0 for both the Advanced word at its resting frame of 200, and the Communications word at frame 240. This will help them gently rest into place. You can view the AVI or QuickTime file of the final animation on this book's CD.

These techniques are basic but fundamental. Setting motions, using splines, and applying images to different parts of your animation are very useful tasks. You can take these steps one bit further with Object Dissolves.

Object Dissolves

An Object Dissolve can add even more creativity and motion to your animations. Remember, a simple logo animated over a static background these days is not much to look at. 3D is more popular than ever, and audiences are used to seeing a lot of motion on screen. You can add other elements, such as moving image maps that dissolve on and off during the course of the animation. As you work through the next exercise, you can see that dissolves can be added to word objects to give them less of a hard look and bring out a more soft-flowing look by cross-dissolving objects.

You can use Object Dissolves for more than making objects appear or disappear. Fading objects and elements throughout an animation can enhance the look and feel of the final scene. The animation techniques in this chapter guide you through a layering process. Using Object Dissolves adds one more creative element to the process, as described in the following exercise.

USING OBJECT DISSOLVES CREATIVELY

1. As an example of using Object Dissolves, with the same scene loaded, load the Atrium.lwo file from the Chapter 13 directory on this book's CD.

2. With the flat atrium polygon loaded, the atrium image should load with it. This object consists of a single polygon with an image mapped onto it. Move this object behind the letters. You may need to advance to frame 200 to see the letters in their final resting place.

3. Move the Atrium object up to the top left of the screen, and create a keyframe at 0. Make the object hang out of the frame a little.

4. Next, move the Atrium object directly down, and create a keyframe for it at 300. Again, make it rest slightly off frame. Figure 12.17 shows the wireframe of the polygon in place at frame 200. Figure 12.18 shows the rendered animation at frame 200.

The atrium image is 30% transparent so that the background image sequence can still be seen. Remember that the background image sequence can be affected by the objects or lights in the scene.

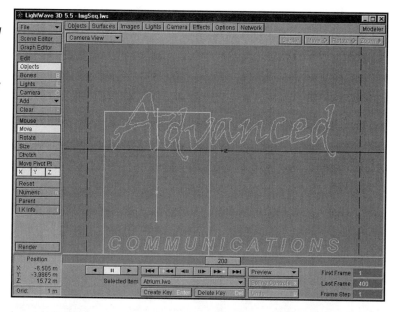

Taking this object one step further, you can fade it on just after it starts moving and just before it stops. This is a good way to keep the animation flowing.

5. Go to the Objects Panel and select the Atrium.lwo as the current object. Lower in the Objects Panel, go to the Appearance Options tab, and click the E button next to Object Dissolve. This will take you into the dissolve envelope for the current object, Atrium.lwo. You may need to remove any transparency maps as LightWave does not enable you to dissolve objects with Transparencies set.

6. The object is already set to 30% transparent. You want the object to fade in from 100% transparency to 30% transparency, not zero. Zero transparency would make it totally opaque.

7. Create a key in the envelope window at frame 5 and another at frame 20. The object will begin dissolving in at frame 5. Go to frame (f) zero in the envelope and set the Current Value to 100%. Also set 100% Current Value to frame 5 as well.

8. At frame 20, set the Current Value to 30%. Figure 12.19 shows what your envelope for the dissolve should look like.

FIGURE 12.19

The Object Dissolve envelope for the Atrium object. Here, the object will dissolve on over half a second, or 15 frames.

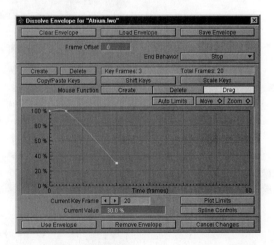

9. Create another keyframe at 280 and one more at 295. Set the Current Value at frame 280 to 30%, and then set it to 100% at frame 295.

TIP

Pressing n while in the Envelope Panel instantly places you in the Current Value window.

Now you need to set spline tensions for the keyframes in the envelope. If you look at figure 12.20, you'll see how the lines representing the dissolve curve slightly. The curves cause the Dissolve value to dip below 30% between frames 5 and 280. Note that the fact that it goes above 100% between frames 0 and 5 can be disregarded because 100% is the maximum effect. Spline tensions at a few keyframes will eliminate your object from drifting in and out of transparency.

FIGURE 12.20

Without spline controls set on the envelope, the object's dissolve will not be clean.

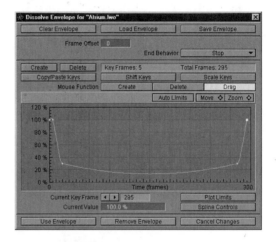

10. Go to frames 5, 20, 280, and 295 and set a spline tension of 1.0. Figure 12.21 shows the final dissolve envelope for the Atrium object.

FIGURE 12.21

The Object Dissolve for the Atrium object is clean and ready after a few spline tensions were added.

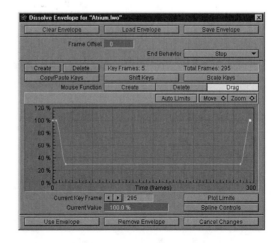

TIP

Whenever possible, try to keep an animation flowing. Dissolving on and off objects when they are in motion is a good way to achieve this. Also, when editing an animation into a video, it's professional looking to have elements continuously moving through complete fade out of the animation. The same rule applies when fading into an animation; elements should already be in motion.

If you render this scene as an animation, you will see that your object will now begin to fade when it is moving, and fade out before it stops moving. Wireframe previews do not show dissolves, only renders. This is typical of many video projects your colleagues might have produced. You can create the same DVE or Digital Video Effects in LightWave with Object Dissolves.

TIP

If you have the ability to grab video with your computer, try loading and mapping an image sequence onto the polygon. Instead of dissolving in a still image, you can have moving video within your animations. Or load a sequence of animation frames for more animations within animations.

Each of the techniques described in the preceding pages is commonly used in day-to-day LightWave work. As you progress and your work becomes more challenging, you'll use tools such as the Object Dissolve envelopes much more frequently. Other things the Object Dissolve is useful for are

- Dissolving on objects for added special effects.

- Dissolving out objects out of range of the camera.

- Performing cross-fades between similar objects to simulate a morph.

- Dissolving between two similar objects to simulate surface attributes changing.

- Using fast and flickering dissolves—great for clip-mapped images of lighting.

You can also add Object Dissolves to cover up an animation as well. Read through the next exercise to see how to do this.

DISSOLVING BACKGROUND IMAGES

1. Load the Bkdplate.lwo file from this book's CD. This flat polygon will be used to cover up the background animation to isolate the final letters as they come to rest.

2. Place the Bkdplate object behind the atrium object, as well as the Advanced and Communications word objects. Create a keyframe for it at 0.

3. Go to the Objects Panel and enter the Object Dissolve envelope (E) for the bkdplate. Because the objects finish their movements by frame 300, you can slowly dissolve on the Bkdplate object over two seconds or so. Create a keyframe at 240 and another at 300. Set the current value to 100% at frames 0 and 240. Set the current value to 0% dissolve at frame 300. Again, set a spline tension of 1.0 for the keyframe at frame 300. Figure 12.22 shows the image at frame 300 with the Bkdplate object dissolved in.

FIGURE 12.22

A background polygon is dissolved on to give the appearance of the background animation fading out.

Object Dissolves can really add some creative flare to your animations. Too often, you may see animations that are stiff and lack movement, or have too much. Finding the right niche for a basic but smooth animation is key to your success. Finding that niche requires the right techniques, many of which you've read about in this chapter.

To add to your knowledge of LightWave animation techniques, you should work with refraction, even to basic log animations. The following exercise is a simple example of how two objects can create an entirely different look for a client's logo.

Refraction

In Chapter 10, "Lighting and Atmospheres," some basic principles of refraction were discussed. Refraction can be used in LightWave to simulate a glass on a table, a magnifying glass, liquids, or perhaps water.

Part of creating realistic animations is to use real-world properties such as refraction. Refraction is the term that describes what happens to light as it passes through different surface properties. This exercise will step you through using refraction in a LightWave scene as an animation technique.

USING REFRACTION

1. Save any work you've been doing in Layout. Next, clear the scene and load the OmniLogo.lwo file from this book's CD. Also load the Water.lwo file. In Layout's Side view, move the Omnilogo down on the Y-axis below the water's surface, as in figure 12.23.

2. Press 6 on the keyboard to view the scene from the Camera view. Move the camera up above the objects looking down, as in figure 12.24.

3. The position of the Omnilogo should be at its resting keyframe. Create a key for it at 200. Set a spline tension of 1.0 also.

4. Move the logo off to the left of the screen. Create a keyframe for it there at 0. You don't need to set a spline tension here because the motion of the object will begin off camera.

If you look at the rendered image now, you won't see much. There are some things you need to do to make this logo look like it is under water. The first is to set the background colors.

FIGURE 12.23

The Omnilogo object is moved down on the Y-axis from the Side view.

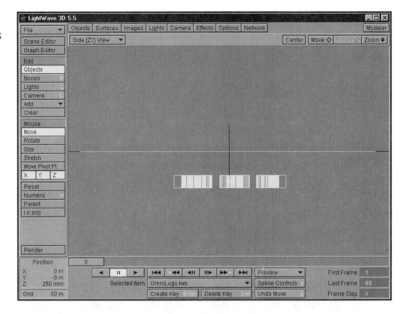

FIGURE 12.24

The camera is moved into position looking down at the objects. A slight angle here couldn't hurt.

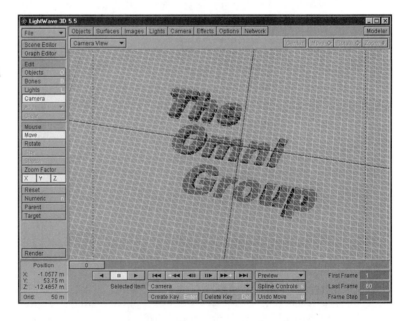

LightWave's default background color is black. However, you have the ability to use the background color settings in the Effects Panel for more than just color gradient backdrops. You can use the color gradient to help create a cloudy sky, or in this exercise, sea water.

5. Go to the Effects Panel, and under the Backdrop and Fog tab, set the Backdrop color to 156,210,237 RGB to create a blue-green sea color. Close the Effects Panel and return to Layout.

6. Now you need to make the water look more realistic. You've set the background color that will appear to be the sea under the surface of the water. Go to the Surfaces Panel and look over the settings for the water. Note that the color of the object is virtually the same as the backdrop color. What makes it stand out is its specular highlights. It is also 80% transparent. When LightWave's refraction rendering is turned on, the object will help refract the logo underneath it.

Water is not usually as flat as this object is. To change your object, go to the Objects Panel, set the current object to water, and under the Deformation tab, click the Displacement Map (T) button. This will take you into the Texture Map Panel for displacement maps.

7. Select Fractal Bumps as the Texture Type. Set Texture Size to 10 M for the X, Y, and Z values. Set Texture Amplitude to 2.0 and Velocity to .2 for the X, Y, and Z values. If you make a wireframe preview, you'll see the rippling water and the logo underneath. However, if you render the image, you'll see that the underwater logo feeling just isn't there. Figure 12.25 shows the rendered image without refraction.

The Water object has been subdivided in Modeler. In order for a displacement map to work effectively on an object, it must be made up of many segments. With an object made up of many segments, it is more malleable and open for displacement effects.

8. Now go back to the Surfaces Panel and make sure that the Refractive index for the water surface is set to 1.333. Go to the Render Panel at the top of the interface, turn on Trace Refraction and render again. This will take substantially longer to render due to the raytracing, but the results are worth the wait. Notice the difference in figure 12.26.

TIP

Because refraction takes significantly longer to render, you can fake the effects. By subdividing the Text object as well as the Water object, you can apply the same displacement map to the text. This effect is not a true representation of refraction, but rather gives the appearance of refraction. With both objects using a displacement map, you don't need to turn on trace refraction in the Record Panel.

FIGURE 12.25
Rendering the image
without refraction
doesn't make the logo
look like it's
underwater at all.

FIGURE 12.25
*Rendering the image
without refraction
doesn't make the logo
look like it's
underwater at all.*

FIGURE 12.26
*With Refraction turned
on in the Render Panel,
the image looks more
convincing.*

Refraction is a complicated study. However, for your animations, you don't need to understand all the principles involved in calculating light. With the help of the Refraction index found in your LightWave User and Reference guides, and knowing to turn on Refraction in LightWave, you can add more realism to your LightWave scenes.

Summary

Animation techniques can range from how you use your mouse to complex keyframing and motions. This chapter introduced you to powerful techniques that you can apply to any of your upcoming projects. However, the animation techniques described here are just the tip of the iceberg. Your practice and patience will inevitably help you create your own animation techniques. Here are a few reminders when creating animations in LightWave:

- Be sure to always check your LightWave User and Reference guides as you come across areas of the program that have you baffled. With a little help, you can be on your way to creating great works of animated art.

- A good way to pick up tips is to follow the e-mail and newsgroup lists on the Internet about LightWave. Look to monthly 3D magazines for current and different LightWave tutorials, such as *3D Design* from Miller Freeman Publishing.

No matter how saturated the field of computer animation becomes, or how much 3D animation is out there, your own techniques will set you apart from everyone else. Now, if you are ready to enhance your LightWave skills and techniques even more, read Chapter 13, "Bones and Character Animation."

Chapter 13

BONES AND CHARACTER ANIMATION

Bones and character animation are hot topics in the anima-

tion industry. These two elements of LightWave are the

reason many animators use the software. With the release of

Version 5.5, LightWave now offers improved bone function-

ality and enhanced inverse kinematics. The bone structures

in your body move the flesh around it. In LightWave, you set

up a bone structure in a character to make it move around.

Bones in LightWave are easy to use, if you set them up

properly. If you work with a poor bone structure, you will

have a difficult time keyframing the object.

This chapter will explain LightWave 5.5's bones and how they can help create realistic character animation. You'll learn:

- Understanding the role of bones in animation
- Choosing the right model for a bone structure
- Setting up bones properly
- Moving bones
- Modeling human objects and bones
- Animating a character with bones

Understanding the Role of Bones in Animation

Understanding what bones are, how they work, and why they are shaped like they are will help you use them to the fullest. Figure 13.1 shows one bone added to an empty scene.

NOTE

You must have an object in the scene to add a bone. A simple null object will suffice.

FIGURE 13.1
This is one bone in Layout.

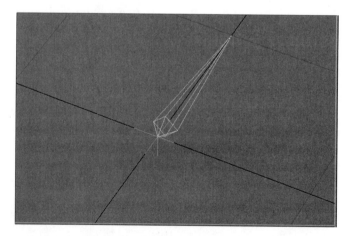

The bone's shape really doesn't mean anything. It is simply a representation of the bone's Rest Length. The fat end of the bone is its pivot point. The bone's Rest Length is its strength. The smaller the Rest Length, the less influence it will have on the object it's associated with. A misunderstanding with many

LightWave users is that they often set a bone's rotation, movement, and size before the Rest Length. This is not the right way to set up a bone. If this happens, the bone will instantly deform the object when it's made active.

When a bone is added to an object in Layout, it is in its inactive state. To load a bone, you can go to the Objects Panel, enter the Object Skeleton Panel under the Deformations tab, and click Add Bone. Or the easier way in LightWave 5.5 is to select the Add Bone command from the Add drop-down menu under the Edit group of items in Layout. Figure 13.2 shows the Add buttons in Layout.

FIGURE 13.2
You can add a bone, draw a bone, add child bones, and draw child bones directly in Layout in LightWave 5.5.

This new feature in LightWave also lets you draw bones and draw child bones, which will be described later in the "Hierarchies" section of this chapter.

When to Use Bones

Bones are used not only for character animation, as in this chapter, but also as "handles" for simple animated objects. A blowing curtain needs to have a little randomness added to the bottom of it, for example. A normal displacement map can create the ripples in the curtain, but to add a touch more movement, a bone can be used to pull the corner at varied keyframes. Something like this requires the use of only two bones, one anchor bone and the handle bone.

Another use for bones is for animating facial muscles. As you'll read in Chapter 14, "Facial Animation and Morph Gizmo," MetaNURBS models and the Morph Gizmo plug-in can animate different phonetic positions. But there are times when a certain expression, cheek bulge, or scowl is better accomplished with a bone. PIXAR, the makers of the hit movie *Toy Story*, used hundreds of controls to animate certain characters. For the character

Woody, it is rumored that the animators used more than 200 controls to animate his face alone, 75 of which were used for the mouth positions. The "controls" PIXAR used with their proprietary software can be compared to LightWave's bones features. That means over 200 bones need to be placed to animate a character like Woody.

Most of your projects won't require 200 bones. As a matter of fact, this is probably overkill. And with the power of Morph Gizmo, much of that work is eliminated.

You can use bones to create fluid human motions. Adding bones to a character's stomach, chin, or arms and moving them or sizing them at key times can create bouncing bodies.

TIP

To animate wobbling objects, be sure to check out Wobbler, one of the many plug-ins from software developer Jon Tindall at MetroGrafx.

You can add bones to objects such as a heart to simulate a beating pulse. Or add a bone or two to your favorite character to simulate breathing. Once you understand how bones work, where they are effective, and where they are not, you will use them more efficiently.

Bones do not move polygons but, rather, they move points. Because polygons are made up of points, the entire object deforms by a bone movement. Choosing the right model for a bone structure and character animation is key to your success in creating character animation.

Choosing the Right Model for a Bone Structure

Creating the right model for a bone structure doesn't mean that you have to model the character yourself. It also doesn't mean that you have to use a character in the true sense of the word, such as a 3D cartoon figure or an animal character animation. With the right bone setup, the right model, and the right keyframing, even a simple tin can or box will come to life. The right movements and timing can make a simple object have more life and character than a fully articulated human object with poor movements. Creating the right model for character animation means building an object that will deform well when animated with bones, whether it is simple or complex. To start out this chapter, you will build something you might have in your wallet or purse and make it come to life. You'll build it and place it in a scene that is on the *Inside LightWave 3D* CD.

Polygonal Models

Modeling for bones with polygons is different than modeling for architecture or modeling for still images. You need to be aware of what your character will do, how it will move, and what poses it will make in the scene. Knowing these details is crucial to properly modeling your object. In the case of the credit card in this section, it is going to be bent and manipulated to look like it has arms, legs, and a head.

This section will show you that a simple object, in this instance a credit card, can take on a human persona. The idea is credited to Mark Thompson and Jeff Goldman of The Big Machine (formerly Fusion Films) and their staff. You may have seen their dancing credit card on NewTek's LightWave 3D demo reels, and now it's time to make a version of your own.

You'll set up a bone structure with child bones for precise character movement. Often, bones that are not set up properly are difficult to control through rotations. The following exercise, as well as the exercises later in this chapter, explain the proper techniques for setting up bones.

TAKE CHARGE, PART ONE

1. Open LightWave's Modeler. Save any work you may have and press Shift+n to create a new work area. From the Objects Panel, select the Disc tool. Enter its numeric controls by pressing n on the keyboard. Enter the following values:

Sides	24	
Segments	1	
Bottom	0m	
Top	0m	
Axis	Z	
Center	X	−3.4659 m
	Y	5.3112 m
	Z	0m
Radii	X	312.6831 mm
	Y	312.6831 mm
	Z	0m

2. Click OK and press Enter to make the disc. Figure 13.3 shows the Disc tool Numeric Requester. This disc will become the corners for the Credit Card object.

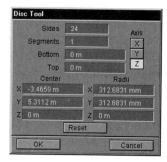

3. Press a on the keyboard to fill all views. Press k to kill the polygons. You are left with only the points. Select the points that make up the disc from 1 o'clock to 8 o'clock, as if the ring of points was a clock. Figure 13.4 shows the selected points.

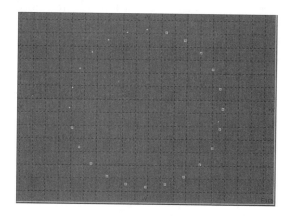

4. With the points selected, press z to delete them.

5. Select the Mirror tool from the Multiply menu (or press Shift+v) and mirror the object on the 0 X-axis. Now mirror again with the two sets of points on the 0 Y-axis. Figure 13.5 shows the set of points in four corners.

6. Select each point in order from left to right around all four corners, in a clockwise direction. Selecting points in a counter-clockwise direction results in polygons facing the opposite direction on the positive Z-axis.

FIGURE 13.5
*The original set of
points has been
duplicated three times
to create four identical
corners.*

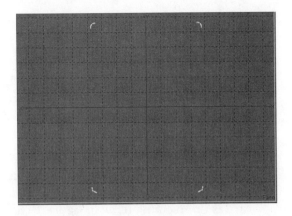

7. Once all points are selected, press p to make the polygon. Figure 13.6 shows the flat Credit Card object.

FIGURE 13.6
*Once the corner points
are selected, a polygon
is made to generate a
flat credit card.*

If you placed bones in this object, they wouldn't have much effect because in order to bone an object and create skeletal deformation, an object needs to be made up of many segments. In this credit card example, it's important to have rounded corners. But at this point, if you tripled and subdivided the polygon, you would get a terrible mesh of polygons, which could create unwanted tearing when rendered. Figure 13.7 shows how the credit card would look with triples and subdivided polygons.

FIGURE 13.7
*Because the credit card
has rounded corners,
tripling and
subdividing the object
results in an uneven
polygonal mesh.*

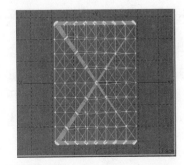

To keep the corners and maintain an even mesh, you can use the Boolean Intersect tool.

8. In a new layer, draw out a box slightly larger than the Credit Card object. Keep the Credit Card object in a background layer as reference. Before you make the box, press the up arrow key 14 or 15 times to increase the number of segments on the Y-axis. Press the right arrow key about 12 times to generate multiple segments on the X-axis. Press Enter to make the polygon mesh.

9. Go back to the Credit Card object, and extrude it about 2m on the Z-axis. Keep the subdivided box in a background layer and make sure the credit card is intersecting it, as in figure 13.8.

FIGURE 13.8

An extruded Credit Card object intersects a box with multiple segments ready to be Booleaned.

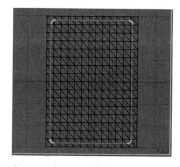

10. Press Shift+b to call up the Boolean CSG Requester, as in figure 13.9.

FIGURE 13.9

The Boolean CSG Panel where the objects will be intersected.

11. Select Intersect and click on OK. The credit card will now be flat, made up of an even mesh of polygons. If you see extra points generated and sticking out of one side of the object, simply select and delete them.

Figure 13.10 shows the credit card with an even polygonal mesh throughout. Now the card can be animated correctly without odd render errors.

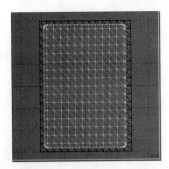

12. Select Intersect and click on OK. The credit card will now be flat, made up of an even mesh of polygons.

13. Press m on the keyboard to merge any duplicate points. Extrude the credit card on the Z-axis about 65mm.

14. Surface the object as front, back, and sides.

15. Save the object as **Ccard.lwo**, or something similar.

Within the next few pages, you'll need to load your creation into Layout to bring it to life.

TIP

Pressing z on the keyboard deletes a selected item and does not leave it in memory. Remember to use this key when permanently deleting selections. Pressing x on the keyboard appears to delete a selection, but actually cuts the points or polygons and keeps them in a memory buffer, which can be pasted into another layer.

Spline Models

Although LightWave needs polygons to render, you can still create objects in Modeler with splines for use with character animation. Objects with intricate curves and corners can be modeled cleanly and smoothly with splines. Figure 13.11 shows a spline curve created to make a mouthwash bottle.

You can load this spline object from the book's CD (Bot_spln.lwo) and make adjustments to it. LightWave 5.5's Backdrop Image loader is used to load a picture of a mouthwash bottle for exact spline creation. Lathing the spline can create a very clean model, ready to be brought to life. Load the Mouthwash bottle object from the book's CD for your own experimentation.

FIGURE 13.11
Splines are great for modeling intricate details in objects for character animation.

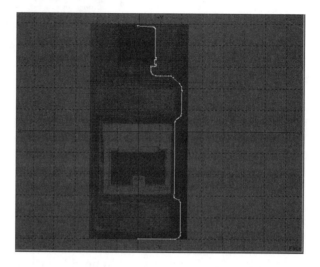

TIP

For more in depth information on LightWave and spline modeling, check out Chapter 7, "Character Modeling with MetaNURBS."

A major benefit of modeling with splines for characters is for tracing images. You might want to create a 3D character from a 2D image. Perhaps it's something you've drawn, or a character a client has provided to you. In either case, scanning the image and tracing over it in the background in Modeler with splines is one the most accurate ways to build a character without a professional 3D scan.

MetaNURBS Models

LightWave 5.0's introduction of MetaNURBS opened the gate to new ways of 3D modeling. MetaNURBS can help you easily create anything from a peanut to a potato chip, hairdryer, a computer printer, an automobile, and more. Of course, building characters with MetaNURBS is one of its best functions.

NOTE _____

See Chapter 7 and Chapter 14 for more information on character modeling with MetaNURBS.

MetaNURBS, or Non-Uniform Rational B-Splines, assists you in modeling characters with incredibly smooth polygonal meshes from very simple objects. This is a huge asset to the character animator in that polygon counts are kept low in Layout, enabling more speed and flexibility when setting up complex character projects.

Seamless Models

Before the use of bones, animated characters needed to be put together in a hierarchy. A hand object needed to be attached to a forearm object, which needed to be attached to an upper arm object, and so on. With bones, models can be seamless. Animating a character in a simple hierarchy resulted in seams at the joints, similar to the mannequin objects in figure 13.12.

FIGURE 13.12
Mannequin objects like these have seams at the joints, which makes the character look less lifelike and more like a puppet.

Bones within an object displace the entire polygonal mesh through its points, resulting in seamless models. Because of this, inanimate objects such as bottles, lamps, buildings, or credit cards can come to life. Try to work with seamless models whenever using bones. Your objects will look more realistic and more believable. Speaking of objects coming to life, it's time to give your credit card a real "charge," using its hierarchical structure.

Hierarchies

A hierarchy is a group of persons or things arranged in order of rank. That means that a bone structure within a character has parent bones and child bones within it. A hierarchical structure is what many of your LightWave animations will be built from, especially when it comes to character animation. The schematic in figure 13.13 shows a diagram of a hierarchical structure of a character, as seen by LightWave's Scene Editor.

FIGURE 13.13

This diagram of a character's bone structure shows the hierarchy. LightWave's Scene Editor shows an overview of the current scene as well as any and all hierarchies.

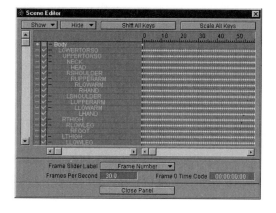

Here you can see that the body is the parent object. From there, the lower torso is a child that is parented to the upper torso, and so on. The head is a child of the neck. This hierarchical structure is set up so that, when the body or main parent moves, the child objects follow. Think of how your own body works to better illustrate things. When you twist your upper chest, your upper arms follow, as does you head. But, your head can turn by itself without affecting the parent objects. If the hierarchical structure were reversed, a head movement could result in the whole body moving as well.

Bone Structures

Simple or complex bone structures benefit from hierarchies. To set up a proper bone structure, you need to first determine what your character or object is trying to accomplish. For the animated credit card or just about any inanimate object, a human-like bone structure works best. Figure 13.14 shows only bones, but notice the human shape they create.

FIGURE 13.14
Here a bone structure is put together like that of a human.

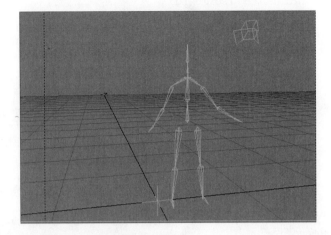

The bone structures you set up can vary from object to object. The following methods can help you minimize setup time and maximize performance.

Setting Up Bones Properly

How to set up bones is a matter of much debate. This book explains a method of setting up bone structures that will virtually eliminate the annoying gimbal lock problem common to bone structures. Gimbal lock is an artifact of specifying rotations. When an object's pitch angle is set to 90° (or –90°), a heading rotation produces the same result as a bank rotation. Physically, the pitch rotation moves the object's Z-axis onto the original Y-axis, which is used for heading rotations. For example, a bone is added into LightWave lying flat on the ground plane on the Z-axis. If the bone were rotated on the pitch at this point, it would rotate correctly.

When the bone is rotated and put into place within an object, it still thinks it's lying down on the Z-axis. What you'll find is that you are forever rotating active bones to move them into place.

The workaround for this is to load your object laying down as well. Typically, characters are built standing up and are loaded into Layout as such. By laying the character down, the bones are generated and made active without changing their original orientation. Bones move with an object, so rotating the object to an upright position results in a properly working bone structure. Follow along with the next exercise to set up a bone structure for the animated credit card.

The following exercise will guide you through setting up bones with LightWave 5.5's new Add Bone feature. From there, you will put the Credit Card object in motion.

TAKE CHARGE, PART TWO

1. From the CD accompanying this book, load the Ccard3D.lwo object into Layout. Notice that the card is loaded lying down on the ground plane, as in figure 13.15.

FIGURE 13.15

Setting up bones in an object while it's lying down avoids problematic rotations when the bones are active.

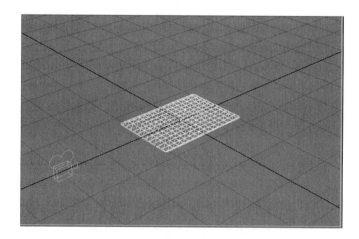

2. Go to the top view (XZ) in Layout (press 2 on the keypad) to see the Credit Card object straight on. Select the object from the Edit group, and then select Bones.

3. Select the Add drop-down menu, and choose Add Bone. You'll see a small bone pop up in the middle of the object. Notice that the bone's rotational pivot point is directly on the 0,0,0 XYZ axis. Figure 13.16 shows the single bone loaded.

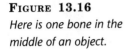

FIGURE 13.16
Here is one bone in the middle of an object.

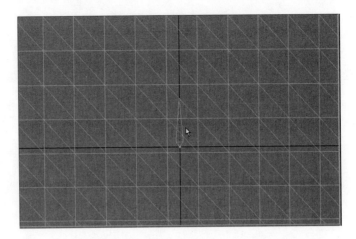

TIP

When setting up bones in any object, turn off the OpenGL display. From the Scene Editor, you can toggle between Wireframe and Shaded Solid display on an object-by-object basis. For this example, Show Objects as Partial Wireframes was chosen from the Show drop-down list.

4. From the Mouse group, select Rest Length for the bone just added. Click in the Layout window and increase the Rest Length of the bone to about 2.2. Watch the Information Panel at the bottom left of the Layout screen.

Never size the bone for setup. If you sized or stretched a bone before it is active, once it becomes active, your object will instantly conform to those bone settings. By setting the Rest Length, you are telling LightWave what length you want the bone, not what size. A bone's size directly affects the size of the object it is assigned to. A bone's Rest Length is the size of the bone's influence.

5. Once you've set the Rest Length, press the equal (=) key to add a child bone. It is important to set the Rest Length for the initial bone first because a child bone will be created with the same Rest Length. With the child bone selected, change its Rest Length to about 1.9.

6. Add a child bone to the second bone, and this time adjust its Rest Length so that the tip of the third bone sits just below the edge of the object, as in figure 13.17.

FIGURE 13.17
Child bones each have their Rest Length set; the last one is set so that it sits just under the edge of the object.

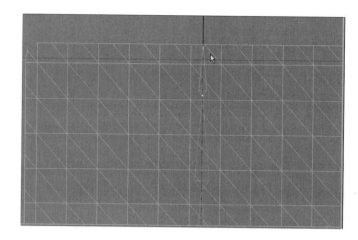

7. Select the first bone. This bone represents the body of the credit card and is the main parent bone. Add another child bone to it. This time, rotate the child bone on its heading about 110 degrees. Increase the Rest Length to about 3.2.

8. Repeat step 7, but rotate the new child bone by –110 so that it rotates the other way. These bones will become the arms of the object.

NOTE

As you add bones to your scene, it may be a good idea to go to the Objects Panel and rename the bones. In this example, you can rename bone 1 **body bone**. Rename the second bone **chest bone**, and so on.

9. Now add another bone. This time, rotate it 180 degrees on the Heading, and move it beneath bone 1 on the negative Z-axis, as in figure 13.18.

This bone will become the lower body bone. It will rotate independently of the upper body bones, such as the chest, head, and arms. Now all you need to do is add leg bones. You can add them as child bones to the lower body bone, or add them as independents. Because the object is not very complex, you can add the bones individually, not as child bones.

10. Add a bone, rotate it 180 degrees, and set the Rest Length to about 4.0 or so. Move it to the bottom left of the object. Repeat the process for the other leg. Figure 13.19 shows the final bone structure for the credit card.

FIGURE 13.18
Another bone is added, but not added as a child bone.

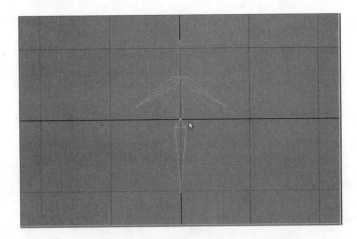

FIGURE 13.19
Using hierarchies and eight bones, this credit card is ready to come to life.

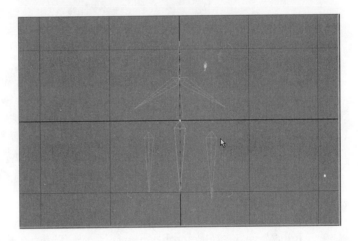

Adding bones to characters in LightWave is easy to do, once you know the steps. When it comes to inanimate objects such as a credit card, a bone structure is complex enough to give the object a persona, but simple enough to let you work efficiently.

Skeleton Maker Plug-In

Setting up bones for the credit card in Layout is the most common way to build the structure. The same goes for other objects such as humans and animals. But LightWave 5.5 offers a new tool, Skeleton Maker, that lets you build a bone structure through the use of splines, in LightWave's Modeler. It saves quite a bit of time when setting up any bone structure, especially more complex ones with Inverse Kinematics. Follow along to see how this new plug-in works.

With Skeleton Maker, you can create a complex bone structure for a human in a fraction of the time it would take to place bones in Layout. Figure 13.20 shows the Casual Guy with clothing.

FIGURE 13.20
The Casual Guy gets ready for some splines.

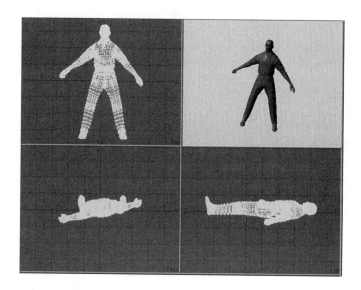

The following exercise will step you through the proper steps for using LightWave 5.5's Skeleton Maker plug-in. This exercise can be applied to any type of object. Here, you will use Casual Guy.

USING THE SKELETON MAKER PLUG-IN

1. Enter Modeler and, in a new layer, load the CasualGuy.lwo object from the CD accompanying this book.

2. Place Casual Guy in a background layer, and in a new foreground layer, select the Polygon tab and then Create Points.

By placing points, the Skeleton Maker plug-in will create a bone in Layout based on the points in the spline curve. For example, if you create three points from left to right and make a spline, Skeleton Maker will make three bones, a parent and two child bones. Because you created the points from left to right, the bones' lengths will be drawn to the right.

3. Start by adding points in the left arm. Place the first point in the shoulder area, the next at the elbow, and one more at the wrist. Because the pivot point of the bone will be generated at each point in the curve, placement is crucial.

Note

Be sure to pay close attention to all views when creating a spline for Skeleton Maker. If the curve is not lined up with the object properly, bones will be created outside of the object.

4. Once the points are created, press Ctrl+p to create an open spline curve. Tweak the position of the points using the Drag tool (Ctrl+t). Figure 13.21 shows the first spline curve created for the right arm.

FIGURE 13.21

The first spline curve is made for the right arm of the character.

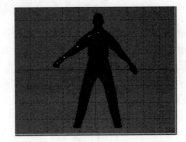

5. Repeat this process for the right leg. Make a point at the hip, another atop the thigh, one at the knee, another at the heel, and one more at the tip of the toe. Remember to move the points in each view. The toe point needs to be pulled out to the end of the foot. Press Ctrl+p to make a spline curve.

6. Once you have the right arm and leg splines created, you can mirror them over for the left side of the body. Because the object is not perfectly even on both sides, use the Drag tool to move the left side points into place. Figure 13.22 shows the arm and leg curves.

7. Starting at the waist, create points up the center of the model, another point at the collarbone, another at the neck, and the last one at the top of the head. Remember that the first point created will become the pivot

point for the bone. That means the fat end of the bone will be generated in Layout where you placed the first point.

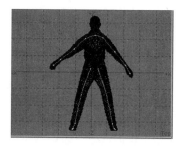

8. Select the waist point, and create another point at the base of the crotch. This will create a bone facing downward as an anchor. Now, create a point underneath one of the arms, toward the rib cage. Create a second point above the waist and create a curve for the two. This will create an anchor bone for the side of the model. Again, remember to watch all views when placing points. Copy this curve and paste it on the other side of the body.

9. For the last part of the curve, select the left shoulder point and the collarbone point. Press Ctrl+w to weld them together. Repeat this for the other shoulder. Figure 13.23 shows the final spline curve structure for Casual Guy.

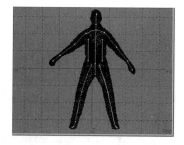

10. From the Tools tab, select the LW_Skeleton_Maker plug-in. Figure 13.24 shows the Skeleton Maker interface.

11. Skeleton Maker is easy to use, once you have the spline curves drawn. Click Enter Bones's Parent Object, in this case, the CasualGuy.lwo on the book's CD. Then, click Enter Scene File Name. Choose a directory on your hard drive to name and save the scene that Skeleton Maker created.

FIGURE 13.24
*The Skeleton Maker
interface.*

12. Check the Rest Bones button. This will activate the bones. Click OK.

13. Enter Layout and load the scene you just created. Figure 13.25 shows the object in Layout and the bone structure Skeleton Maker created.

FIGURE 13.25
*Skeleton Maker
generated this bone
structure, based on
spline curves.*

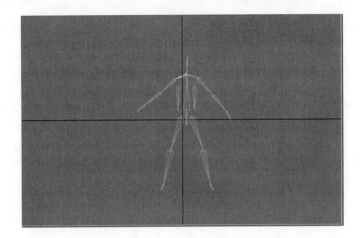

Skeleton Maker adds functionality to your work with bones in LightWave. Note that this is only another way to set up a bone structure in a character. If you are more comfortable setting up bones directly in Layout, you should do so. Skeleton Maker is simply another option for your creative talents in LightWave.

Moving Bones

Moving bones applied to an object in a LightWave scene moves the geometry associated with them. A misconception is that bones move the object when, in actuality, they deform an object based on the displacement of points. Don't expect bones to physically move an entire object.

When a bone is added to an object, it stays with the object. The proper way to move bones is to move and animate an object and use bones to perform skeletal deformations to limbs, faces, or the body of an object. The two combined equal character animation. Follow along with the next project to give that credit card of yours a little boost.

For the animation, you simply want the card to run across the screen. You might think, "how would a card run, if it could?" A common practice with animators is acting out the motions of what otherwise are inanimate objects. If you were placed inside a giant foam credit card for a trade show, how would it look when you walked around? Think about it, and apply the same motions to the 3D character.

The next exercise walks you through moving bones associated with an object. The bones will deform the object's geometry, whereas moving the object physically moves the character.

TAKE CHARGE, PART THREE

1. In Layout, load the ActiveCard.lws from the book's CD. This is the Credit Card object with an active bone structure applied.

2. Select the right leg bone and rotate it forward on the pitch. This will be the first leg the character is kicking forward. In conjunction with this, rotate the right arm bone forward, similar to figure 13.26, and create a keyframe at both for frame 8.

FIGURE 13.26

The right arm and leg bones are rotated forward to begin making the card run.

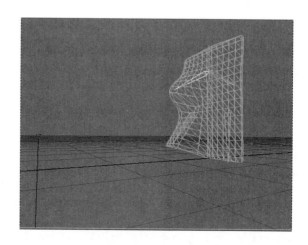

3. Next, rotate the left leg and left arm bones back, opposite of the right side bones. Create a keyframe for these two bones at frame 8 as well. Figure 13.27 shows the other half of the object's rotation.

FIGURE 13.27

The left side of the character begins moving.

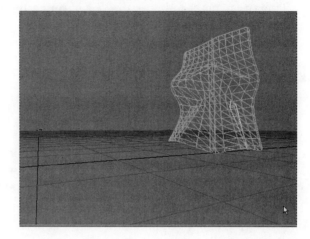

4. Select the chest bone and rotate it back on the pitch and also create a keyframe at 8. Go to frame 0, and create a keyframe for the bone positions there at frame 16. This saves you the hassle of moving each bone back to the original position.

5. At frame 24, rotate the left leg and left arm bone forward, and do the opposite for the right side bones. Create keyframes at 24 for each bone. Again, go back to 0, but this time create a keyframe for each bone at frame 32.

6. Lastly, put some bounce into the simple walk. At frame 8, raise the object up slightly off the ground. At frame 16, the card should be back on the ground, at frame 24, back up, and then down again at frame 32. Make a preview of the animation.

This walk cycle is basic but helps demonstrate how setting a few keyframes can bring a simple character to life. By moving the character from one location to another, in combination with bones displacing the shape of the object, a character is born.

Timing

When it comes to character animation on any platform, timing is crucial. Timing can make or break the look of your animation. It is important for you to study how a person walks and talks, how a person uses expressions to convey a message. Look at figure 13.28.

FIGURE 13.28
A skeleton takes the first step.

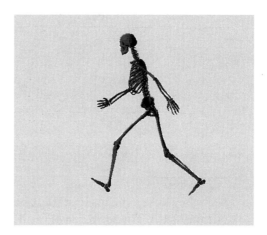

Here, the skeleton begins walking. Notice how more than just the legs are moving. The body moves, and the center of gravity is forward, as it would be when walking. A character that is standing straight up with only the legs moving is somewhat unrealistic. In figure 13.29, the skeleton continues walking, head bobbing along the way.

FIGURE 13.29
The skeleton bobs his head as he walks.

As the skeleton walks, his hips turn, the head bobs, and the arms swing. These are all things people do when they walk without even realizing it. As a 3D animator, it's your job to study people and their movements. Figure 13.30 shows the skeleton pushing his body forward along with his head to make the next step. To better understand the nuances of a walk, load the SkelWalk.AVI movie from the CD.

FIGURE 13.30

The skeleton bobs his head up and pushes it forward for the next step.

The timing of the motions and bones cannot be stressed enough. Timing in character animation is a learned technique. To master timing and keyframing, your best weapon is practice. This chapter guides you through tools and instructions for you to learn with. Timing keyframes and bone movements takes much practice to get it right. Study character work from your favorite animators. Watch videos with a stop watch to see how movements are timed. How long does it take for a pitcher to throw a baseball? How long does it take to walk up a flight of stairs? Study whatever you can and you'll have people studying your work in no time.

Creating a Key for All Items

When you create a keyframe for a bone, an object, a light, or the camera, you can select from Create Key for Selected Item, All Items and Decedents (parents and child objects), or you can create a key for All Items. This function is very useful in that if you are moving a series of bones, you don't have to create a key for each one. However, this section is mostly here as a warning.

If you have been animating with LightWave for a while, you might be comfortable with pressing the Return or Enter key to create a keyframe. When you create a keyframe and select Create Key For All Items, LightWave remembers that with each additional keyframe. Be careful that you don't quickly create a key without looking at this setting. You could have set up just the right motion for a bone, and then go to move another. Accidentally, you selected Saved For All Items, and the perfect keyframe now jumps quickly to the other keyframe, its timing now changed.

Use this only when you know it's exactly what you want to do. When in doubt, leave it out. For most normal keyframes, you can create keys on an individual basis.

Modeling Human Objects and Bones

With the earlier exercises, you saw how setting up a bone structure properly is important. Lying an object on its back while placing bones helps eliminate gimbal lock. Additionally, you saw that the Skeleton Maker plug-in is extremely helpful in creating complex bone structures.

Placing bones in human characters is more challenging due to its complexity. With the use of the Skeleton Maker plug-in in Modeler, a complex bone structure is easier to create. Creating bones in humans means recreating a simplified bone structure of a real human. That is to say, a spine needs to be made, shoulder bones, upper arms, femurs, hand bones with finger bones, and so on. These multiple bone structures can be tedious to set up but worth the effort when it comes to animation. The next section discusses multiple bone structures and how you can use them in conjunction with other bone structures in a scene.

Multiple Bone Structures

Multiple bone structures within an object is more than one hierarchy. When it comes to human bone structures, multiple parent and child structures can be set up in the same character. In addition, you can create scenes in which characters with different bone structures can act independently of each other. Figure 13.31 shows a complex hierarchy.

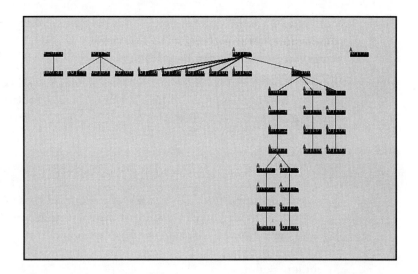

If you load a new scene with a character and another bone structure, you add a different animated character scene. Using the Load From Scene function in Layout's Objects Panel, you can put the contents of one scene into another.

Working this way enables you to work in a clutter-free Layout while maintaining much of your system resources. Using Load From Scene for character animation is an essential key. You can set up bone structure and key movements and save the scene. The only things in this scene are the character and its bone structure. Then you can load this scene into a much larger scene such as an animated city or living room to bring the character to life.

Cloning Bones

Cloning bones is another important step in your study of bones and character animation in LightWave. Because of the way bones work, you cannot parent objects to boned objects. Polygons are made up of points, and they also move with points. For example, you have a little JellyBean character that you are thinking of animating for a commercial. You create the JellyBean, its legs and arms, and save it. You add eyeballs and parent them to the JellyBean in Layout. Once the bones are added and the character is animated, nothing happens to the eyes! The eye objects are parented to the position of the JellyBean and ignore deformations of the JellyBean by bones. Remember that bones pull and deform points, not polygons. There is a workaround to this. Follow along with the next exercise.

Cloning bones is a technique that might come in handy when animating characters with bones. The deformations bones imply do not affect parented objects. This exercise explains how to clone a bone structure to keep parented objects in motion with boned objects.

CLONING BONES

1. Load the JellyBoneActive.lws scene file from this book's CD. This is a little character you can use in your own animations to practice timing and movement. Next, load the Eye.lwo object from the CD. The eyeball is loaded separate from the JellyBean because it needs to rotate independently.

2. Parent the Eye.lwo object to the JellyBean. Move the eyeball to the upper-right area of the JellyBean, as in figure 13.32.

FIGURE 13.32
One eyeball is loaded and moved into place.

3. Now move some of the bones around. Select the chest bone, and rotate it on the pitch. Notice how the eyeball doesn't move? This is the reason you need to clone the bones. Figure 13.33 shows the character bend backward minus his eyeball.

FIGURE 13.33
*Because of the way
bones work, rotating
the bone to bend the
object does not bend
the eyeball along
with it.*

You can easily avoid this problem through the use of clones. By using
dormant bones on the character where the eyes would sit and cloning the
original object, an eyeball can be added. Clones of objects also clone any
associated bone structure.

4. Select the JellyBoneActive.lws scene, and clone the JellyBean object
   once from the Objects Panel. Select Replace Object from the Objects
   Panel for the cloned JellyBean and replace it with the Eyeball object
   found on the book's CD.

5. The Eyeball object's main spine bone (chest bone) needs to be lined up
   with the main spine bone of the body. Because the eyes are modeled at
   0,0,0 XYZ axis for perfect rotation, it does not load into the scene in
   correct position. Moving it will also move its skeletal structure.

6. Deactivate any bones in the Eyeball object, and then move it into its
   position on the JellyBean. Create a keyframe at 0. Select the Eyeball
   object's chest bone, press r on the keyboard to activate it, and then
   deactivate it from the Skeletal Deformation Panel within the Objects
   Panel. You don't want to activate any other bone in the Eyeball object
   other than the main one, the chest bone.

7. Activate the Eyeball object in the JellyBean object. Your eye should now
   track the JellyBean object.

Cloning bones is a good workaround for situations when all other options fail. Although somewhat awkward at first, cloning can help you achieve the look you want. You can also try using LightWave's Motion plug-ins.

T I P

When using the Parent Bone plug-in, you need to create a keyframe for the object to see it follow the motion of a bone.

Animating a Character with Bones

Animating a character can be the most tedious but rewarding work you will do in LightWave. Along with a good story, a character's entire expression, movement, and timing are key to the animation's success. These tips can make the task simpler:

■ Keep a mirror by your desk. Watching yourself move and use expressions can be good reference for animating.

■ For dance, walk, or run moves, perform for yourself and study the movement.

■ Timing is everything, so practice, practice, practice.

■ Avoid repetitive computer-generated cycles, such as a walk or a run. Keyframe the movements for more realistic and random effectiveness.

Another great way to animate a character is to animate over an image sequence. By loading an image sequence into LightWave, you can move your character into position using the sequence as a template. Figure 13.34 shows an example.

Additionally, you can animate a character to sound. Using LightWave 5.5's audio capabilities, you can move a character to sound. Both of these methods are some of the fastest and most efficient ways to make a character come to life with music, because timing is no longer left to chance. What really helps to animate the character is Inverse Kinematics.

Understanding and Applying Inverse Kinematics

LightWave 5.5 has improved the speed of its Inverse Kinematics routines by nearly 500%. This means that adding multiple goal objects is no longer a problem, even on slower computers. You can now easily add a goal object to characters' hands, feet, knees, elbows, and heads while still maintaining control.

Inverse Kinematics, or IK, enables you to pull one object and have the rest follow. This is not only great for animating things such as chains or ropes, but characters. Figure 13.35 shows CasualGal.lwo with an IK chain in place. The crosshairs at the limbs are null objects assigned as goal objects. A goal is what the hierarchy looks to for control.

When to Use Inverse Kinematics

You can use Inverse Kinematics essentially whenever you want. Unlike bones, IK is important to many types of animations: industrial, architectural, and character. Typically, you may see IK chains placed on characters, as in figure 13.37. Moving a null object and having the character's arm follow is an effective way to create realistic motion of limbs.

FIGURE 13.35
The Casual Gal is better controlled with the help of Inverse Kinematics.

However, you can use IK in different way, sort of like a lock. If you want to make a superhero crouch down, pause, and then leap off to fly over his favorite building, how would you do it? Usually by bending the legs, moving the feet, and then moving the objects. But you can use IK goals to lock down feet and use another null to move the legs.

Using Inverse Kinematics, bones, and null objects, you can make a pair of legs jump off the ground without the aid of additional plug-ins. LightWave 5.5's Inverse Kinematics feature enables you to set up an IK goal so that jumping legs and feet stay firmly on the ground. Follow along with this next exercise to create jumping legs.

JUMP!

1. Load Legs.lws into Layout from this book's CD. Animating a jump can seem to be a daunting task. To make your life simpler, you can use IK to control two legs.

2. From the Edit group of items, select the Add drop-down list and choose Add Null Object. Figure 13.36 shows the scene as it's loaded.

3. The new null object should be centered between the legs. Now select each leg and parent it to the new null object. Feel free to rename the new null Leg Mover or something similar from the Objects Panel.

FIGURE 13.36

A couple of legs. You can easily animate these legs with the help of a little IK.

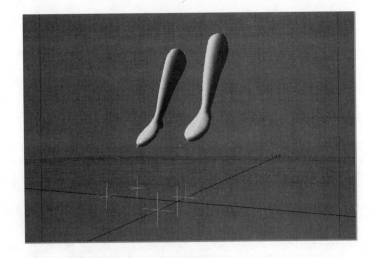

Each leg has an IK chain already set up through the use of two nulls. Figure 13.37 shows the bone structure. Each leg has a thigh bone, shin, and foot bone hierarchy. The last bone in the chain is the toe bone (bone 4) that is barely visible. The foot bone (bone 3) is set to an IK goal at the heal. The toe bone is IK'ed to a null at the toe.

FIGURE 13.37

A bone structure in the legs will move the leg around when set with Inverse Kinematics.

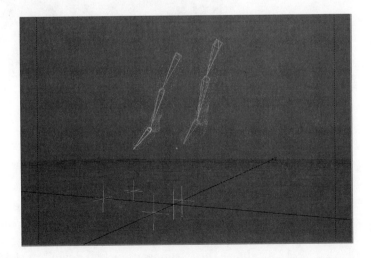

Because adding a goal and IK chain places the control at the pivot point of a bone, adding a very tiny toe bone gives control to the front of the foot. If only one goal was added to the foot bone, the control would be at the heel. If you added a goal to the shin bone (bone 2), you would have a control at the knee. The two IK goals for the leg are placed on the 0 Y- axis.

4. With the two legs parent to the new null (the mover null), you can begin animating a jump.

5. But before you animate the legs, press 3 on the keyboard to switch to a side view. Select the Leg Mover null, and then choose Move Pivot Point from the Mouse group of items on the left-hand side of the Layout screen. Figure 13.38 shows the view.

FIGURE 13.38

The side view shows the Leg Mover null object.

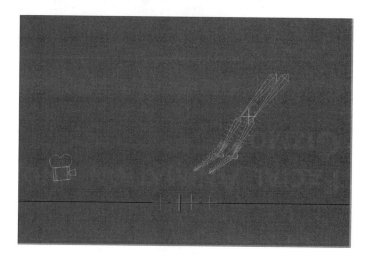

6. Move the Leg Mover null up and to the center area of the legs. Press 1 on the keyboard to switch to a front view, and make sure the null is centered between the legs. Press 6 on the keyboard to return to the Camera view. Figure 13.39 shows the Camera view with the null centered.

7. Now with the Leg Mover null selected, using the right mouse button (use Ctrl and the mouse on the Mac), move the null down. Turn off X movements, and move the null toward the camera on the Z-axis. Figure 13.40 shows the legs now crouched down but the feet stay locked to the ground.

FIGURE 13.39
The Camera view
shows the null ready
to animate the legs.

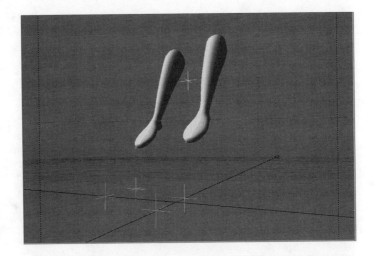

FIGURE 13.40
By moving the Leg
Mover null, the legs
crouch down to the
ground.

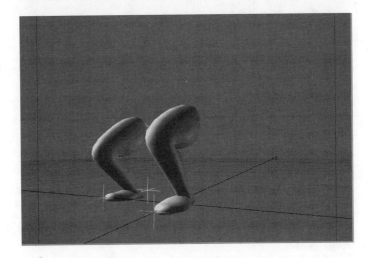

8. Move the null up and the legs will follow, as in figure 13.41.

9. Continue moving the Leg Mover null and then follow with the IK nulls to finish the jump.

FIGURE 13.41
Moving the Leg Mover null up brings the legs into a jumping stance.

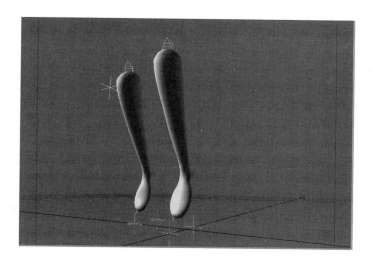

This method works well when legs need to be locked down. This method also works well for that common foot slide problem found with walking or running characters. Using the Muscle Flexing feature of bones, the calf bones and thigh bones in the legs make the leg objects bulge as they crouch together. This adds more realism to a character's movements. Load LegsIK2.lws from the accompanying CD to see a jump in motion.

Making Setup Easier with IK and Bones

Inverse Kinematics and LightWave's bones create a good marriage of tools. LightWave 5.5 makes the setup process a bit easier through the use of Draw Bones.

Drawing bones in Layout is a simpler way to add bones while setting their Rest Lengths at the same time. Typically, you would add a bone, move it, and set its Rest Length. Drawing bones allows you to click and drag out a bone, instantly generating it in place with the desired Rest Length. Read through this exercise to use the Draw Bones and Draw Child Bones features.

DRAW AN IK CHAIN

1. Clear Layout and add a null object. Press 2 on the keyboard to go to a top view. Select the null, and then select Bones for the null. Click the Add drop-down menu as seen in figure 13.42, and choose Draw Child Bones.

FIGURE 13.42

You can select the Draw Child Bones feature directly from Layout's Add menu.

NOTE

When using the Draw Bones feature, you can draw bones only in the Top, Front, and Side views.

2. Once Draw Child Bones has been selected, click in the Layout window with the left mouse button, and drag to the left or right. As you do this, you are doing two things: adding a bone and setting its Rest Length at the same time. Because you selected Draw Child Bones, you can click, drag, and release to make a bone. Then click and drag again to draw the child. LightWave will automatically add the child bone onto the end of the previous bone. Use the Layout grid as reference for drawing equally sized bones. For the last bone, make it very tiny, for the IK null, similar to the heel and toe example earlier in the Inverse Kinematics section of this chapter. Figure 13.43 shows a bone hierarchy created in about 10 seconds.

TIP

Once you select Draw Bones or Draw Child Bones, the mode is maintained until you press a button on the keyboard or select another function. If you change views, you will need to reselect the Draw Bones features.

3. Select Objects, and then add another null object. Move this null to the last bone on the chain you just drew.

4. Select the first null (Null1) and then select Bones. Select the last bone in the chain, the small one you put at the end. With that bone selected, click the IK Info Panel in Layout. Figure 13.44 shows the IK Panel.

FIGURE 13.44

The Inverse Kinematics Panel in Layout.

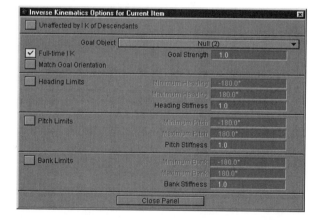

5. Select Null2 as the Goal Object, and turn on Full-time IK. Full-time IK tells LightWave that Inverse Kinematics is always on, not just when a keyframe is created.

6. Go back to Layout and select Null2. Move it around and watch the IK chain in action. Figure 13.45 shows the null's effect on the bone chain.

FIGURE 13.45
*Movement of the null
object bends the chain
around.*

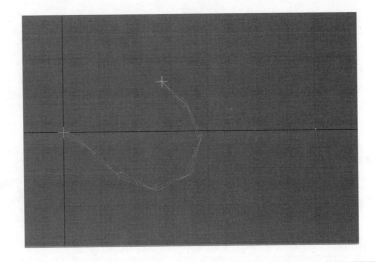

This shows how simple and effective an IK chain can be, especially when used with bones. However, there might be circumstances when you need to add another control in the middle of the chain. This can be done with another null object.

Once an Inverse Kinematics chain has been set up, you might need more control over certain joints such as the knee of a leg or an elbow. You can add additional Goal objects for control over additional areas. This next exercise takes you through adding IK Goals to an existing scene.

ADDING MORE IK GOALS

1. With the same IK chain of bones already loaded (or load the BoneIK.lws from the book's CD), add another null object to the scene. Move it to the middle of the bone chain as in figure 13.46.

2. Select the bone directly to the right of the null, as in figure 13.45. If you drew the bones to the left, select the bone to the left of the null. Whichever way you drew the bones, remember that the null will control the chain from the pivot point of the bone it is IK'ed with.

3. With that particular bone selected, open the IK Info Panel, and set the third null as the Goal Object. Turn on Full-time IK.

FIGURE 13.46
A third null is added to be used for more control over the IK chain.

4. Go back to Layout, and select the Null3 object and move it down. Then move Null2 around. You can see that you have more control over the position of the bone chain as in figure 13.47.

FIGURE 13.47
A third null object adds more control to the bone chain once the IK has been set.

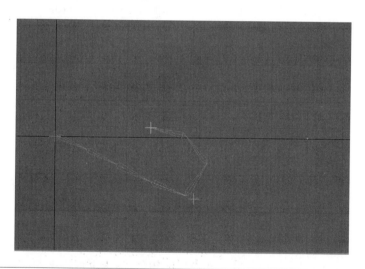

This method of using multiple goals with bone chains is a base foundation that you can employ in any of your animations.

Auto Key Adjust and IK

The Auto Key Adjust and Auto Key Create functions can be helpful when setting up movements with Inverse Kinematics. Turned on from the Options Panel, these features when both activated enable you to move a null in place at a particular keyframe and do nothing else. A keyframe will be created for you automatically.

This is useful when your character is moving around and you need to tweak certain IK positions at particular frames. To use them, turn both Auto features on, and return to Layout. From there, go to the particular frame in which you want to give something a keyframe. Move the null or bone to the desired position at that frame. Then, go to the next frame, and move again.

Working this way takes practice if you have always created keyframes manually. Try creating keyframes both automatically and manually on the same scene to see which method works best for you. Often you may find that manually keyframing and then using the Auto features for tweaking is a good way to go.

Warning

Auto Key Adjust and Auto Key Create will remain selected the next time you start LightWave. Their functions are remembered in LightWave's configuration file. Remember to turn them off after use. Accidentally having these functions on can create unwanted changes to your scene. Remember when left on, Auto Key Adjust and Auto Key Create can be considered Auto Key Destruct!

Summary

Bones and character animation can be the most rewarding aspects of animating with LightWave. You've read in this chapter that when set up properly, bones can truly bring your character to life. In this chapter, you learned:

- Bones deform points, not polygons.
- To set a bone's Rest Length, not its size, for placement.
- To set up bones in a character that is lying flat for greater control over bone rotations.

- To create bones in LightWave 5.5 in Layout or Draw, or with the Skeleton Maker plug-in in Modeler.

- Character animation requires practice. Timing and proper keyframing are key to a successful character animation.

- That you need to practice!

Use the objects and scenes provided on this book's CD-ROM and experiment with the examples and techniques described throughout this chapter. When you are ready, move on to Chapter 14, "Facial Animation and Morph Gizmo," to make your characters talk.

Chapter 14

FACIAL ANIMATION AND MORPH GIZMO

Developing a character for 3D animation involves a good story, proper technique, and, of course, a believable character. No matter how complex or simple a character may be, along with proper motion, the facial expressions bring a character to life. In this chapter, you'll see that reproducing the human facial muscle structure can create phonetically shaped faces that you can use with LightWave 5.5's new Morph Gizmo plug-in.

The following list describes the different techniques you will learn in this chapter:

- Understanding the human face

- Understanding phonetics

- Working with Morph Gizmo

- Lip syncing in LightWave

This chapter will introduce you to techniques to model and animate your character's facial expressions and guide you through setting up a complete animation with lip syncing, character facial expressions, and character movement. You'll also see how to use bones to animate facial area muscles.

Understanding the Human Face

Before you dive into Modeler to create your favorite character, it's important to study how the muscles in the human face work. Figure 14.1 shows a human face with the muscles underneath.

Refer to figure 14.1 and you'll see the corresponding muscles.

1. The Frontalis muscle raises eyebrows and is used for speaking, helping the face create expressions.

2. The Curragator pulls eyebrows down and brings them together. This muscle is used when conveying emotions such as anger and fear. It also comes into play for some people when they are in deep thought.

3. The Levator Palpebrae raises eyelids.

4. The Orbicularisoculi muscle squeezes the eyelids into a squint.

5. The Levator Labii Superioris lifts the upper lip and curls the nose to display rage.

6. Zygomatic Major creates a grin. The zygomatic pulls the entire orbicularisoris, the muscle circling the lips, back toward the ear.

7. The Triangularis muscle moves the ends of the lips downward into a frown.

8. The Orbicularis muscle tightens the lips.

9. The Risorious/Platysma. This muscle pulls the lower lip sideways and shows the lower teeth.

10. Depressor Labii Inferioris muscle. This muscle pulls the bottom lip down.

11. The Mentalis muscle. This muscle pulls the lower lip up to make a pouting mouth.

FIGURE 14.1

The human face is comprised of many intricate muscles. Movement of key muscles generates facial expressions.

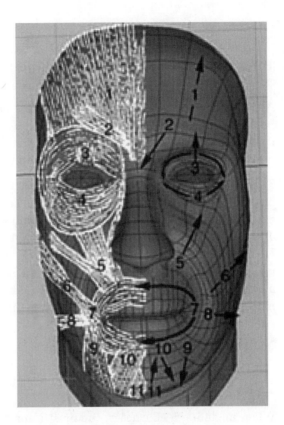

These key muscle groups of the facial structure can aide in your facial animation practices. Placing bones at these key points or modeling the different positions with Morph Gizmo help create the right set of facial models.

Modeling a Human Face

When you understand how a human face is built, you can begin building models. Since characters in animation represent human personas, the same facial structure can be applied and exaggerated to create different morphable face targets as well. These targets in LightWave refer to a face (or head) object that is made up of the same number of points and polygons (in the same order) but with variation. As an example, a facial morph target can vary from the facial morph source in that the source face has no expression where as the target face is smiling. You can use differently shaped facial models as different morph targets—the end result being an animated face.

NOTE

See Chapter 7, "Character Modeling with MetaNURBS," for more information on modeling characters in LightWave with MetaNURBS.

Although there are some excellent models on the CD accompanying this book, you may want to model your own unique human face. Follow along with these exercises to see how LightWave's MetaNURBS can be used to model a human face you can make talk in Morph Gizmo.

For these exercises, you won't build a character face out of a box like you may have seen in many MetaNURBS demos. The following technique is used extensively by Susan Ishida and Joe Clausen, the talented animators at Joe's Digital Bar & Grill (http://www.lightwavelab.com/) and on their LightWave Lab training tape, Volume 1. For this tutorial, you are going to use a variation of their techniques. Joe and Susan begin modeling faces with a box, but a flat one. From there, they add points and begin molding the model. In this tutorial, you will begin with only points, then create quad polygons, and so on.

The Eyes

When modeling a character, the most important area is the eyes. For this reason, the exercises in this chapter will begin with modeling the eyes of a character. When discussing the eyes, the entire eye region of the face is included, such as the eyebrows, eyelids, bags under the eyes, and so on. The eyes are important because it is through them that emotion is expressed, such as fear, sadness, anger, happiness, and so on. Work through this exercise to create expressive eyes in LightWave.

STARTING WITH THE EYES

1. Enter LightWave's Modeler and zoom out or in to a grid size of 200m. Then, place five arched points in the Face view, as in figure 14.2.

FIGURE 14.2

Five points are created in Modeler, ready to make an eye.

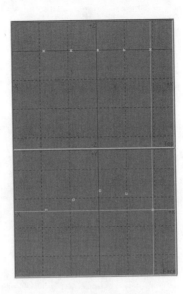

2. Press c on the keyboard to copy the points. Press t to move the points, and move them up slightly from the Face view about 300mm.

3. Press v to paste the original set of points down. Deselect them.

4. Now mirror the points on the Y-axis to create an eye shape outline of points as in figure 14.3.

FIGURE 14.3

One set of points is copied and mirrored to create the outline for an eye.

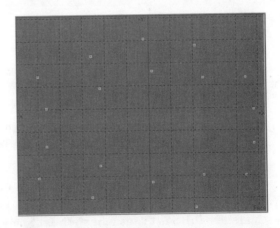

5. After the points are down, begin selecting four at a time to make quad polygons. Starting with the top set of points, select two from the top row left, and two from the bottom row left. Be sure to select the points in a

clockwise direction so the polygons face the right way. After you select four points, press p to make a polygon.

6. Keep selecting four points and pressing p, until you have eight polygons, as seen in figure 14.4.

FIGURE 14.4

Four points at a time are selected to make quad polygons.

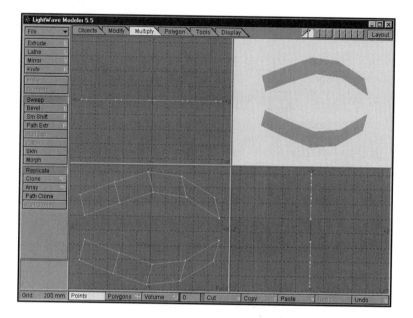

TIP

LightWave 5.5 now supports both three-pointed polygons (tris) and four-pointed polygons (quads) in the same MetaNURBS model. Try to work with quads first, as they work a bit better with MetaNURBS.

7. After your polygons are created, be sure you are in Polygon Edit mode and deselect all polygons. Next, press the Tab key to turn on MetaNURBS. See how the polygons smooth out? Now turn MetaNURBS off again by pressing the Tab key.

You are going to work with polygonal models. The best way to work with MetaNURBS is by modeling straight polygons, switching on MetaNURBS to see how your model is shaping up, and then continue modeling with polygons. This is useful because less memory is taken to display the polygons, and the model is easier to manipulate. When

MetaNURBS is on, finding control points on the Patch surface can be tedious as the model becomes more complex.

8. With the eight polygons in the Face view, start adding more points to the top of the eye. Add five more there, two on each side and then five underneath the eye. Shift+= is the keyboard shortcut for Create Points. Figure 14.5 shows the additional points.

FIGURE 14.5

Additional points are added to the front view in Modeler. These will create additional polygons.

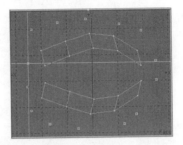

9. Switch to Point Edit mode. Using the points from the existing polygons, select in a clockwise order four points at a time, and press p to make a polygon. Figure 14.6 shows two polygons created.

FIGURE 14.6

After additional points are created, more polygons are made.

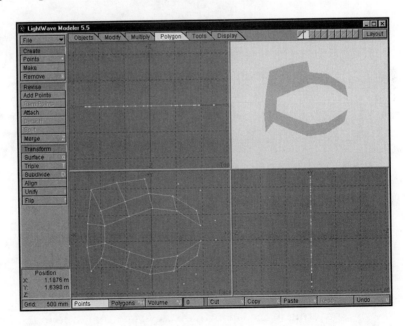

10. Continue making polygons out of the points you have created. Add more points to build out the eye area even more. Now, select the top row of points, and move them all forward. Select the added points in order to continue creating polygons. After you create the polygons, move the top row of points forward on the Z-axis. You may even want to begin bending rows of points for shape. Now, press the Tab key to see how the eye is shaping up in MetaNURBS. It should look something like figure 14.7.

FIGURE 14.7

The human face is comprised of many intricate muscles. Movement of key muscles generates facial expressions.

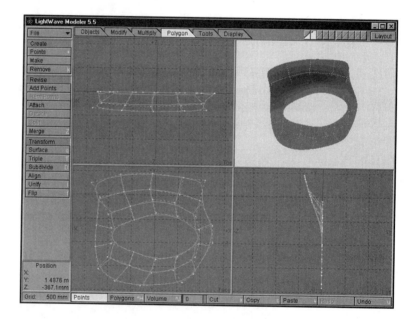

Now the procedure gets a little tricky. The techniques described here show how creating points to make polygons can begin shaping the eye of a human face. From here, you will add more polygons to create eyelids, brows, and the nose, simply by adding points and creating polygons.

You may see that certain polygons aren't visible when modeling. As long as the polygons are all facing the same direction, certain polygons not appearing in the OpenGL display is normal. Due to the severe shape of a few particular polygons, they can become non-planar. Don't worry though, they will be corrected and appear just fine when MetaNURBS is turned on.

By moving the top row of points forward, as in figure 14.7, when MetaNURBS is turned on, you can see that the eye MetaNURBS is beginning to take shape. From here, you can build the eyelids and brow more.

11. Make sure you are not in MetaNURBS mode, and add five more points in the empty area of the eye—in the eyesocket. Join these points to the points above it (your original set of points) by selecting them four at a time, and create more polygons. Do the same for the bottom portion of the eye socket. Now, with these new points selected, move (t) them back behind the original set of points, from the Side view, as in figure 14.8.

FIGURE 14.8

More points are added and moved behind the original set of points to begin shaping the eyelid.

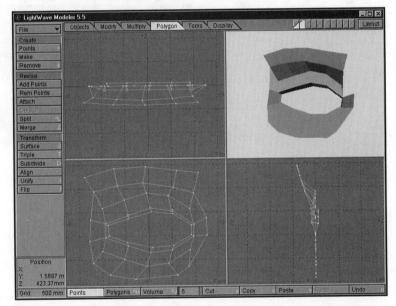

12. Turn on MetaNURBS with the Tab key to see how the eye is shaping up. If you like how this eyelid looks, move on to the lower eyelid. From here, add more points to create polygons for the brow area. Remember to move the points after they're created to help shape the eye.

13. Create points farther out to the left of the eye area. Join them with the side points of the eye to make more polygons. Keep extending the growth of polygons for the other areas of the face, as you did for the eye and socket.

14. Pay attention to the other views, remembering to move points off of the 0 axis to shape the eye. Figure 14.9 shows the eye area with lids and a brow. Use this image as reference for continuing the model of your facial eye area.

FIGURE 14.9

Using the same points creation and polygon creation techniques, an eye area and face begin to emerge.

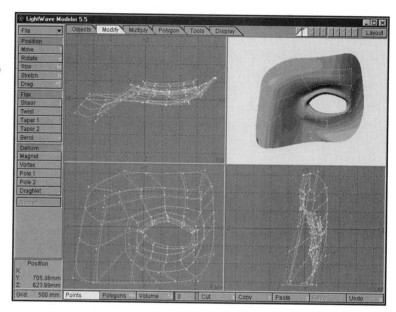

TIP

Don't just move points when creating faces. You can select a group of points and rotate them, twist them, bend them, or use any of the other Modify tools on them. Be sure to experiment with the points while in MetaNURBS mode to see how different positions and rotations affect the shape.

Creating the eyes for a character can be fun. You have the creative freedom to build any type of character you want with the techniques previously described. In addition to this, you have the ability to create numerous expressions by moving only a few simple points in the eye areas. Experiment on your own and adjust select points in the eye areas to create mean expressions, worried expressions, and more. When you're confident with the eye area of a human face, continue reading to learn how to create the nose area.

The Nose

Creating the nose is as involved as creating the eye but not as difficult as the mouth. You need to pay attention to all views. Remember, this is a 3D program you are working with, and it's important to check the Top and Side views as well as the Front view often.

BUILDING A NOSE

1. Load the Eyestart3.lwo object from the book's CD. This is where the previous exercise ended. If you have come this far on your own, feel free to use your own model. Select the bottom-left polygon; the one that would be in the area of the nose, as in figure 14.10.

FIGURE 14.10

Adding points to build faces is how you begin. You can also Bevel or Smooth Shift polygons to create shapes and curves, as shown here.

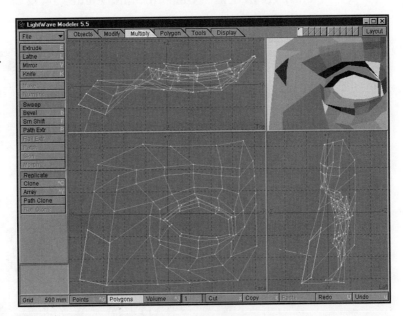

2. With just the one polygon selected, press Shift+f to call up the Smooth Shift function. In the Smooth Shift Panel, enter an offset of 500mm, and leave the Max Smoothing Angle at its default of 89.5 (see fig. 14.11).

FIGURE 14.11

The Smooth Shift function, shown here, enables you to multiply polygons, similar to the Bevel tool. You can apply an Offset and Max Smoothing Angle through its Numeric Requester.

3. After the Smooth Shift is applied, you'll see that the nose area now protrudes. From here, you need to make the nostrils. Deselect any polygons still selected. Now select the bottom polygon of the area you just created with Smooth Shift. Figure 14.12 shows the polygon selected.

FIGURE 14.12

Selecting the bottom polygon of the nose area enables you to multiply just from here. Two bevels on this polygon will create a nostril.

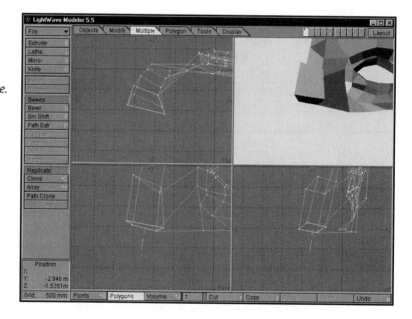

4. With this polygon selected, press the b key to use the Bevel tool. Set the Bevel Inset to 100mm and the Bevel Shift value to 100mm. Click OK to apply the specifications to the Bevel function.

5. Without deselecting the polygon, Bevel it again. With the new polygon selected, move it up into the nose. Deselect the polygon, and press the Tab key to see how the MetaNURBS version of the face is developing. You can see that the nose is somewhat square. Feel free to move points using the Drag tool (Ctrl+t) to adjust, as you like. Also, move the points of the nostril in to narrow its opening. You can even experiment with more Beveling or Smooth Shifting on the nose area. Figure 14.13 shows the face at this point when MetaNURBS is turned on.

FIGURE 14.13

Creating polygons, using Smooth Shift and Bevel to create the contours of a face.

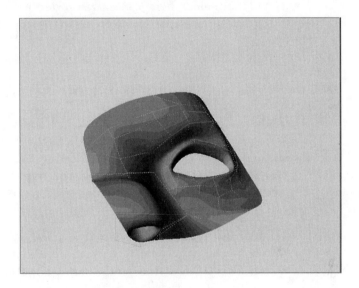

To make a two-sided face, you will use the Mirror tool. The opposite side of the nose has a polygon on it, which won't allow for a clean mirror. Select and remove the single polygon from the opposite side of the nose (the left side) before doing the next exercise.

There is a steady progression to modeling a face starting from the eyes, building the nose, and then creating the mouth. A good way to model a face is to always start with the eyes. The nose area can accentuate the eyes you've created, and the mouth can add to the character as well. The nose you build can have a tremendous impact on the final look of the face. You can build a small pug nose or a large cartoon-like nose. Whichever you choose, think of your character. A nose is a characteristic all its own and as you model, consider how you want your character portrayed within an animation. When you've mastered nose modeling, continue on to create a mouth.

The Mouth

The mouth is as important to the face as the eyes and nose. The eyes bring expression to the character, as does the nose. The mouth is the area you will manipulate to create lip syncing in Morph Gizmo. Follow along with the next exercise to create a mouth.

In this exercise, you add more points to create the mouth. Remember to add points and then select them in clockwise order to join them with the existing object. To create the mouth, place points in the same manner as you did with the eye.

MODELING THE MOUTH

1. Add points along the bottom of the Face object as you did earlier under the eye. Carefully attach the points to the rest of the face. It may be difficult to see the exact points to connect to, so turn on the OpenGL Sketch preview for more accuracy. You want to create the face with an open mouth so that making phonetics is a bit easier.

2. Place the points along the edge of the face, and curve them slightly (similar to the points of the eye) to create the top lip of the mouth. After you have the points down, copy and paste them to generate another identical set. Move the points down slightly to begin creating the polygons. Attach these pasted points to the first set. Do this one more time for three sets of points.

These three sets of points will create the lips of the face. Figure 14.14 shows the points in place.

TIP

Remember to watch the points in all views. A mouth curves with the face. By selecting all the points of the mouth and using the Bend tool, you can curve the mouth.

3. The placement of the points in the lip is exactly like those in the eye. Use the eye as reference if you need to.

4. Pay attention to all views, and move rows of points in the lip area to form the curves. The top row of points can remain in place.

FIGURE 14.14
Closely placed points will give more control to the MetaNURBS cage, allowing the creation of lips on the face.

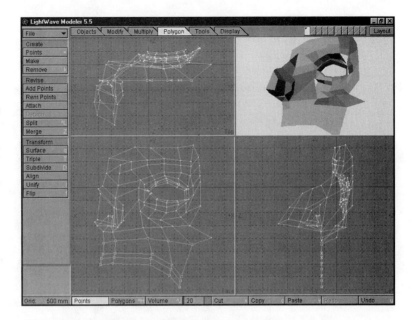

5. The next row down from the top can be pulled forward and up for the top of the actual lip. You can pull the next row down and out a bit more, then add one more additional row, moving it down and back to create the bottom of the lip. Figure 14.15 displays the results of this instruction.

FIGURE 14.15
Close rows of points aligned to form the curves of lips.

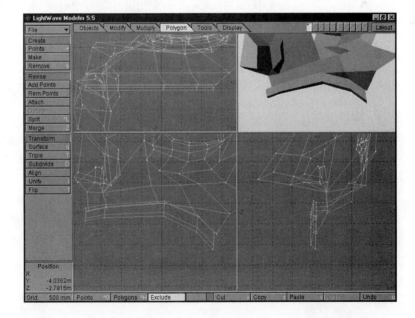

6. To see how the face looks in MetaNURBS, press the Tab key. Figure 14.16 shows the same object as in figure 14.15, but with MetaNURBS turned on.

FIGURE 14.16

The same face and lip object from figure 14.15 with MetaNURBS turned on.

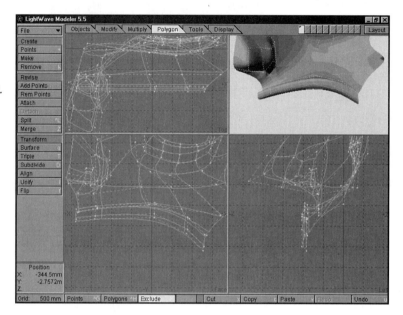

7. The lips in figure 14.16 are shaping up but still need tweaking. Use a photo of a real person as a reference to the proper shape of the lip.

8. Continue with the bottom portion of the mouth, when you have what you like for the top. Mirror the points in the top portion of the mouth to create the lower portion.

9. Join the bottom points with the top at the side of the mouth. You may need to add a few points to the side area of the mouth. Use these points to create the side of the mouth, attaching a point from the top of the mouth, to points on the side of the mouth and then to a point on the bottom of the mouth. Figure 14.17 shows the mouth in polygonal form before a chin.

10. Leave the center of the mouth open, as you did when creating the eye. From here, create points and build a mesh of polygons to create the chin and the rest of the cheek.

FIGURE 14.17

The mouth is taking shape with the addition of some lips.

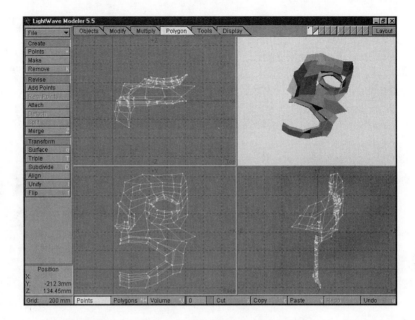

FIGURE 14.17

The mouth is taking shape with the addition of some lips.

11. From the Modify Panel, use the Magnet or DragNet tools to curve the mouth out to give it a more natural facial curvature. You can also select the points in the mouth area and bend them from the Side view (bottom-right viewport).

12. After you create the chin and cheek, you need to mirror the face. Before you mirror, select all the points on the very left edge of the model. When selected, use the Set Value command (Ctrl+v) to move all selected points to an identical location. Move the points to an area beside the face. In this example, the points are moved to 80mm on the X-axis, as in figure 14.18.

13. Lastly, mirror the face at the same location you placed the points at with Set Value. When mirrored, you'll notice a seam down the middle of the face. Press m on the keyboard to merge those points together.

TIP

If you don't like how the face looks after it's mirrored, or the eyes seem too far apart, press undo and move the narrow part of the nose and forehead area. You can set up to 15 Undo levels through the Data Options Panel (o).

FIGURE 14.18

Use the Set Value command to move all the points on the left side of the face to an identical location for mirroring.

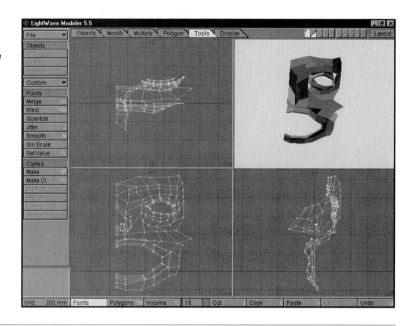

This modeling technique is very effective for creating any type of face or character head. It's good to know how to create your own faces because you can apply the basic concepts to all human races, aliens, animals, or any other human-like creature.

Phonetics

Setting phonetic mouth positions can be time-consuming. References are needed to ensure that the proper mouth positions are being created. But with the use of MetaNURBS, you don't have to model a new face for each phonetic. The following exercise will show you how to adjust the mouth of an existing head object to create phonetic facial objects.

WARNING

Regardless of triangles and quadrangles, your object must be made up of the exact same number of points; your object's point order cannot change if you want it to morph correctly later with the Morph Gizmo plug-in. Do not add or delete points within an object. Only reposition them.

CREATING PHONETIC FACES

1. Load the ManNURB.lwo from this book's CD into Modeler. This head object is one that can be found on many 3D resource sites or bundled with 3D software packages. Because LightWave Modeler 5.5's MetaNURBS now supports triangles as well as quad polygons, you can manipulate this head easily.

2. The Head object is loaded with MetaNURBS already on. Press the Tab key twice to toggle between the polygonal model and the MetaNURBS model to see the difference.

NOTE

Because the ManNURB.lwo Head object is detailed well, you can set the Patch Division to 1; you only need to convert it to polygons so it is animatable in Morph Gizmo. Press o on the keyboard to go to the Data Options Panel, and then set the Patch Division to 1. Keep this setting throughout your modeling. Changing it will change the point count of an object, resulting in an object that you cannot morph.

3. This Head object has its mouth sealed. By using MetaNURBS, you can open the mouth without polygonal errors. From the Left view, zoom into the mouth region. Select the points making up the center area between the lips. Figure 14.19 shows the point selection.

FIGURE 14.19
Selected points make up the center of lip.

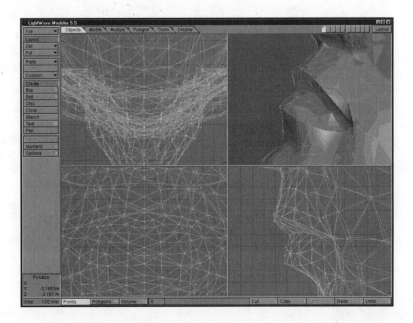

4. With the points selected, move them back into the character's head, as in figure 14.20. You have created a morph target.

FIGURE 14.20
The selected points in the middle of the lips moved back into the character's head to create a mouth opening.

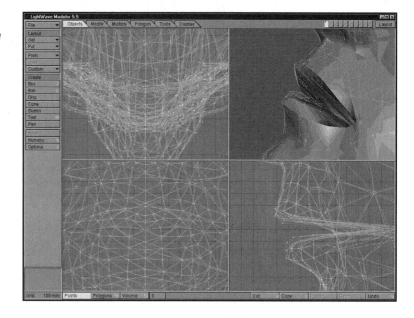

5. Deselect any points and press a to fit the head in all views. Press Ctrl+d to freeze the MetaNURBS cage. Figure 14.21 shows the renderable head object. Save this as **Head_A.lwo**.

This is where making different phonetic mouth positions becomes easier. After the object's MetaNURBS cage is frozen and the object is saved, use Undo to return to the original MetaNURBS model for more changes.

6. Press a to fit the head in all views. Select Undo (u) once to bring your object back to the MetaNURBS version. Now select the points making up the area of the lower jaw.

7. With the lower jaw's points selected, move the mouse to where the jaw rotation is on a human head, in front of the ear. Select the Rotate tool (y) and rotate the group of points up to close the mouth. Deselect the points and freeze the patches (Ctrl+d). Save the object as Man_Anchor.lwo. This will become the Anchor object in Morph Gizmo later in this chapter under the Morph Gizmo section.

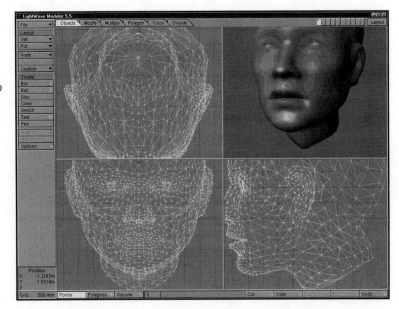

FIGURE 14.21

After you move the points in to place, the head's MetaNURBS patches are turned into polygons with the Freeze command.

8. Press Undo (u) twice to move the points to their original position. With the group of points still selected, use the Rotate tool (y) to rotate the group of points down to open the mouth. Now you have a character with a big mouth.

9. Deselect all points. Freeze the patches (Ctrl+d) and save the object as **Head_Open.lwo**. Figure 14.22 shows the open mouth in MetaNURBS.

10. After the object is frozen and saved, press Undo (u) twice, once to undo the freeze, and the other to move the mouth back into the original position. Now you can make more specific phonetic positions. Select the area of points making up the front of the lips. Using the Magnet tool from the Modify Panel, drag out an effect region with the right mouse button. Then, drag the lips forward from the face to a pucker shape as in figure 14.23.

11. From here, adjust the points to complete the shape of the mouth into a u-shaped phonetic position. Do this by puckering the lips and slightly curling the bottom lip. You are modeling the mouth into a shape to pronounce the letter u. Take a look in the mirror and make the "u" sound. Notice how your mouth is shaped and use it as a reference.

FIGURE 14.22

FIGURE 14.22

The points around the lower jaw area selected and rotated to create an open mouth.

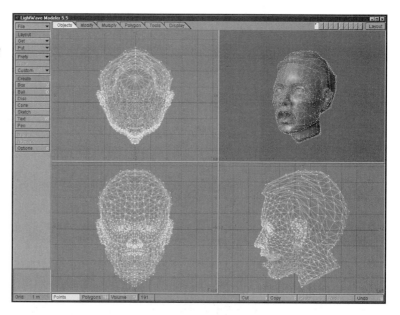

FIGURE 14.23

You can move the points making up the lip area into a u shape with the Magnet tool and Drag.

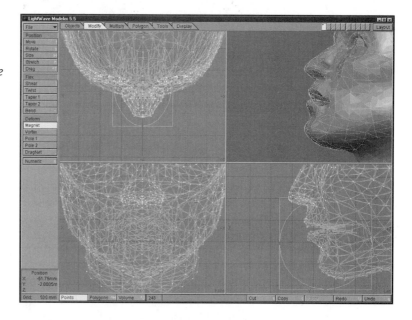

12. Select the region of points in the cheek area, and move them in from the face view using the Stretch (h) tool.

TIP

You don't always have to use the points of an object to manipulate its shape. You can also modify the polygons.

13. Select the polygons that make up the front of the lower lip and move them down slightly. When you have the mouth in place, freeze the patches and save the object as **Head_U.lwo**. Figure 14.24 shows the head with the mouth in a u phonetic position.

FIGURE 14.24

Points and polygons moved to create the mouth shaped like the letter u.

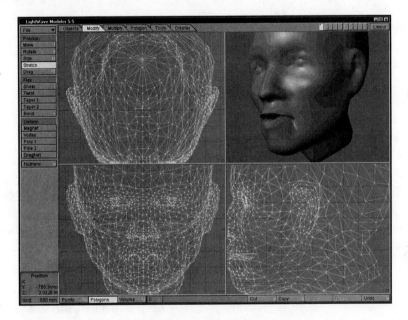

To make the proper u shape of the mouth, your best reference is a photograph or mirror. If you have access to a small mirror, keep it at your desk and say vowels—a, e, i, o, u—to see how your face changes for each. With that as a reference, model your character's different morph targets to be used with Morph Gizmo.

From this point on, you can use Undo to move the mouth shape back to its original position. If you have made more than 15 changes and run out of Undo levels, remember that you have the original ManNURB.lwo object on CD. This is why saving your work in stages is a good idea. At any given moment, you can go back to any stage of your project and continue from there.

Move the mouth into as many positions as you like. Using the basic vowel sounds is often enough to make believable speaking characters. On the book's CD, use the full vowel set of the Head object used in the previous exercises from the Chapter 15 Projects directory.

Expressions

Part of creating facial animation is the expression a character conveys. An animated face uses different mouth positions to express a word, as shown in the preceding exercise. Animating the eyes of a character can add the finishing touches to a talking face.

The following exercise guides you through moving key points and polygons in the face of an object to create different moods.

CREATING FACIAL EXPRESSIONS

1. Load the Man_NURBclsd.lwo into a clean layer in Modeler. This object is a MetaNURBS object with the mouth closed. For this section, you will move the eye elements to create facial expressions. In the next exercise, you will use Morph Gizmo in Layout to combine these eye objects with the head objects created earlier.

2. Move the work area of Modeler to a close-up view of the eyes of the head. Press w on the keyboard to load the Polygon Statistics Panel. Select the Eyelids surface from the drop-down list, pictured in figure 14.25. After you select that surface, press the + key next to the "with Surface" area last on the statistics list. You will see the eyelids become selected. With them selected, you can now enter the Change Surface Requester (q) and turn on Smoothing and change their color if you want.

3. After you select the Eyelid surface, go to the Side view, and press the y key to select the Rotate tool. Move the mouse behind the eye, in the temple area of the head. Rotate the lids down.

Note that Modeler works differently than Layout. Rotation, for example, works based on the mouse position, not the orientation of the object.

FIGURE 14.25

The Polygon Statistics Panel enables you to see information on all polygons, as well as to select certain polygonal groups surfaced with the same name. Here, the Eyelids are selected.

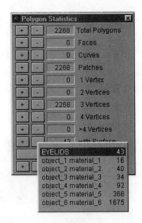

4. If the eyelid does not rotate to your liking, or rotates out too far or not enough, simply press the u key to undo the rotation; then rotate again from a slightly different position. When you rotate the eyelids the way you want, press Ctrl+d to freeze the MetaNURBS patch. Save the object as **ManEyeClosed.lwo** or something similar. Figure 14.26 shows the head with eyes closed.

FIGURE 14.26

Rotation of the eyelid polygons closes the character's eyes.

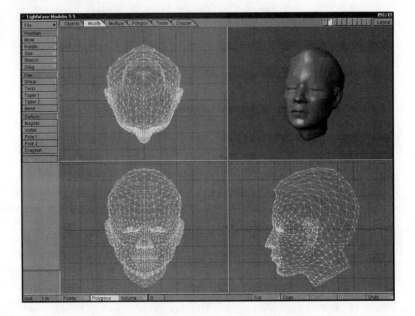

5. Press Undo (u) a few times to bring your model's eyelids back to their original position. Deselect all polygons. Select the polygons in the center of the forehead, right above the nose. These polygons are in the area of the Curragator muscle (refer to figure 14.1 at the beginning of this chapter). Moving this muscle down creates a look of anger or concern, as shown in figure 14.27.

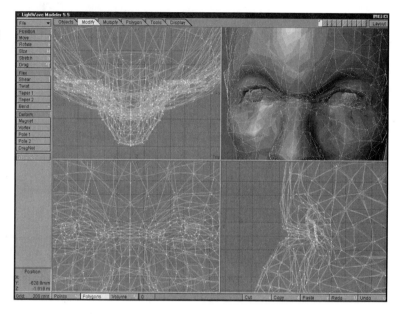

TIP

Don't only use Move on the selected polygons; try using the Stretch tool (h) on them as well to scrunch the nose together.

6. Manipulate points around the eye areas to make an angrier character, or add subtleties of your own. When you have a concerned or angry face you like, save the object as **ManConcern.lwo**.

7. Use Undo (u) to return to the original facial positions. With the same Curragator muscle area polygons selected, move them up to create a worried look. Figure 14.28 shows the head with a worried face.

8. Use Undo to undo the worry. Make other facial expressions based on the muscle chart in figure 14.1 at the beginning of this chapter.

FIGURE 14.28

The Curragator muscle group of polygons moved up on the face to create a worried look.

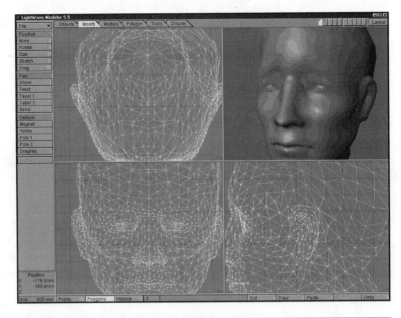

This section has given you the tools to create facial objects with accompanying phonetics and expressions. It is important that you work through the preceding exercises before continuing with Morph Gizmo, because you must be familiar with good modeling techniques to get the most out of this plug-in. Good models, good morph targets, and the proper expressions will benefit you when working with the Morph Gizmo plug-in. The next section uses the Head objects created in the previous section. Now, continue to read to learn how to create talking heads in Morph Gizmo.

Using Morph Gizmo for Faces

Morph Gizmo is a powerful new plug-in included with LightWave 5.5. With Gizmo, you can group areas of objects and set varying Morph percentages between different morphable targets. You can lip sync your characters with Gizmo, and group various areas as well. In the previous exercises, you created different mouth positions and saved each one. Each of those objects is a morph target. You also created varying morph targets but only changed the eye area. These objects can also be loaded into Morph Gizmo simultaneously and grouped, as you'll see in this next exercise.

Morph Gizmo works with Anchor objects and Target objects. Anchor objects are not anything different than the Target objects. Anchor objects are simply the starting morph position before a morph begins with Gizmo. The Anchor object, in this situation, should be the face with a neutral expression. A neutral position is a face with no expression, a closed mouth, and open eyes. All other objects loaded from here are morph targets that have different facial expressions, closed eyes, different mouth positions, and so on. Also, the anchor does not have to be named "anchor" to work; this is done simply for organizational purposes. The first object loaded in Morph Gizmo is always the "anchor" object.

Later in this section on Morph Gizmo, you work with Gizmo's audio features. To use the audio feature, you will need a sound card and speakers in your computer. If not available, you can still follow along with this exercise to familiarize yourself with Gizmo's keyframing. Also note that this audio function of Morph Gizmo is strictly experimental and will be implemented more in future versions.

Morph Gizmo enables you to group different objects. For example, you can load a set of phonetic facial models and group them together as mouth objects. From there, you can load a set of facial models with eye expressions and group them as a set of eyes. This next exercise guides you through grouping and working with the Morph Gizmo interface.

USING MORPH GIZMO

1. Load Layout and go to the Options Panel. From the Generic Plug-ins category under the General Options tab, select the LW_Morph_Gizmo plug-in.

2. When the interface comes up, select Load Object from the Current Object area and load the Man_Anchor.lwo object from the CD accompanying this book. Figure 14.29 shows the Gizmo interface with the Anchor object loaded.

3. After the Anchor object is loaded, select Load Object again and load the Man_A.lwo object.

FIGURE 14.29
*The Morph Gizmo
interface is shown with
the Man_Anchor.lwo
object loaded from the
CD accompanying this
book.*

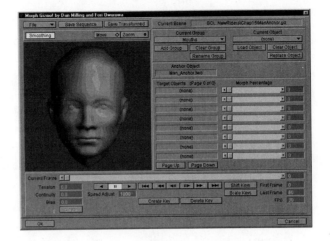

4. If you look to the Current Group area to the right of the OpenGL window, you will see that the Current Group is set to Default. Select Rename Group, and enter the name **Mouths** in the Requester, as in figure 14.30. With Morph Gizmo, you can add up to 64 groups, each with 64 objects.

FIGURE 14.30
*The Add Group
Requester enables you
to add new groups to
Gizmo projects.*

5. Click OK to make the Mouths Group. Now load the rest of the Vowel Sound objects in the directory on the CD, Man_E.lwo, Man_O.lwo, and so on. Don't load the Eye Position objects just yet.

6. After the full set of objects is loaded into the Mouths Group, select Add Group. In the Requester, type the name **Eyes**.

You will see that all the objects loaded in the Mouths Group are no longer listed under the Target Objects list. They are still loaded, but because you created a new group, you are viewing the target list for the Eyes Group.

7. With the Current Group set to the Eyes Group, load the Eye objects, such as Man_Concern.lwo, Man_Puzzled.lwo, and Man_Worried.lwo.

8. From the File drop-down menu, save the project as **Man1.giz**. You don't want to reload all objects should an error occur. Note the extension for a Gizmo file, .giz.

If you begin moving some of the morph percentage sliders, you'll see that the man's mouth is moving. You'll find that Morph Gizmo is great for creating new mouth shapes with different morph positions and percentages. Using a simple phonetic set such as the one you loaded in this exercise, you can make your character talk quite convincingly. Granted, a full accurate set of phonetics is more ideal, but often not needed because of Gizmo's morph controls.

9. The best way to make a character talk is by moving the mouth in sync with sound. Version 5.5 Gizmo has sound capabilities. This audio sync capability is a hidden advanced feature and is still experimental. However, it will provide you with enough sound capability to sync sound with Morph Gizmo, making a much more versatile tool. With the Gizmo interface opened, simply type the word **wave**. This isn't typed into a Requester; simply type it on the keyboard while the Gizmo interface is open. You'll see the audio features appear, as in Figure 14.31.

FIGURE 14.31

Typing the word wave turns on Gizmo's audio controls.

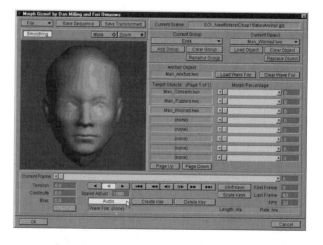

10. Click the Load Wave File button above the Morph Percentage list. Load the Vista.wav file from the book's CD-ROM. Look at the readout on the bottom of the Gizmo interface. You will see that the .wav file information displays, including location and length.

11. Note the length of the file is 2.507 seconds. Look above the display to the Last Frame setting. The Last Frame is defaulted to 60. Reset this to 2.5 seconds, about 80 frames.

12. Make sure all Morph Percentage sliders are set to zero. This means that all mouth targets are set to 0 morph percentage.

13. Create a keyframe at frame zero. Do this by pressing Enter and then pressing it again, just as you do in Layout. You can also press the Create Key button at the bottom of the screen.

14. Move the Current Frame slider to hear the audio. Move it to the point where the voice begins to say "aasta" from the full "Hasta La Vista, Baby" sound. This is at frame 4 or so.

15. Grab the Man_Open Morph Percentage slider and slide it to 100%. This will open the mouth, as in figure 14.32. Create a keyframe at frame 4 with the mouth open.

FIGURE 14.32
The Man_Open morph target is slid to 100%, opening the man's mouth.

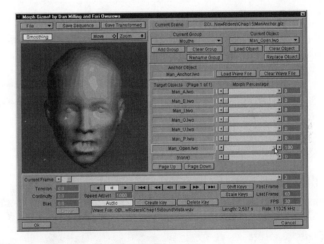

16. Now move the Current Frame slider more until you hear the "ss" sound of "Hassta." This is at about frame 9 or so. At the frame, move the Man_E Morph Percentage to 80%, Man_Open to 0%, and also move the Man_O Morph Percentage to 40%, as in figure 14.33. This will create the shape for the "s" sound.

17. Create a keyframe for this morph position at frame 9. Settings from previous keyframes carry over to the next keyframe, so reset the values to zero. Now move the slider to hear the "t" sound in "Hasta." This is at

about frame 13. Here, move the Man_P Morph Percentage to 100% and create a keyframe.

FIGURE 14.33

A combination of morph percentages creates an "s" sound.

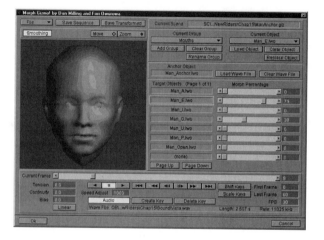

18. At frame 15, move the Man_A Morph Percentage to 100, and the Man_P Morph Percentage to 0. Create a keyframe for it there to create the morph position for the last "a" in "Hasta."

19. Now, move the Current Frame slide a bit more to hear the "La" portion of "Hasta La Vista, Baby." This is at frame 17 or so. Reset previous values to zero, and move the Man_E Morph Percentage to 100, the Man_O Morph Percentage to 55, and the Man_U Morph Percentage to 60%. Create a keyframe at frame 17. Figure 14.34 shows the morph percentages at frame 17.

FIGURE 14.34

Additional uses of combinations create various mouth positions.

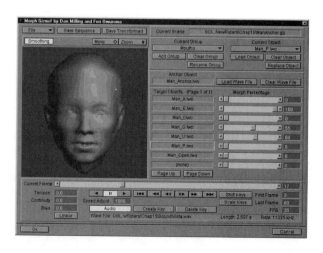

From this point on, continue the same process to finish making the character talk. Simply move the Current Frame slider until you hear the key vowel sounds, and set a morph percentage to match. Often, as you did at frame 17, a combination of morph percentages can create the right mouth shape.

You also created a group for the eyes. You can animate this group separately from the mouth grouping. To do this, you will save the project (for safety) and set the Current Group to Eyes. Again, moving the Current Frame slider to hear the audio, and set the Eye Group Morph Percentages at the times you want during the audio track. Load a finished version of this exercise, the Vista.giz file from the book's CD-ROM, into Morph Gizmo to see how the two groups work together. Please note that on lesser systems, the audio will play back slightly stuttered. Systems such as Pentium 100s or Pentium 133s are a good example.

TIP

Because Morph Gizmo can create interesting mixes between morph targets, a Save Transformed feature has been added to enable you to save current morph positions.

Morph Gizmo is an entirely new way of creating talking characters in LightWave. Using this tool saves enormous amounts of time when it comes to lip syncing, and you should practice using it often. There is more, however, to Morph Gizmo that just lip syncing. You can morph things other than Head objects, such as body parts described in a later exercise. Using the audio feature in Gizmo, you can create objects dancing to music. Before you move into working with other objects in Morph Gizmo, read on to learn about saving Morph Gizmo scenes.

Saving Gizmo Scenes

Saving a Gizmo Scene is actually saving the Morph Gizmo project, with all objects and keyframes remembered. Saving the project is necessary to adjust it later, or more importantly, to animate it. To load the Gizmo file into LightWave's Layout for animation, you must save the .giz file.

WARNING

It's very important to save your Gizmo projects as you go. Mistakenly clicking OK or Cancel in Gizmo clears the project. Gizmo does not prompt you to save your work before closing the plug-in, so save often.

To save the Morph Gizmo project, select the Save Project As from the drop-down File Requester in the Gizmo interface. Figure 14.35 shows the File Requester.

FIGURE 14.35

The Save Project As selector in the File menu is key to using Gizmo in Layout.

Using Gizmo Scenes in LightWave

Morph Gizmo works within LightWave to generate a displacement file that you can load into LightWave's Layout. Using Gizmo to create a talking character is the first step in completing a LightWave scene. When you create a Morph Gizmo file, you can load it into Layout to incorporate it with other scene elements. It's not complicated to use a Gizmo scene in LightWave, only requiring a few key steps.

INCORPORATING MORPH GIZMO IN LAYOUT

1. With a cleared scene in Layout, go to the Objects Panel and load the Man_Anchor.lwo file from this book's CD. This is the Anchor object used in the Gizmo project in the previous exercise. It's important to note which Anchor object you use in a project because it is essentially the morph source for the Gizmo displacement plug-in.

2. Also from the Objects Panel, when the Anchor object is loaded, select the LW_Morph_Gizmo_Render plug-in from the Displacement Map Plug-ins category. When loaded, click the Options button and you'll see the Requester pictured in figure 14.36.

FIGURE 14.36

The Morph Gizmo Render displacement map plug-in enables you to load the Gizmo scene into Layout.

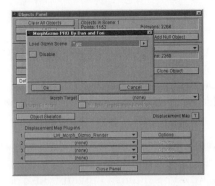

3.   Click the small arrow on the right side of the screen to load the Gizmo project. Select the Vista.giz file from this book's CD. In a moment, the full project's path will appear in the Load Gizmo Scene window. Click OK, and then close the Objects Panel. When you return to Layout, you will see the man's head. Figure 14.37 shows Layout.

FIGURE 14.37

Only one object is loaded into Layout, but because of Morph Gizmo's displacement map capabilities, the Head object will be lip synced to the audio track.

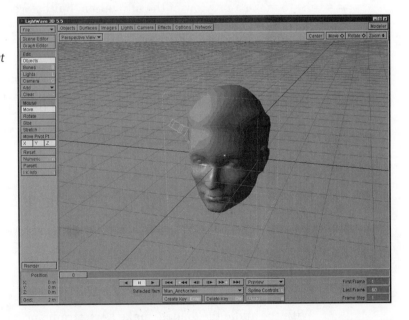

Notice that only one object was loaded. Morph Gizmo generates a displacement map file, which remembers the point order of the morph percentages set in the Gizmo interface. By loading the Anchor object in Layout and then applying the Gizmo displacement map file, the object is told to displace to the instructed point positions. This is extremely helpful because the scene is not loaded with objects to create series of morphs. This frees up memory and cuts rendering time.

Moprh Gizmo's hidden audio feature makes the plug-in complete. The ability to sync audio-visually with a character makes lip syncing a breeze. The ability to sync audio in Layout is also possible with LightWave 5.5. Read this next exercise to learn how to sync audio with your characters in LightWave's Layout.

SYNCING AUDIO AND GIZMO IN LAYOUT

It's time to make a preview of the animation, but before you do, access LightWave's audio playback in Layout.

1. From the Layout window, press Ctrl+Shift+F1. This enables LightWave's experimental features.

2. With the experimental features enabled, go to the Scene Editor. At the bottom of the Scene Editor interface, you will see Load Wave File and Clear Wave File. These are experimental features. Click the Load Wave File and load the Vista.wav file used to sync the Morph Gizmo project earlier.

NOTE

If you load the .wav file and nothing appears in the .wav file display in the Scene Editor, your audio file is technically still being accessed by Morph Gizmo. To correct this, save the LightWave scene, quit the program, and start again. Reload the scene, reset Experimental Features, and load the audio.

3. With the audio file loaded, make a wireframe preview. You will hear a choppy version of the audio play as the preview is generated. When you play back the preview after the wireframe is created, the audio will play truer to life.

WARNING

Depending on the speed and setup of your computer system, some audio playback will be better or worse. The system processor and system memory play key roles. The more the better, especially when it comes to RAM. If your audio is quite choppy, nothing is wrong. Again, this feature is experimental.

Now that you've made a character talk, what do you do with the rest of the body while the face is talking? And how can you make your character interact with other characters? The upcoming sections will provide the answers.

Gizmo and Body Parts

Morph Gizmo is not just for animating faces. You can animate other body parts such as hands. Figure 14.38 shows the HandRLX.lwo loaded into Morph Gizmo.

FIGURE 14.38

Not only faces can be animated in Morph Gizmo. Here, a hand is loaded ready to point.

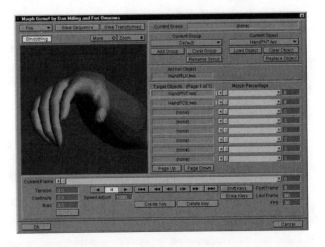

Animating other things in Gizmo works on the same principles as animating faces. Create a MetaNURBS cage of polygons, freeze the patches, and save the object to create an Anchor object. Manipulating the MetaNURBS cage creates different morph targets. Figure 14.39 shows the same Hand object loaded in Morph Gizmo but morphed 100 percent to the HandPNT.lwo.

FIGURE 14.39

The original relaxed hand is now pointing using a 100 morph percentage in Morph Gizmo.

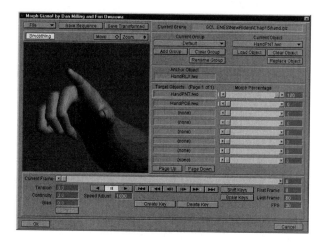

LightWave's morphing capabilities work in a linear fashion. If you carefully look at the hand when it morphs, the fingers travel in a straight line. This is because morphing techniques in LightWave move points in a straight line. Creating more lifelike movements that are less linear merely requires one or more interim morph targets. You can load the Hand.giz file from the CD that came with this book into Morph Gizmo to experiment with morphing the hand. Even though the fingers don't exactly curl, the animation will work. A hand's position changes over just a few frames. What is more noticeable is the final resting position. Animating hands with Gizmo is easy and saves time over working with bones.

If you want to animate a hand gesture, and the hand is not a close-up during the animation, you should use Morph Gizmo to animate the gestures. If you want to animate a hand gesture and want to show it close up, animating the fingers with bones might be a better alternative.

NOTE

The way you to create a look in LightWave is totally up to you. Should you decide that a combination of bones and Morph Gizmo is how something should be animated, do it. If you decide that Morph Gizmo is the only way to animate, do that as well. Do what works well for you. This book helps guide you through different options, but it's up to you to decide the best method for your animations.

Figure 14.40 shows the same hand in Morph Gizmo morphed to a peace sign. The fingers of the hand were bent into each position using MetaNURBS in Modeler.

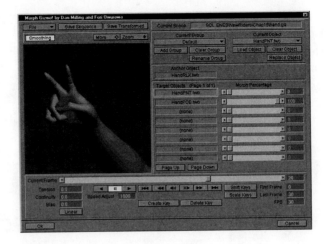

Using Morph Gizmo to animate hand gestures is going to yield a better result in many cases. This is because with Gizmo, you have precise control over the target positions, the morph percentages, and you can animate to an audio track.

Morph Gizmo and Full Bodies

The idea behind using bones in Layout is to animate seamless characters. But if you only create morph targets for head and hands in Morph Gizmo, what about the rest of the body? Attaching them to a full body in Layout results in seams, and then parenting becomes an issue in that you need to parent hands to forearms, forearms to upperarms, upperarms to shoulders, and so on. The way around this is through the use of third-party plug-ins such as Puppet Master, or something you can do yourself.

When creating different phonetic facial positions, for example, create them on the head that is already attached to a full body. Save the full body the same way you would with the different morph targets such as Man_A.lwo. When you load the Man_A.lwo into Morph Gizmo, the full body is already there. Because you only changed the mouth position in Modeler, that will be the only visible change in Morph Gizmo. After you make the .giz file with a talking mouth, you can load it into Layout with the LW_Morph_Gizmo_Render displacement map plug-in. From here, add bones to the body structure and animate.

Load the Cman.giz file into Morph Gizmo. Figure 14.41 shows that the morph source and morph targets are a full body of the caveman.

FIGURE 14.41

Loading a full body into Morph Gizmo with different mouth positions can create a full seamless talking character.

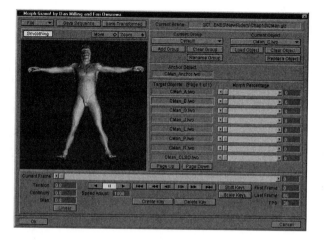

Slide the Cman_J Morph Percentage to 100. Notice that only the mouth position changes. You are still only manipulating and morphing the mouth and eye positions; there just happens to be a body attached.

Combining Tools

You can combine tools and techniques in LightWave to create great-looking character animation. For example, in Morph Gizmo, you created the mouth, eyes, and perhaps other expressions to make a character talk. You can create that Gizmo scene with an Anchor object such as the Caveman. You can save that full Gizmo scene to use later. In Modeler, you can use the same Anchor object, the Caveman, with Skeleton Maker to create a bone structure and IK hierarchy.

Because you based your Skeleton Maker scene on the same object as you did for your Morph Gizmo project, you can joint the two scenes in Layout. First, load the scene created by Skeleton Maker. This loads the bone structure and the Anchor object into Layout. Then, from the displacement map plug-ins, use the LW_Morph_Gizmo_Render plug-in to load the .giz scene created in Morph Gizmo. This loads the displacement map settings for the facial movements without disrupting the body and bone structure. Remember, you created both projects with the same Anchor object, the Caveman.

Now, you can take it one step further. If you created a talking character in Morph Gizmo based on an audio track, you can animate the character to it as well. Using the Load Wave File in Layout described a few pages back, make your character movements based on the sound. When you move the frame slider in Layout, you will hear the audio track you loaded. At certain sounds or words, move the character's head and limbs accordingly. The mouth is already moving to the sound because of the Morph Gizmo scene.

Combining Gizmo Scenes

Perhaps you have characters that need to interact with each other. Say, for example, you created a talking character with Morph Gizmo, set up bones with Skeleton Maker, and put the scene together in Layout. After that scene is saved from Layout, you can load it into other scenes. Perhaps you have set up another animation with a different sort of character talking. You can set up each character's movements in different scenes. When complete, load one scene, and then use the Load From Scene function in the Objects Panel to load the additional scene into the current one. This scene will show the existing bone structures, displacement map information such as Morph Gizmo, and object files.

Syncing Audio Later

After you have created a talking character based on an audio track, you can use the same audio later when exporting the rendered animation. Animation playback units, such as the PVR from DPS or TrueVisions' Targa boards, can sync audio with animation. In addition, you can use nonlinear editing programs along with traditional editing techniques to sync audio to animation. Figure 14.42 shows the Perception interface from Digital Processing Systems.

The PVR can record and play back your animations. It can also tag audio. If the animation is made based on a .wav file, for example, you can load the same .wav file into the PVR. When the animation is played, the audio is automatically cued, creating a perfect sync.

TIP

If you have editing equipment at your disposal, record the audio directly to the finished animation from the original source for best audio and lip syncing results.

FIGURE 14.42

The DPS Perception Video Recorder can record and play back your animations, as well as audio.

Animating Faces with Bones

Morph Gizmo is not the only way to create expressions in LightWave. Using bones, you can deform a face interactively to create some outrageous looks. Follow along with this next exercise to use LightWave's Reference objects to map a face onto an object and move muscle areas with bones.

IMAGE MAPPING THE FACE

1. From the CD accompanying this book, load the DigitalDan.lwo object into Layout. From the Images Panel, load the Daniel_M.tga image. This is a 3D model of Dan captured with a 3D Digitizing camera.

2. From the Surfaces Panel, set a texture map (T button) for Surface Color. In the Texture Map Panel, set the Texture Type to Planar Image Map, and the Texture Image to Daniel_M.tga. Turn off Width Repeat and Height Repeat, set the Texture Axis to Z, and click Automatic Sizing. Turn off Texture Antialiasing, and then click Add Reference Object. This will add a null to the layout, which will directly control the face image map.

3. Click Use Texture and close the Texture Map Panel. Go to the Options Panel, and under the Layout View tab, turn on OpenGL and OpenGL Texture displays. Set the Texture Resolution to 128 × 128. You may also have to change the object's visibility in the Scene Editor to Show Full Textured Solids to see the OpenGL Texture.

4. Before you close the Options Panel, change the Bounding Box Point/ Polygon Threshold to 13310. This is the total amount of polygons in the DigitalDan object. Setting this value stops the object from jumping to Bounding Box mode, enabling you to visually see the texture moving on the object.

WARNING

Depending on the speed of your system and video card, a Threshold setting of 13310 may really slow down your system. Test these settings to see how well your system performs.

5. Return to Layout. You should see something like figure 14.43 on your screen.

FIGURE 14.43

The Digital Dan object loaded into Layout needs a face-lift.

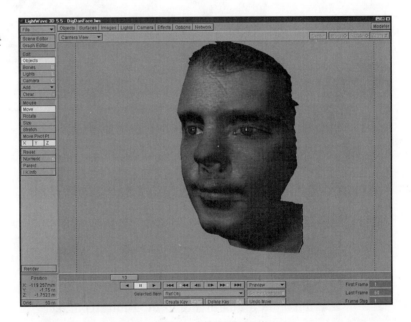

6. Select the Reference object (RefObj) and move it up. You should see the face image moving on the texture. With the Reference object, you can size, move, rotate, or stretch an image on a surface in real-time. This can be animated as well. Move the image so that it lines up with the object, as in figure 14.44.

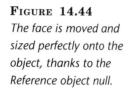

FIGURE 14.44

The face is moved and sized perfectly onto the object, thanks to the Reference object null.

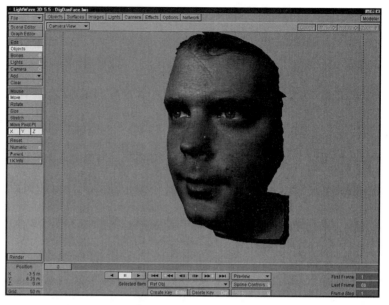

Reference objects are new to LightWave 5.5 and can give added control to your texture-mapped images.

Bone Structures

The bone structure in a face can be complicated or simple, depending on how much deformation you intend to do. For the next exercise, the face needs a few expressions added, therefore, only a few bones are needed. In most cases, you won't need many bones to animate a face if you are using the Morph Gizmo plug-in to create talking. This next exercise takes you through making a few adjustments to the DigitalDan face.

You can set up the facial bone structure according to the muscle diagram at the beginning of this chapter. For this example, you want to create angry eyes and worried eyes, so a bone between the nose will do the trick.

FACIAL BONES

1. Load the DigDanFace.lws scene from this book's CD. Select the DanClosed.lwo object. Turn off OpenGL display to free up your system resources a bit. Select Bones, and select the Draw Bones feature from the Add drop-down menu. Draw one bone on each side of the head, inside the ears as in figure 14.45.

FIGURE 14.45

Two bones are loaded to lock the head in place.

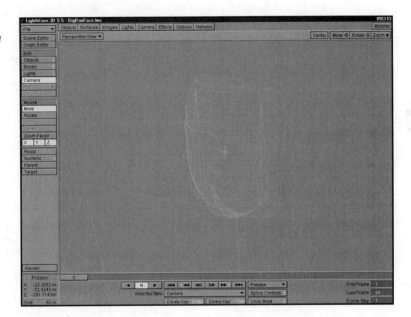

2. From here, add a small bone to the bridge of the nose, as in figure 14.46.

3. Add two more bones, set their rest lengths to about the length of the nose, and place one on each side of the nose. This will help keep the facial structure when the Curragator bone is moved. Figure 14.47 shows the two nose bones.

4. Make all the bones active by pressing r on the keyboard for each bone. If you changed your object display to something other than Textured Solids, now change the display back.

5. Move the Curragator bone down and create a keyframe at 10. Figure 14.48 shows how the face now scowls. Figure 14.49 shows the Curragator bone moved up to create a worried face.

FIGURE 14.46

When the anchor bones are in place, you can add a small bone to the bridge of the nose. This bone will be the control for the Curragator muscle control.

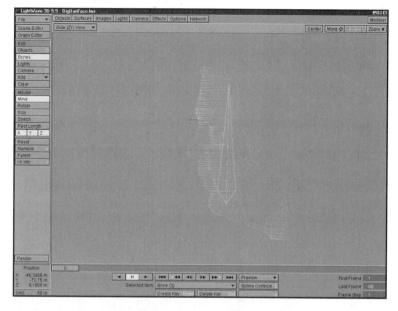

FIGURE 14.47

Two nose bones added to the face to help keep its facial structure when the Curragator bone moves.

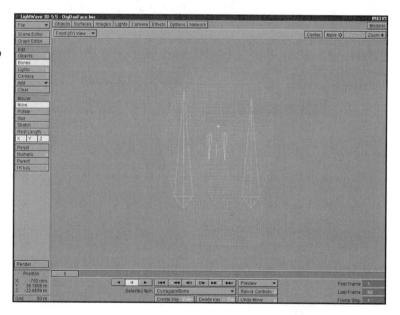

FIGURE 14.48
Moving the Curragator bone makes the face scowl and appear mad. Note that the image map follows.

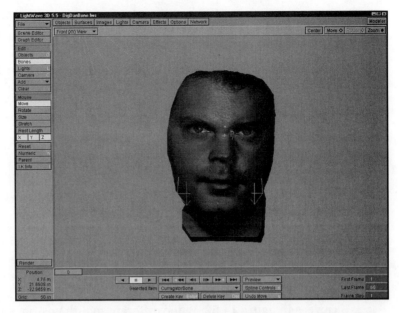

FIGURE 14.49
Moving the Curragator bone up creates a worried face.

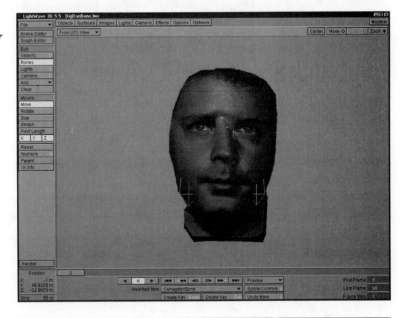

This example showed that a few bones can help create expressions on faces in Layout. You can add more bones to this face, such as a few in the eyebrows, to help create further expressions. Add a bone or two to the cheeks and some around the mouth. Use the facial muscle diagram in the beginning of the chapter to see key areas to place bones. From there, you may need to adjust various Rest Lengths for strengths.

Using Magpie Pro for Lip Syncing

Magpie Pro is a third-party program that works directly with LightWave's Morph Gizmo plug-in.

Magpie displays a .wav file in a track-analysis form. With this program, you can assign different mouth (phonetic) positions at specific times along the audio track. Played together, all mouth positions create a lip-synced character. Magpie Pro also adds the features of .avi files for video reference as you can see in figure 14.52. When different mouth positions have been assigned in Magpie, a Morph Gizmo file (.giz) can be generated for use in LightWave.

On this book's CD, you can find a working demo version of Magpie. Please visit their web site at http://thirdwish.simplenet.com.

Summary

You can apply the techniques described throughout this chapter to any number of characters and creatures you animate. Experiment with different morph positions, exaggerate expressions, and practice timing. Use audio .wav files as guidelines for lip syncing and motion. In no time, you'll create animations more realistic than you ever thought possible. In this chapter, you read about:

- Modeling a human face
- Understanding phonetics
- Creating expressions
- Using lip synching
- Attaching audio in Layout
- Animating faces with bones

This chapter guided you through the use of morphing and bones in facial animation. You have the option to use one or the other, or both, in your animations. A good rule of thumb when deciding which method to use is to consider the desired end result. If your character needs to explicity talk, morphing is the best choice. However, if your character only needs to make different facial expressions and not talk, you can simply apply a few bones to the face in Layout. Work with both methods to get a feeling for each and you'll know which method is best for you. Much of your character work does not necessarily have to be animated. You can create characters and build expressions for still images.

Part IV

RENDERING AND POST PRODUCTION

Chapter 15

COMPOSITING

Compositing enables you to combine images to create a complex image. Compositing originally was a completely optical process, using many mechanical means. Today, the process of compositing has largely been taken over by computers using purely digital methods. Digital compositing is often a straight 2D process, involving no 3D geometry at all. But as you shall see, by using the compositing processes available in LightWave, live action elements and computer-generated imagery can be combined in ways that were never before imaginable.

This chapter covers the following topics:

- Early compositing methods
- LightWave compositing in the digital world
- Compositing shadows
- Seamless compositing

Early Compositing Methods

In early compositing work, some of the effects would be done in-camera, using the latent image technique. Film was shot with part of the lens obscured with black paper; then the film was rewound and the complement of the obscured area was masked off. The rewound film was shot again, giving the film a controlled double exposure.

Early filmmakers also had a rather novel way of adding a foreground. An artist with a large pane of glass accompanied the cinematographer to the site of the shoot. Again the camera was set up; the pane of glass was positioned in front. The artist would then paint additional scenery directly onto the glass. The camera saw the combination of the foreground painted "glass matte" and the background through the clear glass. Though there were obvious problems with alignments, depth of field, and changing lighting conditions, it was still easier then floating castles in the clouds or waiting for jungles to grow.

As compositing became more sophisticated, methods were developed to combine separately shot pieces of film. Optical printers were created that rephotographed the separate images, combining them into one. This enabled finer control but still relied on the latent image technique used when back-winding film.

Sometimes, the unwanted parts of the image could not be conveniently removed through masking of color keying and had to be manually removed a frame at a time by rotoscoping. Rotoscoping is the processes of going to each frame of the film and physically painting out the unwanted elements. This usually resulted in a jumpy edge that surrounded every movement.

What's the point of this history lesson? The techniques developed a hundred years ago for celluloid have their direct counterparts in software. LightWave uses many of the same basic concepts as traditional optical compositing, using many of the same terms to describe the functions. Compositing in LightWave is taken further because you can apply many of the 3D animation tools and functions to accomplish compositing feats undreamed of by early cinematographers.

LightWave Compositing in the Digital World

Combining two or more images can be done much more simply and cleanly using LightWave than using the optical process, where the number of foreground images that can be layered onto a single background is dependent on the physical limitations of the mechanical equipment used. In LightWave, there are no such restrictions. LightWave has the capability to combine thousands of elements. The basic LightWave compositing tools fall into three categories:

- **The background image or plate.** The original acquired image that is the bottom layer of the composite.

- **The foreground image or plate.** The image that is composited on top of the background plate.

- **Images mapped onto geometry.** Between the background and foreground plates there are images that are mapped upon the surfaces of LightWave objects.

Parts of images can be removed through the use of alpha channels, clip maps, and the transparency controls on the Surfaces Panel. Many of these functions can be keyframed and have envelopes adjusting their values over time.

The use of envelopes gives very precise control over the combining of images. Envelopes give you the ability to control the position and opacity of composition elements on a precise frame-by-frame basis. The envelopes used in compositing function in exactly the same way as envelopes used elsewhere in LightWave do. If an object is used as a compositional element, that object can be keyframed to the appropriate translations within the scene. An envelope can be used to dissolve an object in and out at appropriate times.

Background Plate

The background image function is unique in that by itself it has no controls or settings and is unaffected by anything in the scene. Its function is to serve as the bottom-most layer of the composite, the layer on top of which all the other elements are rendered over. The background is not touched by light or shadows, it stays locked in place regardless of camera movement, and it will not be refracted or reflected by objects, even when trace reflection and refraction are turned on. The background image is also unaffected by the depth of the field setting or the Soft Filter option on the Rendering Panel. Also, no way to fade the background in and out or to transition between different images exists.

However, using a background image does not add rendering time and is only antialiased when it comes into contact with a rendered object. Many of the limitations of a background image are countered by using the next process, front projection mapping.

The first step in compositing is to load a background plate from which to build the 3D scene. The following exercise steps you through the loading of the background plate Cloud.tga.

THE BACKGROUND IMAGE

1. From the accompanying CD, load the image Cloud.tga.

NOTE

LightWave has retained the capability to recognize and load various image formats even if the file names do not include the corresponding extension, They will not, however, show up in the Requester unless the Show All Files option is activated.

2. Click on the Effects button to access the Effects Panel.

3. Click the Compositing Page tab.

4. In the top Requester where it says Background Image, select Cloud.tga. The image is now the backdrop for any objects rendered in the scene.

The next step in compositing is to add more layers and create the illusion that a 3D rendered object is existing in the same space as the background plate. To make it appear that the object is interacting with the background plate, you need to give it some depth by using additional layers, which you add in the following exercise.

COMPOSITING A 3D OBJECT OVER A BACKGROUND IMAGE

1. With the Cloud.tga image still loaded as the background, add some objects.

2. Load the object Littlespaceship.lwo from LightWave's Object, Space directory.

3. Now render a frame. You should see the spaceship flying into a cloud bank (see fig. 15.1). Even with all the settings left at their default values, you get a nice image.

FIGURE 15.1

Spaceship object over a cloud background; LightWave compositing at its simplest level.

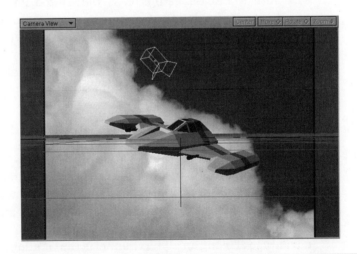

As you can see, the background image is the first step in understanding the basics of compositing in LightWave. You take an image and render a LightWave object over it, giving you the first two levels. The next step is to composite the parts of an image that appear to be in front of the rendered object, the foreground elements.

The Foreground Image

The foreground image is very similar to the background image but it has a number of extra functions. An image loaded as a foreground will be in front of everything else in the scene. The foreground dissolve control enables for the foreground image to be mixed with the rest of the scene. The foreground dissolve has an envelope control to fade the image in and out of the scene. Most of the time, you want to use the foreground image as a matte, which means that part of the image must be transparent. This is done either by using an alpha image or by color keying.

The Foreground Image option is well-suited for use when the rendered objects appear behind the foreground elements and do not need to cross in front of them. Because the foreground image is the top layer of the composite, to see anything other than the foreground image, you need to cut some holes in it to see through. There are two ways to make selected parts of the foreground images transparent, by using an alpha channel and by color keying.

The Alpha Channel

Compositing often uses alpha channels to combine elements. An *alpha channel* is like a transparency map applied to an image. Typically, you would load your background plate into a paint program and modify it to become a grayscale image that looks like a stencil of the original image. The big advantage of using an alpha channel is that it allows for a smooth transition between being transparent and opaque. The variable transparency is important for antialiasing and compositing partially transparent objects.

The alpha channel for the foreground works the same as it does elsewhere in LightWave. When an image is loaded as a foreground plate, a second image is loaded as an alpha channel. Areas of the alpha channel that are 100% black will cause that area of the foreground image to be completely transparent. 100% white areas of the alpha channel will show only the foreground image.

If the foreground image is to be composited using an alpha channel that was not rendered over a pure black background, it will be necessary to activate the Foreground Fader Alpha. Because LightWave's compositing is an additive process, if the Foreground Fader Alpha is not checked when needed, the portions of the foreground that have been added to the image will appear much too bright.

For some odd reason, this is the only place that LightWave does not have the option to use a negative alpha, so if the alpha image is giving you the exact opposite of the desired transparency, it will be necessary to reverse the image through some other means.

Foreground Key

Using a color range for the Foreground key is the other way to make parts of the foreground transparent. By using a defined color range, specific portions of a foreground image can be removed. Using a color range for a Foreground key is similar to a clip map in that each pixel is either 100% visible or completely gone, with no transition between. The Foreground key option is rarely used because of the harshness of the edge of the key and the difficulty in properly setting the color range, but it can still be useful for certain situations. When using a foreground image, it is necessary to remove selected portions so that other elements of the scene can be seen. Here are exercises using the alpha channel and the Color Clip option.

In the following exercise, you have a hilly desert scene on which you want to composite a giant cow. If the cow were simply placed in front of the background, you would not have a sense of scale. The cow needs to be inserted into the image in such a way that you are given visual clues as to the size of the beast.

COMPOSITING USING THE FOREGROUND IMAGE AND ALPHA CHANNEL

1. Clear the scene. From the accompanying CD, load the image Valley.tga and the image ValleyMask.tga.

2. Load the Cow.lwo from LightWave's Objects, Animals directory.

3. In Layout, rotate the Cow.lwo 90 degrees on its heading axis so you are not staring straight at its backside (see fig. 15.2).

FIGURE 15.2

A giant cow is positioned to appear over mountains by using the alpha channel to remove part of the foreground.

4. Go to the Effects Panel Compositing tab. In the middle of the panel are the Foreground Image options (see fig. 15.3). Select Valley.tga as the foreground image and the ValleyMask.tga as the alpha image. The color image should be on the left side, and a black and white image that follows the contour of the horizon should be on the right. Activate the Foreground Fader Alpha option by clicking on its box on the lower left of the compositing options screen.

5. Do a test render. You should now have a picture of a giant cow standing behind a mountainous ridge with a black sky (see fig. 15.4).

6. Go back to the Compositing Panel and select the Valley.tga image, which is currently the foreground image, as the background image also. Another test render will show the giant cow neatly sandwiched between the foreground hills and the horizon.

FIGURE 15.3

A screen shot of the Compositing section of the Effects Panel showing how to use the foreground alpha channel.

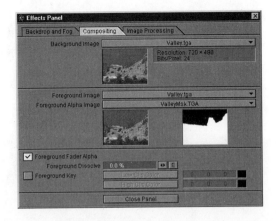

FIGURE 15.4

A rendered image of the cow overlooking the mountain using a foreground image with an alpha channel.

In some situations, it is possible to key out the unwanted sections of the foreground by keying out a range of colors from the foreground image. This continues from the previous example.

7. Go back to the Effects Panel Compositing tab. Change the foreground alpha image from ValleyMask.tga to none.

8. Check the box for Foreground Key. For low clip color, enter the values 70,85,120. For the high clip color, enter the values 120,85,205 (see fig. 15.5).

FIGURE 15.5

The Compositing section of the Effects Panel showing how to set the values for a color clip.

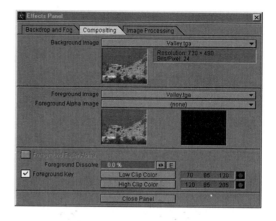

9. Do a test render.

Notice that the blue sky portion of the foreground image has been removed, leaving a jagged edge between the areas that are inside and out of the specified range. The colors given for this example were obtained through trial and error, judging by eye the lightest and darkest value of the area to be keyed and doing test renders to fine-tune the values. Generally, if you need to do a color key for a composite, there is other software better suited for generating an alpha channel for use as a matte.

Images Mapped onto Geometry

The process of applying an image to the surface of an object is referred to as *mapping*. Though LightWave enables you to apply mapped images to control many different attributes, color mapping is used almost exclusively.

For more information on mapping images onto geometry, refer to Chapter 9, "Managing Textures and Materials."

Front Projection Mapping

Front projection mapping can be difficult to grasp because there is no real-world analogy for it. Front projection mapping is an option in the Surfaces

Panel. It can be used for some of the attributes to apply a map to an object, as if it had global coordinates that were perfectly scaled and positioned to match the same image loaded as a background.

The camera and object can both be repositioned and rotated, but that will have no effect on how the map is registered on the scene. Keep in mind that front projection mapping is for perfect registration, and will not match the same image used as a background unless care is taken in adjusting the lighting and other surface attributes of the object.

The following exercise is an example of how images placed on geometry by front projection will line up perfectly to the same image loaded as a background. In traditional composition, this is referred to as *registration*. In LightWave, the Front Projection Map has no texture scale or texture centering values because the image is locked into the exact area of the frame.

USING FRONT PROJECTION MAPPING

1. Clear the scene. From the accompanying CD, load the image Cloud.tga and have it selected as the background image.

2. From the LightWave Objects, Animals directory, load the Cow.lwo object and keyframe it so that it fills most of the screen (see fig. 15.6).

FIGURE 15.6

The Cow object in position to illustrate the effects of front projection mapping.

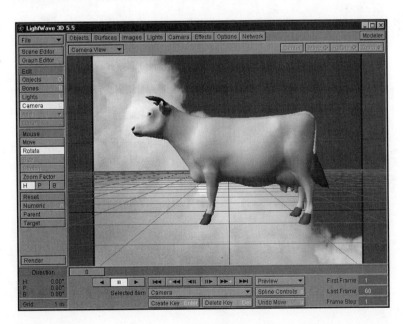

3. In the Surfaces Panel, go to the surface called Cowhide and select the Color Texture button. Change the texture type from Fractal Noise to Front Projection Map, and select Clouds.tga as the texture image.

4. Do a test render.

Notice how the hide of the cow tends to pick up the background image (see fig. 15.7). Any changes to the cow's geometry or position will not alter the position relative to the camera of the front projected mapped image. The basic shape of the cow's body is still discernible because the light source is creating brightly lit areas and shaded spots. You can render the cowhide invisible by having it ignore all lights.

FIGURE 15.7
The effects of applying front projection mapping as a color map.

5. In the Surfaces Panel under Cowhide, set the Luminosity Value to 100% to make it completely self-illuminated. Set the Diffusion Level at 0% so that light striking the surface has no effect.

6. Do a test render.

The render shows that all the polygons with the cowhide surface seem to have disappeared, but all polygons have remained (see fig. 15.8). The cowhide polygons are still there; they are just so perfectly aligned with the background image that they blend in seamlessly.

FIGURE 15.8

The effects of applying front projection mapping as a color map with luminosity added.

7. Load a second object. Keyframe it so that it is partially behind the Cow object, and render a test frame (see fig. 15.9).

FIGURE 15.9

The Cow object and the Spaceship object in position to illustrate the effects of front projection mapping with a second object.

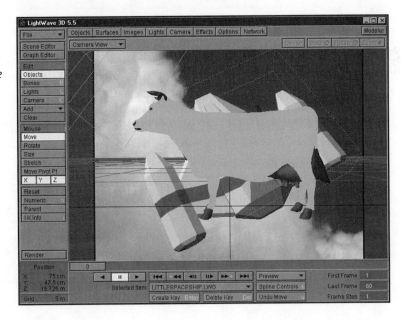

Notice that where the geometry of the Cow.lwo crosses in front of the second object, that part of the object appears to get sliced away (see fig. 15.10).

The two main uses for front projection mapping are to give 3D attributes to a background plate and to modify the image used as a background. The mapped objects then can have the attributes of a typical LightWave object, as seen in the cow example. They cast and receive shadows, can be reflected and refracted, and are affected by lighting, depth of field, and the soft filter. By adjusting the luminosity and diffusion, the surfaces can also be set to not react to the other settings in the scene.

You can also apply front projection mapping to surface attributes other than color. Luminosity, diffusion, transparency, and reflection all have front projection mapping as a texture option. Even clip mapping has the option of a front projection map and can be used for compositing.

In the following exercise, you will use front projection mapping of a clip map to make it appear that a Cow object is placed behind part of the background.

USING A FRONT PROJECTION CLIP MAP

1. Clear the scene and load a fresh Cow.lwo.

2. From the accompanying CD, load the Cloud.tga image and the Cloudmask.tga image.

3. Select Cloud.tga as a background image. In the Options, Layout View Panel, activate the background image for the Layout view that will make the background image visible in the Camera view of the Layout screen.

4. Clone the Cow.lwo once so you have two cows. Go to the Objects Panel, and with the Cow.lwo object selected, click on the Clone Object button and make one clone of the cow. For Cow.lwo(1), click on the Clip Map Texture, select Front Projection Map, and use Cloudmask.tga as the texture image. The white areas of the map will be the areas that are to be removed, so select Negative Image for the Clip Map.

5. In Layout, select the Camera view so that the background image is visible. Position Cow.lwo (1), the one with the clip map applied, so that its head is just poking out from behind the clouds. Position Cow.lwo (2) closer to the camera facing the other way.

6. Do a test render (see fig. 15.11).

FIGURE 15.11
Two cows, with the rear cow having a clip map applied to make it appear that it is poking out from behind the cloud bank.

This shows clip maps can be used on a per object basis for the purposes of compositing. The front projection map will always be perfectly registered to the frame.

The test render shows the first cow coming out from behind a cloud bank and the second cow already in front of the clouds. You can use the clip map method on a per object basis. You can achieve the same transparency effect with soft edges by using a front projection transparency map on a per surface basis.

One of the wonderful things about LightWave is that there are often many different ways to get the job done, each with unique properties and capabilities. By understanding how all of LightWave's functions work together, particularly in compositing, you can achieve very sophisticated effects.

Creating Multiplane Animation

In traditional animation, 2D images are painted on planes of glass and stacked to give the flat images the illusion of depth. You can use the same technique by applying front projection maps to a series of polygons. The advantage that you have in 3D animation over traditional cell animation is that you can fly your 3D objects between and through the various levels.

In the following exercise, you will use a series of flat polygons with front projection maps to give depth to your background plate. Each polygon will have the same color map but different transparency maps.

CREATING A MULTIPLANE ANIMATION

1. Clear the scene. From the accompanying CD, load Hill.tga and the associated alpha masks, Frontmask.tga, Middlemask.tga, and Backmask.tga.

2. From the accompanying CD, load the polygons Front.lwo, Middle.lwo, and Back.lwo.

3. Keyframe the Front.lwo in the center of the screen at the position 0,0,0. Keyframe the polygon Middle.lwo at 0,0,5. Keyframe the polygon

Back.lwo at 0,0,10. Scale the polygons so that the sides are past the edges of the camera frame.

4. Go to the Surfaces Panel. The surfaces Front, Middle, and Back will have the same settings applied to them. The front projection color map of the Hill.tga image has a luminosity value of 100%. For each of the surfaces Front, Back, and Middle, select the image Hill.tga as a color texture front projection map and set the luminosity to 100%. Do not use the alpha images here; the masks are for defining a transparent region.

5. The surfaces for three polygons will be made partially transparent by applying the appropriate transparency front projection map to them. For the surface Front, use the image Frontmask.tga for a front projection transparency map. For the surface Middle, select the image Middlemask.tga as the front projection transparency map. For the surface Back, select the image Backmask.tga as the front projection transparency map.

6. In the Effects, Compositing Panel, select the image Hill.tga as the background image.

7. Load the Cow.lwo and clone it three times so there are four cows. Position the cows between each of the polygons and place them so they appear at various latitudes on the hill (see fig. 15.12). Do a low-res test render and reposition the cows as necessary (see fig. 15.13).

FIGURE 15.12

A Perspective view showing the positioning of the Cow objects for the multiplane rendering.

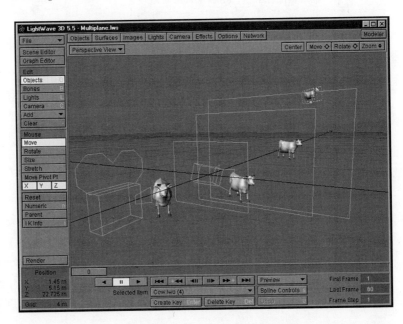

TIP

To speed the rendering of the scene, it is possible to use the alpha masks as a clip map instead of a transparency map. The transparency map gives a softer transition on the edge, but clip maps render much more quickly.

What you have done so far is already beyond much of the capabilities of traditional compositing. Moving your elements around in 3D space gives you incredible amounts of flexibility when combining images. Until now, you have been inserting your rendered objects in between layers of other images. In order to make the LightWave object appear to be more integrated with the original images, having the object cast shadows that appear to interact with the background goes a long way to "marry" the rendered objects with the background.

Compositing Shadows

Shadows are an important part of compositing. If all the other objects in an image are casting shadows, it is necessary to have the rendered object appear to cast a shadow to have it fit in with the rest of the image.

Not only does the rendered object need to cast a shadow, the shadow needs to fall in such a way that it makes sense. A perfectly flat shadow falling over a group of beach balls would not be very convincing. The angle and sharpness of the shadow must also match the shadows in the original image.

There are two ways to have the rendered object cast an interactive shadow on the background plate: a single-pass method involving front projection mapping and a two-pass method using the shadow alpha function. Both methods involve the use of stunt objects used as shadow catchers. A *shadow catcher object* is geometry modeled to approximate an object in the background plate and has its object appearance options set to receive shadows only.

Single Pass Shadowing

You can render shadows into a scene in a single pass simply by using front projection mapping and stunt objects. The difficult part is balancing the luminosity and diffusion values of the surface catching the shadow. If the surface with a front projection map has the luminosity set at 100% and the diffuse value set at 0%, the surface will perfectly match the original background image, but because the surface is adjusted not to react to light, it will not show a shadow. A lighting setup will perfectly illuminate the front projection surface and is unlikely to light the objects properly or have the shadows casting in the correct directions.

Two Pass Shadowing

The shadow alpha function is a simple process that is hard to describe. The shadow alpha requires both a rendering pass and a compositing pass. With shadow alpha, two images are rendered for each frame, an RGB image and an alpha image. The alpha image will render for not just the objects in the scene but also the areas where the shadows fall. The RGB image will render the wanted images in full color and all the shadow catching objects will be completely black. The alpha image will show white for all the solid objects and black where there are no objects. The areas where the shadows fall on the stunt objects will be gray.

Once the RGB images and alpha images are rendered, LightWave then composites the images. The original image is loaded as a background. The RGB rendered image is loaded as a foreground with the associated shadow alpha file loaded as the foreground alpha image. LightWave will then combine the foreground and background images using the alpha mask as a map. The RGB image will be mostly black except where the object is rendered. The gray area of the alpha mask representing the shadow will mix some of that black into the background image to darken it. Because the foreground elements to be composited have been rendered over black, it is not necessary to use the Foreground Fader Alpha option to get the desired results.

In the following exercise, you will use geometry that approximates the size and position of buildings in your background image. You will use the objects as "shadow catchers" when you introduce a LightWave-rendered rocket ship to the scene. You will render it once to get the foreground elements and the shadow alpha, and then finish it by compositing the original background image with the newly rendered spaceship and its shadow foreground using the shadow alpha image.

CREATING A SHADOW ALPHA COMPOSITE

1. From the accompanying CD, load the image Industry.tga. Go to the Effects, Compositing Panel and use Industry.tga as the background image.

2. From the accompanying CD, load the objects IndustryBldg.lwo and IndustryGround.lwo. In the Scene Editor, select the objects to be shown as wire frames (see fig. 15.14).

3. In the Options, Layout View Panel, select Background.

4. Adjust the camera height and angle so that the layout grid approximates the ground in the background image.

5. Moving and scaling only on the X and the Z axes, keyframe the Ground object so that it covers the ground shown in the background image.

6. Move the IndustryBldg.lwo object into position so that it lines up with the right side of the center building with the white-sloped roof. Rotate and move the object so that it comes close to appearing in the same space as the building in the background photo.

FIGURE 15.14

A Camera view showing the placement of the shadow catching objects.

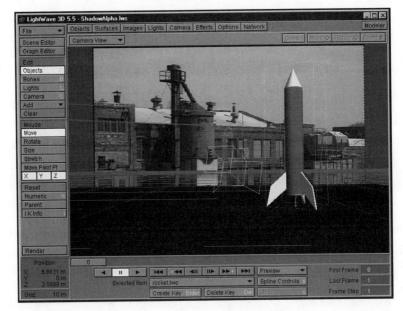

7. From the accompanying CD, load the Rocket.lwo object. Using the Overhead view, move the Rocket.lwo object to a position slightly in front of the building and keyframe it there. Double-check its position in the Camera view.

8. Adjust the light. Select and edit the light and choose the Light view. Position the light so that it sees the Rocket object with the building behind it. The light should shine so that the rocket casts a shadow on the building. Do a test render with Trace Shadows turned on to make sure this is so.

9. Apply a front projection map to the building and ground for the purposes of aligning the shadow. The top of the rocket's shadow should fall on the flat part of the roof. If the shadow falls on the chimney or the grain silo, adjust either the rocket or the light.

10. Adjust the surface for the shadow catchers. In the Surfaces Panel, select the shadow catcher surface. Remove all maps and textures and change the color to black. In Surfaces, Advanced options set the Alpha Channel box to Shadow Density. Shadow density is the attribute known in previous versions as shadow alpha.

11. Remove the background image, and in the Render Panel set the Save Image Panel to save both the RGB images and the alpha images. Be sure to save them in different directories or with different names.

12. Render and save the RGB and alpha images.

13. Clear the scene and prepare to composite the images. In the Images Panel, load the RGB image and the alpha image. Also load the original background image, the Industry.tga file.

14. Go to the Effects, Compositing Panel. For the background image, select Industry.tga. For the foreground image, select the newly rendered RGB image and the shadow alpha for the Foreground Alpha Image. Do a test render. If the composited part of the image has a "washed out" look, go back to the Effects, Compositing screen and toggle the setting on the Foreground Fader Alpha box. Figure 15.15 shows the spaceship image integrated into the background.

FIGURE 15.15
The spaceship integrated into the background image using the shadow alpha method to cast a shadow that falls on the buildings in the background.

TIP

The compositing pass that LightWave does to combine the background, RGB, and alpha image takes very little time. Because there are no objects to render, it is not necessary to antialias, trace shadows, or even turn on any lights. As a result, it renders the frames very quickly.

Though using the shadow alpha technique seems to take many steps, it is the best and most convenient way to incorporate shadows into a composited rendering.

The shadow alpha technique is just one example of the numerous tools that LightWave offers for compositing. In order to "sell" a composite, that is, to make it seem natural to the environment, there are a number of things you can do to make the introduction of new elements to the scene as seamless as possible.

Seamless Compositing

Compositing 3D objects into existing footage is a tricky business. It has been said that computer graphics are being seen more but noticed less. To seamlessly introduce objects, whether beach balls or dinosaurs, requires a good working knowledge of nearly all of LightWave's functions. Fortunately, with the power of LightWave, not only can you make your composite wonderful, but invisible as well.

The following list contains several tips that will help you create seamless composites with LightWave:

- When compositing a 3D object into a footage shot on video, use field rendering. If the source footage originated on film, turn off field rendering and use dithered motion blur.

- The Soft Focus option in the Camera Panel helps blend the objects with the background. Background and foreground images will not be affected by soft focus, but surfaces with a front projection map will.

- Foregrounds and backgrounds do not have to be the same image. You can take an isolated tree branch, create an alpha mask for it, and use it as a foreground image.

- Front projection maps cannot be used for bump maps and displacement maps. You can simulate them by scaling the size of a polygon so that the edges align with the sides of the screen and then use a planer map with automatic sizing.

- Get as much information as possible on the source material. The type of camera used, its focal length, and the amount of zoom. Also get any positional data on the objects in the scene and the height of the camera. You can enter all of this information numerically into the layout screen to use as a starting point for aligning the compositing elements.

- An object with a front projection map, 100% luminosity, and 0% diffusion can still raytrace reflections.

Compositing covers a lot of territory. It can be as simple as flying a logo over a new background image or as complicated as inserting a dinosaur jumping out of a forest and running through traffic. As your skill tools for compositing become more sophisticated, so do your audiences. Keep in mind that it is often the perfection of the composited element that draws the audience's attention. It is necessary to develop an objective eye that can see how the finished composite will look to someone who has not seen the separate elements or knows of the amount of work involved.

Summary

Not only does LightWave composite images, it also has the power to alter the source images in ways that make the various elements appear to be inserted into the scene, not just sandwiched between a foreground and background. Interactive shadows, reflections, and lighting all work together to seamlessly integrate images to make a believable and transparent composite. This chapter covered the following:

- Using the background plate
- Working with the foreground image
- Images mapped onto geometry
- Front projection mapping
- Multiplane animations
- Single pass shadowing
- Two pass shadowing

The next chapter takes you into the world of output options and techniques in LightWave.

Chapter 16

OUTPUT OPTIONS AND TECHNIQUES

Being a professional 3D animator requires you to have knowledge in areas beyond just animation. You need to be a director, camera person, gaffer, salesperson, and business person, and be creative as well. As an animator, you need to know how and where your 3D animation will be used to complete a project. This chapter will discuss the following topics you need to be familiar with to be a successful animator:

- Digital disk recorders

- Internet and FTP sites

- File formats

- Film recording

- LightWave and non-linear editing

- Editing animations

Once you create your 3D animation, you need to output it. This can be to anything from VHS tape to Digital Beta to Internet transfers and AVI or QuickTime movies. Whatever the situation, you need to be prepared to fulfill requests from clients successfully.

Understanding Digital Disk Recorders

Digital disk recorders are a remarkable asset to 3D animators. These handy hardware and software combos enable you to directly record and play back an animation within the same computer. Just a few years ago, these units were not very common, and most rendering was recorded one frame at a time to a frame-accurate video editing deck. Digital disk recorders are much more beneficial to you as an animator for many reasons. Most of the reasons are based on solutions to problems with single frame recording to a video deck. The following list gives a few examples of why recording animations to a digital disk is better than recording directly to tape:

- Frame-accurate video decks are very expensive, as much as $60,000, as opposed to DDR's anywhere from $2,000–10,000.

- Recording directly to tape creates a huge margin for error. Videotape can slip, resulting in frame "drop-outs" throughout the animation.

- Using a digital disk keeps the files in a digital state, enabling you to recycle images in other applications, or another animation, without any loss in quality.

- Digital disk recorders can store large amounts of data and that data can be backed up electronically for future use. Rendering to tape requires making a copy of the tape, instantly creating a quality generation loss.

Digital disk recorders are becoming better and cheaper as the 3D industry continues to grow. There are a few companies right now creating these helpful units, many of which have Internet web sites with more information. Several models are discussed in the following sections.

The Personal Animation Recorder (PAR)

The PAR was one of the first major breakthroughs for digital disk recording for LightWave animators. Released initially for the Amiga, the makers of the PAR, Digital Processing Systems, Inc., could not keep up with orders. This device consisted of a card that installed inside the Amiga computer, with its own dedicated hard drive. Animation can be recorded directly to the drive and played back instantly in real-time broadcast quality. Soon after the Amiga version of the PAR, Digital Processing Systems released the PAR for the PC, still used by many animators. If you work on an Amiga using LightWave, you can find many used PAR systems available through the Internet and through your local LightWave dealer.

The Perception Video Recorder (PVR)

Shortly after the release of the PAR, Digital Processing Systems announced the Perception Video Recorder. The Perception offered the same technology and functionality as the PAR, but with much greater quality. This device will run with DEC Alpha- and Intel-based computers running Windows NT for Windows NT Workstations. The PAR uses 8-bit encoding technology, whereas the PVR uses 10-bit encoding, which renders higher quality. The PVR also offers component, composite, and SVHS outputs. Composite video signals have one single video line, whereas component video signals have the red, blue, and green signals separated. SVHS or Super VHS video lines maintain color saturation better than composite signals.

Some major differences between the PAR and the PVR beyond quality are the tools each uses. In order to play animations continuously in the PAR, an animator needs to "join" them. This process physically joins the animations together on the digital hard disk. Often, this procedure damages one of the joined animations, as the files are moved and rearranged on the hard drive. The PVR, however, offers a play list in which any animation from anywhere on the drive can be added to the list. The PVR then plays through the list seamlessly.

The PVR also supports audio files. By creating a play list of animations, an audio track can be tagged and played along with the set. In addition, the PVR offers simple editing such as cuts and dissolves between animations. The DPS Perception Video Recorder is a PCI card-based digital video disk recorder. This means that video signals can be recorded into the PVR at digital quality. Recording time is limited only by the capacity and number of attached drives. The PVR also has an optional real-time video capture daughter card to record video. Its dedicated hard drive can be written and rewritten as often as you like.

Used with animation software or other computer graphics applications such as LightWave, the Perception Video Recorder can directly import RGB files. The PVR integrates with software packages using a DPS file system in which video frames appear simultaneously in different file formats. Any software package capable of saving RGB images to or loading them from a hard drive can be used. Stored files can be instantly played back in real-time or slow motion.

An automatic entropy prediction circuit is used to determine the optimum amount of video compression on a frame-by-frame basis. This circuit looks at each frame recorded and sets the appropriate amount of compression. This works during real-time recording as well. The user also has complete control over the compression/quality level settings. Captured video can be exported as sequential RGB files for rotoscoping and other compositing applications.

Hollywood Digital Disk Recorder

The Hollywood Digital Disk Recorder from Digital Processing Systems, Inc., unlike the PAR and PVR, records and plays back uncompressed animations and video. Every time an animation is compressed, it loses some quality. Because the Hollywood doesn't use compression, its quality surpasses that of the PAR and the PVR.

Even though it is 100% decompressed, Hollywood offers the lowest cost per minute of any D1 system. D1 is a component signal whereas D2 is composite. D1 is one of the highest quality video formats available. In a computer equipped with four 4GB hard drives, five or more minutes of video can typically be recorded. The DPS Hollywood system plugs directly into the PCI bus of an Intel or DEC Alpha Windows NT workstation. Graphic files can be rendered directly to Hollywood using the exclusive DPS Virtual File System, which also provides instant RGB file format conversion for all popular formats.

The DPS Hollywood D1 recorder consists of three cards: Luminance processor (PCI), Chrominance processor (PCI), and Genlock Timing/Serial D1 interface (ISA). An optional fourth card adds a real-time alpha channel

(4:2:2:4 mode). The cards are connected by a ribbon cable that transmits parallel 10-bit video data between the boards. The luminance and chrominance boards are connected to separate chains of SCSI drives via on-board Fast-Wide SCSI-II controllers.

Targa 2000 Series

Another brand of Digital Disk Recording comes from Truvision, the makers of Targa 2000 boards. These boards work well with LightWave, and are available for both the Macintosh and Windows platforms. Truvision offers a variety of boards, each one slightly better and more expensive than the next. The Targa 2000 PCI for Macintosh or Windows NT offers full motion video input and output of both composite and s-video formats at resolutions up to 640×480, 648×486 NTSC, or 768×576 PAL. Targa 2000 Pro is capable of up to CD or DAT quality audio on board. The Pro version also supports 720×480 resolution in BetaSP quality. The Targa 2000 will also output CCIR 601 resolution video. The Targa 2000 Pro is ideal for 3D animators and commercial producers.

The Targa 2000 DTX is the next generation Targa 2000 product. Its data rate delivers excellent image quality at 2:1 compression, making the Targa 2000 DTX ideal for traditional broadcast non-linear editing, compositing, animation, and 3D applications.

Targa 2000 DTX offers the same features as the Targa 2000 RTX, but in a single-stream configuration. Targa 2000 DTX ships standard with an Audio/Video cable to connect to an analog environment or it can be configured with a Breakout Box. Targa 2000 RTX also drives an RGB display at up to 21" at 24-bit color and supports full-motion previewing on RGB and video displays.

Truvision's new Targa 2000 SDX is based on the Targa 2000 RTX and includes dual M-JPEG codecs for real-time, full resolution effects processing at up to 300KB per frame. This compression language enables the Truvision board to compress and record video in real time without delays. The more compression there is, the poorer the picture will be. However, the more compression there is, the more storage there will be. This is a common dilemma for non-linear users. A good rule of thumb to work with is to not record video at a higher quality than the original source. If you shoot a wedding on SVHS format video, for example, don't record it at Digital or Broadcast quality. Record it at SVHS or Industrial quality. Working this way saves hard disk space but maintains good compression. Digital disk recorders keep getting better, faster, and cheaper. However, that doesn't mean you should wait to add one to your 3D toolbox. The use of a digital disk recorder not only enhances your animations by keeping rendered frames in a digital format, it offers you more control over the final destination of your project. Whether you plan to output to film, video, CD, or the Internet, digital disk recorders are a necessity. Research the following companies to learn more about digital disk recording devices.

Digital Processing Systems, Inc.
www.dps.com
HEADQUARTERS
70 Valleywood Drive
Markham, Ontario
L3R 4T5
Canada

USA
11 Spiral Drive, Suite 10
Florence, Ky 41042
USA

EUROPE
Unit 9, Romans Business Park
East Street, Farnham
Surrey GU9 7SX
U.K.

ASIA/PACIFIC
Unit 11, 10-12 Woodville St
Hurstville, Sydney
N.S.W. 2220
Australia

Truvision, Inc.
www.truvision.com
2500 Walsh Avenue
Santa Clara, CA 95051
408/562-4200,
FAX 408/562-4065

Internet and FTP Sites

As a LightWave animator, the information and resources available to you over the Internet are mind-boggling. Through the Internet, you can study the art of 3D animation, learning about theories and techniques such as Inverse Kinematics, Forward Kinematics, and physics in 3D, just to name a few. You can participate in newsgroups and discuss all aspects of LightWave with other animators from around the globe. *Newsgroups* are forums based on a set topic in which you can contribute messages. Most service providers offer news services, and Internet browsers such as Netscape and Internet Explorer offer newsgroup functions. You can participate in chat rooms if your system enables you to and discuss LightWave in real time with other animators. Add to this the ability to view and see LightWave and 3D work from artists in all walks of life, without leaving your desk—quite amazing.

NOTE

To access IRC on the Internet, you need to use IRC software such as MIRC. You do not need additional hardware, but you must have an Internet connection. You can often find trial and shareware versions of IRC programs across the Internet. Once you set up an IRC program, use the #lightwave command to access the LightWave IRC channel. Also, the IRC programs can inform you how to sign on to other IRC channels. Check it out when you can.

LightWave's growth through the years has spawned countless LightWave-specific, LightWave-generated, and LightWave dealer sites on the World Wide Web. In addition to this, many LightWave FTP sites are available for you to explore, share, and download LightWave files with friends and strangers. *FTP*, or File Transfer Protocol, is a direct link between your computer and an Internet server. This server contains folders in which all forms of content, LightWave or otherwise, are stored. FTP sites are a great way to transfer and receive files from clients as well. There are so many LightWave-related sites on the Internet, the best way to discover them is through an Internet search. Go to www.yahoo.com or www.hotbot.com, or any of the other popular Internet search engines to find interesting LightWave-related web and FTP sites.

Film Recording

Much of your LightWave work will eventually be output to video tape, either VHS, SVHS, ¾ ", BetaSP, MII, D2, Digital Beta, or D1. However, you might secure a project from a client who needs an animation to be output to film. This might be for a television commercial, television show, or theater. You might be fortunate enough to have an animation job for a local movie theater in which your LightWave animation will be shown before each movie.

Film recording is an easy process for animators. It's not a cheap process, but an easy one. It's easy because all you need to do is send the frames to a film recording house. These specialty houses use expensive film recording devices that can range upward of $50,000. The process is simply a matter of transferring the rendered images through the film recorder.

Cost and Usage

The cost of recording animations to film depends on many factors:

- The number of images needing to be transferred

- The number of copies needed

- Types of conversions: NTSC, PAL, or SECAM

- How quickly you need the final products

Film recording requires more than money and a film recording facility, it requires more rendering time than normal. A resolution of 720×480 is typical for 3D animation. Recording for film, however, requires up to four times that amount, with a screen resolution of 2560×1920. Four times the resolution equals four times the rendering. Often, a client may suggest or supply a specific resolution higher than 2560×1920. Perhaps you have a client who needs animated titles for a 70mm IMAX film. Each situation is different, but LightWave can handle rendering resolutions up to 8000×8000 pixels. Be prepared to have significant time available for rendering, as well as storage. Files rendered at very high resolutions are essentially larger images and require more disk space.

Getting files from your computer to a film recording facility requires good size storage. Systems such as Iomega's JAZ drive can transfer 1 gigabyte of data on one cartridge. A DLT drive from Optima Corp. can handle up to 15 gigabytes of data. Find a solution that works best for your needs from your local video/computer dealer.

Finding a Film Recording Facility

In order to find the right film recording facility for your needs, you need to research a few factors.

- Use client referrals for finding film recording facilities.

- Compare pricing between facilities.

- Find out time frames for each facility.

- Sample a previous job.

Finding a film recording facility is easier near major cities. For 3D animators in smaller towns, you may need to find a resource in the nearest city that has a film recording facility. If you don't live near a film recording facility, you may have to send files on a JAZ cartridge or some other type of removable media. Files to be sent to a film recording facility are usually too big for Internet transfers.

Like various LightWave World Wide Web and FTP sites, the Internet is a great resource for hunting down a film recording facility near you.

NOTE

Not all businesses are listed on the Internet. Be sure to check your local phone book or local creative directory for complete listings of film recording studios.

Here are just a few of the film companies you can find on the Internet:

- www.safelight.com/labserv.htm

- www.prismstudios.com

- www.thephoto.com

- www.photoregon.com

- www.igraph.com

Using LightWave and Non-Linear Editing

The advance of digital technology through the 1990s has placed you in a fantastic position as a 3D animator. Finishing a project, recording to tape, editing, audio mixing, and dubbing used to be headaches animators often had to consider. Now with the growth of non-linear editing, costs have dropped, making even the hobbyist LightWave animator a part-time video editor.

Non-linear editing enables you to rearrange, organize, and manipulate video clips in a digital setting. Your home VCR is a linear device, for example. In order to get to the end of a movie, you have to physically fast-forward the tape. In a non-linear setting, such as inside a digital disk recorder or a DVD (digital video disk) system, forwarding to the end of a movie (or video clip) is instant. The information is stored digitally, so accessing specific clips simply requires selection.

Non-linear editing solutions enable video and animation footage to be edited internally on a computer system. This allows for seamless transitions, multiple passes, multiple keys, titling, and audio all to be put together in one single environment without any loss of quality. A final product such as a 3D animation with video and audio added can be recorded directly to video tape for delivery to the client.

Types of Non-Linear Systems

The market for non-linear editing is growing rapidly. Your choice of editing systems depends greatly on cost, existing computer, and intended application. As a 3D animator, a non-linear editing system can add to your creative talents by enabling you to:

- Edit 3D animations
- Create demo reels of animations for clients
- Update demo reels often
- Add audio to animations
- Edit video

Non-Linear editing systems vary in price and performance. Typically, they are Mac- or PC-based and offer a variety of effects. AVID's MCXpress for Macintosh and Windows NT offers affordable editing solutions for independent and small animation and production facilities.

MCXpress is a high-performance, cost-effective, real-time digital video editing and finishing system for video professionals who create content for tape, CD-ROM, or the Internet. It features professional picture and audio editing tools, broadcast-quality images, real-time 2D and 3D effects and is fully compatible with, and upgradable to, any Media Composer system.

The MCXpress is only one type of non-linear editing solution. Other types of systems, such as NewTek's Flyer, Scitex's Stratasphere, VideoActionNT, and others, are systems that all perform similar functions. In-Sync's Speed Razor editing software works with a Perception Video Recorder or Targa Truvision Board. Because many 3D animators use these boards to output animations, Speed Razor, priced below $1,000, is often a great solution.

Speed Razor features multiple input and output, up to D1 quality, full field rendering, no project length limits, flexible effect compositing tools, and real-time audio mixing (from 6 to 20 tracks).

Editing should be a natural transition for 3D animators as it offers more flexibility for clients. The ability to add audio, edit transitions between animation clips, add animated countdowns, titles, and more are all excellent reasons for animators to add non-linear systems.

Editing Non-Linear Within the Same Computer

Adding on a non-linear editing system is often cost effective because it can be added to the same computer workstation you use for 3D animation. This all-in-one environment is ideal for 3D artists. As mentioned, In-Sync's Speed Razor is a great add on as it works directly with your existing Perception Video Recorder or Targa board. Other types of systems can also be added to your workstation for digital editing of animations.

Digital Fusion is a nonlinear compositing and special effects system for Windows NT. It will run stand-alone and also offers direct support for the DPS Perception and Hollywood DDRs. It is a fully multithreaded, multiprocessor-optimized package with a powerful and flexible flow layout for visualizing and layering effects. Digital Fusion supports unlimited layers, is resolution independent, has unlimited undo's and redo's, has powerful warps and effects, can directly load most image format types, and also features animatable effects-masks that use polygonal shapes to apply effects to user-definable regions of any image. When layers are composited together, each layer's resolution remains intact. The final result of this system is a clean and sharp picture, with very little or no picture loss. Every aspect of Digital Fusion's tools are fully animatable, with powerful spline controls. There are three levels of the product: Digital Fusion Lite v1.1, Digital Fusion v2.0, and Digital Fusion Film v2.0.

Although Digital Fusion is a true non-linear editing system, it can perform many linear effects. Digital Fusion is a great tool for post-process and compositing work in the digital environment.

Editing Non-Linear in Another Computer

Creating your animations on one computer and editing them on another has its pros and cons. A benefit of editing in another computer is that your workstation is free to create and render more animations. The downside to editing in another computer is finding a workable solution to transferring data. A typical 15-second animation can be as large as 400MB in size. Unless a digital transfer is used through a network or removable media, the animation needs to be output to tape and then rerecorded in the editing systems. This step takes away a generation of quality from your animation.

Digital backups, such as removable media or CD-ROM, are always a good investment for the 3D animator. Not only can you back up your work and system files, you can transfer images to other systems quite easily.

Manipulating Video in LightWave

A strong advantage a 3D animator with non-linear editing equipment will have over other animators is the capability to use video in LightWave. As a LightWave animator, you can load images and apply them to objects such as labels, textures, and backgrounds, but you can also load sequences. LightWave's image loader enables you to add a sequence of images for further manipulation in LightWave.

With a sequence of video, you can create the most realistic 3D warps and effects, better than most available editing systems. Why? Because manipulating video in LightWave truly creates a 3D effect and the antialiasing is good.

With video in LightWave, you can animate objects in real-world environments, wrap moving pictures around geometric shapes, or project images on a virtual wall. Be sure to read more about Video and LightWave in Chapter 17, "Video Post Effects."

Editing Animations

The art of a 3D animator can be made even better through the use of editing. Like movies or videos, the final presentation works best when edited. Your animation may only be 15 or 30 seconds long, but think of how many edits there are in a television commercial. Imagine how interesting your animation would look if it were created and edited like a television ad.

Editing animations requires planning. Knowing what you can edit and what you cannot will help you when creating an animation. You know that by using bones in a character, for example, you can't create a full range of motion. To combat this, you may work to model and animate the character so that the bones do not deform the character improperly, but to no avail. Suppose you are animating a character who needs to pick up a box and place it on a top warehouse shelf. If you know you are going to edit, you can use two characters and cut the shot. Instead of animating one long camera shot, animate the first part of the scene with a character whose arms are modeled downward. Then, animate the next part with the arms modeled up. Create the two animations and edit them together, creating a clean cut between shots.

Another example of how you can use editing for 3D animation is an animated sports arena. Your client needs a 30-second animation that calls for quick camera angles from all corners of the stadium, as well as close-ups. You can render each individual shot and edit them together for precise frame cuts. Editing your animations opens new doors of creativity for you and your project. By editing, you can take animations to the next level. You can "finish" your project through editing and audio.

Editing does not mean just cuts between animations either. Editing can be anything from dissolves, to wipes, to screen pulls, to processed video. Many video editing devices enable you to blur, slow down, speed up, or manipulate video sources just about any way you want. Additionally, you can use other software-related products such as Adobe's Premiere or After Effects to edit your animations. Adobe Premiere supports Apple QuickTime and Microsoft

Video for Windows (AVI) formats, so a wide range of hardware and software products is compatible with Adobe Premiere. Adobe After Effects lets you composite and animate in layers.

Adobe Premiere

Whether you're an expert or neophyte, you can easily create high-quality digital movies and video with Adobe Premiere software. This powerful editing software enables you to combine video, animation, still images, and graphics with the same high-quality control and results generated by professional editing systems. It also enables you to incorporate video images and LightWave animations into multimedia presentations.

Adobe After Effects

Adobe After Effects 3.1 provides the power and breadth of features required by filmmakers, video producers and editors, graphic designers, multimedia professionals, 3D animators, and web developers to produce high-end, unlimited composites, fluid animations, and sophisticated special effects.

After Effects is available in Standard and Production Bundle versions for Windows and Macintosh. The Standard package comes with core features and plug-in effects for adding motion to graphics. The Production Bundle is packed with additional functionality, features, and controls.

Summary

LightWave animations, video-editing tools, and image processing programs are created by manufacturers to help you do your job. Used effectively, you can convincingly tell a story through creative ideas and graphics. Add in sound and clever editing, with a few effects transitions, and you have a finished presentation. This chapter guided you through:

- Understanding digital disk recorders
- Working with the Internet and FTP sites
- Using film recording with your animations

- Working with LightWave 3D and non-linear editing

- Types of non-linear systems

- Editing your LightWave animations

No matter what software you use to edit your animations, and no matter how many effects you add to your animations, be sure to do one thing—create. Throughout the animation projects you embark upon, always keep in mind your goal. Learn and understand the resources available to you. Knowledge is power, and when it comes to LightWave, knowledge is creative freedom. Now, to add more creativity and a different look to your 3D animations, read Chapter 17 to learn how to create high-end digital graphics with LightWave.

Chapter 17

VIDEO POST EFFECTS

This is an exciting time to be a 3D animator because there is so much happening in the world of 3D that you can experience and grow with. However, clients and audiences demand more. They do so because the technology is everywhere, on television, videos, the Internet, CD-ROMs, and, of course, in the movies.

To stay competitive in the 3D world, you need to look beyond traditional uses of LightWave to get the job done. And, even though you are a 3D animator, you often need to finish up your animations in post-production to make them stand out.

This chapter will guide you through Video Post Effects and you can create them in LightWave and enhance your existing animations. You'll learn how to do the following:

- Simulate motion control.
- Create Digital Video Effects in LightWave.
- Add 2D effects to 3D renders.
- Use layers of pictures and images in LightWave.
- Create animations for Digital Keying.

Enhancing 3D Animation with Digital Video Effects

If you've ever worked in video production, you are familiar with the terms DVE and ADO. Animators use DVE (or Digital Video Effects) and ADO (or Ampex Digital Optics) to animate still and moving images. Many times, these units simulate 3D warps and image manipulation to video and text. Enhancements like these can make a video production come alive.

There are a number of Windows and Macintosh programs that enable you to put the finishing touches on a 3D animation on your hard drive. Traditional DVE and ADO have limited channels in which effects can be layered. This means that multiple passes need to be made, resulting in lost generations of video or animations, as well as sound. Multiple passes mean that a video effect needs to be made and recorded to tape. That tape must then be run through the editing system again in order to add another video effect. This process must continue until all the effects are added, resulting in loss of quality. But, through the power of LightWave, you can mimic the high-end DVE and ADO effects in your computer without any worry of quality loss. You can manipulate text and video and add warp effects to as many images as your computer memory and software allow. Your effects in LightWave will truly be 3D, unlike video equipment's simulated 3D effects.

Creating Digital Video Effects in LightWave

Adding Digital Video Effects in LightWave means adding another way of looking at how things can be done—something that you should always be considering.

TIP

Always look for new ways of creating animations and graphics with LightWave. If you become bored and feel your work often looks the same, find a different way to create the effect. Push the limits of your imagination, and watch what animators are doing on the major television and cable networks, as well as in the movies.

Creating DVE in LightWave can be great for faking motion control moves on still or moving pictures. Say, for example, that you are editing video and need images of people and places floating around the screen. You need to take a few photos and slowly have them grow toward the camera, at which point you will dissolve to another picture. To accomplish this, you need to obtain a high-quality photo, place it on a stand, light it, and then hopefully video tape or film it smoothly.

By using LightWave, you can eliminate most of the problems. The other alternative is to rent out a studio with a motion control camera, costing hundreds of dollars an hour. Although the results can be exceptional, you can't afford to do this for this project. And frankly, you shouldn't have to. You need to realize that you can animate your pictures and video clips in LightWave and avoid renting motion control suites and digital editing suites.

NOTE

In a major city, Post-Production Digital Suites can range anywhere from $200 an hour and up. If you've ever worked on a video, you know that it takes more than an hour to edit a final piece. Elsewhere, the services are unavailable.

The following project will take you through the simple steps needed to create four moving images in LightWave. From there, you'll create soft moving backgrounds, and then add some 3D effects to create a digital transition.

This tutorial begins in Modeler and ends up in Layout, as many of your projects do. You'll find that you may need a paint or image program such as Debabilizer from Equilibrium Software or Photoshop from Adobe to assist in this exercise. Also, shareware programs such as Paint Shop Pro work well for image cleanup. If you don't have access to an imaging program, it's a good idea to add this software to your toolkit when you can. Cleaning up, translating, and painting images for your LightWave work are essential, and you can only accomplish these tasks with the proper software. Often, your client will give you artwork that needs to be cleaned up or manipulated for use as a bump map or clip map in LightWave. This is another reason to use an imaging program. For this exercise, the sample images are included on the CD that came with this book.

NOTE

Good paint and image programs can cost upward of $600. Check your local retailer or LightWave dealer for recommendations.

2D DVE IN LIGHTWAVE

1. Enter LightWave's Modeler and go to a clean layer. Check the Information Display at the bottom-left part of the interface to make sure that the grid size is set to 1m, as in figure 17.1.

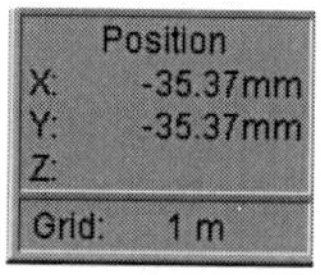

FIGURE 17.1

Use the Information Display in LightWave's Modeler to make sure you are using the proper grid size.

Position	
X:	-35.37mm
Y:	-35.37mm
Z:	
Grid:	1 m

2. You're going to map horizontal images first, so you need to create a polygon to map them onto. Select the Box tool from the Objects Panel (or press Shift+x) and draw out a box in the Front view.

3. The footage you will use for this exercise is from a still camera and from video so you need to create a box with the right aspect ratio. The aspect ratio is 4×3, or 640 by 480. Press n on the keyboard to enter these numeric values:

	Low	High	Segments
X	-4.9872m	6.0129m	1
Y	-3.9968m	3.9968m	1
Z	0m	0m	1

4. Press q on the keyboard to call up the Change Surface Requester. Change the name of the surface to **Image_One**. As you progress with the following techniques, you can change the name of the polygon's surface to exactly what the image or video sequence is. Click OK.

5. Press Enter to make the flat polygon. Select the Center plug-in to center the polygon on all axes for easy rotation in Layout.

6. Next, from the Objects Panel, select Put, New to save and load the flat polygon into Layout.

NOTE

LightWave's Layout must be running to use the Get and Put commands. You can press the Layout button in the upper-right corner of Modeler to start Layout.

7. Click on the Layout button to switch screens from Modeler to Layout. You can also use the Alt, Tab buttons if working on a PC. Once in Layout, you'll see your flat polygon in Layout, as in figure 17.2.

FIGURE 17.2
One flat polygon in Layout ready for an image map.

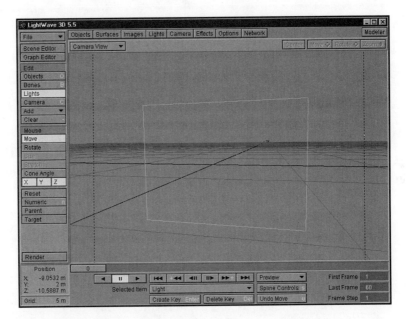

For now, this is all the modeling that needs to be done to achieve digital video effects in LightWave. As you begin to create warps and such for your images, you will modify the existing polygon.

8. In Layout, go to the Images Panel and select Load Image. Load the Rainy.tga file from this book's CD. Figure 17.3 shows the image loaded with its information.

FIGURE 17.3

The rainy image loaded through the Images Panel.

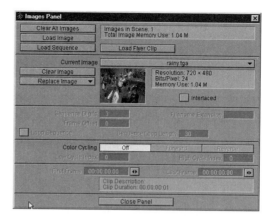

TIP

You don't have to close a panel to open a new one. If the Images Panel is open and you want to go to the Surfaces Panel, simply select the Surfaces Panel button at the top of Layout. One panel will close and the other will open. Conversely, you can close a panel by clicking on the same button.

9. Close the Images Panel and go to the Surfaces Panel. Make sure the Image_One surface is set in the Current Surface drop-down menu.

10. From Surface Color, select the T button to go to the Surfaces Texture Panel. Select Planar Image as the Texture Type, and select the Rainy.tga file as the Texture Image.

11. Turn off Width Repeat and Height Repeat, make the Texture Axis Z, and click Automatic Sizing. Also, turn off Texture Antialiasing. Because you will use antialiasing in the final render of the animation, your image will be antialiased twice if this button is left on, resulting in a blurry image.

12. Click Use Texture and return to Layout. From the Options Panel, go to the Layout View tab and turn on Use OpenGL and Enable OpenGL Textures.

13. Set the Texture Resolution to 128×128. If you have a strong video card, one that has 4MB or more, feel free to increase the Texture Resolution to 256×256 or 512×512. Figure 17.4 shows the Layout View tab.

FIGURE 17.4

OpenGL Textures are available in 5.5 through the Options Panel.

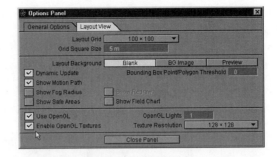

NOTE

Setting the Texture Resolution in the Options Panel does not affect the rendered image. This setting is for display purposes only. For example, a Texture Resolution of 64×64 will yield a pixilated image in Layout. When rendered, the image will look like the original image loaded into Layout.

14. Close the Options Panel and return to Layout. Can you see your image on the polygon? When using the OpenGL display settings, you need to tell LightWave to display OpenGL in two places. You've set the Layout View OpenGL settings through the Options Panel.

15. Now go to the Scene Editor and display the current object as a Textured Solid. You can do this by clicking on the small icon in the second column within the Scene Editor. Cycle through the nine choices until the t appears (for texture). To make things easier, choose Show All Objects as Textured Solids from the drop-down Show menu, as in figure 17.5.

FIGURE 17.5

From the Show drop-down menu, you can tell LightWave to Show All Objects as Solids or Texture Solids.

16. Close the Scene Editor and return to Layout. In a moment, your polygon will redraw and the applied texture will appear on the surface, as in figure 17.6. This new feature in 5.5 enables you to see applied images without rendering. This feature can save a lot of time, especially when more image-mapped polygons are added to the scene.

FIGURE 17.6

*The applied image
appears on the
polygon in Layout.*

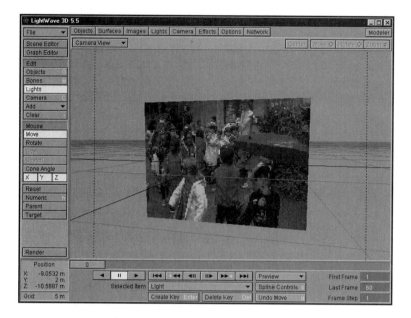

17. Move the camera so that it is facing the polygon straight on. An easy way
    to do this is to select Camera as the Edit item and then select Move as
    the Mouse function. Then, press the Reset button. Do the same for
    Rotation. This eliminates the need for tediously moving the camera into
    place and resets it to its default position.

This is basic, but it is important to know the full process because this is
the basis for any video post effect you will create in LightWave. Still
images, as shown here, can be mapped on, and rendered image sequences can be applied, as can video clips.

18. Go to the Options Panel, and from the Layout View tab, select Show Safe
    Areas. This will place an industry-standard safe area outline in Layout.
    It represents the limits for your animation to fit in a television viewing
    area. Showing Safe Areas is only a reference and does not show up in the
    rendering. The outer ring is the limit for elements, and the inner ring
    represents the limit for text elements.

19. With the camera in its default position, move it back on the Z-axis only
    until the polygon goes just beyond the outer ring of the safe area, as in
    figure 17.7. Be sure to create a keyframe at zero to lock it in place.

FIGURE 17.7

The camera is moved into place for a test render, using the Show Safe Areas feature from the Options Panel. OpenGL has been disabled for this image to show the safe areas.

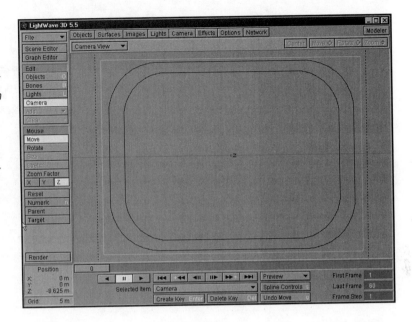

20. Press F9 to render the current frame. Your image renders cleanly. Because the image is mapped onto a polygon in Layout, it is open to any lighting situations set up. For this animation, all you need is a general light source. The default Distant Light will be fine. You may need to rotate it slightly to evenly illuminate the surface of the polygon.

From this point on, you can set up your camera moves easily and quickly. Instead of moving the camera, you can zoom it for a more realistic effect.

21. Go to the Camera Panel and set the Zoom Factor to 6.5, the equivalent of a 48mm lens. Doing this will keep the image from appearing too warped as the camera rotates.

22. Keeping the camera in place at zero, rotate the camera toward the boy with the umbrella. Use Layout's interactive Zoom Factor to zoom into the portion of the image with the boy and umbrella. Create a keyframe at zero. When asked to create an envelope, click Yes.

Thanks to 5.5's OpenGL Texture support, you can see exactly where to line up the camera, as in figure 17.8. Remember to wait for the image to redraw onto the polygon after making any adjustments.

FIGURE 17.8

OpenGL Texture support enables you to easily place the camera on a specific portion of the image.

23. Press f on the keyboard to call up the Go To Frame Requester. Enter 100 and click OK. Rotate the camera over to a close-up of the little girl, as in figure 17.9. One important thing here is to create an envelope key for the camera as well as a motion key for it.

24. After you create a keyframe for the rotation (the motion key), select Zoom Factor and press Enter to create an envelope key. This locks the camera's Zoom Factor in place at frame 100. To use LightWave 5.5's interactive zoom in Layout, you must create a keyframe for the camera's Move and Rotation, and also for the camera's Zoom Factor.

25. Now go to frame 220 and zoom the camera out to about 6.5. Rotate the camera up and over to the right to fit the image into view. Figure 17.10 shows frame 220.

26. Your animation needs one more element: spline control. To make the camera move smoothly across the image, set a Spline Tension of 1.0 for each of the three keyframes at 0, 100, and 220.

27. Now, make a preview of your animation. You just mimicked a motion control camera. Now render the animation to your hard drive or digital disk recorder.

FIGURE 17.9

The camera is rotated over to the left side of the image at frame 100.

FIGURE 17.10

The last frame of a simple animation to simulate motion control camera moves.

As you can see, with LightWave, you can animate pictures as well as 3D objects. Think about some of the possibilities with this technique:

- Scan images from your own photos and animate them.

- Create visually appealing slide shows.

- Animate images to highlight certain portions of a presentation.

- Animate images for sync with voice narration.

These are just a few of the possibilities you have at your fingertips. You can even advertise your DVE/ADO services to your local production community for added business. But what if you need to do more than this? What if animating just one image is not enough? Because these images are mapped onto polygons in the computer, you can add layer after layer after layer, without any quality loss by repeating the steps shown previously.

If you are working with a video postproduction company, you can animate an image for them that they can add to their own videos. But, your image animations do not have to be limited to simple rectangular polygons either. You can also animate cutouts over other images, images with odd shapes, and soft-edged images for added video post effects.

Keying an Animation in LightWave

Keying animation is very common for many animators. Although much of the final product can be put together in LightWave, minus the audio, animators are becoming more familiar with compositing and blue screening. Production houses often like a 3D animator to supply the animation over a black background, which will be dropped out during editing. An example would be a flying logo that the client wants over footage of his restaurant or auto dealership. This is one form of keying animation. Rendering over a black background can sometimes lead to problems, however. If there are dark shadows or dark colors within a logo, that portion of the animated 3D object will be subject to keying as well. Digital Video Effects units often have trouble keying when dark colors bleed together. To avoid this, many post houses may ask you to render an animation over a blue or green background at a specific RGB level. Often, an RGB value of 0,255,0 or 0,0,225 will work well.

However, if you want control over all of the elements of your animation, you should create keyed animations within LightWave. You can also ensure your images will have soft edges, something many post houses are equipped to provide. The following exercise will demonstrate how to create soft-edged images and keys. This exercise will take you step by step through setting up soft-edged images in LightWave that you can use for still or moving sequences. Be sure to see Chapter 15, "Compositing," for more information on keying animations.

The goal here is to animate the image moving in a linear fashion over a nice background, similar to a familiar 2D DVE or ADO type of move.

SOFT-EDGED IMAGES AND KEYS

1. In Layout, save any work you've been doing and clear the scene. Load the Image_one.lwo file from the book's CD-ROM. This is the object created for the exercise earlier in this chapter.

2. Go to the Images Panel and load the Sunstorm.tga file from this book's CD, and place it as a background image through the Effects Panel, Compositing tab.

3. In the Options Panel, you can turn on BG Image for the Layout Background. This will display the image in Layout. If the OpenGL display is turned on, the background image will appear in color.

Figure 17.11 shows how the mapped polygon with the rainy image sits over the cloud image.

FIGURE 17.11

Adding an image as a background element creates an instant "keyed" effect.

4. Now soften the edges of the image for a better look. Load the Img1_sft.tga file from the book's CD. This image, shown in figure 17.12, is a white square with its edges blurred and softened to black. This will be used as a transparency map in LightWave.

FIGURE 17.12

A simple black-and-white image with softened edges is all that you need to create soft-edged images in LightWave. Use your paint program to create them.

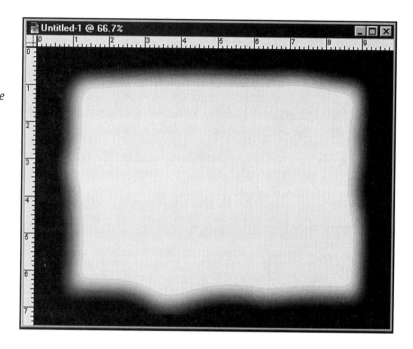

5. Go to the Surfaces Panel and click the T button next to Transparency. Here, you can set a transparency map for the object.

6. In the Texture Map Panel, select Planer Image, and place the Img1_sft.tga file as the Texture Image. Turn off Width Repeat and Height Repeat, select Z as the Axis, and then click Automatic Sizing. Because the white areas of the image become transparent, click on Negative Image. This time, you can leave Antialiasing on, as this image's purpose is to create a soft edge. Click Use Texture and return to Layout. Press F9 to render the current frame. Figure 17.13 shows the rendered image.

NOTE

With a transparency map, the brighter areas of the applied image will become transparent while the dark areas become solid. The gradation from black to white then, creates a gradation from solid to transparent.

FIGURE 17.13

A transparency map applied to the image suddenly softens the edges and adds a different look to the animation.

You can apply this technique to different images, fonts, or pictures. The background image is just a still image in this example, as is the mapped polygon. You can easily replace the still images with sequences. For example, from the Images Panel, simply select the Rainy.tga image and select Replace With Sequence. You can use one of the sample sequences included on this book's CD-ROM. If you want to change the background image, you can select the Sunstorm.tga image and replace it with another image or sequence.

You can take this look a step further by adding motion to the mapped images, as well as adding more images. To give your animation some variation, you can use different-shaped transparency maps for added dimension.

LightWave 3D is capable of creating more than just 3D images. You can use your LightWave system to create great-looking two-dimensional images as well. This exercise will show you how to create 2D video moves in LightWave.

ADDING 2D EFFECTS TO 3D RENDERS

1. Load the SoftEdge.lws scene from this book's CD. Figure 17.14 shows what the scene looks like when frame 0 is rendered.

FIGURE 17.14

Multiple polygons with images mapped along with transparency maps create a 2D video effect.

2. The image maps were created the same way as described earlier, along with a transparency map placed on each to soften the edges. All you have to do is move the polygons. To mimic 2D DVE moves, keep the images on an axis. That is, move them on the X- or Y-axis only. If you take a look at the Top view in Layout, you'll see that each polygon is separate from the other.

3. Select Image_Five.lwo and move it to the right of the Layout view, on the X-axis only. Create a keyframe for it at 280. Select Image_One.lwo and move it to the left of the Layout screen, and create a keyframe at 300. Repeat this process with the other images.

When you make a preview of this animation, you'll see that the images float across the screen just as if they were edited together in a DVE or ADO.

N OTE

You can load an existing preview of this animation from this book's CD. From the Preview drop-down menu in Layout, select Load Preview, and choose the SoftEdge.pvw file on the CD. This won't load the scene, just a wireframe preview. You can save your own previews after you generate them, as well.

In figure 17.14, the render of the Image_Five.lwo object wasn't square, but rather the shape of the image. This is something you can achieve easily to create soft-edged cutouts in LightWave. A clip map (from the Objects Panel) would work, but often limits what image you can use. Clip maps work with the dark and light of an image, and sometimes certain images, such as the image of the old man in this example, don't clip properly. Instead, a transparency map similar to the square one used in this chapter's first exercise was created. Figure 17.15 shows the transparency map for the Image_Five.lwo object.

FIGURE 17.15

A black-and-white version of the image of the old man used to create a soft-edged image for use as a transparency map.

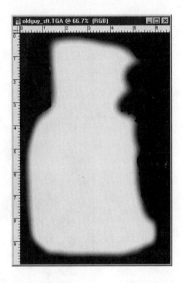

To create this transparency map, you need to color the outside areas of the image black in your paint program. In this case, Adobe's Photoshop 4.0 was used to paint the areas other than the man black. Once painted black, the area was selected and then inverted. The inverted selection, the man himself, was painted white. From there, the edges were softened and the image was saved and applied as a transparency map in LightWave. Figure 17.16 shows a close-up render of the Image_Five.lwo object with the old man image mapped on and a transparency map applied.

Figure 17.16 shows how cleanly LightWave can soften edges. The reason this is done in LightWave rather than a paint program is because of the animation. If you need to create one still image such as figure 17.16, you would be wasting time creating it in LightWave. A simple paint program is all that you would need. But by creating it in LightWave, you can animate the image across the screen, over a background, with other images, and even with text.

FIGURE 17.16

A transparency map of the color image applied to clip out the areas other than the man.

As an example of animating text with multiple images, load the SoftText.lws scene from this book's CD-ROM. Figure 17.17 shows a rendered still of the animation with floating text moving in the background.

Remember, you can replace each of these still images with moving picture sequences or animations. By adding text, you are enhancing the look and feel of the animation to something better looking than an everyday DVE or ADO type of effect.

In figure 17.17, the text is not extruded. There are four text objects, each one sized a bit differently than the other. Their surface is quite simple—the background image Sunstorm.tga is applied to the text. Then, a glow is added and the text is 50% transparent. The movement of the text is soft and subtle, left to right and up and down at a slow speed. See the AVI or QuickTime movie of the animated text and pictures on this book's CD.

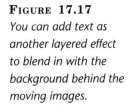

FIGURE 17.17
You can add text as another layered effect to blend in with the background behind the moving images.

Creating Animated Wipes

With LightWave, you can animate cool 3D objects, space stations, flying logos, and more. But the idea of creating animated wipes for use in postproduction is often overlooked. An animated wipe is something you'd see on television, such as the popular animated wipes uses on Tim Allen's Tool Time show. It is an animated element that is used to create a transition from one video clip to the next. In this next section, you'll be guided through the steps to create animated 3D wipes.

If you pay close attention to television commercials and most television sitcoms, you can see that simple cuts and dissolves are the only transitions used. Yet when it comes to corporate video, training videos, wedding videos, or specialty videos, creative wipes are used. The technology today offers a wide range of wipes and transitions for video editors, many of which are customizable. But as the case often is, the customizable wipes sometimes aren't enough. A good example of customized wipes appear in Tim Allen's *Home Improvement* show on ABC TV. Each week you can see different customized wipes that relate to the topic of the show. This is easy to do in LightWave 5.5.

The following exercise will take you through the creation of a page curl, a good wipe that can look very sharp when added to an edited video. By creating the curl in LightWave, you are adding a true 3D look and feel to the wipe. In addition, your image of video clip applied to the curling page will be sharp and clear because of LightWave's renderer.

THE PAGE CURL

1. Open LightWave Modeler and create a box with the following settings:

	Low	High	Segments
X	-6.0405m	6.0052m	1
Y	-4.9808m	4.9808m	1
Z	0m	0m	1

2. Click OK and press Enter to make the box. When this box is animated, you will want to place an image on each side. You don't want the box extruded, so you need to select the surface on each side of the flat polygon.

3. Select the single box polygon. Go to the Tools Panel and from the Custom drop-down list, select the LW_Make-DoubleSided plug-in.

4. This plug-in makes the object double-sided. However, simply clicking on the polygon selects and deselects the entire box. You need to use Modeler's Information Panel to select each polygon. But first, with both sides selected, press q to call up the Change Surface Requester. Name the entire object **BackSide**.

NOTE

Using Layout's Double Sided option from the Surfaces Panel does not enable you to place different images on either side of the flat box. Using the LW_Make-DoubleSided plug-in enables you to place two surfaces on the flat object.

5. Once the surface has been named, and with both sides still selected, press the i key to call up the Polygon Info Panel. Figure 17.18 shows the panel.

6. In the Information Panel, press Next and then Deselect. This tells Modeler to go to the next polygon and deselect it, leaving only the front side polygon selected. Click OK, and press q to change the surface name to **FrontSide**.

FIGURE 17.18

The Polygon Info Panel.

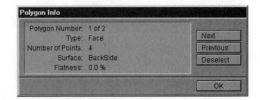

7. Deselect the front polygon once the surface name has been changed. Since this object is not made up of two solid polygons, it won't bend in Layout. Press Shift+d to call up the Subdivide Polygons Panel. Figure 17.19 shows the Subdivide Polygons Panel. Click OK to subdivide the polygon. Now you have eight polygons, four on each side. Repeat this process four more times until you have 2,048 polygons, 1,024 on each side.

FIGURE 17.19

The Subdivide Polygons Panel.

This technique of naming two-sided polygons is extremely useful. You can use it for naming thin objects that need two surfaces, such as leaves, papers, glass, and eggshells.

8. Save the object and enter Layout. Or if Layout is already running, use the Put, New command from the Objects Panel.

9. Press the 1 key on the keyboard to switch to a Front view. With the object selected in Layout, select Bones from the group of Edit items on the left-hand side of the Layout screen. Then, click the Add button and select Draw Bones from the list. To draw bones, you must be in either the Front, Top, or Side views.

10. In the Front view, draw two bones from the top down on the polygon. One should be on the left, and the other should be on the right, as in figure 17.20.

FIGURE 17.20
*Two bones are added
to the polygon to bend
and warp it.*

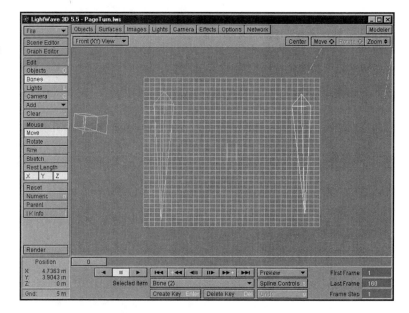

11. Go to the Images Panel and load the Ape.tga image and the Clouds.tga image from the CD accompanying this book. Next, go to the Surfaces Panel and place the cloud image on the back-side surface and the ape on the front-side surface.

NOTE

Since the cloud image is abstract, its orientation when mapped onto the back polygon is fine. However, if you compare the original image with the mapped image, you'll see that the mapped image is backward. To fix this, go to the Texture Map Panel for the cloud image. Simply make the X size a negative value. For example, if the texture size on the X-axis is 12.0457m, make it −12.0457m and the image will be mapped correctly.

12. When the page turns and warps, you want to have some dimension added to it. Before closing the Surfaces Panel, add some specularity to the front and back surfaces. Set Specular Level to somewhere around 70% or 75%. Make the Glossiness Medium (64).

13. Close the Surfaces Panel and return to Layout. Turn on OpenGL Textures from the Options Panel to see the mapped images in Layout. Figure 17.21 shows the image in Layout with OpenGL Textures turned on.

FIGURE 17.21
Two images mapped onto the flat polygon. Here, the front side shows the ape image in OpenGL mode.

14. Now all you need to do is move the bones to warp and turn the image. Select the bone on the right side. Move it toward the camera and over to the left. Rotate it slightly so that the bottom edge curls up a bit.

15. Select the bone on the left side of the screen and move it back and to the right. Figure 17.22 shows what happens to the image when you move the bones.

16. Continue moving each bone toward the center of the screen. As the bones near the center, create a keyframe for each of them at frame 70. Select the Page object and rotate it on its heading about 70 degrees and create a keyframe for it there also.

NOTE

Bones only move the points of an object. The bones in this animation warp and bend the object with the images mapped on it. The object needs to be rotated in conjunction with moving the bones.

17. Rotate the object 180 degrees from the original position to reveal the back-side surface. Create a keyframe for it at frame 160.

FIGURE 18.22
Two bones are all that you need to begin warping and turning the image in Layout.

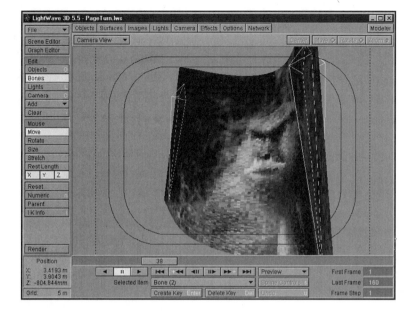

18. To move the bones into place to unwarp the object, don't worry about physically moving them. Select the first bone, and then choose Move from the Edit items group. Click the Reset button. Do the same for Rotate. Also, create a keyframe for the bone at frame 160. Repeat this reset process for the second bone. Now, make a preview. Figure 17.23 shows a rendered view of the warped object at frame 44.

FIGURE 17.23
The rendered image shows how clean the warped object is in LightWave. The full animation can be keyed over existing video.

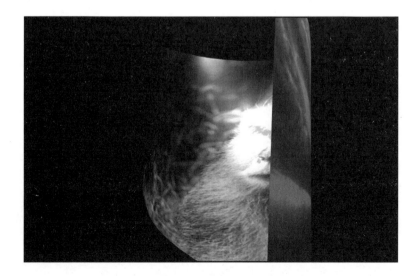

Experiment with the positions of the bones and the speed at which the object turns around. For your use, this final animation can be found on this book's CD. Look for PageTurn.lws. To enhance the animation even more:

■ Bring the Ambient Intensity down to 0% for a more dramatic look.

■ Add a light source to hit the curved polygon to enhance the specularity.

■ Use Field Rendering so the image stays clear and sharp when animated.

The rendered animation of this warping and turning object can be exported to tape and edited into a video. Use a blue background color of 0,0,255 RGB when rendering the animation. The blue can be dropped out and the rendered animation can be seamlessly keyed over a video source.

Warping objects in LightWave puts a new twist on the idea of 3D animation. Using bones is just one way to accomplish the task. In LightWave 5.5, you can take the same two-sided object and use the new Deformation plug-ins to add interesting effects. The following exercise is an example.

ANIMATED VORTEX

1. Load the WipeBox.lwo object file from this book's CD. Add two Null objects to the scene, and rename them Corner_Null and Center_Null.

2. Create a keyframe at zero for the Center_Null object in the center of the WipeBox.lwo object. Move the Corner_Null object up to the top-right corner of the WipeBox.lwo object and create a keyframe for it at zero. Figure 17.24 shows the object with the nulls in place.

3. Go to the Objects Panel and select the WipeBox.lwo object as the current object. From the Deformations tab, select the LW_Deform:Vortex plug-in. Click on the Options button and place the Center_Null object as the Effect Center and the Corner_Null object as the Effect Corner. Figure 17.25 shows the Model Deformation:Vortex Panel.

FIGURE 17.24
*The object is loaded
and two Null objects
are put into place
ready to animate the
object.*

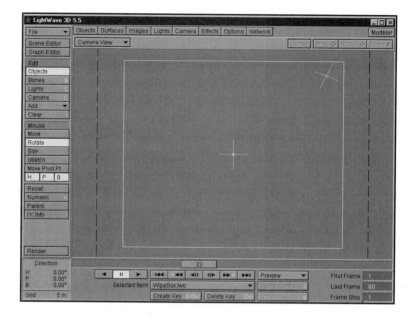

FIGURE 17.25
*The Model
Deformation:Vortex
plug-in's Options Panel.*

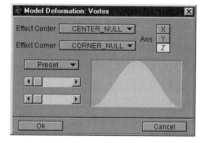

4. Click OK and close the Objects Panel. Select the Center_Null object and rotate it on the Bank –90 degrees. Create a keyframe at frame 60. The image now warps based on the rotation of the Null object, as in figure 17.26.

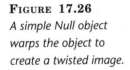

FIGURE 17.26
A simple Null object warps the object to create a twisted image.

Experiment with the other Deformation plug-ins. Use a transparency map and a vortex deformation at the same time over an animated background. The tools in LightWave are powerful enough to open the doors to creativity for you.

Adding Sound to Your Animation

Working in the field of 3D animation no longer means just "animation." As a 3D animator, you need to be a cameraman, director, graphic artist, gaffer, and grip. You also need to be knowledgeable in video and audio editing. This doesn't mean you have to know how to edit, but that you understand the principles of editing and how important audio is to not only video and film, but animation as well.

Sound can make a good animation great. Have you ever watched a movie without sound? Not very effective, is it? The same rule applies to your animations.

Enhancing the Feel of an Animation

Audio can significantly enhance the feel any animation, even if it's only music. Finding music and sound effects for your animations is not difficult. Putting them together with your animations is usually the hard part, but there are a few ways you can add audio without much effort.

If you are working with a Perception Video Recorder from Digital Processing Systems, you can tag audio with your animation. If you call up the animation you want to play and then open an audio file (such as a .wav file), the Perception will play the audio in sync with the animation when the Play button is pressed. Other digital recording programs also support audio, so check with your LightWave dealer for your best option.

Attaching audio to your animations is not as much work as adding sound effects. A music bed within your animations is easy to accomplish in that it's one continuous track. Sound Effects, however, need to be perfectly timed to key areas within an animation.

Sound Effects and Multiple Sounds

Even if your animation is a flying logo with dancing lights and floating crystals, adding sound effects to match the visuals will make your work more professional. Sound effects bring elements to life within an animation. Your flying logo, for example, uses particles that explode behind the logo as it moves into view. You can add a twinkling sound to enhance the crystals. When a light streaks across the screen, add the faint sound of a jet, and so on.

Figure 17.27 shows a frame from the animation described earlier in the chapter.

FIGURE 17.27
You can enhance this animation significantly with different audio tracks for each floating image.

In the animation pictured in figure 17.27, different sounds can draw attention to different areas of the animation. The sound on this animation can start out mixed with sounds from all the different images. When the image of the children in the rain travels by, audio of kids playing can be brought up to full volume. When the Eskimo image floats down, the sound of the children can come down and sounds of the Eskimo and wilderness can be brought up, and so on. Underneath all of this is a well-designed music track.

Enhancing animations with audio should be almost as important to you as the animation itself. Audio completes a story, as well as an image. There are a number of ways you can find audio to add to your animations. One way is through Music Libraries. Check the back of video and computer magazines for CD collections of music, some of which are royalty-free. Find public domain audio and music through newspaper ads. This type of music is free of royalties as well. In addition, perhaps you know a musician who can create custom music for you. You can also buy music from a recording facility or hire musicians to record custom soundtracks.

Another way to find audio for your animations, and probably the best method, is to have it custom-made. This may sound expensive, but it doesn't have to be. There are many talented musicians looking for ways to get their music heard. Hire one of them for a small fee to score your animation. Instead of payment, offer to list him at the end of your animation. This is smart business, and, what's better, your music is one of a kind.

Special Effects Plug-Ins

Video post effects in LightWave mean manipulation of what is a normally rendered animation. It also means audio and sound effects. But there are third-party developers who make products for you to use to add a different sort of video post effect. Figure 17.28 shows the WaveFilter 2.0 plug-in.

FIGURE 17.28

WaveFilter from Unlimited Potential offers a wide range of video post effects for your LightWave animations.

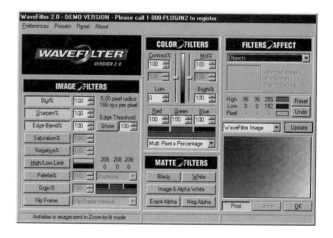

The WaveFilter 2.0 plug-ins from Unlimited Potential offer the LightWave animator more tools so that post process work can be done inside LightWave. Often, you will need to boost the contrast, change the luminance, adjust the graining, adjust the color levels, sharpen, or make an animation blurry or negative. To accomplish this, you need to have a video post house edit the video and make the changes, or process each frame with an image processing tool in a separate pass after the animation is rendered. With WaveFilter, you can control each of those elements directly from the Image Filter plug-ins.

LightWave has some of its own video post effects, too. Figure 17.29 shows the effects of PennelloLite.

FIGURE 17.29
You can apply Molecular Bubbles to a rendered animation using LightWave's PennelloLite plug-in.

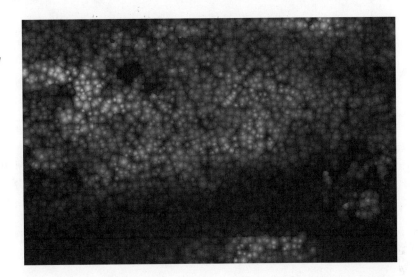

Other effects plug-ins in LightWave include NightVision, Emboss, Blur, Vignette, Watermark, and more. Take a look at the Image Filter plug-ins in the Effects Panel and apply some to your existing animations. Be sure to check the LightWave Internet web sites, and visit your local LightWave dealer to find all the effects plug-ins available for LightWave.

Summary

Video post effects in LightWave can be an art form all their own. Each part of an animation is important, from the storyboards to the models, to the surfacing and lighting, to the sound and editing. Your expertise in these areas will only prove positive on the road ahead as a LightWave animator. Knowing that you can make an animation and either correct or enhance certain areas later with image processing filters puts you a step ahead. Understanding how to add sound effects to your animations puts you another step ahead. In this chapter, you read about:

- Enhancing 3D animations with video post effects

- Creating Digital Video Effects in LightWave

- Keying animations

- Creating animated warps

- Adding sound to animations

- Using sound effects in animation

- Special effects plug-ins

Another positive element in your arsenal of knowledge is how to create cel animations. With LightWave, you can create your own cartoons using the new 5.5 Super Cel Shader plug-in. Read Chapter 18, "Using Cel Animation," to learn more.

Chapter 6

USING CEL ANIMATION

This chapter will show you how to create 2D animation with LightWave 5.5 using the Super Cel Shader plug-in. Using Cel animation may almost seem as if you are defeating the purpose of buying and using a 3D animation program. Why would you spend money and invest time in a three-dimensional modeling and rendering package to turn around and create flat images? It's not as crazy as it may sound.

A Cel animation is traditionally an animation created one "cel" at a time. The worlds between traditional cartoonists, Cel animators, and 3D animators are both very different and similar at the same time. They are different because Cel animators literally draw each frame of animation, working with ink, paint, and flat images. However, 3D animators work in the computer environment and have mathematical tools and functions to get the job done. A 3D animator lets the computer generate many of the frames while only creating "key" frames.

Their worlds are similar in that each requires a significant amount of talent and expertise. Computer animators are no less talented than those in the 2D-Cel-animation world, and vice versa. As the computer graphics industry grows at astonishing rates, animators have a plethora of tools to use to create their craft. Given that, many traditional 2D animators now use a computer to create their masterpieces.

Using LightWave's Cel Shader plug-ins, you can take your mathematically made models and simple characters made out of balls and turn them into believable 2D characters without having to be a sketch artist. Added to that is the power to animate, sync sound, and render images directly to a digital video recorder.

This chapter will guide you through the following topics:

- Understanding traditional Cel animation
- Using traditional Cel animation in 3D
- Changing 3D objects into cartoons
- Using the Super Cel Shader plug-in

Understanding Traditional Cel Animation

Even though you are using a 3D-computer animation program to create 2D animations, a fundamental understanding of traditional Cel animation is key. The foundation you learn from studying the timing and movement of Cel animation can improve your work in computer animation, both 2D and 3D.

There are a number of books that can help you launch a successful career in character creation in LightWave. The first book is by George Maestri entitled *Digital Character Animation* from New Riders Publishing. Another great resource is *The Illusion of Life* by Frank Thomas and Ollie Johnston, published by Hyperion Books. Thomas and Johnston were longtime artists for Disney and have created a countless number of frames of animation over the years. Both books help you to understand the concepts and theories behind character animation in timing, movement, and expressions.

Another great way to learn about 2D Cel animation is to watch videos. Cartoons may be created for children, but many are also art. Studying cartoons such as the Disney classics is an excellent way to learn the nuances that bring a character to life, both in 2D and 3D.

Once you've studied the books and watched the videos, you need to work at your craft. As you progress, your skills and talents as a professional character artist will become natural and instinctive. These fundamental skills are necessary to achieve the best animations.

Traditional Cel Animation Applied to LightWave

Studying the works of Cel animation pioneers such as Frank Thomas and Ollie Johnston can help you build the right characters with 3D to be used for creating 2D animations. In order to create 2D Cel animation in LightWave, you must first create everything in 3D. Remember, though, that you are creating objects that will only be seen in 2D and appear flat when compared to 3D animation. However, 2D animation simulates depth through shading and scaling. Characters and objects can remain simple. On this book's CD, you will find a simple character (Rat_1.lwo) that works well in both 3D and 2D. The model works well for 2D because it's not surfaced with bump maps or intricate details. The character is made to look cartoon-like. You are simply bringing it from 3D to 2D.

Traditional Cel animation can teach you much about the possibilities of 3D animation. You can apply the traditional Cel animation techniques of motion, color, and character design to your 3D animations.

Cel Motions Applied in 3D

You can use the techniques of traditional Cel animation in your 3D animations to create a look that combines the best of both arts. Watch some of your favorite cartoons and you will see the over-compensated character movements and exaggerated expressions. These are the elements you need to employ in your 3D animations for transformation into Cel art. You'll also notice the colors and light are bright and vivid in cartoons. Although many 3D animations are also bright and vivid, lighting in a program such as LightWave is another aspect to consider over hand-drawn traditional Cel animation.

In order to achieve such a look in LightWave, the colors should be flat and even without specular highlights. The lighting should also be even and neutral. Note that you can use specular highlights if you want. Experiment with both to see the differences.

NOTE

Some animation available on television and video is dark and doesn't use exaggerated movements as much as traditional Cel animation. The information in this chapter is geared toward achieving cartoon-like images from LightWave. However, you can use the basic Cel shading techniques to create your own look.

Character Design for Cel Animation

The character you decide to use for your next Cel animation project should be chosen wisely. Most objects will work well when the Super Cel Shader or Cel Shader plug-in is applied in Layout. The Cel Shader plug-in applies an algorithm to make large bands of color across a surface. The Super Cel Shader offers additional control over the applied bands of color from Diffusion, to Brightness, to Specularity. Building your character for Cel animation is somewhat easier than building for 3D in that you can leave out many details. You can leave these out because the surface of the objects will become washed out and flat when rendered with the Cel Shader plug-ins.

Simple balls are sometimes all you need for a character's head and eyes. A rounded box can be used for the body and extruded discs can be used to create limbs.

TIP

Although simple objects are discussed and used as examples, you should experiment with more complex models when using LightWave's Cel Shader. Complex models will work as well with the Cel Shader, but simple versions of the objects are all that is needed.

This chapter concentrates more on the animation aspects of Cel animation in LightWave. You can use the Rat_1.lwo character that has been created for you and placed on this book's CD-ROM. You can modify it in LightWave's Modeler if you want.

Changing 3D Objects into Cartoons

When you decide what character(s) you are going to use in your Cel animation, you can first change its surfaces to use the Cel Shader plug-ins. This is done by applying the Super Cel Shader plug-in to each surface. The following project will show you how to set up an animation to be rendered as Cel animation, using the Rat_1.lwo from the book's CD.

MAKING 3D OBJECTS FOR 2D IMAGES

1. Save anything you've been working on and clear the scene in Layout. Here, you're going to set up the Cel Shader for the cartoon rat. The Cel Shader plug-ins create large bands of color across a surface to create a flat two-dimensional look. Without it, color is more gradient across a surface in LightWave, creating a three-dimensional look.

2. From the Objects Panel, load the Rat_1.lwo file from this chapter's project directory on the book's CD-ROM. Also load the Stool object and the Room object. Move the stool to the back corner of the room.

3. Close the Objects Panel after the objects have been loaded. Press 6 on the keyboard to view the scene through the Camera view. Move the camera up and to the right to gain a perspective on the cartoon rat. Figure 18.1 shows the rat as it is loaded into Layout.

4. Go to the Surfaces Panel, and then click the Advanced Options tab. Here, you'll find LightWave's Shader plug-ins, two of which offer Cel shading in LightWave 5.5. LightWave 5.0 users will find only one Cel Shader.

5. Make the current surface Body. From the first drop-down list under the Shader plug-ins, select the Super Cel Shader.

6. Press the F9 key to render the current frame. Figure 18.2 shows that the image still looks like a 3D render.

FIGURE 18.1

The cartoon rat is definitely three-dimensional, but not for long.

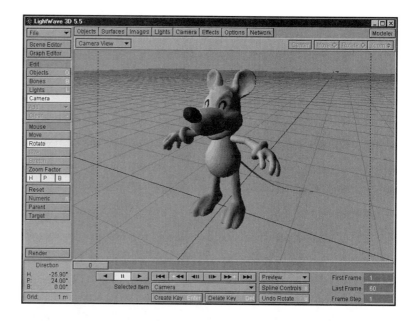

FIGURE 18.2

The cartoon rat is still looking like a three-dimensional character. A few more adjustments will turn the character into a 2D rat.

If you look at the body of the rat, you'll see what looks like three shades of color. The Super Cel Shader you set was only applied to the current surface, the body. The way LightWave uses Surface Shaders is both good and bad. It's good because you have control over each and every surface. Any Shader plug-in can be applied to any individual surface. However, this can be bad when you have many surfaces to work with. Unfortunately, LightWave 5.5 does not offer a Global control over all surfaces. This simple rat character has only six surfaces. The stool has two, and the room has two surfaces. Setting the Super Cel Shader or any Shader plug-in is not that time consuming for this scene. However, if your scene has many surfaces, the process can be tedious.

7. Go back to the Surfaces Panel and select the Nose surface as the current surface. Again, choose the Super Cel Shader plug-in from the drop-down list under the Advanced Options tab. Repeat this for the Legs, Head, Tail, and Iris surfaces. You can select surfaces with the up and down arrow keys using your left hand on the keyboard. Select the plug-in with your right hand and the mouse.

8. Apply the Super Cel Shader to the Room and Stool objects. Press F9 to render the current frame. Figure 18.3 shows the entire scene with the Super Cel Shader applied.

FIGURE 18.3

The rat character and room are starting to flatten out and look more like a cartoon.

Figure 18.3 is starting to look more like a cartoon but it's missing something. If you've paid close attention to cartoons, you may notice an outline around characters and elements in a scene. Because traditional Cel animators first draw the outline of their cartoons and then color them later, the outline remains in the final animation. To help you create the most realistic Cel animations, LightWave lets you add that familiar outline to your characters.

9. Go to the Objects Panel in Layout. Select the Rat object as the current object and then select the Appearance Options tab. Two-thirds down the interface on the left side, select the Polygon Edges check box, as in figure 18.4.

FIGURE 18.4

The Polygon Edges check box within the Appearance Options tab under the Objects Panel. Below it is the Cel-Look Edges check box.

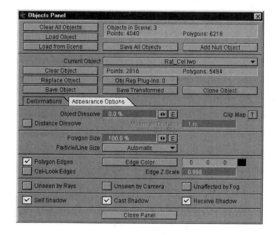

Once this is selected, more options appear on the panel. The Cel-Look Edges check box is available, as is the Edge Z-Scale check box. The Cel-Look Edges check box tells LightWave to add that drawn outline around the selected object, in this case, the Rat object. The Edge Z-Scale check box controls the scaling factor so that the polygon edges are always drawn on top of their respective polygons. The default setting of .998 works well in most cases. If you notice that polygon edges or Cel-Look edges are not being drawn correctly, adjust the value very slightly.

10. Select the Cel-Look Edges check box, and then choose the Medium/Small setting from the Particle/Line Size option, as in figure 18.5.

FIGURE 18.5
*The Particle\Line Size
option enables you to
change the thickness of
the Cel-Look edges.*

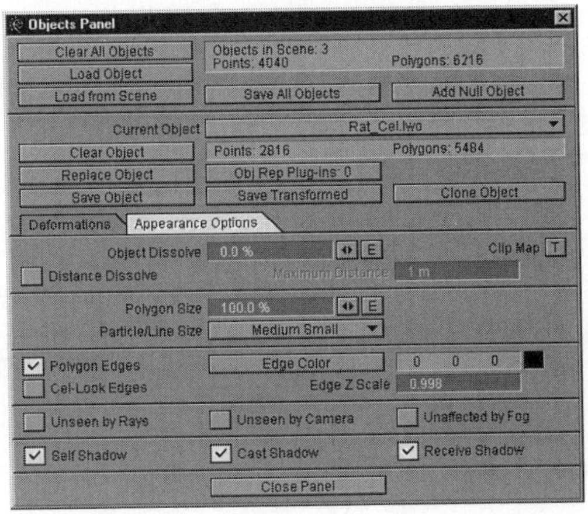

11. The Edge Color can remain at the default of black, 0,0,0 RGB. With the Rat object's Cel edges applied, do the same for the Stool and Room. Press F9 to render the current frame. Your image should now look more like a cartoon, as in figure 18.6.

FIGURE 18.6
*Cel-Look edges are
applied to the objects
to give them a hand-
drawn look.*

Using plug-ins in LightWave can often add to your render times, such as the Steamer and SkyTracer plug-ins. The Cel-Shader plug-ins, however, do not add to rendering time.

You have made a 3D character look like a cartoon, but if you look carefully, the image is not quite complete. This is because you never changed the default lighting. There's only one distant light in the scene, and for cartoons, you need light that is more even. The next section will discuss how to light Cel animation.

Lighting for Cel Animation

The default distant light is fine for the first light. However, this light is not enough for a Cel animation. One simple light will not light the characters and scene evenly, which in turn creates more depth. On a 3D animation, that's great. On a 2D Cel animation, that's not the look you should want. Follow along with the next exercise to light the Rat scene.

When setting up lights for a Cel animation in LightWave, there is no set method you must follow. This chapter demonstrates some lighting situations that you can start with. On the average, a flat general lighting condition works well when using either the Cel Shader or Super Cel Shader plug-ins. You may need to be more creative with your lighting, or you may need to generate special effect lighting, or simply want a look all your own. This exercise will work well for basic cartoon style animation.

SETTING UP LIGHTS FOR A CEL LOOK

At this point, you should begin where the previous exercise left off. This exercise will guide you through lighting for Cel look animations.

1. Go to Layout and select Lights from the Edit sub group menu on the left side of the screen. You can also press Shift+L on the keyboard.

2. From the drop-down Add menu, choose a distant light. This will add an additional distant light to the Layout.

NOTE

Additional lights that are added to a scene, either from the Add button in Layout or through the Lights Panel, will have a default Light Intensity value of 50%. Cloned lights retain the existing light's intensity and other values.

3. Distant lights don't need to be moved, because their effects come from the rotation only. Rotate the light so that it hits the right side of the rat. Figure 18.7 shows the position of the light's rotation from the Front view.

FIGURE 18.7

A second distant light is added to the scene to light the rat and room from the right side.

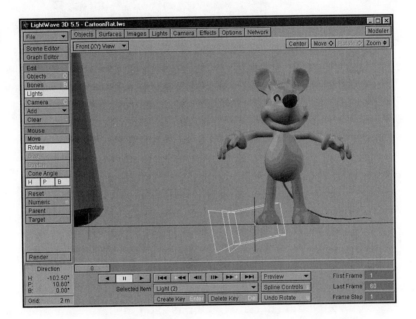

4. To make the lighting more even, go to the Lights Panel and change the Light Intensity on both lights to about 75% or 80%. Press F9 to render the frame. Figure 18.8 shows the scene with the two distant lights.

Look at figure 18.1 and compare it to figure 18.8. You can easily make out the difference between the original 3D image and the new 2D Cel-shaded image.

FIGURE 18.8
*Two distant lights
evenly light the rat,
stool, and room.*

You may think that the Cel-shaded image needs some enhancements. With LightWave 5.5 and the Super Cel Shader plug-in, this is easy to do.

Super Cel Shader Plug-In

The Super Cel Shader plug-in that ships with LightWave 3D 5.5 offers control over color zones within a surface. There are up to four color zones to work with, based on the surface's brightness or diffuseness. Each zone can range from dark to light, based on the minimum and maximum settings to define the colors. The minimum and maximum values range from 0 to 1 in increments of .10 and must progressively get higher. As an example, the minimum value of zone two must be higher than the maximum value of zone one, and so on. Without this progression, a hard edge will be created between bands of color.

Figure 18.9 shows the Super Cel Shader Options Panel where each zone is controlled.

FIGURE 18.9

The Super Cel Shader offers control over four zones of color on each surface.

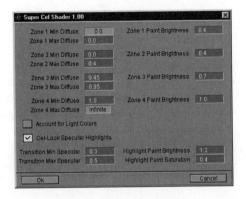

Each zone also has control for brightness: 0 is black, and 1 is the brightest. These are the most common settings, but you can set other values. Each zone brightness corresponds to the respective zone's minimum and maximum ranges. From here, you can set Account for Light Colors, which will tint the particular surface with the color from a light source. You can also add Cel-Look Specular Highlights, which give your surface very cartoon-like specular highlights. Without it, the specular highlights will appear as they normally would with just the Cel Shader plug-in.

At the bottom of the Super Cel Shader Options Panel are two controls for Transition Min Specular and Transition Max Specular. These settings tell LightWave which part of the specular highlights to show. Similar to the Brightness values, 0 shows the darkest part of the surface whereas a value of 1 shows the brightest part. Like LightWave's regular Specularity control, the higher value creates a tighter hotspot, or smaller specular highlight. Lastly, on the bottom right of the Super Cel-Shader Control Panel, you'll see two controls to Highlight Paint Brightness and Highlight Paint Saturation. Highlight Paint Brightness controls the amount of overall highlight on the surface, whereas Highlight Paint Saturation determines how much surface color should be used to saturate the highlight.

These controls are like many of LightWave's settings, each giving you more control as the software matures. With the Super Cel Shader, you have much more control over the final look of your cartoon animations. Experiment with various settings to see what variations you can create. You may find that the default settings work well in many instances.

Mimicking 2D Art in LightWave 3D

Recreating 2D art in LightWave can enhance the look and feel of your character animations. Character animation originated as 2D art, so the transition to 3D art makes perfect sense. A 2D artist often conveys more control over a character's movements because work is done on every frame. Each movement is studied and applied. A 3D artist studies previous frames and sets only "key" frames. The computer calculates frames between the key frames. Often, a 3D artist will need to "tweak" frames drawn by the computer to achieve a certain look.

Reproducing 2D art in LightWave can be accomplished by studying the motions and exaggerations of existing Cel animations. Once you understand some of the basic principles of 2D Cel animation, you can apply that knowledge in LightWave. The following exercise will take you through exaggerated movements in LightWave to make the 3D rat character act like a 2D Cel animation.

NOTE

If you are using LightWave 5.0 and don't have the Super Cel Shader, apply the original Cel Shader plug-in. For users who have slower systems, the same scene is supplied without Inverse Kinematics on this book's CD-ROM. Look for Rat_no_ik.lws.

This scene will use basic character techniques to make the rat discover a big piece of cheese, only to realize that he needs a big fork and knife to eat the cheese. From here, you can add to the scene a cat ready to pounce or another rat fighting for the cheese. To make exaggerated movements, you can employ the use of the bones and character animation. But LightWave 5.5 includes a new plug-in that is an enhancement to 5.0's LazyPoints plug-in. The new LazyPointsGUI (LW_LazyGUI) plug-in gives you more control over the object. Figure 18.10 shows the 5.5 LazyPoints plug-in.

The LazyPoints plug-in creates a lag on points of the object, based on the selected object's pivot point. If you wanted to make an object appear to be sucked down a drain from the nose, for example, move the pivot point of the object to the nose. This point will move first while all others behind it will lag. This plug-in is perfect for simulating exaggerated character movement for Cel-type animations. The LazyPointsGUI plug-in offers two new controls over the 5.0 version. The Lag Rate is the amount that the points in an object will lag behind. The Lag Rate Ctrl Object is an object you assign, such as a null, to control the lag of the points, overriding the Lag Rate setting. Adding a Pivot Point Ctrl Object will change the center of the effect for the selected object.

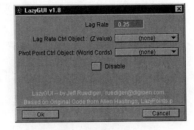

FIGURE 18.10

The LazyGUI plug-in for LightWave 5.5. Here, more control can be given to the lagging points in an object.

RAT ATTACK

1. In Layout, save your existing work, and from the File menu, select Load Scene. Load the Rat_ik.lws. This scene is the rat surfaced for Cel animation with the Super Cel Shader, and set up with a bone structure with Inverse Kinematics Goal objects. Select the Goal objects for the hands and feet, and move them around to get a feel for the IK and mouse setup. Later, you can try using this scene for more 2D character work.

2. In Layout, load the Rathole.lws scene. Here, the mouse is in a room with a big piece of cheese. First, create a keyframe at 7 for the rat exactly where he is when loaded, as in figure 18.11.

3. Now move the rat back in the room to the rathole, sizing the rat down as you go. By sizing the rat down, he'll fit into the rathole and also appear to be farther away. Create a keyframe for the rat at frame 0 once in place. Figure 18.12 shows the rat ready to come out of his hole.

4. Now make a preview. The rat moves quickly from the hole to the cheese. But it needs to be more cartoon-like and exaggerated. Go to the Objects Panel and select the Ratbone object as the current object.

5. Select the LW_LazyPoints as a Displacement Map plug-in.

6. Close the Objects Panel and make a preview. Your rat suddenly sticks to the original keyframe and gets pulled apart like taffy while moving toward the cheese. Figure 18.13 shows frame 7 of the animation. Because the LazyPoints plug-in makes your points lazy, you need to allow time for them to catch up. If your object moves over 7 frames and

the points are lazy, add another 10 frames or so to give the points time
to regroup with the original object.

FIGURE 18.11

The cheese loads directly in front of the rat. This becomes the rat's resting position at frame 7.

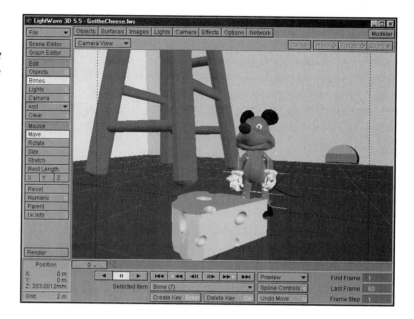

7. If you look at a wireframe preview of the rat's motion, you'll notice that he stops abruptly at the cheese. Instead, it would be more cartoon-like if he overshot his resting frame and then swung back into place. To do this, go to frame 7, and move the rat closer to the cheese. Make a keyframe at 7.

8. Now move the rat back a bit and create a keyframe at frame 11. This will make the rat's LazyPoints overcompensate, fling themselves forward, and then flip back to regroup with the Rat object. Make a wireframe preview to see the motion. Figure 18.14 shows frame 11, where the rat is being displaced due to the LazyPoints plug-in.

With a few more frames, the points catch up to the original object. If you noticed in your wireframe preview, even the tail gets displaced, eliminating the need to add a bone structure.

FIGURE 18.12

The rat is sized down and moved to the back of the room in his hole.

FIGURE 18.13

With the LazyPoints plug-in applied, the rat is pulled like taffy.

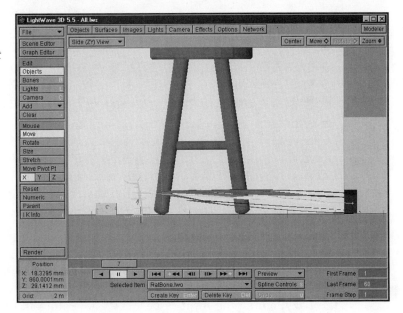

FIGURE 18.14

At frame 11, the points of the rat are trying to catch up to the object, displacing the geometry of the rat.

Often in cartoons, the character decides to quickly leave the screen and come back with a clever device or tool to perform the task at hand. In the rat animation, you can make him decide to leave and quickly come back into the frame with a huge fork and knife, ready to eat the cheese. What will make the scene work is the addition of LazyPoints and large utensils.

By adding the LazyPoints to the rat and then quickly moving him out of camera range, say, over 5 frames, you can accomplish a quick exit. Hold the character off screen for 10 or 15 frames, and then have him dart back into Camera view. This time, the rat can have a large utensil in each hand. By large, consider utensils as tall or taller than the rat. Figure 18.15 shows the LazyPoints plug-in at work as the rat jumps off-camera.

Experiment with the LazyPoints plug-in and the rat scene on this book's CD. Adjust the Lag Rate to see what kind of looks you can create. If you work with bones and LazyPoints together, you may run into trouble. If your bone structure is set up and working and suddenly does not work when you apply the LazyPoints plug-in, it is because LazyPoints is applied to the entire object, so the bone movements don't show up immediately. Bones also move the points within an object.

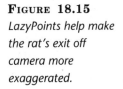

FIGURE 18.15
LazyPoints help make the rat's exit off camera more exaggerated.

To work around this situation, morph the object into different positions when using LazyPoints. As an alternative to that, animate the character off screen with LazyPoints, and then change to a version of the character or object without the LazyPoints plug-in applied.

TIP

As an added effect when using the LazyPoints plug-in, render the animation with motion blur. This will give the animation more of a cartoon-character look.

Here are a few pointers for creating Cel type animations in LightWave:

- Keep lights general and scenes evenly lit.
- Bring up Ambient Intensities.
- Apply the Cel-Look Edges option from the Objects Panel.
- Use the LazyPoints plug-in to help exaggerate movements.
- Use Motion blur to accentuate movements.

Using the Deformation Tools for Cel Animation

You can use LightWave 5.5's new plug-ins in the Deformation tools area of the Objects Panel in a range of animations. Instead of setting up complex bone structures to animate snakes, or bending trees, or wobbling rat characters, you can use the LW_Deform plug-ins, as seen in figure 18.16.

FIGURE 18.16

LightWave 5.5's new Deformation plug-ins are in the Objects Panel's Displacement Map Plug-Ins area.

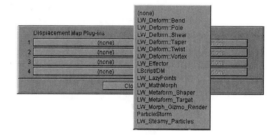

The Deformation plug-ins are essentially deformation tools that bring Modeler functions into Layout. By assigning two nulls to an object, you can easily manipulate an object's physical structure as you would in Modeler, using the following tools:

- Bend

- Pole

- Shear

- Taper

- Twist

- Vortex

You can use each of these plug-ins for animating characters for Cel-type animations. As an example, follow along with the next exercise to make the rat character bend and deform without the use of bones.

A BENDING, TWISTING RAT

1. In Layout, save your existing work and, from the File menu, select Load Scene. Load the BlueRat.lwo object from this book's CD. Figure 18.17

shows the rat loaded into layout with the camera moved to a slightly better perspective.

FIGURE 18.17

The BlueRat loaded into Layout with a good Camera view.

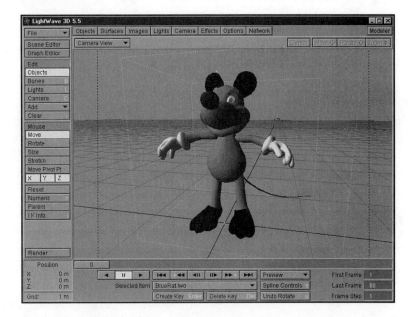

2. Select Objects from the Edit group on the left-hand side of the Layout screen. Select Add, as in figure 18.18, to add a null object.

FIGURE 18.18

The new Add command in Layout enables you to add Null objects to a scene.

3. Add another Null object to the scene. With two Null objects added, create a keyframe at 0. Next, move Null 1 to the top center of the object and create a keyframe at 0.

4. Go to the Objects Panel and select Null 1 as the current null. Press the Save Object button to change the name of the null to Handle. Repeat this for Null 2 and change its name to Base. Figure 18.19 shows the Rename Requester.

FIGURE 18.19

*You can change the
name of your Null
objects in the Objects
Panel by pressing Save
Object. This helps
organize your
LightWave scenes.*

NOTE

Pressing Save Object for a null brings up the Change Name function. This is only for Null objects and not regular polygonal objects.

5. In the Objects Panel, select the BlueRat.lwo as the current object. From the Deformations tab in the Objects Panel, select LW_Deform:Bend from the list of plug-ins in the first drop-down area of displacement map plug-ins. Press the Options button to enter the controls for the Deform Bend plug-in.

6. In the Effect Base Requester, select the Base Null. In the Effect Handle requester, select the Handle Null. Select Y as the axis, and click OK.

7. Go to Layout and select the Handle Null. If you move the handle around, nothing happens. When using these displacement map plug-ins, their effect doesn't take place until a keyframe is made. Being able to see the displacement as it's happening would be much more beneficial, however. Go to the Options Panel and turn on Auto Key Adjust. Go back to Layout and move the Handle again.

8. If you still don't see the results, go back to the Options Panel and under the Layout View tab, change the Bounding Box Point/Polygon Threshold to 5500. Since the object is almost 5,500 polygons, setting this threshold tells LightWave to only draw bounding boxes when the polygon count is about this amount.

TIP

Depending on the speed of your computer and the strength of your graphics display card, results from setting the threshold value will vary. As you can expect, the stronger your system and display, the better this feature will work. A basic 4MB video card will work well.

9. Now go back to Layout and move the Handle Null. The object should bend like a rag doll. Figure 18.20 shows the rat bent over after moving just the one null. Notice that using this plug-in bends the object cleanly. The normal worry of polygons pulling and stretching using bones is eliminated.

FIGURE 18.20

Assigning two Null objects and using the Deform/Bend plug-in can easily bend a character around.

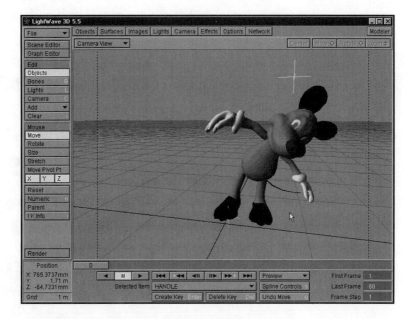

10. The Base Null controls the origin of the deformation, in this case, where the object bends from. Figure 18.20 shows the object bending from the feet. Move the Base Null up to the neck area and then adjust the Handle Null. Now only the head portion of the object bends. Figure 18.21 shows the rat with the Base Null raised up to the neck area.

TIP

Don't be afraid to assign more than one displacement map deform plug-in on an object. For the rat, you can assign two more nulls to control the swaying of the tail. With added nulls, be sure to rename them for good organization. To rename nulls, select Save Object in the Objects Panel for the particular null. Check out DeformRat.lws on the book's CD.

11. Go to the Objects Panel and select the BlueRat as the current object. Change the Deform/Bend displacement map to Deform/Twist. As with the Deform/Bend, set the Base and Handle Null objects. Figure 18.22 shows the Twist Options Panel.

12. Return to Layout and rotate the Handle Null on its Heading. Notice how the object twists? Again, you can move the Base Null object to adjust the point of control for the twist. Figure 18.23 shows the entire object twisting based on the movement of one null object.

FIGURE 18.21

You can move the Base Null to control the origin of displacement, such as the point of bending, as in this image.

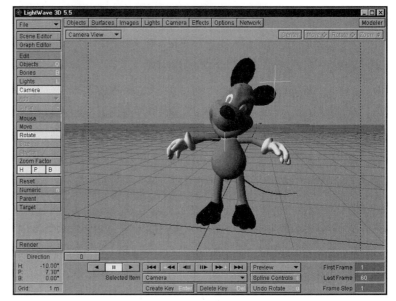

FIGURE 18.22

The Model Deformation Panel for the Deform/Twist displacement map.

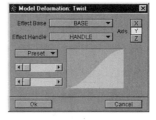

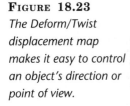

FIGURE 18.23

The Deform/Twist displacement map makes it easy to control an object's direction or point of view.

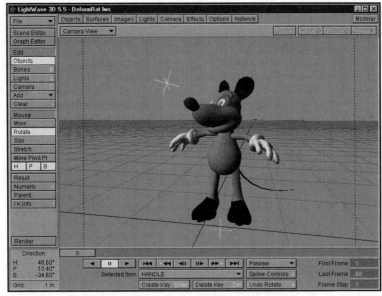

The new displacement map plug-ins can significantly improve your character animation abilities both in 3D and in 2D. Experiment with the Shear and Vortex deformation tools as well; they perform the same functions that they do in Modeler.

Using More Than One Deform Plug-In

It is possible to use the same Base and Handle Nulls with two deform plug-ins. If you load the Deform2.lws scene from this book's CD, you'll see the Deform/Bend and Deform/Twist using the same two Null objects for the Base and Handle. If you make a preview of the animation, you'll see the little rat turn its head and sneeze. You can also use three deformation plug-ins with the same Base and Handle.

Animation like this took very little time to set up. No bones were used, no Inverse Kinematics, and no Morph Gizmo. Two nulls are sometimes all that you need to control an object. Consider all of LightWave's tools when assessing your next project. Animators sometimes discount the easiest methods and simplest tools when animating a project.

Summary

This chapter introduced you to a few concepts and thoughts for 2D animation. You were shown how to use LightWave 5.5's new Cel Shader plug-in; what types of models to use; and ways to animate the character to exaggerate motions. To fully master the art of character animation both in 2D and 3D, however, you need to practice. Some things come naturally to one animator, while another must study hard. Both will do well to learn one of America's oldest crafts, cartoon animation.

In this chapter, you learned that LightWave's Cel Shader plug-ins offer an entirely different look to your animations. This chapter introduced you to:

- Understanding traditional cel animation
- Traditional Cel animation applied to LightWave
- Changing 3D objects into cartoons
- Using the Super Cel Shader Plug-In
- Using the Deformation tools for Cel animation

Remember that you can apply all the information about character modeling and animation to your Cel animations in LightWave. Be creative, be innovative, and take the time to experiment and learn on your own. In time, people will be learning from you.

Chapter 19

LSCRIPT

Programming can be a very complex—and to some individuals, a very terrifying—activity. It is the case, however, with any discipline that the inner workings might seem forbidding until you actually take the time to understand the rules and procedures. Programming is no different. It can be as complex or as simple as you want, and can solve problems for you that would otherwise be impossible to solve.

Scripting, which is what this chapter focuses on, is programming, but at a more abstract level. In computer languages, a higher level of abstraction means that more can be accomplished in fewer lines of code. Scripting with the LightWave 3D LScript system can help the animation programmer (or "scripter") to concentrate on the task to be accomplished instead of what tools to use.

This chapter covers the essentials of LScript and how to utilize the LightWave scripting language in your projects. Specifically, the chapter covers the following topics:

- LScript features
- LScript for LightWave Modeler
- Scripting LightWave Layout

LScript Features

LScript provides access to the internal of LightWave. Such access can provide greater control over LightWave's operation than is possible through its user interface. This access is programmatic in nature, much the same as that provided by the LightWave plug-in SDK.

However, LScript offers this access without the bulk of the overhead required by the SDK. For instance, no platform-specific software compiler is required (an additional software purchase, in most cases). More importantly, except in certain limited cases, LScripts are completely platform independent. Scripts written on one LightWave platform are instantly usable on any other LightWave platform.

LScript provides many features to the LightWave scripter. Here is a partial list of those features, which are discussed later in this chapter:

- Familiar, modernized language syntax advanced enough for seasoned software developers, yet simple enough for the programming novice.
- Structured programming controls and constructs for cleaner, easier-to-understand script writing.
- Scripting of six Layout plug-in architectures: Item Motion, Displacement Mapping, Image Filter, Procedural Texture, Object Replacement, and Generic.

These are only a small percentage of the features that LScript offers the LightWave user. As you begin to use the LScript software, referencing its documentation and reviewing the work of other LScript writers, you will likely begin to realize the true power of scripting. Among the most important, you will find that scripting will enable you to solve more day-to-day animation problems on your projects.

Now, move forward to your first step into the realm of power and control. You will begin by examining the basics of scripting with LScript for Modeler.

LScript for LightWave Modeler

All Modeler scripts are required to contain a single user-defined function (UDF), identified as main. A *user-defined function* is a group of script lines, enclosed in a well-defined and uniquely identified structure, that can be invoked (or called) to have its script code executed. This function name is a marker for the LScript for Modeler scripting plug-in, letting it know the entry point of the script, which is the location where execution of the script should begin. Each function in your script must be identified with a unique name so that it can be distinguished from any other functions; however, the required entry-point function in Modeler LScripts must be named "main" so LScript can locate it.

Functions have bodies or sections of script code that are enclosed between body markers. In LScript, body markers are identical to those used in C— opening and closing curly braces ({}). All UDFs require these body markers, regardless of how many script commands are embedded between them.

Armed with this basic knowledge, you can now create the template that will be used for your first Modeler LScript:

```
main
{
}
```

Now, were you interested in doing nothing more than running the LScript Modeler plug-in, you could simply save this complete (yet useless) LScript to a disk file and execute it.

Note

One thing to note, at this point, is that LScript is case-sensitive. What this means is that the case of a character has significance when LScript interprets a script. For instance, if you uppercased the entry-point identifier Main, LScript would not have recognized it.

Variable names and other such identifiers can suffer from this case-sensitivity problem, too. If, for example, you assign some value to the identifier num, and in the next line you try to display the value contained in an identifier called Num to the user, you will find that what is actually displayed is the value nil. This occurs because you've inadvertently created a new variable called Num whose value is initially set to nil by the LScript Engine (remember that explicit variable declarations are not required in LScript).

Using Explicit Declaration

The combination of LScript's flexibility where variable usage is concerned and its case sensitivity can cause problems with first-time script writers. The Num-versus-num case you just examined was a simplified and easy-to-detect instance. More subtle problems, much harder to locate and eradicate, can occur as a result of this type of situation.

LScript provides the means to override its default behavior by placing LScript into a state where both variables and arrays must be explicitly declared before they can be used. Had you activated this state in the Num/num example, LScript would have generated a compile-time error message regarding both variables, informing you that undeclared variable references were detected.

Usage of this explicit declaration state of LScript is recommended to beginning script writers. It can greatly aid in preventing potential problems that can occur. You activate explicit declaration requirements by placing the strict pragma directive at the top of your LScript. A *pragma* is a message that you send to LScript that provides instructions on how it should behave in certain predefined situations. The following code shows the strict pragma in use with the Num/num example. Refer to the LScript documentation for more information regarding using pragma directives.

```
@strict
...
main
{
```

```
...
var num = 10;
info(Num);      // this line will now generate an "undeclared
➥variable" error
...
```

The example scripts in this chapter will not employ the strict pragma directive. The scripts included in this chapter have been tested to ensure their functionality and usability, so they can be used directly without such safety measures.

"Hello" LScript!

One of the traditional and obligatory tests of any computer language is "Hello World!" This is a simple and unscientific test of a language's complexity. The test shows how many lines of code are required to display the message "Hello World!" The fewer the lines of code compared to other languages, the higher the level or more abstract the language. For your first complete LScript, you will adhere to this tradition and create a script to test the complexity.

```
main
{
    info("Hello World!");
}
```

This LScript will post an informational window with the message "Hello World!" displayed. Pressing the OK button on the window will terminate the script.

This first script, while an authentic and complete LScript, was not very practical. So, to illustrate the power and simplicity of LScript, in the next section, you will create an LScript that performs a function that is very difficult to accomplish if it were performed by hand: creating single-point polygons from the vertices of an object.

Creating Single-Point Polygons from the Vertices of an Object

For this exercise, you need to switch Modeler into a mode known as Mesh Data Edit in your LScript. In Mesh Data Edit mode, you can freely add and delete lower-level data such as points, polygons, and curves. You must be in this mode in order to utilize LScript commands and functions designed to operate directly on this data.

Within LScript's repertoire of commands and functions, some cannot be used in Command Sequence mode, some cannot be invoked during Mesh Data Edit operations, and others can be used regardless of the state in which Modeler is currently functioning. Refer to the LScript documentation provided by NewTek for more precise information concerning which LScript commands can be used during which Modeler states.

The editbegin() LScript command is used to switch Modeler into Mesh Data Edit mode, and the companion command editend() switches Modeler out of this mode and back into its default state of Command Sequence.

The following exercise shows you how to set up the LScript in Mesh Data Edit mode and test for the presence of points in your object.

TESTING FOR THE PRESENCE OF POINTS

1. To get your starting points for this exercise, load an object into LightWave Modeler and press the k key to kill all the object's polygons.

2. Add the editbegin() command to your LScript. Use the following code listing as a guide.

```
main
{
    count = editbegin()
    ...
}
```

An integer value representing the number of points in the currently active foreground layer(s) is returned by editbegin() when you switch into Mesh Edit mode. You will use this value to determine if there are any points in the active layers and as a limit for some looping code.

3. Now check for the existence of points, and terminate the script if none are present.

```
main
{
    count = editbegin()
```

```
    if(count == 0)
    ...
}
```

In the final step of the previous exercise, you are testing for the presence of points in the active layers. If none are present, then the variable *count* will hold a value of zero (0), or a Boolean true. The if() control is used to make a decision based upon the Boolean value (true/false) of an expression. If it does not, meaning that you have points in the active layers, then the expression evaluates to a Boolean false.

NOTE

Notice that you are using the C equation operator (==) to test for equality. As you go along, you will find that many operators and controls in LScript are taken from or modeled after the C language.

Now that you've employed a decision control, you must provide LScript with a path for logic to follow depending upon the outcome of the test. If the test proves false, then you want to continue on with your script. If the test proves true, however, then you know that you have no points to process, and you terminate the script immediately.

In the following script, you want to tell the user that there are no points to process, and you will want to terminate the script. Because this will require two executable statements, you will need to enclose them in body markers.

```
main
{
    count = editbegin()

    if(count == 0)
    {
        error("No points to process!");
        return;
    }
    ...
}
```

You invoke error(), one of three message-display routines available in LScript (along with info() and warn()), and let the user know that you cannot continue processing. You then execute a return command, which has the effect of terminating the script. If a script executes all the way to the end of the main() UDF, then an implicit return command is executed, also terminating the script.

NOTE

You will notice that when you terminate the script using return, you are still in Modeler's Mesh Edit mode. This is not a problem because LScript cleans up many things if you leave in a hurry without cleaning up after yourself. If you fail to reset Modeler into Command Sequence mode upon exit, LScript will detect this condition and correct it for you. This is also the case with other state-driven conditions, such as data requesters.

Now that you've taken care of obvious error checking, you can move on to the real processing of the script. When you switch into Mesh Edit mode, behind the scenes LScript has done some convenience work for you. In particular, two new internal linear arrays have been created, one called points[] and one called polygons[]. These arrays contain the point and polygon IDs of the data in the active layer(s). Whenever you communicate with Modeler regarding a particular point or polygon, you must provide its identifier, so these convenience arrays will certainly come in handy. Because you want to process all points found in the currently active foreground layer(s), you can simply use all the point identifiers found in the points[] array.

To process all available points, you will need to loop through the points[] array from the first element to the last. LScript provides two primary looping controls, the for() loop and the while() loop control. Both are modeled after their C counterparts, with the for() loop control being more complex in its structure. Being new to scripting, you will opt for the simpler of the two (but will use the more complex version hereafter).

PROCESSING THE AVAILABLE POINTS

1. First initialize your counter variables outside the loop itself using a variable called pnt to hold the integer value of the current loop iteration. You will also use this variable as the index value into the points[] array.

```
main
{
    count = editbegin();

    if(count == 0)
    {
        error("No points to process!");
        return;
    }

    pnt = 1;
    while(pnt <= count)
    {
        . . .
}
```

As you retrieve each point identifier, you will perform whatever processing is necessary on that point. In this case, that will entail the use of multiple lines of script code, so you will need to enclose them in body markers. The expression you will evaluate in the `while()` control will simply ensure that you do not use an index value greater than the size of the `points[]` array, which would generate a run-time error and terminate the script.

2. Next, you must ensure that you increment the `pnt` loop counter somewhere inside the loop body because you are using a `while()` loop control.

```
    . . .
    pnt = 1;
    while(pnt <= count)
    {
        . . .
        ++pnt;
    }
    . . .
```

WARNING

If you neglected to increment the value in the `pnt` counter variable, you would get the condition known as an infinite loop, where the loop would never end. In such a situation, the only recourse would be to terminate Modeler.

3. In step 2, you used a C-like increment operator (++) to add one (1) to the
    pnt counter variable as the last action of the loop itself. You also can use
    a more traditional and BASIC-like method of incrementing the counter:
    pnt = pnt + 1. Both commands produce the same result.

4. Now you want to get the location of the current point so that you can
    duplicate it as a single-point polygon. You glean this information using
    the pointinfo() LScript function. You pass the point identifier taken
    directly from the points[ ] array as the parameter required by pointinfo():

```
...
pnt = 1;
while(pnt <= count)
{
    loc = pointinfo(points[pnt]);
    ...
    ++pnt;
}
...
```

5. Addpoint() creates a point in Modeler's space at the specified place by
    the value contained in the loc variable. If the call to addpoint() is
    successful, it will return to the identifier for the new point. You will save
    this new point identifier for use with other functions.

```
...
pnt = 1;
while(pnt <= count)
{
    loc = pointinfo(points[pnt]);
    pid = addpoint(loc);
    ...
    ++pnt;
}
...
```

NOTE

Points and polygons added during a Mesh Data Edit session are not automatically appended to
the points[ ] and polygons[ ] arrays during that session. You must make arrangements to
preserve these returned identifiers while you are within your data-editing session if you need
to provide them to other data-edit functions. These new identifiers will, however, be available
in the Mesh Data Edit arrays in any subsequent session.

At this stage in your script, you have added a new point that occupies the same three-dimensional position as another point. If you were to execute your script now, you would effectively duplicate the existing arrangement of points in the active layer(s). You would have two points for every one you had originally.

In the next exercise, however, you distinguish this new point from the original. Not only will it become visible when rendered in Layout (the original point would be invisible), it will no longer be a point at all. You will promote this single point into a polygon.

MAKING THE POINT INTO A POLYGON

1. Continue from the previous exercise.

2. Call the LScript addpolygon() function.

```
...
    pnt = 1;
    while(pnt <= count)
    {
        loc = pointinfo(points[pnt]);
        pid = addpoint(loc);
        addpolygon(pid);
        ...
        ++pnt;
    }
    ...
```

3. The next command (rempoint()) you will add to your loop permanently deletes the original point, leaving only the new single-point polygon in its place. Add rempoint() to the script.

4. Finally, you will add the editend() command as the last action for the script to perform, which will terminate the Mesh Data Edit mode you started with editbegin().

```
main
{
    count = editbegin();

    if(count == 0)  // what?  no points?
    {
        error("No points to process!");
        return;      // terminate script
    }
```

```
pnt = 1;
while(pnt <= count)
{
    loc = pointinfo(points[pnt]);   // where is it?
    pid = addpoint(loc);
    addpolygon(pid);         // new single-point polygon

    rempoint(pid);           // delete original point

    ++pnt;
}

editend();   // apply changes
}
```

If you fail to call editend(), or you pass editend() a value that can be evaluated as a Boolean false, then all the work you performed during the Mesh Data Edit mode will be discarded. This mechanism is provided to allow a script to abort changes it may have made to any existing mesh data in Modeler. Changes you make during this state will be buffered by Modeler, and not actually applied to any existing data as changes and additions are made. It is not until you give Modeler the "A-Ok" that it will apply your changes.

Calling editend() with an expression that evaluates to a Boolean true (which is the default if no parameter is provided) is the equivalent of giving Modeler permission to modify your existing mesh data.

More functionality can be added to this basic script, such as placing the new single-point polygons into a separate layer without destroying the original points. Such enhancements would make it more functional and convenient to use. On your own, try adjusting this script to make it the most effective for your needs.

The following list explains in detail some of the commands that you used in the exercises in this section. For more information, see the LScript documentation from NewTek.

■ **pointinfo().** Returns a vector, which is one of LScript's internal data types. This vector contains the location, on the X, Y, and Z axes, of the point you identified. A vector is not restricted to merely containing axis data and can hold any three numeric quantities.

- **addpoint()**. Creates a point in Modeler's space at the specified coordinate.

- **addpolygon()**. Returns the identifier of the new polygon just created.

- **rempoint()**. Deletes the original point, leaving only the new single-point polygon in its place.

- **editend()**. Terminates the Mesh Data Edit mode you started with editbegin().

Using a Requester

So far, you've seen how LScripts can interact with Modeler to affect its behavior. However, you can add another dimension to LScripts by enabling them to interact with script users as well. You can accomplish this by using a dialog-generator interface, known as the *Requester*. The Requester allows the script writer to post a dialog window that can gather data and operational instructions from the script user, through the use of Requester controls. As you will see in this section, creating and managing a Requester from LScript is quick and easy.

Because you will concentrate on the Requester itself in this exercise and less on the actual processing of the script, you will begin with the complete processing code of the script you will create. The script, called Snap! will make points selected by the user snap to a location on any axis, both of which will be specified by the user through the Requester Panel. The following listing shows the processing code that Snap! will use to relocate selected points. Most of this processing code should already be familiar, as it was taken largely from the Points-to-Polygons LScript you just created.

```
main
{
    ...
    selmode(USER);
    count = editbegin();

    if(count == 0)   // are any points selected?
    {
        error("No points to process!");
        return;      // terminate script
    }
}
```

```
    pnt = 1;
    while(pnt <= count)
    {
        loc = pointinfo(points[pnt]);   // where is it now?
        ...
        ++pnt;
    }

    editend();   // apply changes
}
```

New to your examples is the selmode() command. This command tells Modeler which types of data you want to work with, either data that has been explicitly selected by the user (USER), or all data that is currently in the mesh regardless of what may be currently selected (GLOBAL). In this case, you are only interested in those points that may have been selected explicitly. As far as Modeler is concerned, if none are selected explicitly, then all are selected implicitly.

When you interact with the user, you will need to know a number of items that will be used when moving a point. You must know which axes will be used (or ignored), and you need to be aware of where on each axis the point should be placed.

The following exercise takes you through the steps to script the Requester.

SCRIPTING THE REQUESTER

1. First, initialize some working variables that will be used both by the Requester and the processing code. Add the following working variables to your Snap! LScript:

```
main
{
    useX = false;
    locX = 0.0;
    useY = false;
    locY = 0.0;
    useZ = false;
    locZ = 0.0;
    ...
    selmode(USER);
    count = editbegin();
    ...
```

2. You will add some Requester code. Posting a data Requester in LScript begins with a call to reqbegin().

```
...
    locY = 0.0;
    useZ = false;
    locZ = 0.0;

    reqbegin("Snap!");
...
```

3. After the Requester is initiated, you can begin adding controls. In your Snap! script, you will allow the script user to indicate each axis to use, as well as a location along that axis. Because of this, you will create six controls, two for each axis. You accomplish this by using LScript's addcontrol() function call.

```
...
    reqbegin("Snap!");

    c1 = addcontrol(useX,"Use X?",@"Yes","No"@);
    c2 = addcontrol(locX,"X Location");
    c3 = addcontrol(useY,"Use Y?",@"Yes","No"@);
    c4 = addcontrol(locY,"Y Location");
    c5 = addcontrol(useZ,"Use Z?",@"Yes","No"@);
    c6 = addcontrol(locZ,"Z Location");
    ...
```

4. When you have added all the controls that you need to the Requester window, you can post the window to the users with a call to reqpost(), allowing them to edit the values to suite their needs.

```
...
    c5 = addcontrol(useZ,"Use Z?",@"Yes","No"@);
    c6 = addcontrol(locZ,"Z Location");

    if(reqpost())
    {
        ...
    }
    else
        return;
...
```

Notice that you use an else clause to provide a logic pathway if the return value of reqpost() proves to be other than true. In such a case, you simply terminate the script and allow LScript to perform any necessary clean up. Also note that because you only used a single line of script code, you did not need to enclose the return command in body markers.

If the OK button is pressed on the Requester Panel, you must query the controls for their new values. The values themselves may not have changed from the values used to initialize the controls, but it makes your script much simpler if you assume that they have.

5. To query the requester controls, you will employ the LScript getvalue() Requester function.

```
   . . .
        c5 = addcontrol(useZ,"Use Z?",@"Yes","No"@);
        c6 = addcontrol(locZ,"Z Location");

        if(reqpost())
        {
            useX = getvalue(c1);
            locX = getvalue(c2);
            useY = getvalue(c3);
            locY = getvalue(c4);
            useZ = getvalue(c5);
            locZ = getvalue(c6);
        }
        else
            return;
   . . .
```

6. When you are through with your Requester, you need to issue the LScript command reqend() to allow LScript to free up any internal resources it may be using, and to allow LScript to launch into a Mesh Data Edit session later.

```
   . . .
            useZ = getvalue(c5);
            locZ = getvalue(c6);
        }
        else
            return;

        reqend();
   . . .
```

7. Now that you have the operating instructions from the user, you can update your processing code to utilize the new data. The complete Snap! LScript adds the final script code to the processing loop to place the current point into the new location indicated by the working variables. If the script users don't alter any values in the Requester Panel, then the point will simply be moved to its current location.

```
main
{
    useX = 2;     // button #2, "No"
    locX = 0.0;   // location is in meters
    useY = 2;
    locY = 0.0;
    useZ = 2;
    locZ = 0.0;

    reqbegin("Snap!");

    c1 = addcontrol(useX,"Use X?",@"Yes","No"@);
    c2 = addcontrol(locX,"X Location");
    c3 = addcontrol(useY,"Use Y?",@"Yes","No"@);
    c4 = addcontrol(locY,"Y Location");
    c5 = addcontrol(useZ,"Use Z?",@"Yes","No"@);
    c6 = addcontrol(locZ,"Z Location");

    if(reqpost())
    {
        useX = getvalue(c1);   // returns 1 for "Yes", or 2 for
➥"No"
        locX = getvalue(c2);
        useY = getvalue(c3);
        locY = getvalue(c4);
        useZ = getvalue(c5);
        locZ = getvalue(c6);
    }
    else
        return;

    selmode(USER);
    count = editbegin();

    if(count == 0)  // are any points selected?
    {
        error("No points to process!");
        return;     // terminate script
    }
```

```
pnt = 1;
while(pnt <= count)
{
    loc = pointinfo(points[pnt]);   // where is it now?

    if(useX == 1)
        loc.x = locX;
    if(useY == 1)
        loc.y = locY;
    if(useZ == 1)
        loc.z = locZ;

    pointmove(points[pnt],loc);   // move the point to 'loc'

    ++pnt;
}

editend();   // apply changes
}
```

The following list explains in detail some of the new commands that you used in this exercise. For more information, see the LScript documentation from NewTek.

- **selmode().** Tells Modeler which types of data you want to work with, either data that has been explicitly selected by the user (USER), or all data that is currently in the mesh regardless of what may be currently selected (GLOBAL).

- **reqbegin().** Accepts a character-string parameter that will be used as the title of the Requester window, and performs necessary internal preparation for adding controls to the Requester.

- **addcontrol().** Accepts a variable number of parameters and returns a control identifier, a numeric value. At a minimum, addcontrol() requires the initial value of the control and the title to be used to identify the control in the Requester window. To simplify the usage of addcontrol(), the parameter used as the initial value of the control is also used to determine the type of control to be created. A third, optional parameter to addcontrol() would be a reference to an array (or an inline initialization block) that would cause the creation of a selection control, a row of push-buttons whose labels are constructed from the array of string values provided.

■ **reqpost().** Returns a Boolean value to indicate which button the user pressed to terminate the Requester, either OK or Cancel. If OK was pressed, then reqpost() returns a Boolean true value, otherwise a Boolean false is returned indicating the user's wish to halt processing. The reqpost() call can be used as the expression to be evaluated by the if() control.

■ **getvalue().** Accepts a single parameter that is the identifier of the control to be queried and returns the data that is found in that control. The data type returned is identical to that used to initialize the control, so you can easily assign the return values directly to your storage variables.

■ **reqend().** Allows LScript to free up any internal resources it may be using and enables LScript to launch into a Mesh Data Edit session later.

Closing Thoughts on Modeler LScript

A good rule of thumb to remember as you are writing scripts is to start out simple and add functionality as you go. If you go back and review the Snap! script, you'll remember that you created it in steps, adding the components you needed in the location where they needed to be, and building upon work that you had already accomplished.

Certainly, if you were to first look at an LScript in its entirety, it can seem quite daunting. If, however, you consider each script as a collection of components or sections—a section to gather user input, a section to add points, a section to write data to a file, and so on—then you will find that no script is as complex or mysterious as it might first seem.

Thinking in terms of discrete sections will help you better understand the construction of LightWave Layout scripts. You will begin discussing this topic in the next section.

Scripting for LightWave's Layout

There is a fundamental difference between the philosophies governing the design of Modeler and Layout plug-ins. Under Modeler, plug-ins are given control of Modeler's CPU time and are expected to complete all their processing before returning control to Modeler. Layout differs in that, with the exception of the Generic class, plug-ins are expected to activate and then remain passive until Layout calls them back to perform processing appropriate to the current state of Layout's execution. This state varies, being a file save of the scene at one point, and the rendering of an animation frame at another. Layout plug-ins must be prepared to activate at any time and to process appropriately at whatever state Layout might be in.

LScripts designed to execute under one of Layout's plug-in architectures must follow this convention as well. However, because of its built-in convenience, LScript does not require the script writer to include code to support a particular Layout execution state if it is not appropriate. LScript simply provides an internal function for Layout to execute instead.

LScript provides scripting capabilities to six of Layout's plug-in architectures:

- Image Filter
- Object Replacement
- Procedural Texture
- Item Motion
- Displacement Mapping
- Generic

However, before you begin delving into the scene-related scripting classes, you will take a brief look at the exception: LScript Generic.

LScript Generic Scripting

Unlike all other plug-in classes, the Generic class of plug-in is unassociated with a scene, and as such does not adhere to the call back mechanism enforced upon other Layout plug-ins. This plug-in class is structurally similar to Modeler plug-ins in that they have a single entry point and are expected to complete all processing during their first and only invocation. However, because of its lack of association with a Layout scene, Generic plug-ins have the capability to load and save scene files directly into Layout during activation.

LScript Generic scripts not only have access to all the internal features of LScript, they also have the power to access objects, along with their attributes, in a currently loaded Layout scene. Add to this the power to load and save Layout scene files, and the LScript Generic scripts can be exceptionally powerful.

LScript Generic (known as LS/GN in LScript) scripts have a single point of entry. Like LScript for Modeler's main() UDF, LS/GN scripts have an entry point identified as generic. The following listing illustrates this design.

```
generic
{
}
```

In this section, you will create an LS/GN script that reads the motion of each object currently in the scene, and reports the name of each that remains motionless throughout the range of animation frames. You will call this new script Slacker. Slacker could be useful in projects where you have large numbers of moving objects in your scene, or perhaps where you imported keyframed objects from scenes created by other members of the project. Using Slacker, you can perform some measure of "quality assurance" on your animation, double-checking that only those items designed not to move are without keyframed motion.

Because you've switched to Layout scripting, your goals are now different. In Modeler, you are concerned with editing mesh data and creating new objects. In Layout, animation of existing mesh objects is your primary concern. Now that your goals differ, your available functions for achieving those goals will also differ. While there is a core set of functions and commands available in LScript (and therefore available to all scripts, regardless of application or architecture), Layout LScript requires a different set of functions and commands to facilitate Layout's goals. Indeed, these functions and commands can vary by architecture (Displacement Mapping, Generic, Item Motion, and so on).

Posting a Requester in Layout scripting involves script code that is nearly identical to that used by Modeler. In fact, you can simply copy and paste requester code from a Modeler script and it will work identically under Layout. However, Layout does present some special conditions that the LScript for Layout software has been designed to handle—specifically, the use of the LightWave Panel Services global-class plug-in.

This plug-in, which ships with LightWave 3D, is intended to provide Layout plug-ins with the capability to create and post requester panels. Under Modeler, this functionality is built into the application. Until the creation of the Panel Services plug-in, Layout plug-ins were left to create their own Requester Panels using the resources available under the current operating system (Windows NT, SGI X Window, Power Macintosh QuickDraw, and so on). Invariably, each unique Requester Panel not only required additional—and platform-specific—code within each plug-in, but the visual appearance of each Requester differed dramatically from the overall look-and-feel of the LightWave 3D interface. Panel Services solved these problems also, reducing and standardizing the amount of Requester code needed in each plug-in, and making the look of each plug-in's Requester Panel match that of the LightWave 3D interface.

LScript for Layout employs the Panel Services global-class plug-in to generate Requester Panels. The use of this plug-in is, for the most part, invisible to the Layout LScript writer. However, because it is a plug-in, the possibility exists that it will not be available (that is, installed) in LightWave Layout at the time the script is executed. Because this condition cannot possibly exist under LightWave Modeler (the Requester code is built into the application), the behavior of the reqbegin() command has been altered under LScript for Layout. When you use reqbegin() under Layout, it will return a Boolean value that indicates the presence of the Panel Services plug-in. If reqbegin() returns a false value, then the Panel Services plug-in is not accessible, and execution of any further Requester code should be avoided. Typically, because your script will need information from the user to complete processing, a termination of the script is usually the most appropriate recourse.

The following exercise takes you through the creation of the Slacker script, which includes steps on creating a Requester in Layout.

CREATING THE SLACKER SCRIPT

1. The first order of business in your Slacker script is to acquire an LScript Object Agent for the current scene information, and one for the first mesh object in the scene. You will utilize the LScript for Layout function call getfirstitem() to create this Object Agent.

As a precaution, you verify the return value of getfirstitem() to ensure that there are actually mesh objects in the scene. The return value of getfirstitem() will be nil if there are no objects of the specified type in the scene.

```
generic
{
    scene  = getfirstitem(SCENE);
    object = getfirstitem(MESH);
    if(object == nil)
    {
        error("No mesh objects in the current scene!");
        return;
    }
    ...
```

2. Next, you need to request some information from the user regarding how you should function. Use the reqbegin() command to do this.

```
    ...
            error("No mesh objects in the current scene!");
            return;
        }

        if(reqbegin("Slacker") == false)
        {
            error("Cannot access the Panel Services plug-in");
            return;
        }
    ...
```

The Panel Services plug-in provides control types that are not available under LightWave Modeler. LScript for Layout extends to its scripts access to a selected number of these new controls. You will employ one of these extended control types in your Requester.

3. In order to complete your processing, you need to know whether or not the user wants you to ignore mesh objects that are children of other objects. To do this, use addcheckbox() to place a check box control into the Requester Panel that is initialized with a Boolean true/false value and returns the same.

```
    ...
        if(reqbegin("Slacker") == false)
        {
```

```
        error("Cannot access the Panel Services plug-in");
        return;
    }

    ignoreChild   = true;

    c1 = addcheckbox(ignoreChild,"Ignore children of other
➥objects");
    ...
```

Notice that you used a new control-creation function in this LS/GN script code. More are available under Layout LScript, and each of them is specifically designed to create extended controls made available by the Panel Services plug-in. These functions do not exist under LScript for Modeler.

4. Once your controls are created, you post the Requester and query the control values just as you would under LightWave Modeler.

```
    ...
        c1 = addcheckbox(ignoreChild,"Ignore children of other
➥objects");

    if(reqpost())
        ignoreChild = getvalue(c1);
    else
        return;

    reqend();
    ...
```

5. After you have the necessary information from the user, you can begin your object processing. You will use a while() loop to step through each mesh object in the scene. For each object you encounter, you will employ a second loop to gather information about the object's whereabouts at each frame to see if it is a productive member of the animation.

```
    ...
    reqend();

    while(object)
    {
        for(frame = 1;frame <= scene.frameEnd;frame++)
        {
            ...
```

```
      }
        . . .
    }
      . . .
```

You may have noticed that, where the while() loop is concerned, you have a potential infinite loop condition. The object variable must be altered in some way within the while() loop so that the loop condition (object is not equal to nil or zero [0]) fails at some point.

6. You ensure that object does not equal zero by adding a call to the Object Agent method next() at the end of the while() loop. This returns the next object in the list of object types. In the case of mesh objects, another Object Agent will be returned for the next mesh object (if any) in the scene. If no further mesh objects are available, then next() will return nil, thus causing the while() loop to terminate.

```
    . . .
    while(object)
    {
        for(frame = 1;frame <= scene.frameEnd;frame++)
        {
            . . .
        }

        object = object.next();
    }
    . . .
```

7. For each frame in the animation, you need to know the position of the current object. You acquire this information using the Object Agent's param() function call.

The indicator types you will be providing to param() cause a series of three floating-point values to be returned. If you assign the values returned by a multiple-item-return function (such as param()) to a single variable, LScript will automatically create an array for you to house those returned values. If the number of returned items exceeds the number of variables to which assignments can be made, the excess items will be discarded by LScript. Be sure associative assignments are what you want so that you do not inadvertently lose data.

8. To calculate the time index you want, take the current frame being processed (contained in the loop counter frame) and divide that by the frames-per-second setting in the scene.

```
...
while(object)
{
    for(frame = 1;frame <= scene.frameEnd;frame++)
    {
        (x,y,z) = object.param(POSITION,frame/scene.fps);
        ...
    }

    object = object.next();
}
...
```

9. You will be comparing each frame's position information to that of the first frame. In order to reduce the amount of script code you need, you will remember the first frame's position information in a shorthand variable, and then use that variable for comparison with later frame information.

```
...
while(object)
{
    moved = false;

    for(frame = 1;frame <= scene.frameEnd;frame++)
    {
        (x,y,z) = object.param(POSITION,frame/scene.fps);

        if(frame == 1)
            firstFrame = <x,y,z>;
        else
        {
            thisFrame = <x,y,z>;
            if(firstFrame != thisFrame)
            {
                moved = true;
                break;
            }
        }
    }

    if(moved == false)
        warn("Slacker alert!   ",object.name);
```

```
        object = object.next();
    }
    ...
```

When comparing later frames, if you find any position that deviates from the first, you can simply skip any further processing for this object. If, however, you scan through all frames without finding movement, you need to post a warning message to the users to let them know of a potentially dysfunctional member of their scene.

10. The last code you need to add to your Slacker script enables you to ignore an object if it is a child of another object. You can check for this condition by accessing the Object Agent data member parent. This public data member will point to an Object Agent that represents the object (mesh or otherwise) to which the current object is parented. If the current object is unparented, parent will be nil.

```
generic
{
    scene  = getfirstitem(SCENE);
    object = getfirstitem(MESH);
    if(object == nil)
    {
        error("No mesh objects in the current scene!");
        return;
    }

    if(reqbegin("Slacker") == false)
    {
        error("Cannot access the Panel Services plug-in");
        return;
    }

    ignoreChild    = true;

    c1 = addcheckbox(ignoreChild,"Ignore children of other
➥objects");

    if(reqpost())
        ignoreChild = getvalue(c1);
    else
        return;

    reqend();
```

```
while(object)
{
    moved = false;

    for(frame = 1;frame <= scene.frameEnd;frame++)
    {
        (x,y,z) = object.param(POSITION,frame/scene.fps);

        if(frame == 1)
            firstFrame = <x,y,z>;
        else
        {
            thisFrame = <x,y,z>;
            if(firstFrame != thisFrame)
            {
                moved = true;
                break;
            }
        }
    }

    if(moved == false)
    {
        if(ignoreChild)
        {
            if(object.parent == nil)
                warn("Slacker alert!  ",object.name);
        }
        else
            warn("Slacker alert!  ",object.name);
    }

    object = object.next();
}
}
```

The following list explains some of the new commands that you used in this exercise. For more information, see the LScript documentation from NewTek.

- **getfirstitem().** Creates Object Agents that enable you to access the attributes of scene-owned objects. Object Agents returned by `getfirstitem()` are internal, as opposed to those regarded as external that can be created by the user using native code.

- **`param()`.** Accepts two arguments, the first being an indicator as to the type of information you are seeking, and the second a time index that represents the point in the animation in which you are interested.

Slacker has shown you the power that LScript Generic script can provide. It can be used as a supervisor for scene files, offering the power of LScript for Layout system with the simplicity of structure provided by LScript for Modeler. Next, you will examine the potential of manipulating surface settings using the LScript Procedural Texture scripting plug-in.

Using LScript Procedural Texture to Pulsate

LScript Procedural Texture (LS/PT) enables you to affect the settings and appearance of surfaces assigned to objects. In this section, you will quickly create a simple LS/PT script that will ramp a surface's luminosity setting up and down throughout an animation. You will call this LScript Pulse. Pulse will demonstrate a technique for accomplishing something that is not currently possible in LightWave: the ability to provide motion to surface attributes as the time index of your animation advances. This is equivalent to keyframing certain surface attributes, a capability that LightWave does not offer through its interface.

All non-Generic LScript for Layout scripts conform to the notion of call backs, as was discussed at the beginning of this section. Each LS/PT script you create will contain at least two UDFs that LScript will invoke at appropriate times. The first is identified as `create` and is invoked when the LScript for Layout script is first activated. It is called only once and is intended to be a location and a time when one-time setup of the script is to be performed. The second is where processing will take place as each frame of animation is evaluated. This UDF is identified as `process`, and it is within this section that the main processing of each script takes place.

LS/PT scripts also require the use of two other UDFs to support their particular processing. These UDFs are `newtime` and `flags`. The first is called each time a new time index is encountered in Layout (the frame number changes), and its main purpose is to remember information passed to it for subsequent UDFs to use. The `flags()` UDF is called only once, like `create()`, and is expected to return a list of flags that indicate the settings that the plug-in will be modifying for the surface. In your example, you will only be modifying the luminosity setting of the surface, so you return only that flag. You can find information about other available LS/PT flags in the LScript documentation.

CREATING THE PULSE SCRIPT

1. You begin your Pulse script by creating some global variables that will be used by various UDFs in the script.

    Global variables are those that belong to the script and not to a particular UDF. Their visibility, or scope, is universal, meaning that all UDFs can read from and write to them as though they were their own, but their values will persist across UDF invocations.

    ```
    thisFrame;
    thisTime;
    fps
    ...
    ```

2. You now add your `create()` UDF. In this example, the `create()` UDF will establish the value for one of the global variables, so that you do not waste time doing it every time your `process()` UDF is invoked.

    In this step, you also introduce a command unique to LScript for Layout that enables you to set the text of the description displayed by Layout on the plug-in panel for this particular plug-in: the `setdesc()` command. If you want, you can employ this command to display operating parameters to the Layout user without the need to bring up the options panel. However, for your current purposes, you simply display the title of the script.

    ```
    thisFrame;
    thisTime;
    fps

    create
    {
        scene = getfirstiem(SCENE);
        fps = scene.fps;

        setdesc("Pulse (LS/PT)");
    }
    ...
    ```

3. Place your `newtime()` and `flags()` UDFs into Pulse. `Newtime()` is passed several parameters by LScript concerning the current index settings of the animation, and you use those to update the global variables for the script.

```
    ...
        setdesc("Pulse (LS/PT)");
    }

    newtime: frame, time
    {
        thisFrame = frame;
        thisTime = time;
    }

    flags
    {
        return(LUMINOUS);
    }
    ...
```

4. With these items in place, you can look to the meat of the script in the `process()` UDF. LScript calls this UDF with a single parameter, an Object Agent that provides the LScript with an interface to operation values for the surface to which it is assigned.

```
    thisFrame;
    thisTime;
    fps

    create
    {
        scene = getfirstiem(SCENE);
        fps = scene.fps;

        setdesc("Pulse (LS/PT)");
    }

    newtime: frame, time
    {
        thisFrame = frame;
        thisTime = time;
    }

    flags
    {
        return(LUMINOUS);
    }
```

```
process: sa
{
    if(thisFrame == 0)
        return;       // avoid problems in your math

    j = thisFrame;

    if(thisFrame > fps)   // has the count exceeded 'fps'?
    {
        // if so, fold it into the 1-to-fps range to
        // simplify your caculations

        i = integer(thisFrame / fps);

        if(i != 0)
            j = thisFrame - (i * fps);
    }

    // you ramp up in the first half of 'fps', and
    // ramp down in the latter

    k = fps / 2;

    if(j <= k)   // pulsing up
        sa.luminous = j / k;   // use the percentage of j in 1-
        ➡(fps/ 2)
    else
    {
        // pulsing down

        j -= k;       // fold down so percentages are correct

        sa.luminous = 1.0 - (j / k);
    }
}
```

Altering a surface's luminosity is as simple as assigning a new value to it. This value is a percentage of the luminosity's intensity at the current time index. Most of the code in your Pulse script's process() UDF is nothing more than simple math that will ramp this percentage up to 100%, or down to 0%, as the time index advances.

You have only touched the tip of the LScript Procedural Texture plug-in's capabilities with Pulsate. Many other surface-related settings can be altered to affect an object's surface appearance. Refer to the LScript documentation for a complete list of the attributes that can be modified using LS/PT scripting software.

Along with the ability to affect an object's appearance using LS/PT, you can also alter the appearance of each complete frame of rendered animation using the LScript Image Filter scripting plug-in. You will examine this software next.

Making Some Noise with LScript Image Filter

Now you proceed into the world of LScript Image Filter, or LS/IF. In this architecture, you will post-process rendered frames of animation just prior to their final destination, whether that destination is a disk file, animation file, or visual display to the user. For this exercise, you will create an LS/IF script that will add an amount of noise, or snow, to each frame of rendered animation. Because each frame will have its own randomly applied noise factor, the effect will create an additional layer of animation to the project. This LS/IF script can be useful for applying a certain amount of grain to the visual appearance of your animation, providing the look and feel of age, as happens to celluloid film as time passes.

The structure of LS/IF scripts is quite similar to that of LS/PT. Like that architecture, it employs both create() and process() UDFs. In your sample script, you will also employ the options() UDF, wherein the user can alter the operating parameters of the Noise LS/IF script.

In your create() UDF, you will be using the LScript recall() function to retrieve values that may have been stored previously on behalf of the script. Later in the script, you will utilize the companion function store() to place values into storage after they have been altered by the user. Subsequent invocations of Noise will retrieve the user's last settings, adding a nice element of continuity.

CREATING THE NOISE SCRIPT

1. As with the LS/PT Pulse script, you will add some global variables along with the create() UDF.

```
noiseColor;
noisePercent;
noiseVariance;
```

```
create
{
    noisePercent  = recall("noisePercent",.2);
    noiseVariance = recall("noiseVariance",.2);
    noiseColor    = recall("noiseColor",<200,200,200>);

    setdesc("Noise (LS/IF)");
}
...
```

2. Processing the image comes next. LS/IF `process()` functions are called by LScript with a number of parameters. These parameters provide information, such as image width and height, so the script can access pixel information correctly. You will use this information heavily in `process()`.

```
...
    setdesc("Noise (LS/IF)");
}

process: width, height, frame, starttime, endtime
{
    red[width] = nil;
    green[width] = nil;
    blue[width] = nil;
    beenThere[width] = nil;
    out[3] = nil;
    ...
}
...
```

NOTE

Every row of an image must pass through each filter applied to it. If you neglect to read and then write any of the image information through your script, those areas in the final image will be filled with a default color of black (<0,0,0>). This is not a behavior of LScript, but rather the way Layout Image Filtering has been designed to function.

3. You are ready to add your main processing loop, which cycles through all the rows of pixels that are available in the image buffer.

```
...
    beenThere[width] = nil;
```

```
        out[3] = nil;

    moninit(height);
    ...
    for(i = 1;i <= height;++i)
    {
        ...
        if(monstep())
            return;
    }

    monend();
}
...
```

4. The script code to acquire and forward pixel data from/to Layout goes into the `process()` UDF next. You will use a row-at-a-time processing function provided by LS/IF called `processrgb()`. This command processes all four default pixel buffers at the same time, which achieves significant gains in processing speed.

```
    ...
    moninit(height);
    ...
    for(i = 1;i <= height;++i)
    {
        red = bufferline(RED,i);
        green = bufferline(GREEN,i);
        blue = bufferline(BLUE,i);
        alpha = bufferline(ALPHA,i);
        ...

        processrbg(i,red,green,blue,alpha);

        if(monstep())
            return;
    }
    ...
```

The remainder of the `process()` UDF for the LS/IF Noise script consists of the script code you need to randomly insert noise into the image. You use the settings in your global variables (potentially set by the user) to determine where and how a pixel will be shaded. The method you will use is largely just a determination of how many pixels per row will be altered, and of those, which will have the noise color and which will have a variant of that color. All of these factors can be affected indirectly by values entered by the user in the options() UDF, which you add in step 7.

5. When you select a pixel for alteration, you need to keep track of it in an array so that you do not waste time processing the same pixel again. Because you randomly select pixels in each row, not tracking those pixels you've already modified would likely result (incorrectly) in lower densities of noise. Use the beenThere[] array to track the pixels.

```
    . . .
        blue = bufferline(BLUE,i);
        alpha = bufferline(ALPHA,i);

        beenThere[] = nil;
        for(j = 1;j <= max;++j)
        {
            pixel = random(1,width);
            while(beenThere[pixel])
                pixel = random(1,width);

            beenThere[pixel] = true;
            . . .
```

6. You will finish off your process() UDF by adding the script code that is responsible for actually altering selected pixels to simulate video noise.

```
    . . .
        alpha = bufferline(ALPHA,i);

        max = random(1,integer(width * noisePercent));
        beenThere[] = nil;

        for(j = 1;j <= max;++j)
        {
            pixel = random(1,width);
            while(beenThere[pixel])
                pixel = random(1,width);

            beenThere[pixel] = true;

            switch(random(1,3))
            {
                case 1:
```

```
            red[pixel]      = noiseColor.x - vary;
            green[pixel]    = noiseColor.y - vary;
            blue[pixel]     = noiseColor.z - vary;
            break;

        case 2:
            red[pixel]      = noiseColor.x;
            green[pixel]    = noiseColor.y;
            blue[pixel]     = noiseColor.z;
            break;

        case 3:
            red[pixel]      = noiseColor.x + vary;
            green[pixel]    = noiseColor.y + vary;
            blue[pixel]     = noiseColor.z + vary;
            break;
    }

    if(red[pixel] < 0) red[pixel] = 0;
    if(red[pixel] > 255) red[pixel] = 255;

    if(green[pixel] < 0) green[pixel] = 0;
    if(green[pixel] > 255) green[pixel] = 255;

    if(blue[pixel] < 0) blue[pixel] = 0;
    if(blue[pixel] > 255) blue[pixel] = 255;
}

processrbg(i,red,green,blue,alpha);

if(monstep())
    return;
}
...
```

7. You will finish off your Noise LS/IF script by adding the options() UDF. LScript invokes this UDF when the user presses the Options button to the right of the plug-in button. It is in this UDF that you place your requester code for acquiring data from the user.

```
noiseColor;
noisePercent;
noiseVariance;

create
{
```

```
        noisePercent  = recall("noisePercent",.2);
        noiseVariance = recall("noiseVariance",.2);
        noiseColor    = recall("noiseColor",<200,200,200>);

        setdesc("Noise (LS/IF)");
    }

    process: width, height, frame, starttime, endtime
    {
        red[width] = nil;
        green[width] = nil;
        blue[width] = nil;
        beenThere[width] = nil;
        out[3] = nil;

        moninit(height);

        vary = noiseVariance * 75;

        for(i = 1;i <= height;++i)
        {
            red = bufferline(RED,i);
            green = bufferline(GREEN,i);
            blue = bufferline(BLUE,i);
            alpha = bufferline(ALPHA,i);

            max = random(1,integer(width * noisePercent));
            beenThere[] = nil;

            for(j = 1;j <= max;++j)
            {
                pixel = random(1,width);
                while(beenThere[pixel])
                    pixel = random(1,width);

                beenThere[pixel] = true;

                switch(random(1,3))
                {
                    case 1:
                        red[pixel]    = noiseColor.x - vary;
                        green[pixel]  = noiseColor.y - vary;
                        blue[pixel]   = noiseColor.z - vary;
                        break;
```

```
            case 2:
                red[pixel]      = noiseColor.x;
                green[pixel]    = noiseColor.y;
                blue[pixel]     = noiseColor.z;
                break;

            case 3:
                red[pixel]      = noiseColor.x + vary;
                green[pixel]    = noiseColor.y + vary;
                blue[pixel]     = noiseColor.z + vary;
                break;
        }

        if(red[pixel] < 0) red[pixel] = 0;
        if(red[pixel] > 255) red[pixel] = 255;

        if(green[pixel] < 0) green[pixel] = 0;
        if(green[pixel] > 255) green[pixel] = 255;

        if(blue[pixel] < 0) blue[pixel] = 0;
        if(blue[pixel] > 255) blue[pixel] = 255;
    }

    processrbg(i,red,green,blue,alpha);

    if(monstep())
        return;
    }

    monend();
}

options
{
    if(!reqbegin("Noise"))
    {
        error("Cannot access the Panel Services plug-in!");
        return;
    }

    c1 = addcontrol(noisePercent * 100.0,"Noise amount (%)");
    c2 = addcontrol(noiseVariance * 100.0,"Noise variance (%)");
    c3 = addrgb(noiseColor,"Noise color");

    if(reqpost())
    {
        noisePercent  = getvalue(c1) / 100.0;
        noiseVariance = getvalue(c2) / 100.0;
        noiseColor    = getvalue(c3);
```

```
        store("noisePercent",noisePercent);
        store("noiseVariance",noiseVariance);
        store("noiseColor",noiseColor);
    }

    reqend();
}
```

Certainly, more can be added to this LS/IF script. Noise can be enhanced to add scratch lines to your images, increasing the illusion of age. Other channel information can be accessed and utilized to provide you with more detail about the structure of the image itself. For instance, the Alpha channel data can be accessed to allow you to create even more special effects with the image's pixels.

LScript Image Filter scripting provides a great means of prototyping image processing techniques. Many different techniques can be created, such as embossing or edge detection, using the conveniences provided by LScript.

Next, you use the LScript Item Motion scripting system to put a new "spin" on things in your animation project.

Spinning Your Wheels with LScript Item Animation

For your last Layout LScript, you will create an LScript Item Animation (LS/IA) script. Item Animation plug-ins (also known as Item Motion) have the power to alter an object's position, rotation, and scaling factors on a frame-by-frame basis. Using Item Animation, you can completely replace an object's keyframed motion with your own.

In the exercise in this section, you will create an LS/IA script called Spinner that produces accurate revolutions-per-minute rotations on an object. This can be useful for items such as propellers, wheels, and machinery.

Spinner will begin much like your other Layout LScripts, with global variables and a create() UDF. However, you will move a step higher in your usage of LScript by employing the language's preprocessor to establish some macro definitions. The macro identifiers will be replaced wherever they are found later in the script by their assigned values. Macros are handy for centralizing script values, allowing you to change them in one location while the preprocessor propagates that change throughout the script code.

CREATING THE SPINNER SCRIPT

1. Spinner's `create()` UDF initializes most of the global variables you will use. You need to add these initial elements to your Spinner script.

```
@define CW    1
@define CCW   2

rpm, rot, fps;
degreeIncr;
toH,toP,toB;
direction;

radrev = 2*PI;

create
{
    scene = getfirstitem(SCENE);
    fps = scene.fps;

    rpm       = 100;
    toH       = false;
    toP       = false;
    toB       = true;
    direction = CW;

    totaldegrees = rpm * 360;
    degreeIncr = totaldegrees / (fps * 60);

    rot = nil;

    setdesc("Spinner: ",rpm," rpm/",(direction == CW ? "cw" :
➥"ccw"));
}
...
```

2. You now can begin your `process()` UDF. You have a delayed initialize variable called `rot`. This global variable was set to `nil` in the `create()` UDF, so you can check to see if it has been initialized the first time the `process()` UDF is invoked.

```
...
    totaldegrees = rpm * 360;
    degreeIncr = totaldegrees / (fps * 60);

    rot = nil;
```

```
        setdesc("Spinner: ",rpm," rpm/",(direction == CW ? "cw" :
➥"ccw"));
    }

    process: ma, frame, time
    {
        if(rot == nil)
            rot = ma.get(ROTATION,time);
        ...
    }
    ...
```

You will use the `rot` variable to hold the object's initial rotation settings (heading, pitch, and bank), giving you a launching point for any subsequent rotations that you will apply. You do this to prevent a violent snap of the object as would happen if it were to have to adjust to new rotational parameters that might be radically different from its current settings. This method allows the animator to set a keyframe for a starting rotational position without having Spinner instantly destroy it.

Along with the current animation index, expressed as both time and frame, LScript passes to the `process()` UDF an Object Agent that provides the script with an interface to read and affect the objects Item Animation settings. You will use this Object Agent to access and alter the object's rotation values based upon settings given to you by the user in the `options()` UDF.

3. Check to see which rotational axis (heading, pitch, or bank) has been selected for spinning, and then apply the rotation setting based on the direction selected, that of clockwise or counterclockwise.

```
    ...
    if(rot == nil)
        rot = ma.get(ROTATION,time);

    if(toH)
      {
        if(direction == CW)
            rot.x -= rad(degreeIncr);
        else
            rot.x += rad(degreeIncr);
      }

    if(toP)
```

```
{
    if(direction == CW)
        rot.y -= rad(degreeIncr);
    else
        rot.y += rad(degreeIncr);
}

if(toB)
{
    if(direction == CW)
        rot.z -= rad(degreeIncr);
    else
        rot.z += rad(degreeIncr);
}
...
```

4. You want to wrap rotations, keeping them in the range of 1 to 360 degrees.

```
    ...
        rot.z -= rad(degreeIncr);
    else
        rot.z += rad(degreeIncr);
}

if(rot.x > radrev) rot.x -= radrev;
if(rot.x < 0)      rot.x += radrev;
if(rot.y > radrev) rot.y -= radrev;
if(rot.y < 0)      rot.y += radrev;
if(rot.z > radrev) rot.z -= radrev;
if(rot.z < 0)      rot.z += radrev;
...
```

There is likely an upper limit to the number of revolutions LightWave Layout will track for an object. Because you do not know just how long an animation will last, or where this limit is and how Layout will react if you achieve it, this code will ensure that the value will not reach or exceed this limit.

5. For your process() UDF, you will update the object's rotational values by using the set() method of your Item Animation Object Agent.

```
    ...
    if(rot.z > radrev) rot.z -= radrev;
```

```
        if(rot.z < 0)        rot.z += radrev;

    ma.set(ROTATION,rot);
}
...
```

6. The `options()` UDF adds the finishing touches to your Spinner LS/IA script.

```
// direction?
@define CW   1
@define CCW  2

// some globals
rpm, rot, fps;
degreeIncr;
toH,toP,toB;
direction;

// how many radians for a full revolution?
radrev = 2*PI;

create
{
    scene = getfirstitem(SCENE);
    fps = scene.fps;

    rpm        = 100;
    toH        = false;
    toP        = false;
    toB        = true;
    direction = CW;

    // calculate the per-frame degree increment to
    // achieve the require RPMs

    totaldegrees = rpm * 360;
    degreeIncr = totaldegrees / (fps * 60);

    rot = nil;

    setdesc("Spinner: ",rpm," rpm/",(direction == CW ? "cw" :
    ➥"ccw"));
}

process: ma, frame, time
{
```

```
    if(rot == nil)
        rot = ma.get(ROTATION,time);

    if(toH)
    {
        if(direction == CW)
            rot.x -= rad(degreeIncr);
        else
            rot.x += rad(degreeIncr);
    }

    if(toP)
    {
        if(direction == CW)
            rot.y -= rad(degreeIncr);
        else
            rot.y += rad(degreeIncr);
    }

    if(toB)
    {
        if(direction == CW)
            rot.z -= rad(degreeIncr);
        else
            rot.z += rad(degreeIncr);
    }

    if(rot.x > radrev) rot.x -= radrev;
    if(rot.x < 0)      rot.x += radrev;
    if(rot.y > radrev) rot.y -= radrev;
    if(rot.y < 0)      rot.y += radrev;
    if(rot.z > radrev) rot.z -= radrev;
    if(rot.z < 0)      rot.z += radrev;

    ma.set(ROTATION,rot);
}

options
{
    if(!reqbegin("Spinner"))
    {
        error("Cannot access the Panel Services plug-in");
        return;
    }

    c1 = addcontrol(rpm,"RPMs");
    c2 = addcontrol(direction,"Direction",@"CW","CCW"@);
    c3 = addcheckbox(toH,"Effect heading");
```

```
    c4 = addcheckbox(toP,"Effect pitch");
    c5 = addcheckbox(toB,"Effect bank");

    if(reqpost())
    {
        rpm       = getvalue(c1);
        direction = getvalue(c2);
        toH       = getvalue(c3);
        toP       = getvalue(c4);
        toB       = getvalue(c5);

        // update your working values to catch any changes

        totaldegrees = rpm * 360;
        degreeIncr = totaldegrees / (fps * 60);

        rot = nil;

        setdesc("Spinner: ",rpms," rpms/",((direction == CW) ?
"cw" : "ccw"));
    }

    reqend();
}
```

Spinner provides a set-it-and-forget-it solution to rotating items in an animation. While a similar effect can be achieved by repeating an object's motion, such repetition would not provide an accurate simulation of the real-world revolutions-per-minute rotations offered by Spinner.

An LS/IA script can also modify other items, such as an object's position and scaling factors. Some amazing effects can be achieved by manipulating this combination of an object's attributes.

This section has covered, rather quickly and directly, some of the more-popular Layout scripting architectures. You've created some comparatively simple-but-practical Layout LScripts, studying along the way some of Layout's peculiarities as they differ from Modeler LScript and pertain to plug-in development.

Creating or affecting animation programmatically can bring into existence visuals that are beyond the capabilities of LightWave 3D as it comes out of the box. Any one of these particular Layout scripting architectures can achieve such results in and of themselves; by working in combination, whether directly or indirectly, the potential is staggering, and the results can be equally so.

The limiting factor is nothing more or less than your imagination.

Conclusion

This chapter merely touched the tip of the LScript iceberg. There are other LScript for Layout architectures that you haven't examined, as well as more advanced uses of the LScript software system—enough to fill several chapters. However, the intention here was not only to show you the usefulness and power of the LScript software system, but also to whet your appetite to begin writing your own useful scripts.

Along with the LScript documentation provided by NewTek, an excellent source of reference for the budding LScript writer is the large number of existing LScripts. Examining the works of others can always teach you things more quickly and efficiently than learning by your own means of trial and error.

You can find the LScript documentation (in HTML format) and many sample LScripts on the LightWave 5.5 CD-ROM. You can also find more information about the LightWave LScript system by visiting NewTek's Web site at http://www.newtek.com.

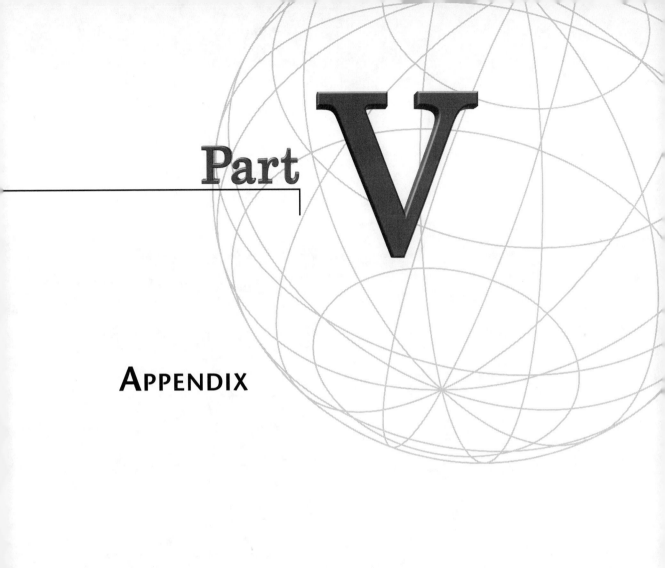

Part V

APPENDIX

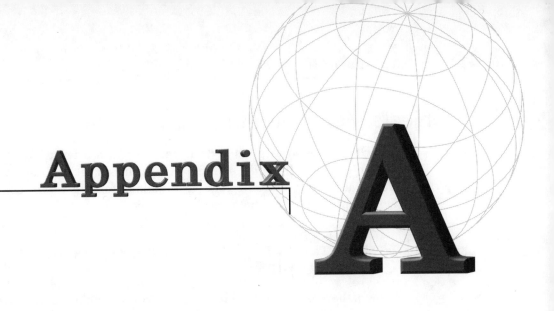

Appendix A

MODELER AND THIRD-PARTY PLUG-INS

Plug-ins in Modeler are divided into two categories: the first is accessible in the Custom group in the Objects menu and the second is accessible in the Custom group clustered in the Tools menu.

Objects Menu Plug-Ins

The Objects menu plug-ins perform various object-oriented functions such as Center, Text, Julienne, and more. This plug-in set is different from the Tools menu plug-ins that perform functions to help create objects. The Objects menu plug-ins help manipulate objects.

The Center Plug-Ins

Some of the most useful Modeler plug-ins are the simplest. Center, Center1D, CenterScale, and CenterStretch fall into this category. They are so useful that many professional LightWave users set up the various function hot keys to correspond to one or more of these plug-ins. For example, you can apply the Center plug-in to a function key such as F2, through the Edit Keys command under Preferences within the Objects menu.

While an object is loaded in Modeler, applying the Center plug-in automatically centers the object on its central pivot point. This is great for control of objects in Layout. The other Center plug-ins perform variations of the Center command and can also be set to keyboard hot keys. The only drawback with these plug-ins is that they do not work on subsets of selected points or polygons; they will always apply the operation to the entire foreground layer(s).

Julienne

A project will often call for greater segmentation along an axis, or perhaps the need to convert a single polygon into a grid of polygons for further sculpting. For any of these purposes, Julienne works perfectly (see fig. A.1). Simply specify a slicing axis and the number of segments desired, and Julienne will slice up your object. The only shortcoming is that Julienne doesn't work well with polygons that are completely flat along an axial plane, such as a shape completely resting on the X-Y plane. When this happens, you must rotate the polygon slightly around the X-axis, apply Julienne, and rotate the polygon back into place.

FIGURE A.1

Using Julienne to "grid-ify" a polygon.

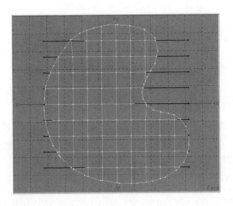

FIGURE A.1

Using Julienne to "grid-ify" a polygon.

LightSwarm (LW_LightSwarm)

LightSwarm is a very interesting and powerful plug-in. Using it, you can turn a single light into a cloned bank of lights using the selected points in the foreground layer. You can use this to quickly generate a scene of streetlights, lights along a tunnel, and so on. Using the LightSwarm plug-in eliminates the need to set up and place many lights in LightWave's Layout. Using points in Modeler, the plug-in will create a LightWave scene file of lights that can be added to an existing scene through the Load From Scene command in Layout's Objects Panel.

USING LIGHTSWARM

This plug-in will generate a scene file that contains an oriented group of lights. Once the scene is created, it can be imported into other scenes, eliminating the need to set up multiple lights.

1. To use this plug-in, you need to create a scene with the light you want to clone and save it in Layout.

2. Create the points that represent where you would like to clone the saved light.

3. Run LightSwarm to create the bank of lights. This light bank can then be loaded via a Load from Scene in the Objects Panel in Layout.

Illustrator_Import Plug-In

Illustrator_Import (LW_Illustrator_Import) can be a great time-saver in logo animation. If the client can provide the logo in Adobe Illustrator (.ai) format, chances are that this plug-in will load it automatically into Modeler.

It should be noted that the version that ships with LightWave 5.5 might not be the latest version (for example, the version shipping with the 5.50e rev of LightWave does not properly import Corel-generated AI files). To ensure that you have the latest version, visit the following site:

ftp://ftp.dstorm.co.jp/pub/lightwave/plugins/

MathMotion

MathMotion can also be a handy plug-in for creating mathematically interesting motion envelopes (which can be attached to objects in Layout from the Motion Graph Panel). Most animators overlook highly mathematical plug-ins, as they appear daunting.

PathToMotion

PathToMotion converts a spline path into a motion file for use in Layout. By making a spline curve in Modeler, you can run the plug-in to create a motion path from it. The motion path can be loaded into a Layout element's Motion Graph Panel. There are, however, a few issues to note in using this plug-in:

- This plug-in has no options to specify the key spacing between subsequent keyframes, but instead defaults to a spacing of 5. Once the motion is attached to an item in Layout, it may be necessary to scale the keys to fit the motion within the frame parameters desired.

- The points will be added to the motion file in the order that they were created, or if explicitly selected, in the order of selection. If a curve has been created where points were created and added to the curve after-the-fact, then it will be necessary to explicitly select points in order to preserve their order in the motion file.

- When the file requester appears, prompting for the file name, the file name extension will probably not be a .mot file, which is what this needs to be. Therefore, when saving the motion file, change the extension to .mot.

PolyEdgeShaper (LW_PolyEdgeShaper)

PolyEdgeShaper can easily turn a single polygon into myriads of shapes such as simple extrusion, beveling, round-edged, and neon, to name a few. As an example, create a flat disc in Modeler. Run the LW_PolyEdgeShaper plug-in. Select Bevel in the Plug-in Requester and watch what happens. The plug-in shaped the edge of the polygon. Press u to Undo and try the other options of the plug-in. Figure A.2 shows this plug-in creating an artist's palette from a single polygon, automatically rounding the edges and saving the work involved in performing multiple bevels to achieve similar results.

FIGURE A.2
Round-edged artist's palette created with PolyEdgeShaper.

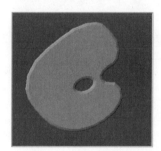

ParametricObj

ParametricObj is another mathematical plug-in. It weaves together polygons created by applying a formula for X, Y, and Z along increasing U and V values.

In its standard form, ParametricObj will create a sphere, but if you know the proper functions to apply, it can create much more. As an example, many modelers will create satellite dishes and such using simple half-spheres. While they may look correct visually, they are not mathematically correct. Satellite dishes are actually parabolic in shape, not spherical. Following is a simple formula for creating a parabolic dish with the LW_ParametricObj plug-in (see fig. A.3):

```
X: v*cos(2*_pi*u)
Y: v*sin(2*_pi*u)
Z: v*v
```

Leave everything else at its default value.

Once the shape has been created, merge all points to join all overlapping points together. Finally, stretch the shape along the Z-axis until it is the desired shape.

FIGURE A.3
Parabolic dish created using the ParametricObj plug-in.

Plot2d (LW_Plot2D)

Plot2d is used to define a mathematical function of Z based on X and Y. Mesh resolutions defined higher than the default will cause mangled polygons. The workaround for this is to define the plot in Curve mode and then use the Auto-Patcher plug-in to patch the spline curve cage with polygons.

Quadric (LW_Quadric)

The Quadric plug-in creates a class of shapes known as Superquadrics (see fig. A.4). These can range in shape from a slightly rounded-edged cube to a hubcap-like torus, and anywhere in between.

To properly use this plug-in, adjust the Side and Top Roundness values independently anywhere between 0 to about 100, as well as the Hole value from 0 to 1 and beyond. Play with these values and see what shapes you end up with.

FIGURE A.4
A menagerie of shapes created with the Quadric plug-in.

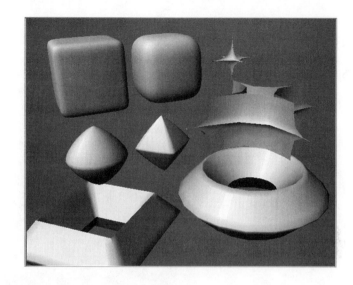

Primitives (LW_Primitives)

The Primitives plug-in adds a new variety of basic shapes to Modeler. Spline cages, platonic solids, toroids, random distributions of points, gears, and circular wedges are all made quite easily by this plug-in. Figure A.5 shows an object created with the Primitives plug-in.

FIGURE A.5
A soccer ball created with platonic primitives.

TextCompose (LW_TextCompose) and TextCurve (LW_TextCurve)

Both of these plug-ins easily generate text effects in Modeler. Text compose enables multiple lines of text to be modeled simultaneously, with options for justification, beveling, rounding, and others. TextCurve enables the creation of text along a circular curve (see fig. A.6).

FIGURE A.6

Text created with the TextCompose plug-in.

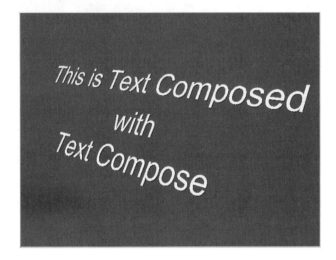

Tools Menu Plug-Ins

You can find the following plug-ins under the Tools, Custom menu in Modeler.

Add-MetaBall and MetaBalls

MetaBalls provide another method of modeling objects, in which metaballs are placed in varying 3D configurations and then a smooth skin is created from them. These two plug-ins represent the current extent of the MetaBalls implementation in LightWave. Figure A.7 shows a hand created with the MetaBalls plug-in.

FIGURE A.7
*Hand created with the
MetaBalls plug-in.*

Using the Add-MetaBall plug-in, you can create metaballs of varying strengths, positive or negative. The surface applied to each metaball at creation determines the strength that particular metaball will have when the MetaBalls plug-in is applied. You can change the strength of a metaball after the fact by changing its surface name. Positive metaballs will pull the final skin outward, whereas negative metaballs will push the skin inward.

When trying to sculpt a larger metaball form, it may be helpful to use the Rail Clone tool to create strings of metaballs. Once all metaballs are in place, the MetaBalls plug-in can be run to define the metaballs surface. The grid size specified will determine how fine the surface will be divided and will also determine the smoothness of the final mesh.

TIP

When creating objects with MetaBalls, it is recommended that the metaballs be built in one layer and the mesh in a separate layer. This can easily be achieved by selecting the metaballs layer and a lower-numbered empty layer. When the MetaBalls plug-in is applied, the mesh will automatically be generated in the lower-numbered layer, allowing it to be quickly deleted if further adjustments need to be made to the metaball positioning.

Auto-Patcher

Auto-Patcher can automatically patch relatively simple spline cages. More complicated spline cages may confuse this plug-in, so your results may vary. Perhaps the best candidates for auto-patching are spline cages created with the Primitives plug-in or with the Plot2D plug-in. You can run the plug-in from the Custom list under the Tools menu. When the dialog box appears, enter the number of subdivisions desired for each patch; the higher the number, the more detailed the patch mesh will be.

Extender

The Extender plug-in is another plug-in whose simplicity belies its usefulness. Select two or more points along the edges of a polygon and run the Extender plug-in. After running the plug-in, the points will still remain selected, but once you move the points, it becomes clear that there is a new set of quad polygons (all-important for MetaNURBS modeling) between the selected points and the original positions of the points. Using Extender, it is easy to build up regions of quad polygons as necessary for use with MetaNURBS.

MetaFormPlus

Originally designed as a plug-in that enabled metaforming of polygons of greater than three or four sides, MetaFormPlus has become much more. This is because it's tied into the Metamation plug-in used in Layout. MetaFormPlus is a Layout plug-in that enables boning and animating of a rough meta-cage of an object and then has the transformations applied to a smoothed, high-resolution version of the same object.

The MetaFormPlus plug-in converts a low-resolution cage into the high-resolution version of the same object. Be sure to click on the Metaform Triangles as Triangles button when metaforming an object for use with MetaFormPlus when prompted.

NOTE

It is also a good idea to jot down somewhere the subdivision level used, as that value will be used to set up Metamation in Layout. It should also be noted that if you intend to deform your objects using bones, the Triple All Quads button should be checked as well. While a quad may be planar in its resting state, it is highly unlikely that it will remain so as its vertices are pushed about in Layout.

PointClonePlus

The PointClonePlus plug-in is a useful tool in its own right. Using a background layer of points as a template, it will clone a copy of the foreground geometry for each point, with optional jittering during the cloning process.

SmartTriple

The SmartTriple plug-in will automatically select all non-planar polygons in your geometry and triple them. Be advised that this may not be enough if you plan on deforming your geometry during the course of animating it. If so, triple all polygons.

SkeletonMaker

SkeletonMaker is a new plug-in introduced with LightWave 5.5 that makes creating object skeletons a snap. To use this plug-in, create a series of spline curves, each representing a chain of bones in your final object. Run the SkeletonMaker plug-in, and it will convert these curves into bone chains in a LightWave scene. It can also optionally rest the bones, derive the bone names from the spline curve surfaces, and add IK goals to the end of the chain.

Index

U-V

Digital Character Animation

by George Maestri

Add the spark of life to your computer-generated animations! Animation expert George Maestri provides you with all the essential information needed to create convincing CG characters in 2D and 3D. The full color presentation and step-by-step tutorials make this nonsoftware-specific book a must for every animator library.

ISBN: 1-56205-559-3
$55.00 USA/$77.95 CAN, CD

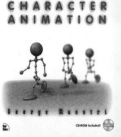

Inside Adobe Photoshop 4

by Gary David Bouton, Barbara Mancuso Bouton, Gary Kubicek

You can master the power of the world's most popular computer graphics program. Easy-to-follow tutorials, in Gary's famous style, teach you the full spectrum of Photoshop's powerful capabilities. The most comprehensive book available on Photoshop 4!

ISBN: 1-56205-681-6
$44.99 USA/$63.95 CAN, CD

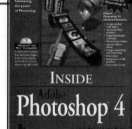

Teach Yourself Photoshop 4 in 14 Days

by D. Bront Davis, Steven Mulder, Carla Rose

In just two short weeks, you'll understand the essentials of Adobe® Photoshop, master professional imaging techniques, learn how to effectively use all the tools and features, and get tips on creating spectacular designs quickly and easily. Using the step-by-step approach of this easy-to-understand guide, you'll be up to speed with Photoshop 4 in no time!

ISBN: 1-56830-403-X,
$39.99 USA/$56.95 CAN, CD

LightWave Power Guide

by Dan Ablan

LightWave Power Guide focuses on the most powerful functions of LightWave, highlighted by examples of those functions in use. Topics such as LightWave's plug-in architecture, character animation, inverse kinematics, and advanced modeling are covered in-depth and accompanied by tutorials that teach real-world skills.

ISBN: 1-56205-633-6
$44.99 USA/$63.95 CAN

A V I A C O M   S E R V I C E

The Information SuperLibrary™

Bookstore	**Search**	**What's New!**	**Reference**	**Software**	**Newsletter**	**Company Overviews**
Yellow Pages	**Internet Starter Kit**	**HTML Workshop**	**Win a Free T-Shirt!**	**Macmillan Computer Publishing**	**Site Map**	**Talk to Us**

CHECK OUT THE BOOKS IN THIS LIBRARY.

You'll find thousands of shareware files and over 1,600 computer books designed for both technowizards and technophobes. You can browse through 700 sample chapters, get the latest news on the Net, and find just about anything using our massive search directories.

All Macmillan Computer Publishing books are available at your local bookstore.

We're open 24 hours a day, 365 days a year.

You don't need a card.

We don't charge fines.

And you can be as **LOUD** as you want.

The Information SuperLibrary

http://www.mcp.com/mcp/ftp.mcp.com

MACMILLAN COMPUTER PUBLISHING USA

A VIACOM COMPANY

Technical ---- Support

If you need assistance with the information provided by Macmillan Computer Publishing, please access the information available on our web site at **http://www.mcp.com/feedback.** Our most Frequently Asked Questions are answered there. If you do not find the answers to your questions on our web site, you may contact Macmillan User Services at **(317) 581-3833** or email us at **support@mcp.com.**